To:
Ralph and Barbara
with thanks.

Nature Writing and America

The prose is
convoluted and
dense, but then so
are the conditions of and
from which it speaks.

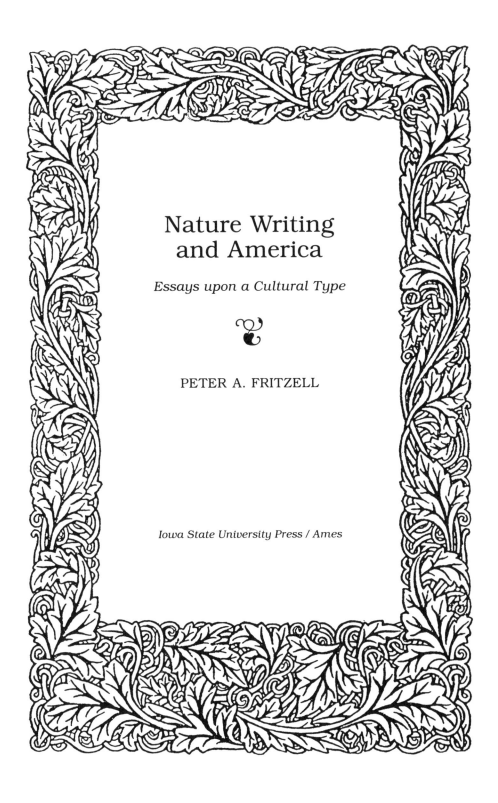

Nature Writing and America

Essays upon a Cultural Type

PETER A. FRITZELL

Iowa State University Press / Ames

© 1990 Iowa State University Press, Ames, Iowa 50010
All rights reserved
Manufactured in the United States of America
⊗ This book is printed on acid-free paper.

Library of Congress Cataloging-in-Publication Data

Fritzell, Peter A.
    Nature writing and America : essays upoon a cultural type / Peter A. Fritzell.—1st
    ed.
        p. cm.
    Bibliography: p.
    Includes index.
    ISBN 0-8138-0117-6
    1. Natural history literature—United States. I. Title.
    QH104.F74   1990
    508.73—dc20   89-15377

For Peter, John, and Marlys

and, as they know,

for two Teagues and one Trace

CONTENTS

ACKNOWLEDGMENTS

his book has been many seasons in the making. Formative parts of it doubtless go back to early childhood, to a pregnant mother shooting teal in a prairie sunrise from a grassy rockpile, with her three-year-old, black-raincoated son as retriever—to a father flycasting crappies on the edges of lilypad beds, or glassing warblers in the tops of backyard elm trees, or pointing to avocets and phalaropes in late-summer potholes. Thanks be to them.

Thanks be as well to members of the faculty of the University of North Dakota: to the ant man, George Wheeler; to Dale Riepe of the philosophy department; to Robert Caldwell of the English department. Thanks too to Peter Heath, then a lecturer in philosophy at St. Andrew's; and to several faculty associated with Stanford University: to John Clyde Loftis, the student of the Enlightenment, who inspired a first-term graduate student to scrounge the libraries for the periodical writings of John Burroughs; to David Levin, who fostered my interest in William Bartram and in all landscapes early American; to Howard Mumford Jones, a visitor whose urgings toward the literature of mining in early America I did not take; to William Clebsch, for bag-lunch training in matters stylistic, philosophic, and academic; to Wallace Stegner, for a sympathetic introduction to *A Sand County Almanac* and for enduring, kind encouragement in the study of natural things; and especially to Lawrence V. Ryan, Renaissance man, who not only took under his wing the fledgling from North Dakota, but who has supported him in each of his later moltings.

Thanks, too, to the National Endowment for the Humanities for the two fellowship-years without which this book would have been inconceivable—to Dartmouth College for a year's association as a visiting scholar in environmental studies—and to the many friends and colleagues at Lawrence University whose ongoing aids to my unconventional interests have sustained me in ways both economic and psychic: to the three Lawrence presidents whose material grants-in-aid have been much valued, and especially to President Richard Warch; to Thomas Headrick, then vice-president for academic affairs, for the time in England, Scotland, and Wales that enabled me to extend my reading and build my library in the nature writing of Britain; to J. Michael Hittle, less finally for his support as dean of the faculty than for those moments on the North Fork of the Flambeau or in early-autumn snowshowers when you know you are not alone; to Leonard Thompson, for continued readings in theory and counselings in practice; to Jerald Bullis, not only for his understanding verse but also, and more, for many sunlit, alder-swamped memories that oblige far more than a modicum of praise; and to Richard Yatzeck, for the "thrum-whooshing" of many grouse and several very late, discursive nights.

Beyond these to thank, there are the many writers and scholars I have tried to acknowledge in both text and notes, and the many more whose influences inevitably go unmentioned. And, finally, of course, there are those to whom the book is dedicated, the members of the family who have had to tolerate my convoluted mind-tracks— Marlys, who has supported and suffered my frequent trips afield— and two sons and three Brittany spaniels, each of whom has given me almost constant lessons in epistemology and metaphysics—in the bone-chilling, snow-blown dusk of Christmas Eve cornfields, in the rainy aspen suckers of mid-October, and over the bluegill beds and smallmouth runs of bright early summers. If I have misread the moments and mislearned the lessons, it is no fault of theirs.

Chapter 6, "*Walden* and Paradox: Thoreau as Self-Conscious Ecologist," is reprinted by permission, in but slightly altered form, from *New England Review* (now *New England Review and Breadloaf Quarterly*), Vol. III, No. 1 (Autumn 1980): 51–67. Copyright © 1980 by Peter A. Fritzell. To the editor of *New England Review*, Sydney Lea, I extend the kinds of gratitude due both to a keen reader's eye and to the generosity that admits an outsider to the intricacies of local coverts. Chapter 7 is a slightly revised version of an essay that appears in *Companion to A Sand County Almanac*, ed. J. Baird Callicott, copyright © 1987 by the Board of Regents of the University of Wisconsin System, and used here by permission of the University of Wisconsin Press. An earlier and slightly longer version of the same essay appeared in *Transactions of the Wisconsin Academy of Sciences, Arts and Letters* 64 (1976): 22–64; and I gratefully acknowledge the permission of the same officials for its use here as well. To the editors of both these publications and to the family of Aldo Leopold I offer my continuing appreciation. Throughout they have understood the qualms of consciousness and conscience that are endemic to the thoughtful management of natural resources.

For permission to reprint the "Homestead Act" that appears as an epigraph to chapter 4, I thank Jerald Bullis again. This poem, composed of a place called "the cabin," on a marshy lake in northwestern Wisconsin, was originally published in the short-lived *Cornell Review*. To Annie Dillard, in turn, I can do little more than extend the thanks and the recognition due from one pilgrim to another.

Finally, I extend my grateful acknowledgment to the following for permission to reprint excerpts from these books:

To Harper & Row Publishers, Inc., for extensive quotation from Annie Dillard's *Pilgrim at Tinker Creek*. Copyright © 1974 by Annie Dillard.

To Oxford University Press for selections from Aldo Leopold's *A Sand County Almanac and Sketches Here and There*. Copyright © 1949, 1977 by Oxford University Press, Inc.

To Yale University Press for selections from *The Travels of William Bartram: Naturalist's Edition*, edited by Francis Harper. Copyright © 1958 by Yale University Press.

To Ohio State University Press for selections from *The Centenary Edition of the Works of Nathaniel Hawthorne, Volume VIII: The American Notebooks*, edited by Claude M. Simpson. Copyright © 1932, 1960, 1972 by the Ohio State University Press.

To Princeton University Press for selections from Henry D. Thoreau's *Walden*, edited by J. Lyndon Shanley. Copyright © 1971 by Princeton University Press.

To Marcelle L. Krutch for quotations from Joseph Wood Krutch's "Prologue" to *Great American Nature Writing* (New York: Wm. Sloane, 1950). Copyright © 1978 by Marcelle Krutch.

A NOTE ON "MAN" AND NATURE

Throughout this book, and with some regularity, I have used the terms *man* and *mankind* as synonyms for what Western peoples have been given to calling *the human species*, as synonyms for the likes of *humankind, Homo sapiens, humanoid, hominid*, and *anthropoid*, all but the last of which encodes one or another echo of the masculine "man" or "homo." Where I have so used the terms *man* and *mankind*, I have done so either because they have seemed truer to my historical subjects (male or female) than other available alternatives, or because I have been seeking to expose and dramatize the underlying logic and ontology of the tradition in which they speak—its psychological, sociological, and, finally, even its biological and ecological incongruities.

In the Western world we have not yet learned to speak with quietude of "human and nonhuman nature"; and in America, especially, we are not inclined to appreciate the differences between that phrase and the far more popular and traditional "man and nature"—or such variants of the latter as "woman and nature" or "man and land." We are still much taken, too much it seems to me, by "man's (or woman's) relations to nature," too much worried about "what man (or woman) has done to nature," and not enough, not nearly enough, about what man or humankind or Homo sapiens or even humanity (of either sex) does, and has done, *in* nature—as if we do (or could do) what we do in any other venue. In America, especially, we are still very much given to those ancestral visions in which we say men and women are or will become parts of nature, as if any of us could ever be a part of anything else, whatever our conceptions or phrasings of our conditions. In the same inherited vein, we are still much inclined to speak of someone or other (Thoreau or John Muir or Annie Dillard, perhaps) as being more sensitive to "nature" than someone else (say John D. Rockefeller or the members of the U.S. Army Corps of Engineers)—as if any of us (for all our differences) has ever been sensitive to anything else—as if we ever could be. We are still much given, in other words, to that version of the American dream in which "man (as humankind or anthropoid, of either sex or either gender) is (or becomes) a part of nature"—that inherited dream of the New World which, in its not so variant phrasings, most often unwittingly betrays the very disjunctive and dualistic (and by now occasionally even "alienated") heritage it is conceived by many—and most often unwittingly—to rectify, redeem, or subvert.

When I deal in *man* and *mankind* as synonyms for *humankind* and *humanoid*, then, I do so in large part because the hundreds of figures (of both sexes) about whose writings I am speaking themselves speak in such terms, and would only be misrepresented by such alternative phrasings as "humanity's relations to nature" or "humankind's relations to land"—but also in part because I am trying to address and expose a heritage and a pattern of usage for and of which such alternatives as "humankind and nature" or "humanity and nature" or even "woman and nature" are at best (or would be) but comparably telling echoes, echoes of the sort that continue to present man or woman or humankind as somehow the coequal of nature—rather than as a diminutive and relatively short-lived scrap of same, an utterly dependent and subordinate part, one might say.

Part One

Introduction

Chapter One

Preliminary Concerns

he initial chapters in this book are presented, finally, as a series of speculations—a set of woefully incomplete conjectures, surmises, and hypotheses—about the origins, the functions, the history, and the attributes of what we popularly and far too loosely call "nature writing." The later chapters, close readings of exemplary individual works, are my attempts to illustrate what can and ought to be done in the critical analysis of nature writing, both by way of connecting it with the broad contours of Western thought and by way of elucidating its underlying drama.

In the last analysis, I will be pleased if these essays do something to stimulate ongoing discussion and even argument about a form of writing that, for all its continuing popularity and occasional real achievements, has generally been neglected (and even disparaged) in serious literary history and criticism. The essential argument of the book as a whole is, I suppose, fairly simple: that nature writing, in its preeminently Thoreauvian form, is fundamentally an American phenomenon; that it arose from an uneasy, inherently unstable, and especially American attempt to meld or blend the traditions and forms of Aristotle's *Historia Animalium*, on the one hand, and Saint Augustine's *Confessions*, on the other; that nowhere in the world are (or were) disinterested biological or geological science and personal or spiritual identity (or autobiography)—the two defining components of Thoreauvian nature writing—as closely or deeply related as they are (were and have been) in America; and that the underlying drama deriving from that relationship reflects or, better, captures one of the signal, definitive tensions of American and Western culture.

3

To some readers this book will seem to reflect an obsession with things American, to the exclusion of forms and types of art, literature, science, and thought found in other cultures, and generally believed quite akin (if not identical) to their American counterparts. To people of this persuasion, I can only say, at the moment, bear with me; I hope not only to show how and why the best American nature writing is distinct from the "nature writing" of other cultures, but also to suggest, at least, that natural history, natural science, and even ecology perform discriminably different functions in America than they do elsewhere.

To other readers this book will seem to reflect an obsession with a rather narrow conception of genre, specifically with that form of prose typified by *Walden*, and later extended and amplified in the prose of Aldo Leopold, Loren Eiseley, Edward Abbey, Annie Dillard, Barry Lopez, and John Janovy, among others. To people of this persuasion, in turn, I can only say that I am fully aware that the tensions I identify as definitive to the best American nature writing are also, in broadly philosophical terms, the tensions that define much of the "nature poetry" of the West—from Wordsworth through Dickinson, Frost, and Jeffers to Roethke, Snyder, Ted Hughes, and Ammons. It could even be said that the paradoxes and tensions I here identify as central to the best American nature writing are fundamentally and finally the defining tensions in the work of Plato, Dante, and Shakespeare—or Melville, Woolf, and Eliot—as they are as well, I suppose, in the works of Saint Teresa, Kant, and Wittgenstein, among many many others.

The case I would make here is not that the dialectic of the best American nature writing is somehow "logically" unique, but that the commitments of the best American nature writers, their allegiances to the antipodal elements of that dialectic, are different (and often more extreme) than they are in classical and contemporary verse or fiction or philosophy. No poet (with the possible exception of Lucretius) or philosopher or writer of fiction whose works I know, not even the most serious "nature poet," has ever demonstrated Thoreau's or Dillard's or Janovy's—much less John Muir's or John Hay's—allegiance to extended scientific catalogues, descriptions, or explications; and the extent of that commitment, it seems to me, necessarily makes the reading—the psychology and the grammar (if not the "logic")—of such nature writing different from, say, the reading of Ammons's more figural or typological uses of scientific terminology.

There are, of course, many poets, writers of fiction, and even philosophers whose works, while lacking that allegiance to the vocabularies and styles of natural history and science, are quite as intensely engaged as the best American nature writers in knowing self-conception, self-reflection, and self-analysis. There are also many literary naturalists, scientific essayists, and what W. J. Keith has called rural writers as committed as the best American nature writers have been to taxonomic identification and scientific exposition; but none of them is similarly committed to the composition and analysis of the isolate, individual self.[1] In short, I would defend my obsessions with American nature writing by arguing that it partakes, at its best, both of the form of spiritual autobiography or diary and of the form of natural history or systematic biology—both of Rousseau's *Confessions* or Wordsworth's *Prelude* or Camus's *L'Étranger* and of *Gerard's Herbal* or Linnaeus's *Systema Naturae* or Eugene Odum's *Fundamentals of Ecology*—both of Jonathan Edwards's "Personal Narrative" and of the catalogues of species one finds in so many narratives of exploration and travel—both of Emerson's journals and of Louis Agassiz's *Contributions to the Natural History of the United States*—and that it does so in a way technically distinguishable from other kinds of writing, a way that typically confounds conventional literary categories and often violates conventional criteria for consistent narrative and exposition.

There is no way, it seems to me—certainly no easy way—of decently comprehending the combination of Ishmael's (and Melville's) alternating self-assertions and self-doubts (humorous or otherwise), on the one hand, and his "Cetology" (humorous or serious), on the other, unless one comprehends something as well of the interplay in much of early America between uncertainties (often fairly radical) ❯ about personal and spiritual identity, on the one hand, and driving dedications, on the other hand, to compose systematic and scientific accounts especially of one's nonhuman surroundings. Something very broadly similar might readily be said of the reciprocation between the personal and the scientific in the works of Cooper, Audubon, and Franklin—or William Bartram, Jonathan Edwards, and Poe—as it might reasonably be said as well of William Byrd or Caroline Kirkland or Mark Catesby. That interplay, more than anything else—or so it seems to me—is ultimately and historically responsible not only for America's extensive (perhaps, even extreme) dedication to natural science, but also for the remarkable favor its citizen-readers continue to grant first-person singular narratives of all kinds. That interplay is not only responsible for the continued currency (often the near idolization) of even the most mundanely assured nature writers—and their numerous, supporting botanical, ornithological, and now "environmental" clubs and organizations (associations and clubs in many ways almost religiously ritualistic)—but responsible as well for the Montaignes and Pascals on the

American "natural" scene, for the dialectic of the best American nature writing, for the ambiguities of *Walden* and the paradoxes of *Pilgrim at Tinker Creek*.

In my view, *Walden*, and *A Sand County Almanac*, and *Pilgrim at Tinker Creek*, and *Desert Solitaire*, and Janovy's *Keith County Journal*, and Lopez's *River Notes*, and the nature writing of Loren Eiseley are the archetypification of that historic interplay between personal narrative and systematic science, perhaps even the perfection of it—not only the fairly straightforward reportage that characterizes the majority of nature writing in America—not the systematic exposition or enthusiastic publication of "nature" only—but the composition, examination, celebration, and doubt of individual human self as well, including doubts about the efficacy (and, perhaps, even the honesty) of one's writing—sometimes, indeed, the efficacy of any writing at all, and of human language generally. This troublesome and often paradoxical blend of impersonal (and largely descriptive) science, on the one hand, and intensely (and often egoistic) personal narrative and reflection, on the other, continues to seem to me distinct and peculiar to the best American nature writing. It seems to me as well to derive ultimately from a combination of psychological, social, and biotic conditions peculiar to landed
• early Americans, specifically to peoples attempting to settle the United States.

In fact, the best American nature writing is honestly and heavily committed both to the normal and to the abnormal, simultaneously given both to settling the world and to unsettling it. In *Walden*, as in the writings of John Muir and Edward Abbey, or Annie Dillard and Loren Eiseley, such nature writing reflects and expresses not only that deep, original American desire to escape history or civilization, to return to Eden and become again an unthinking, unsinning part of nature, as we say, but also that just-as-original and contrary American drive to improve upon history, to practically, if not programmatically, advance and even perfect it—often, ironically, by attempting to retire from the social and civilized scene and, even more tellingly, by *writing the document* or recording the experience that will tell all history what it's like to know The Natural or The Wild.

Inevitably, I suppose, the conflicts between these two formative desires have produced a dialectic of systematic assertion and acute skepticism in the best American nature writing, an unusual drama of extended and often fairly mundane expositions of fact, on the one hand, and unremitting and often fairly intricate self-reflections, on the other. The result, at its best, is a literature of extreme positions: egoistic celebrations of self alternating with various forms of self-deprecation or self-effacement; what to many readers is excessive and almost catechistic description or exposition juxtaposed with extravagant forms of self-consciousness; extended and straightforward accounts of nonhuman nature played against radical doubts, doubts not only about the efficacy of civilized institutions, but deep suspicions as well about one's own impositions upon (and even pollutions of) that same nonhuman nature.

The best American nature writers are (and have been) so taken with, committed to, and consumed by "nature in the original"— and simultaneously so skeptical of the methods of historic civilization—that they have come perilously close to extreme forms of self-consciousness and self-doubt. They have so identified with "nature" that they have come to suspect deeply their own motivations as writers, and seriously to view their own writing, even their most scientific writing, as plain animal behavior, however "articulate." At their most extreme, they have come close to identifying and, hence, "confusing" the conventional categories of modern Western thought and sanity. Even as they have knowingly and methodically used those categories—man and nature, subject and object, art and science, emotion and reason, fiction and fact—to represent and examine their relations to their surroundings, they have also sought to confound those categories (and their implicit methods) and to prove them inadequate as explanatory terms for the human individual's relations to nonhuman nature. They have often presented and considered what we (and they) would conventionally call the artificial as if it were natural—and, conversely, what we would conventionally call the natural as if it were artifice, as if it were the product of human ingenuity, imagination, or design. With comparable regularity, they have conceived both art and science (including their own efforts at same) as natural devices or adaptive strategies—as psycho- and sociobiotic developments of evolution or as expressions of ecosystemic interactions.[2]

It is almost as if their confrontations with and absorptions in these *American* lands—the combination of their needs literally to locate themselves (to come to daily, practical terms with the elements of their surroundings) and the ongoing power of their inherited conceptions of America—have driven them to question seriously the prevailing logic of their inherited culture even as (or *because*) they have been forced to use and, hence, to ratify (if not affirm) that very logic (and its attendant vocabularies) in their primary accounts of themselves and their environments. Like many an early American settler, America's nature writers have been caught between their needs to locate themselves, to place themselves systematically, and their desires to quit the business of hav-

· ing to locate things, their dreams of immersing themselves in a prehistoric, unconscious, and Edenic NATURE.

In fact, their dilemmas and their awkwardnesses, their vacillations and alternations, echo and perpetuate in some detail the elementary experience of many early, landed Americans. Though, unlike the early settler, they have been aided by detailed topographic maps, field guides, taxonomic manuals, and scientific textbooks, they have otherwise sought, in Thoreau's famous words, "to drive life into a corner, and reduce it to its lowest terms," to confront nonhuman nature alone, without further significant institutional, social, or familial support. What they have found, of course—however reluctantly—is that the lowest "terms" for themselves (if not for other members of the species) are troublesomely institutional, fundamentally linguistic and stylistic. The underlying drama of their writings—their allegiances, their conditions, and even their skepticism—has thus mirrored one of the essential forms of American experience, both actual and mythic: the experience of a self-conscious human individual attempting to come to terms with what we far too innocently and unconsciously call "the land."

In a "world" of few maps, fewer guidebooks, and no established funds of local lore—in the world of the early American settler—the process of literally locating oneself requires, among other things, the making of primitively operative distinctions; and it certainly increases one's awareness both of one's basic needs for such distinctions and of their final flimsiness, fragility, and artificiality. Artificial and arbitrary though names and place-names may seem under such conditions, one's needs for same may well appear essential, as it were—if not downright natural or organic—and the distinction between art or artifice and nature (between name and nature, if not between appearance and reality) will seem both less significant and less clear than it does in the warming confines of a local pub or in a lecture hall.

The effort to maintain one's inherited conceptions of America under such conditions requires, in turn (if it doesn't entail), the reduction of all such historic distinctions into one natural, paradisaic whole, a perpetual place of places where distinctions between name and nature, art and science, or appearance and reality are not only unnecessary, but to and in which they are the ultimate betrayal. There is pride after all (as one version of the story goes, ultimate pride), if not in the making of such distinctions, then certainly in the belief that they will somehow enable humankind to transcend its limitations or, finally and historically, to comprehend its condition. There is humility as well (as the same version of the story goes), the humility (and despair of all worldly distinctions) which is the necessary prerequisite to salvation—a final condition easily thought of, perhaps, when one's terms for a New World don't seem to be working.

But then there is the other version of the story as well—the story, as we say, of the "fortunate fall"—which here might be viewed as the decay of medieval and feudal Europe, the entire fortune of which is then vested and invested in *America*, specifically in the United States. As Tom Paine was wont to say:

> TIS TIME TO PART. Even the distance at which the Almighty hath placed England and America is a strong and natural proof that the authority of the one over the other, was never the design of heaven. The time likewise at which the continent was discovered, adds weight to the argument, and the manner in which it was peopled, encreases the force of it. The Reformation was preceded by the discovery of America: As if the Almighty graciously meant to open a sanctuary to the persecuted in future years, when home should afford neither friendship nor safety. . . .
>
> . . . Freedom hath been hunted round the Globe. Asia and Africa have long expelled her. Europe regards her like a stranger, and England hath given her warning to depart. O! receive the fugitive, and prepare in time an asylum for mankind.

In this version of the story, pride is not sin or ultimate betrayal, but patriotism; and humility is (or soon becomes) the recognition that one is destined in one's unpretentious, agrarian way to herald the continuing, historic advance of humankind. In the six years between the publication of *Common Sense* (1776) and the appearance of Crevecoeur's *Letters from an American Farmer* (1782), Paine's "asylum" becomes "this great American asylum," an asylum on the move, and replete with only the best of human achievement. In the seemingly unassuming view of Crevecoeur's farmer, James:

> Here individuals of all nations are melted into a new race of men, whose labours and posterity will one day cause great changes in the world. Americans are the western pilgrims, who are carrying along with them that great mass of arts, sciences, vigour, and industry which began long since in the east; they will finish the great circle.

And in the words of William Ellery Channing:

> The great distinction of our country is, that we enjoy some peculiar advantages for understanding our own nature. Man is the great subject of literature, and juster and profounder views of

> man may be expected here than elsewhere. In Europe, political and artificial distinctions have, more or less, triumphed over and obscured our common nature. In Europe, we meet kings, nobles, priests, peasants. How much rarer is it to meet *men*; by which we mean human beings conscious of their own nature, and conscious of the utter worthlessness of all outward distinctions compared with what is treasured up in their own souls.[3]

The refrains are familiar. The stage is set—predestined even—for the reformation and renaissance of history across and upon the American landscape. But there is another, and potentially upsetting, side to even this version of the story.

When, as happens, one's inherited preconceptions of America—as a place where appearances and disguises do not (or will not) finally matter—are utterly disappointed, and daily or hourly impossible to maintain, the issues may well be confounded again. When ancestral conceptions dictating "the utter worthlessness of all outward distinctions" (including the distinction between appearance and reality) prove not only utterly misleading but at gross odds with one's hourly and daily efforts to locate oneself, the defining terms, categories, and images of those disappointed conceptions may again come into question. One may easily feel betrayed, in this case no doubt by one's ancestors—left out in the cold, as it were—and yet with little else upon which to proceed other than the very terms and categories one has inherited, the very terms and categories *America* was originally destined to do away with, or at the very least to improve upon.

Conceived of the late Middle Ages and the Renaissance, nursed and raised by the Enlightenment and Romanticism, America—the *New* World—proves itself, in the words of Wayne Franklin, "an epistemological problem"—and more than that even.[4] Since it is difficult, finally, to separate epistemology from ethics or politics, or metaphysics or science, or aesthetics or logic, America proves itself one vast and evermore intricate problem indeed. And the intricacies of that problem are dramatized in the works of the best American nature writers, as they are in *Moby-Dick* or Cather's *My Ántonia* or Faulkner's *The Sound and the Fury*.

Reading and rereading the works of America's best nature writers, one is tempted to say that there is something in the experience of the *American* land—or, better perhaps, the experience of *American* self in land—that tilts the epistemic and metaphysical underpinnings of historic Western culture and threatens to disturb its modernly dominant logic. Far from being able to transcend the limitations of their conditions or to comprehend and understand themselves and their environments, the best nature writers of America (including the supposed "transcendentalist," Thoreau) have found themselves almost constantly faced with the evidence—the inescapable facts, as it were—of those limitations. At its best (or worst), in fact, the best American nature writing has borne a striking similarity to the works of those classical mystics who have attempted to capture their experience in language. Like Saint Teresa or Kierkegaard or the T. S. Eliot of "Ash Wednesday" and *Four Quartets*, the best American nature writers have frequently found their words straining, cracking, and sometimes breaking "under the burden," most often at the very moments when they have needed those words to stay in place. And "staying in place," of course—composing or fixing the details of coherent, local places—has been one of their driving impulses, and one of the characteristics of their writing that distinguishes it finally from personal narratives of travel or scientific exploration.

Theirs has not been a literature of spatial journey or geographic quest. Instead, as Thoreau early indicated, it has been a literature of staying, (or, better, trying to stay) at home, trying to stay at a detailed and engaging, if frequently troubled, psychobiotic home—by no means a domicile in the conventional sense of the word, but (if things go well) a familiar and, above all, local ecosystem, the bounds of which cannot be separated from the terms, conceptions, and desires of its human maker, user, and appreciator—and the systematic detailing of which may provide, if only momentarily, the kinds of contingently reassuring root-systems to which one can return whenever flights of fancy or wit, or metaphysical dilemmas and epistemic paradoxes, threaten to disrupt the tentative centers of one's life.

The "quests" of the best American nature writers have finally been psychobiotic, metaphysical, and even psycholinguistic. In a sense, I suppose, they have attempted to construct and plumb "sacred places," but generally without dramatized institutional support (with the aids only of their personal libraries and especially those kinds of taxonomic guides that have enabled them to get a tentative grip on their surroundings), and always with the suspicion that institutionally and historically supported "sacred places," however necessary, are misleading, that truly sacred places are functions of growth rather than cultivation. So that, while they have been dedicated to the scientific delineation of their places, to the vocabularies and even the styles of systematic biology and ecology, they have also been suspicious of those styles and vocabularies—in open need of the fixings such science can provide, but uneasy about the un-self-conscious habits (and even naiveté) their use regularly seems to occasion.

Typically, the central narrators and expositors of American nature writing have been isolate figures, shunning the security of extended friendships or neighborhoods, wary of social and political commitments, and (with the one notable exception of their recurrent scientific descriptions and explanations) distrustful of the forms of established institutions. In any conventional sense of the term, they have been conspicuously "protestant" thinkers and writers. Far more than most, they have tried to do it on their own, to define their own places, and generally to establish direct, unmediated relations between themselves and their nonhuman others.

Their affinities to Saint Teresa or Saint John of the Cross or Petrarch on Mont Ventoux have been (and are), then, not a function of institutional affiliations, but of their having substituted (or attempted to substitute), however periodically, one catechism for another—the terms and figures of systematic biology and, now, ecology for the terms and figures of systematic theology—and of their continual and deep-rooted awareness of its final inadequacy. Generally, they have been all too aware not only of their limitations but also of their dependencies—especially, of course, their biotic and ecologic dependencies, but also their linguistic and psychic attachments, if not indeed their reliance on science as mediator and metaphor. For all their apparent "protestantism," and contrary to their popular reputations, they have been wary both of the saints of self-reliance and of those who would trumpet the eventual ascendance of the human species.[5] About the only terms they have been able to leave unexamined for more than a paragraph or two have been the ordinary terms of geobiotic science, and these terms have served them just as the terms, figures, and phrases of the religious calendar and the mass have served their classical theological counterparts, at best as something upon which self-consciously to construct what in handbooks of meditation are called compositions of place, contingent sets of images upon which to concentrate and reflect.

Anti-institutional in one sense, they have been solidly conventional in another, as deeply conservative and as plainly methodical as any self-conscious person in open need of elementary terms for self and surroundings. In the face of extreme self-doubt, despairing of themselves and humankind, they have regularly turned (or returned) to the descriptive basics of their nonhuman surroundings. When epistemological or metaphysical explorations have gotten out of hand, they have invariably brought themselves back to earth by authoring rudimentary accounts of an oak leaf, a beehive, or a chickadee—as if, having run amuck of Truth or Knowledge or Nature, they were seeking (or trying to seek) the security of things more routinely "known" or "knowable." The central figures in their writings have thus moved, with some awkwardness and pain, between extraordinary and even "abnormal" states of mind—states expressed in consciously mixed metaphors and pointed contradictions—and quite ordinary and even common states—states initially achieved with some degree of self-consciousness, but states in which their compositors have temporarily been able to lose themselves in the usual and the customary.

Their experience of what we call the overwhelming or incomprehensible has not, of course, been conventionally theological or religious. It has, rather, been deeply biotic or extensively ecological and evolutionary. Their epistemological doubts and metaphysical despairs have arisen not from contemplation of what we call the super- or supranatural, but from their desires and attempts to comprehend what we call "the natural," those nonhuman things and relationships that have traditionally been thought to go (or have been dreamed of going) before human language and history—those things and relationships quintessentially and originally Edenic and *American*, those aboriginal, prehistoric, and prelinguistic Realities which Western peoples were to discover (or rediscover) in the New (Old) World, "the state of nature" as it was before humans conceived or perceived it, or interfered with it and corrupted it—biotic relationships and chemical elements as they are "in nature," as we say—the logically strict implications being that neither we nor our laboratories are "in nature," that our efforts and discoveries are somehow "unnatural," that we by nature and condition are at odds with NATURE (or that we ought to be), and that we have somehow left it and our natural instincts behind and beneath us (or that we *must* do so).

Inevitable and at least half-committed heirs to these traditional ways of speaking and thinking, the best American nature writers have nonetheless found few things more foreign (and less adequate) to their experience. In part no doubt because those same traditional ways of speaking and thinking have foretold, as they still foretell, a "return" to prehistoric Nature in America—in part no doubt because they themselves have been at least half-dedicated to that ancestral end—and in part, finally (and I would argue most tellingly), because in their daily efforts to locate themselves they have indeed found themselves "closer to nature"—America's best nature writers, like many landed Americans, have had great difficulty with the notion that the human species is somehow unnatural or outside nature—great difficulty accepting the notion that humankind has (or can) somehow leave nature behind.

Traditional though such ways of thinking and speaking may be, in the best nature writing of post-Enlightenment (and Romantic) America they have done little but muddy prospective paradisal waters, nothing if they have not confused, befuddled, and (in a mathematical sense) radicalized the underlying logic and even the morality of classical Western thought—and for at least two reasons: first, no doubt, because in early and elementary America it is difficult, despite one's heritage, to convince oneself either that one is "outside" nature or that one has somehow left it behind (much less that one can); and, second, because—given the ancestral prospect of America, its sustaining preconceptions and images—it is by no means clear that one *should*.[6] Since the underlying, ancestral vision of America means a return to an unspoiled, prehistoric "nature," if it means anything—the discovery (or rediscovery or achievement) of a prelapsarian condition—it seems at least half like heresy to suggest that man in America should be at odds with nature, something like the ultimate betrayal of one's heritage to suggest or believe that one *ought* to leave nature behind or to overcome one's natural instincts. And when the paradisal version of one's heritage is coupled with the ostensible demise of original sin in the late eighteenth and early nineteenth centuries—when America more than any other place is defined by that apparently liberating prospect—when America becomes, as it does, not only the hope but the redemption and eventual salvation of humankind, it can easily seem the height of apostasy to say that man is (or should be) at odds with nature. American people, at least, must *not* put nature or natural instinct behind them; for to do so would be to forsake the original foundations of Western culture, its original paradisal myth in almost every Western language.

There are, then, at least two good reasons why it is difficult to separate man and nature in early and elementary America, two solid incentives not to dissociate the human and the nonhuman (or for that matter, reason and instinct or emotion, and even, I suspect, subject and object). One reason is daily, practical, and all too immediate: the almost constant awareness that one is very close to nature indeed. The other is mythic, theological, ideological, and perhaps even philosophic; and it derives in a troublesome way from the very heritage that otherwise declares not only that human and nonhuman nature are at odds with one and other (or that humanoids have somehow left nature behind) but that they must continue to distance themselves from it.

There are also, of course, at least two good reasons why it is easy to separate man and nature in early America, at least two solid incentives to continue to dissociate the human and the nonhuman (as well as reason and instinct, or word and thing, or subject and object). One reason, again, is daily, practical, and all too immediate: the almost constant need to establish familiar, accurate names for the objects and elements especially of one's nonhuman surroundings, and to do so in ways that are consonant with the prevailing usage, not to say the logic and the philosophy, of one's inherited culture—the only culture one has—and yet simultaneously suitable to environments and phenomena almost completely foreign to that culture—to enforce and reinforce traditional distinctions not only between man and nature, but also between name and nature, and most fundamentally perhaps, between self and others—if for no other reason than that those distinctions seem almost constantly threatened by one's immediate needs and conditions. The second reason for continuing to dissociate the human and the nonhuman in America is once again mythic, theological, and ideological—preeminently historical and even perhaps historiographic; and it, too, derives, at least a bit annoyingly, from the heritage that otherwise prophesies the discovery or rediscovery of paradisal symbiosis in America. It rests, first, in the mythology and the belief that, though humankind may once have lived in unconscious harmony with nature (or that "primitive" peoples still do), both she and he and all their heirs are now forever fated to make and understand of the world what they can, necessarily inadequate though their efforts and their terms must be; and it rests as well, and today perhaps even more powerfully, in the conviction that America must carry with it, for better or worse, that historic mass of "arts, sciences, vigour, and industry" that once emerged in the East—must come to know (and, hence, to manage or redeem) not only itself but the whole of creation systematically and scientifically.

Whether the terms are sacred or secular, as we say (and even if the latter are "confused" with the former), the logic and the psychology of the experience are terribly familiar. Whether the ding an sich is God or Nature unobserved and unconceived—whether the ineffable other is It or Thou—the psychology and even the philosophy abide. Though The Wild or The Natural or The Canada Goose may replace The Divine, the logical, epistemological, and psychological dilemma remains: how to know (or "experience" or describe) that which is, as we say, "beyond words"—without mucking it up, altering its condition, or otherwise influencing it—and then, recognizing in some form of classical despair (now an *American* despair, par excellence) that one can't know or comprehend or even "experience" The Wild or The Natural, feeling either that one has failed or that one has somehow polluted and betrayed it—how to get around, through, or behind the uncertainty principle on one's way to knowledge or paradise. The mind's road to The Muskrat or The Phoebe, if one is truly given to it, is just as difficult as the mind's road to God; and for the best American nature writers the roads have been essentially one, evoking the same fundamental awareness of the limitations of human language and conception.

The various dimensions of the heritage have been troublesome enough in their European shapes and stylings. In self-conscious Americans they have tended to create radical disjunctions and at least mild forms of a kind of cultural schizophrenia—extreme tensions between several senses of dislocation, on the one hand, and deep (even obsessed) desires to locate, on the other—and nowhere more so than in the best nature writers.

Most American nature writers, obviously, have been nowhere near as self-conscious as Thoreau or Dillard or Janovy. Most have been unable or unwilling to cast either their own needs and impulses or the underlying terms of their inherited culture (much less their own phrasings) into critical or biotic perspective—and not surprisingly. For the kinds of self-consciousness that typify and define the *best* American nature writing require a tolerance for ambiguity that is very difficult to sustain—a dedication to paradox, and even an occasional delight in uncertainty, that can be extremely unsettling. The dominant rhetorical stance of modern science, moreover—the biology, the geology, the physics, the chemistry, and now the ecology, which (along with Romantic landscape art) have been the sources of most American nature writers' essential terms and conceptions, the groundwork to their principal modes of thought— has been, as it no doubt must continue to be, fundamentally positivistic and representational. That rhetorical stance enforces and entails a view of relations between language and experience in which words are tools or devices wherein and whereby to represent the truths of phenomenal reality, a reality of which language is not generally considered a part (and certainly not a determinant), but a kind of transparent medium which, if precisely and systematically used, will enable us to see things (and, hence, to locate ourselves) with verifiable (or at least "highly probable") clarity.

That rhetorical stance was, of course—as it continues to be— utterly essential to the elementary and "early" experience of America. In almost daily need of primitively descriptive terms for their surroundings, in the face of a plethora of denominational and cultural creeds (all of them deriving from one old world or another, and few of them clearly sanctioned beyond one's own congregation or parish), and in lieu of other warranted methods of accounting for themselves and their environments, many (perhaps most) Americans (and the vast majority of American nature writers) have inevitably (and most often unwittingly) turned to the logic and terminology of modern scientific culture for their primary authorizing means to identity and location. Most American nature writers, like most Americans, have thus responded almost solely to those original incentives to dissociate language and experience, or word and thing, or man and nature, even when they haven't "meant" to. For those dissociations and discriminations, like the modern science built upon them, are designed precisely to counter the psychic and social instabilities, the epistemic uncertainties, that elementary American experience seems so easily to occasion, in *Moby-Dick* as in *Walden*, or in Faulkner's *The Sound and the Fury* and Barry Lopez's *River Notes*. Indeed, modern science is dedicated to resolving the tensions and ambiguities of that experience and to minimizing (if not eradicating) the literally anthropo-logical, biotic, and linguistic self-consciousness that may otherwise seem almost endemic to an American's condition.

Most American nature writers, then, have replicated and reinforced the dominant rhetorical stance of modern science, in large part because the underlying logic and epistemology of that stance have compensated for the daily uncertainties of their rudimentary experiences—because that stance does nothing to encourage (and much to discourage) the kinds of self-consciousness that trouble a Thoreau or an Eiseley—and because that logic and epistemology are devoted to eliminating the kinds of paradox that define *Walden* and *The Immense Journey*, if not even to subduing the humbler doubts of *A Sand County Almanac*.

It is hardly surprising, therefore—and nothing but understandable—that the vast majority of America's nature writers have turned toward one form or another of conventionally disciplined science, and away from the potentially exhausting effects of self-consciousness—away from self (insofar as they have been able to) and toward their nonhuman others. It is even understandable, perhaps, that they have written what are largely "undramatic" works, works not so much of interrogation or inquiry (and certainly not of introspection) as works of identification, information, and appreciation, works that establish and assert rather than doubt or question, works of explication rather than complication:

> Shrubby cinquefoil, another shrub of this layer, also belongs to the rose family. This is the only bush cinquefoil, the others being graceful herbs. "Cinquefoil" refers to the five-fingered leaves.

Like the rose, the flower has five brilliant petals; its color is yellow right out of the paint tube, set against five green sepals, and a profusion of stamens. The shredded gray-brown bark, hanging in ribbons, and the dried sepals identify the shrub even without leaves. Cinquefoil is browsed by deer only when better forage is not available; wildlife biologists use it as an "indicator plant." If the cinquefoils are heavily eaten, the range is over-populated with deer.

Squaw currant and gooseberry both have tiny pink flowers early in the summer, and they are easiest to tell apart when they bear their characteristic berries. Grouse are fond of them both for food, and the dried berries sometimes persist on the plant all winter long. Both shrubs send out long arching canes which root at the tip, and when growth is heavy in moist places, provide shelter for rabbit and bird. (ANN ZWINGER, *Beyond the Aspen Grove*, 200)

At Moraine Lake the cañon proper terminates, although apparently continued by the two lateral moraines of the vanished glacier. These moraines are about 300 feet high, and extend unbrokenly from the sides of the cañon into the plain, a distance of about five miles, curving and tapering in beautiful lines. Their sunward sides are gardens, their shady sides are groves; the former devoted chiefly to eriogonae, compositae, and graminae; a square rod containing five or six profusely flowered eriogonums of several species, and about the same number of bahia and linosyris, and a few grass tufts; each species being planted trimly apart, with bare gravel between, as if cultivated artificially. (JOHN MUIR, *The Mountains of California*, 72)

This year has also been rich in Indian pipes. This is that unreal, pure-white plant, which, in more mythical times, has been called the corpse plant, or ghost flower. It blooms by itself, though out of the moist woodland humus like the mushrooms, lacking chlorophyll as they do. There is some dispute apparently, consistent with the Indian pipe's ghostly nature, about what it really is. Some books refer to it as a "saprophyte," which means a plant that absorbs its nutrition from dead or decaying organic matter, but in others it is called a "parasite." A parasite gets its nourishment from a living host. The Indian pipe has a very small mat of rootlets where the thick stems join together at the base of the plant. If you dig it out of the ground it looks as if it were resting on bare knuckles. These roots, according to the botanists, have an outer layer of funguslike tissue, which means that the fungus rather than the roots has actual contact with the soil. So it sounds as though the Indian pipe, being dependent for its food on the fungus and not the soil or humus, were a parasite. Another alternative, if the fungus gets any nourishment from the plant, is that they live in a state of mutual association, or symbiosis. Thus science, still trying for exactitude, and the Indian pipe, still unaccountable. It seems to be on the verge of several worlds rather than an integral part of one, a plant you might meet in a dream.

Other old and once popular names for it are: Dutchman's-pipe; fairy smoke; convulsion weed; eyebright; bird's nest; and American ice plant. It was called ice plant, according to Alice O. Albertson in her *Nantucket Wild Flowers* (1921), because "it resembles frozen jelly and is juicy and tender and dissolves in the hands like ice." One contemporary authority calls it "clammy," which is accurate enough, and keeps it in the realm of ghosts and chills, but I think it was an exaggeration to say that it dissolves in the hands. I find it solid enough, not fragile or perishable to the touch. Its stems have a fibrous, tough core, which is sometimes hard to tear. It also has a pungent, woody smell, though this probably comes from the soil it grows in.

All the same, it is an elusive, beautiful flower, a miraculous specialty. Coral pink shines almost translucently through the stems, which are covered with tiny white bracts, or scales, taking the place of leaves—scales of a tiny albino fish perhaps—and the bell-like flowers hang their stiff white heads straight down, with pink seed pods standing up between them, round, decoratively grooved little crowns. When the plant dies, it stands for months as a thin, brownish black string, having turned from beautiful ghost to lifeless reality. (JOHN HAY, *Nature's Year*, 76–77)[7]

The vast majority of American nature writing has functioned almost solely to settle the country—to compose it and delineate it, to give its elements sanctioned identities, and then to appreciate them—to establish (and perhaps occasionally to puzzle over) names and classifications, to fix (or attempt to fix) the terms of the nonhuman environment, and, if or when terms prove hard to select or difficult to certify, to celebrate in some customary way the country's mysteries and elusiveness—in one way or another to ordain American lands, without thinking too much about the process (or the particular terms) of ordination.

Though even the most popular American nature writing may sometimes seem to query the functions and outcomes of Western and American civilization (often in the abstract), its terms and phrasings have regularly mirrored and reinforced the underlying and dominant logic of that civilization—either the controlling rhetorical stance of modern science, or its philosophic backside, the dominant, popular, post-Cartesian and Romantic aesthetic of "nature," according to which science is a coldly rational enemy and we must learn to reinsert "emotion" or "sympathy" into our understandings and appreciations, in this case especially our appreciations of our nonhuman surroundings. Whatever side of the philosophic coin appears up, the conventional (and largely unknowing) dualism has prevailed. The vast majority of America's nature writers, like the vast majority of America's "environmentalists," have been precisely what one would expect them to be, inevitable and for the most part unwitting creatures of their culture, even when (or, rather, especially when) they have consciously sought to be otherwise. There are, after all, few Thoreaus or Dillards or Eiseleys in this world, few who are willing or able to cast their ancestral logic (much less themselves and their own language) into critical perspective, few in the sciences and (perhaps more troublesomely) few in the humanities who have been willing or able to consider themselves and their efforts to understand what we call nature as constantly and inevitably constrained by language.

Though even the most popular and conventional American nature writers may occasionally seem to have despaired of human history and civilization, they have not, and pointedly have not, queried the functions, status, or stature of nonhuman nature (or the languages, scientific and aesthetic, conventionally used to represent them). Hence (unlike Thoreau or Eiseley or Abbey), they have done little but bolster those classical Western distinctions between moral (or immoral) man and amoral (or Moral) nature; between the unpredictable, variable, and fickle world of Man and the dependable, harmonious, perennial world of Nature; or, in one of today's alternative arrangements, between the now determinant and even pernicious global dominion of the human species and the fragile or vulnerable condition of the ecosphere. In classic and conventional Western fashion, they have given the powers and the pains of "ought" and "ought not"—the capacities for guilt or shame or vengeance (and, hence, the prerogatives and licenses of responsibility and irresponsibility)—solely to humans, while reserving the dependable and trustworthy "is," the absence of conscience and consciousness, for nonhuman nature. If they have seemed occasionally to despair of Man, they have never despaired of what modern, Western peoples conventionally call Nature (though they have often, of course, despaired *for* Nature). They have placed their undying faith in the "facts" or "processes" (in the "patterns," the "rhythms," the "cycles," the "beauty," and even the "Morality") of the natural world "out there," as we say. In the process they have echoed both that traditional faith (originally a European faith) in America as "Nature's Nation" and that classical and especially post-Cartesian way of thinking that dissociates mind and body, or reason and emotion, or fiction and fact, and that finally finds salvation in "practical philosophy," a philosophy of "methods and results," scientific or aesthetic, which may enable mankind not only to become "masters and possessors of nature," enjoying "the fruits of the earth and all its commodities," but improving "health" as well, "which is undoubtedly the first good, and the foundation of all other goods of this life."[8]

What Descartes saw (or hoped for) in medicine—"some means of rendering men as a whole wiser and more dextrous than they have been"—the prospect of freeing "ourselves of an infinity of illnesses" and perhaps even "the decline of age"—the majority of America's nature writers, like many (if not most) American people, have seen and dreamed of in images and concepts of ecosystemic and environmental health, in improved and increased knowledge of "our natural environments" or in a "better understanding of man's relations to nature," in a "return to nature" or a "return to the land," in "a life in balance with nature" or in "nature study" and "natural areas," and finally perhaps in "the restoration or preservation of natural environments," in "wilderness areas" and "wild rivers," and now even in "environmental management" and "ecological engineering." In fact, a large part of the story of "Man and Nature in America" could be reasonably and accurately told by conceiving and considering it as an attempt to extend medical science to nonhuman organisms and systems.

In each of these phrases and in each of their coordinate efforts, America's nature writers—like their popular, political, and now professional empathizers—have underwritten the fundamental faith of the modern, Western world, not simply the faith that Man's (or Nature's) lot can be improved, for that is obvious enough, but (and more importantly) the faith in our conventional (and largely unexamined) phrasings of same, phrasings that by now function almost as a creed. It is simply not possible, after all, to speak of (and certainly not to advocate) "a life in balance with nature" without disconnecting "life" and "nature," without implying and assuming a view of the cosmos in which that life (in this case a human life) is separate from (and, most tellingly perhaps, coequal to) the entirety of nature. It is not possible to speak of a "return to nature" without implying and assuming that humans (or at least Western, and especially perhaps American, humans) either are not parts of nature or are at some partial remove from it—that they have somehow left it behind or beneath them, or that they can (or could). The proof in the Western and American pudding here is that no one has as yet felt it necessary to speak of or advocate the return to nature of the wood duck or the quaking aspen, or even of the Holstein or the Brittany spaniel.

It is not possible to speak of (much less to advocate) a "return to the land" without assuming and implying both that humans (or, at least, some humans) *have* "left" the land, and that they *can* (or could) and thus defeating one's apparent "purpose," to remind people that they *cannot* "leave" the land, that they cannot take their sustenance from any other source. It is not even possible to speak of a "better understanding of man's relations to nature"—or to advocate "nature study" and "natural areas"—without separating man and nature, or setting human and nonhuman nature apart—and, hence, both undermining one's apparent argument and syntactically, logically, psychologically, and sociologically replicating the understanding and the logic of one's presumed opponents, opponents who in recent decades have come to be identified as unthinking, insensitive Western dualists.

To recognize that "wild rivers" and "wilderness areas" are not wild—or that one cannot speak of "man's relations to nature" without divorcing man and nature—requires an attention to language, and an understanding of what one might call its natural functions, that have been (and continue to be) almost entirely foreign to the majority of America's nature writers, as they have been foreign to the majority of Americans generally. Such a recognition requires that language be seen as something other than an innocent, transparent medium wherein and whereby truth or experience is represented—something more or less than an inexpensive device whereby we may come to easy terms with ourselves and our surroundings. Such a recognition requires that language be considered—with more frequency than most Americans, at least, find comfortable—not simply as a historical and societal event, but as a physical, biological, and psychobiotic phenomenon (even in this sentence); and it requires as well that the physical, biological, and psychobiotic functions of language be taken seriously, more seriously than most Americans—and most American nature writers—have been willing or able to take them.

To recognize that the phrase "natural areas" is either redundant (that all areas are natural) or self-contradictory (that any "area" so labeled is *not* "natural") requires (if it does not entail) at least occasional reminders of what most Americans do not want to be reminded of, that no word or sentence is ever spoken or authored without interest, especially perhaps psychobiotic interest, and that all words and sentences are contingent, in this context perhaps especially biologically and psychologically contingent. To recognize

the civilized in the wild, or the human in the Indian pipe and the
saprophyte, or the linguistic in the nonlinguistic (without endless
series of subscripts or continuous quotation marks) requires, in
short, precisely that consciousness or self-consciousness that was
(and continues to be) an all too present threat in (and to) the elementary and original experience of America. It requires an awareness of
language and style that almost everything in American history and
culture has been designed to avoid and subdue or escape.

Most American nature writers, then, have regularly and methodically reinforced conventional distinctions between man and
land, or name and nature, or metaphor and fact, even when they
haven't "meant" to. In the face of daily experiences that might easily have suggested otherwise, they have maintained their faith in
"nature's ways" or, what is the same thing, in the capacities of
humankind to know and understand—in the abilities, for example,
of the monarch butterfly (*Danaus plexippus*) "to sequester the
highly toxic glycosides present in milkweed plants . . . thereby providing a highly effective defense against bird predators," or in the
tendencies of "any ecosystem not subjected to strong disturbances"
to change "in a progressive and directional way," or, quite simply,
perhaps, in the "Persimmon (*Diospyros virginiana* L.)," which is

> a tree with distinctive dark thick bark typically broken into
> *small squarish blocks.* Leaves somewhat thickened, egg-
> shaped, and *not toothed.* Buds *very dark with 2 scales.* End
> buds false. Pith sometimes divided into chambers by weak parti-
> tions. Var. *pubescens* (Pursh) Dippel (found south from Virginia,
> s. Illinois, and s. Iowa) has hairy twigs and leaf undersides.
> Leaves 2″-5″. Height 30′-50′ (130′); diameter 10″-12″ (7′).
> Flowers yellowish, May–June. Fruits slightly larger than culti-
> vated cherries, orange-colored, edible when ripe, Aug.–Oct., or
> later. . . . The green fruit causes the mouth to "pucker up" for
> some time after being tasted. However, cool, ripe Persimmons
> that are soft and fully colored are delicious. They are eaten by
> nearly all birds and mammals, from songbirds to turkeys and
> from dogs to deer. The Persimmon, a member of the ebony fam-
> ily, has strong, heavy, close-grained wood, occasionally used as
> shoe lasts and shuttles.[9]

Like John Hay's narrative figure above, the majority of Ameri-
·ca's nature writers have regularly distinguished between more and
less "mythical" times, the implicit (and often more than implicit)
suggestion being, of course, that we in the modern and American
West live not in mythical times—however troublesome *our* times

may be, however harmonious those earlier, mythical times must have been—but in times of fact or truth or, at the very least, probability and hypothesis. In so discriminating our time from mythic time, and our ways from mythic ways, the vast majority of America's nature writers (and their narrators) have reiterated and underlined (however unknowingly) the original Western vision of an Eden or a Golden Age when and where things were right, and from which we have been thrust (or, worse perhaps, have thrust ourselves) and to which we must make every effort to return. Even Hay's mildly troubled appreciator of the Indian pipe, though he is considerably more conscious of stylistic and linguistic nuance than his more conventional counterparts, can speak with only the slightest and entirely customary irony about what "the Indian pipe" (the definite article is telling) "really is"—while almost simultaneously asserting its unaccountable, ghostly nature—about "saprophyte" and "parasite"—without allowing his quotation marks or the implications of his slight ironic comment on scientific taxonomies and taxonomists to trouble in any serious way his own categorical efforts. Though he is considerably less naive than his counterparts in the works of Muir or Zwinger, he too, finally, is able to maintain his conventional concentration. At no point in the passage does he allow his consciousness of language or style to become self-consciousness, and he readily preserves an easy control over concerns that, in a Thoreau or a Dillard, would occasion both open self-reflection and self-doubt. In short, he allows nothing, finally (not even his awareness of names and naming), to undermine his determination (and his need) to label "it" a mystery; and his "it" remains solely "the Indian pipe itself," so to speak, at no point becoming an overt sign of the desiring human (botanist or nature writer), much less the process of attempting to pin things down.

In his own mind, if one can put it that way, he is unlike both the mysterious Indian pipe and the struggling scientists who seek to name and classify it. He is mystified (clearly mystified) rather than troubled, and he will do almost anything to avoid suggestions to the contrary. Despite his awareness of language and names, at no point does he openly consider any of his own (or others') terms as a figure of thought or speech for the indeterminate condition of the human observer and would-be classifier. Indeed, he cannot afford to. He thinks, for example, that "it was an exaggeration" for Alice Albertson to have written that "it dissolves in the hands"; for "it" must not be allowed to dissolve in his own mind or phrasing. "I find it solid enough," he says, "not fragile or perishable to the touch"; and in just this way he keeps all suggestions of befuddlement and uncertainty well under control. The nonhuman "it," which is variously (too variously, one suspects) Indian pipe, ice plant, Dutchman's-pipe, corpse plant, convulsion weed, ghost flower, eyebright, fairy smoke, and bird's nest, he thus keeps epistemologically and logically (if not psychologically) constant—"out there," as we say—and neither "corpse" nor "convulsion" is allowed to threaten in any serious way its apparently nonlinguistic status or stature, much less its "beauty" or its final "lifeless reality."

As in so much American nature writing, there is more uncertainty (and even uneasiness) here than meets the naive eye. The ambiguities of self-consciousness are under control (even well under control), but they are nonetheless readily apparent, well beneath the surface certainly, but nowhere near as restrained as they are in the passages from Ann Zwinger and John Muir. In fact, the narrating and expository figures in John Hay's writings, both here and in other works, provide some signal clues to the nature and underlying functions of almost all conventional American nature writing—better (or at least more sustained) clues than do the writings of a Thoreau or an Eiseley.

In the passage above, Hay's narrator and expositor vacillates (at best half-knowingly) between what, were it not for the constraints of language, would be two mutually exclusive states of mind and psyche: between an almost consciously held desire to pin down "the Indian pipe," to determine with scientific finality whether it is "saphrophyte," "parasite," or symbiont, and a slightly more conscious determination to "let it be," to assert its final and complete mysteriousness. On the one hand, he seeks to cut through its many names, to determine with clarity whether it or its fungal associate has "actual contact" with the soil—perhaps even to dispense with it and its almost too-present reminders of the limitations of anthropologic and language. On the other hand, he insists (however unobtrusively) on maintaining its complete "otherness," its status and stature as "miraculous specialty."

What gets in the way of his resolution (and "its" final elusiveness) is, of course, language, though by the end of his attempted meditation, he is not in a position (or condition) to admit or recognize its vagaries. For to admit now the inadequacies of his language would be to acknowledge a fundamental similarity between his own categorical (and terminological) needs and the categorical needs of the scientists, who he has quietly insisted are "still trying for exactitude." To consider now the exactitude of his own terminology—"ghostly nature," "unaccountable," "elusive," and "miraculous" (if not "coral pink" or "bracts" or "bell-like")—would be to undermine completely his conclusion, and his concluding state of mind. Like many a would-be worshiper, he would know and establish in completely human terms an object of worship completely beyond human ken; and for that reason he cannot afford to acknowledge either that the effort is logically and stylistically impossible (if not self-contradictory) or that the form and content of his phrases are here at odds with one and other.

He can allow his consciousness of language almost full play when he considers the efforts of others (in this case the efforts particularly of botanists); but he cannot afford the same awareness of his own needs and efforts. Though he makes mild fun of "the botanists" (the definite article may again be telling), though he qualifies the discriminations of his local and apparently less "scientific" source (*Nantucket Wild Flowers*), he does not (and cannot) openly consider the implications of the many and various common names he has unearthed; and he keeps both himself and his subject in constant check with seemingly modest assertions of what one might call ordinary facts, many of them borrowed from otherwise struggling scientists (with "A parasite gets its nourishment from a living host," for example, or "Its stems have a fibrous, tough core" or "the bell-like flowers hang their stiff white heads straight down"). By juxtaposing the logical fun of "There is some dispute apparently . . . about what it really is" with the clearly established fact that "Some books refer to it as a 'saprophyte' "—in short, by not allowing logical fun to become epistemological or stylistic or psychological dilemma—he is able to sustain his own (and most readers') faith in human language, to keep himself (and most of his readers) from considering "the Indian pipe" or chlorophyll (or worse, perhaps, soil) as an expression of human need.

By establishing and maintaining a trustworthy understory of unqualified and unexamined assertions, he is able to keep himself from the potentially unsettling conjecture that his own phrases may be psychobiotic mechanisms—or worse, perhaps, the ornery speculation that all our phrases, assertions, and classifications are sociobiotic (and historic) strategies, adaptive devices designed to keep us from the thought that our age, like all ages, may be mythic. The effort and, for the moment, the success are to maintain, against all suggestions to the contrary, some fundamental and unexamined distinctions between one's self and others (in this case both the mysterious Indian pipe and those human others who have attempted to account for it)—to maintain, in other words, both the status and stature of Nature and the status and stature (however slight) of one's self and one's language. The effort and the success are also to maintain a basic, unqueried, representational (mimetic or categorical) relationship between one's own words and the things one would characterize or describe—certainly not to identify the two, but to assume that one's words (at the very least, such words as "unreal," "ghostly," "elusive," and "miraculous") are fully adequate indicators of the phenomenon—and without thinking about one's needs to establish such relationships.[10]

If the majority of America's nature writers have not queried Nature, neither have they queried themselves as organisms or as writers and users of language. Unlike Thoreau or Eiseley, or Abbey or Dillard or Janovy, they have been loath to consider themselves as organisms, and even more loath (if that is possible) to consider their writing as in any way an instance of mammalian or anthropoid behavior. In this sense, if no other, they have regularly mirrored the dominant logic, epistemology, and even metaphysic of modern scientific culture—and for this reason the narrating and expository figures of their works have been less conspicuous narrators or expositors (less pointedly egoistic and less openly humble or self-doubting) than have their counterparts in *Walden* or *Pilgrim at Tinker Creek* or *River Notes*. Though they have almost invariably written in a formally controlling first-person singular voice—and, hence, may be said to have departed from the strictest rhetorical stance of modern science—they have nonetheless preserved the underlying logic of modern science. By keeping their personal narration and their impersonal descriptions largely distinct (as Ann Zwinger and John Muir do in the passages above), and by not allowing the implications (or the strictures) of the first-person singular to interfere with their presentations of nonhuman phenomena (in short, by not allowing their biology and ecology to extend to themselves and their writing), they have been able to objectify their shrubby cinquefoil and compositae, their monarch butterflies, and even their gardens and groves—and simultaneously to keep themselves at a methodologically and philosophically respectable (and appreciating) distance. In a fashion that dates at least to the Renaissance—to the styles of many early naturalists and explorers—a style later found not only in Gilbert White and Darwin but also in the less autobiographical works of Scott, Cooper, and Austen—they have been able to frame personal narration with impersonal description or, alternatively, to provide set-pieces of impersonal exposition within personal narration—thus keeping human subject and natural object separate, and sustaining conventional discriminations between metaphor (or mystery) and fact. In the other way, of course, lies aberration—or, worse, madness.[11]

Ostensibly more confident and less "troubled" than their Thoreauvian compatriots, the central narrative and expository figures of conventional American nature writing have also been in considerably greater need of the fixings taxonomies and systematic descriptions or expositions can provide. Reluctant, on the one hand, to consider their descriptions or taxonomies "artificial" or arbitrary, they have been even more reluctant (even extremely reluctant) to consider them as natural or organic expressions of human impulse or need. In short, they have been uneasy about exploring or examining the established categories of modern Western thought and sanity—even (or, perhaps, especially) when the essentials of their endeavors have seemed to lead logically and naturally to such explorations. More often than not, their first-person narrators have been singular only in a strictly grammatical sense (and even that but periodically), or in the limited sociological sense that they, like their counterparts at Walden Pond and Tinker Creek, have lacked dramatized and developed friends, relations, or acquaintances. Thus, though they may seem "lonely" or "isolate" when compared to their counterparts in most British and European "nature writing," and though they may seem to share the dedication to the first-person singular of their more self-conscious American associates, their "loneliness" and their "singularity" have seldom been anything other than staunchly formulaic. Seldom have they allowed their grammatical (or logical) and sociological "isolation" to become in any serious or open way psychological or philosophical.

Finally, perhaps less confident or "secure" than their Thoreauvian compatriots, the narrators and expositors of the vast majority of American nature writing have been dedicated to subduing both ego and self-doubt, while simultaneously accenting the formally conventional, both in themselves and in their surroundings, both scientifically and aesthetically. Though they have seemed to want to underscore (and even highlight) the "personal" qualities of their experiences, and though they have written in at least a nominal first-person singular voice, they have regularly shunned suggestions of eccentricity and peculiarity in their conditions. They have tended instead to generalize (and even abstract) the "personal" and the "subjective" in their engagements with nonhuman nature, to render themselves and their environments soundly customary, scientifically and aesthetically clean, and most often morally pure. Unlike Thoreau or Abbey or Dillard or Janovy, they have generally avoided appearing selfish or angry or jealous, much less hungry or predaceous. To a large degree, in fact, they have appeared solely as disinterested (and, in a technical sense, "innocent") recorders of information, or as enthusiastic (and right-minded) appreciators—in short, as almost anything other than active, interested human organisms. Few of them have been openly engaged in *using* the elements of their environments, except in the so-called nonconsumptive way of depending on them for meaning or value or truth. Few have been engaged in active or tense pursuit of the objects of their appreciation; and few have been openly frustrated either by their surroundings or by their own efforts to capture same. Few, in fact, have struggled with the undergrowths of their places, much less stepped on or killed any of their organic associates.

By thus exempting themselves and their writing from biotic and ecological action—by alternating formulaic first-person narration or observation with patented impersonal description or exposition—they have succeeded in restraining both the often disquieting philosophic self-concerns of their American associates and the sociohistorical concerns for local human community and character that distinguish most British and European "nature writing." On the whole, they have succeeded in avoiding not only the barbaric yawp of Whitman and the often uncompromising ego of Thoreau, but also the local characters and customs that typically grace the pages of Richard Jefferies or W. H. Hudson or the Russian "nature writer" Mikhail Prishvin. By keeping their formulaic "personal" distance and by objectifying (if not reifying) their nonhuman environments, they have kept language and biotic impulse from becoming entangled, and thus have avoided both that Thoreauvian state of mind in which the Indian pipe becomes a personal metaphor, an expression of personal condition or need, and that Hudsonian or agri-cultural state of mind in which it becomes a social or historical phenomenon, an expression of dramatized communal custom and association.

In a sense, then, the narrators, expositors, and appreciators of conventional American nature writing might be said to have subdued not only self but history as well, and thus to have kept both themselves and their American Nature as "free" as possible both from basic, psychobiotic self-interest and from the conflicting interests and inroads of historic human institutions. By portraying themselves and their surroundings in ways that "free" them from institutional and communal entanglements, and by making their "discoveries" of their environments "personal" (if not "private") and yet simultaneously "scientific" (as well as "sublime" or "picturesque"), they have been able to avoid suggestions that the things they describe (or the actions they have taken) are matters of social, economic, political, or philosophical debate, or that they are in any way tied to institutionally sponsored methods and associations. More than that, perhaps, by keeping a methodological (scientific and aesthetic) distance upon the undergrowths of the valley or the forest, they have been able to skirt potential undergrowths of the mind, and generally to avoid that often outlandish, and sometimes even whimsical, human ego that alternately asserts and effaces itself throughout the likes of *Walden* or *Desert Solitaire* or *The Immense Journey*—that sometimes seemingly capricious, devouring, and even occasionally frightened self that scratches and claws its way up colorful canyon walls, or delights in watching captured ants gnaw each other to death, or floats, backside down, in the primal ooze of the River Platte. In short, they have been able to avoid those things in *Walden* (and not a few in *The Voyage of the Beagle*) that for many readers disturb the modern sense and sensibility of Nature.[12]

Like the narrator and expositor of John Hay's *Nature's Year* (and like many a vicariously "frontiered" American), the central figures in conventional American nature writing have imagined their Indian pipes—their eagles, their wolves, and their orchids— "on the verge of several worlds"—but without openly facing the psychological or philosophical implications of such a condition. At least half-unwilling (and perhaps finally unable) to place themselves as integral parts of one, local world—a historically and biotically constraining world—they have sought to take themselves to the "verge" of several, though only indirectly, and certainly without suggesting what might happen if one steps over the edge. Driven at the same time, and for obvious reasons, to seek systematic definition for their local worlds, they have been similarly unwilling (and again, perhaps, finally unable) to press the implications of precisely defined locations to their stylistic, psychological, philosophic, or historiographic conclusions. In essence, they have wanted their wolves and their Indian pipes (if not indeed themselves) to be simultaneously of one integral place and of all possible places—or, to phrase the drama another way, they have wanted to make the elements of one integral and operative local place into an almost mystic and Edenic place of all places. The Indian pipe, with its "bell-like flowers" and its "very small mat of rootlets," is thus "a plant you might meet in a dream"—the clear, though unacknowledged, and more-than-slightly worrisome implications being both that you might not meet it "in reality" and, perhaps most tellingly, that dreams (like this "unreal, pure-white plant") are not real.

Few matters have given more trouble to the characters and narrators of classic American literature, from Ishmael and Huck Finn to Jim and Jack Burden, to Nick Carraway and Quentin Compson. We have here—in miniature, as it were—Huck dreaming westward on the shore of the great river, Ishmael (the character) in the crow's nest, Nick vicariously participating in Gatsby's contemplations of the green light across the eastward bay, and Cather's classicist-lawyer, Jim Burden, dreaming westward of Ántonia and the mixedgrass prairie while he composes his manuscript (and attempts to compose himself) on an eastward-moving transcontinen-

tal train. At their respective dreaming moments, none of these quintessentially American characters is any more self-conscious than
Hay's expositor of the Indian pipe. Nor can any of them readily
afford to be. For pressed to (or even toward) their logical and philosophic conclusions, each of the elements of their worlds (with the
possible exception of language) becomes (in the parlance of modern
scientific culture) insubstantial, at best a figure or myth or icon—a
figment of imagination, as we say. Similarly, the Indian pipe,
pressed beyond its conventional, ghostly conclusion, becomes an
illusory fabrication—and pressed further, a metaphor, conceit, or
sign—an emblem, or a figure or a word—a human emission of
sound, perhaps, or worse, what we call "sound waves," themselves
encodings of other encodings of still other encodings, until one is
driven back, perhaps, to common, ordinary "Indian pipe" and,
perhaps, even to "saprophyte" and "parasite."

Tellingly, and perhaps a bit ironically, few have been the American authors whose central characters or narrators have been able to
tolerate the suggestion that dreams (or words) are real, as real certainly as oak leaves and chickadees. Even fewer have been the nature writers (much less the narrators or expositors of nature writing) who have been able to tolerate, even for brief moments, the
kinds of three or more dimensional wordplay (and even letter-and
soundplay) one finds when the central figure of *Walden* contem-
plates "the forms which thawing sand and clay assume" in
"Spring":

> I feel as if I were nearer to the vitals of the globe, for this sandy
> overflow is something such a foliaceous mass as the vitals of the
> animal body. You find thus in the very sands an anticipation of
> the vegetable leaf. No wonder that the earth expresses itself out-
> wardly in leaves, it so labors with the idea inwardly. The atoms
> have already learned this law, and are pregnant by it. The over-
> hanging leaf sees here its prototype. *Internally,* whether in the
> globe or animal body, it is a moist thick *lobe,* a word especially
> applicable to the liver and lungs and the *leaves* of fat, (λείβω,
> *labor, lapsus,* to flow or slip downward, a lapsing; λοβος, *globus,*
> lobe, globe; also lap, flap, and many other words,) *externally* a
> dry thin *leaf,* even as the *f* and *v* are a pressed and dried *b.* The
> radicals of lobe are *lb,* the soft mass of the *b* (single lobed, or **B,**
> double lobed,) with a liquid *l* behind it pressing it forward. In
> globe, *glb,* the guttural *g* adds to the meaning the capacity of the
> throat. The feathers and wings of birds are still drier and thinner
> leaves. Thus, also, you pass from the lumpish grub in the earth
> to the airy and fluttering butterfly. The very globe continually
> transcends and translates itself. . . . and towns and cities are the
> ova of insects in their axils.

Few indeed have been the nature writers disposed to consider the "*glb*" in globe or to declare that "the lip (*labium* from *labor* (?)) laps or lapses from the sides of the cavernous mouth" (a sentence to be read aloud, and self-consciously). Few have been those willing to follow their "genius" to extremes, certainly not at the risk of "insanity" or "bodily weakness," much less environ-mental or eco-logical disequilibrium.[13]

For quite understandable reasons, then, most American nature writers (and the vast majority of their narrators and expositors) have played it much safer than have Thoreau, Eiseley, Dillard, or Lopez. Though their basic needs have been quite similar, obviously—and though we may describe the underlying culture of their works in virtually the same terms—their awareness of those needs (and their understandings of those terms) have been far less open or manifest, far less extensive and extreme, than the awareness and understanding of their Thoreauvian cousins. On the whole, they have been far more "comfortable" than their more self-conscious compatriots. Most have been far less knowingly (and, hence, far less troublesomely) caught between their needs to place themselves and their needs to sustain ancestral dreams of unfettered placelessness. Though they have shared much with their more knowing and witting compatriots, to only a very few of them, in fact, has it ever occurred to think of ecological science or conventional landscape art or history as efforts to "free" humankind from what we call the necessities and constraints of historic and ecological times and places. To most it has never occurred to consider evolutionary theory or evolutionary facts as evolutionary devices to deal with what we call evolutionary time. Though all have known and celebrated biotic cycles and circles—energy circuits and uptake loops—most have shied away from the facts or implications of logical circles.

Like Huck Finn and Nick Carraway, most of the central figures in American nature writing have been inveterate naive dreamers, unable or unwilling to query or examine their inherited dreams of protohistoric and preecological or preevolutionary placelessness. At the same time, of course, they have been caught or driven (most often, again, unknowingly) by the contrary dream, wherein American places especially—scientifically understood and sensitively handled or appreciated—become the perfection of history and the hope of humankind (or at least of their own hopes and "histories"). As a result, by all odds the great majority of them have unknowingly (and, perhaps, even unintentionally) "placed" their Indian pipes and their eagles or buffalo (if not indeed themselves) as firmly as possible outside historic, institutional, and methodological time (and well outside linguistic, stylistic, and textual time). With their dedication to good science and sublime or picturesque art as interest-free endeavors that may enable us to transcend the vagaries of local, regional, and even national history, they have "located" their Indian pipes, their glaciers, their peregrine falcons, and their squaw currents in "places" where all (or almost all) consciousness of human categories dissipates, where one is "conscious of the utter worthlessness of all outward distinctions," without thinking of the necessary and inevitable imperfection of that phrase.[14]

Even the least witting American nature writers, then, have dealt in the underlying paradoxes of American history and culture. Though they have not been plagued with "thinking" in the way of an Eiseley or a Dillard or a Lopez—and though their works, as a result, may seem terribly even-tempered and placid—their dogged sanguinity is at least a bit deceiving. Considered over the longer historical and cultural haul as kinds of cultural artifacts, their solidly conventional works routinely mask the same uncertainties that appear so frequently and directly on the pages of *Walden* or *Pilgrim at Timber Creek*. Even if unknowingly, they have shared the burden of trying to settle the country.

Together with Thoreau and Leopold and Janovy, they have sought to develop and record a colloquial language for their local and American environments, and then to wed that language to the pointedly noncolloquial and apparently sanctioning terminology of an originally European science (now called "international science") and to a fundamentally European landscape art. Their efforts, and a good part of the efforts of their Thoreauvian compatriots, have been to wed Indian pipe (or fairy smoke and convulsion weed) to *Monotropa uniflora* and to link raccoon and mugwump (or shytepoke or stake-driver) to *Procyon lotor* (or *Procyon cancrivorus*) and *Botaurus lentiginosus*—while simultaneously rendering the likes of buffalo and timberdoodle sublime and picturesque—in short, to give both scientific and aesthetic stature to the elements of their American surroundings, without sacrificing their local identities or in other ways undercutting personal experience of place. The task has been substantial, to say the least.

In several senses, then, the vast majority of American nature writing (including a large part of the writing of Thoreau and his self-conscious successors) has functioned to compose the country, to codify it in conventional terms, and then to ratify those terms—to adjust (or attempt to adjust) the terms of its ancient, pre-Renaissance origins to the terms of modern scientific and aesthetic culture—and perhaps more than anything else, to link and underwrite the two "truly original" and "distinctive" features of America, its so-called natural environments and its dedication (however formulaic) to "the individual"—the two features that, it is still often said, historic Europe simply cannot match.

The differences between Thoreau and John Hay on each of these scores—like the differences between Hay and Muir or Ann Zwinger—are finally less a matter of distinctions in kind than they are a matter of variations in degree or extent. The world in which all American nature writers have acted is, of course, a globe spinning upon the classical antipodes of Western thought: on the one side the wild, on the other the civilized; on the one the natural, on the other the human; on the one experience, on the other language; and so on through other and self, nature and science (or art), body and mind, and by no means least, fact and metaphor. The difference between the narrator and expositor of *Walden* and his counterpart in *Nature's Year*—like the difference, in turn, between John Hay's figure and the figure of John Muir—is a matter of their willingness (and perhaps of their ability) to explore the antipodes and the relationships between them. On the one hand, there is ego and the desire (not to say the need) to assert oneself, to acquire, and even to possess. On the other hand, there is the nonhuman natural other and the desire or need to immerse oneself in it, to lose one's sense of self, to be acquired, possessed, and even dispossessed. On the one hand, there is the terribly local, familiar, and singularly unpicturesque mugwump. On the other, there is the conventionally "unemotional" and ratiocinative (though nonetheless sanctioning) *Botaurus lentiginosus*, not to say the $dV/dt = KV$ of energy flow in ecosystems.[15] On the one hand, there is the spiritual restoration (and even salvation) one knows must come from being with nature. On the other hand, there is the singularly uninspiring business of collecting, classifying, measuring, and codifying individual specimens, a labor that, given one's ancestry, is not supposed to be necessary to salvation or restoration.

What distinguishes the works of Thoreau—and Eiseley and Abbey and Dillard—from John Hay's works—and Hay's, in turn, from the works of Muir and Zwinger—is the extent to which they press these needs and notions (as well as the forms and implications of same) to their extremes, the extent to which they express them openly and sometimes even baldly, even to the point of upsetting conventional equilibria of control, even to the point of disturbing their audiences, not to say their own apparently dominant logic or style. At his most extreme, Thoreau is thus both more wild and more civilized than the vast majority of his American compatriots, more wild not only in his extreme egoism but in his extreme expressions of his desire to be dispossessed, and more civilized not only in the explicit attention he gives to etymology and wordplay (in short, to wit) but also in the attention he pays to formal logic and rhetoric. The central figure of Hay's *Nature's Year* is simply less willing to reach out or extend himself than is the central figure of *Walden*, less willing to risk either the wild or the civilized, less willing to risk either his sense of self or his sense of nonhuman others. The central figures of Muir's *The Mountains of California* and Zwinger's *Beyond the Aspen Grove* are, in turn, even less willing than Hay's to risk uncertainty. In their dedication to scientific classification and arrangement, as in their devotion to customary forms of aesthetic appreciation and personal identification, both are far more typical of American nature writing, and almost strictly conventional, even (or, rather, perhaps especially) when they take ostensibly eccentric or unconventional stances.

In one sense, at least, then, the underlying circumstances and occasions of American nature writing have changed little from the time of William Bartram to the time of Annie Dillard. Self-consciously considered or unconsciously illustrated, the essential drama of the story has remained constant. Basically, it is a story of an individual confronting a pointedly nonhuman environment, without significant aid from associates or community, without much in the way of the trappings of civilization, and generally with both individual and environment set firmly outside the intricate scaffoldings and relationships of established institutions. Though the Thoreaus and Dillards and Leopolds have viewed the securities of orthodox understandings and customary terms far more suspiciously and self-consciously than have the Muirs and Zwingers— though the Eiseleys and Abbeys and Janovys have pursued wildness and eccentricity (if not even "abnormality") far more actively and intensely than have the Henry Bestons, Sigurd Olsons, and Helen Hoovers—the essential, ancestral conditions (the obsessions and needs, the ideals and fears) have underwritten both those openly extra-vagant works, like *Walden*, that have sought the antipodes of American experience and those that have stayed closer to the customary equators of home.

Chapter Two

The History and Criticism
of Nature Writing

or almost a century now, students of literature, history, art, and science with vocational or avocational interests in country life and the outdoors—in wilderness, wildlife, and landscape art—or birding, amateur botanizing, and "living off the land"—have been collecting and sharing information about "nature writing" and "nature books"—personal narratives of experiences in or with "nature," as we say, semi-scientific accounts of individual animals or species, records of travel in "wildlands," stories of meditative residence in the not-so-wild, field guides, guides to nature study, and various kinds of how-to-books, including even guides to legislation and political action—all in all the kinds of books that occupy the "Nature" shelves of British and American bookstores and even, to a great extent, the QH division of the U.S. Library of Congress classification system, the division which otherwise contains highly technical studies in such things as entomology, limnology, evolutionary theory, and population biology. No more than the bookstores or the Library of Congress have we devotees of nature writing been able to systematize our readings or our ruminations about them; but over the last half-century, at least, we and our immediate predecessors have begun to develop, almost willy-nilly, the rudiments of a historico-critical canon of sorts for nature writing—a set of loosely related but generally shared understandings of some of its places and functions in Western and, especially, American history, and an even more loosely related (and far less developed) cluster of literary notes and studies concerned with its characteristic forms and styles.

In one of my minds, I doubt that we will ever succeed in further developing this nascent canon or in agreeing upon the kinds of characteristics that should discriminate among the many sorts of books and essays now appearing on our shelves. At present, each of our collections of nature writing and nature books is to a great extent personal and accidental—a function, in part, of individual preferences, habits, and enthusiasms; in part, of local (or regional) residence, experience, and affections; in part, of the limitations of regional or, at best, national associations and markets; and, perhaps for the most part, of coincidental institutional affiliations and chance acquaintances. In lieu of a major, and almost revolutionary, change in conventional systems of bibliographic classification—a change that would entail prior (and comparably revolutionary) changes in popular views of science, literature, and nature (and, hence, extensive developments in literary theory and the philosophy of science, if not in metaphysics, anthropology, and the philosophy of language)—we are unlikely to agree on the means and methods of discriminating entomology, say, from natural history, or natural history from nature writing, or nature writing from nature appreciation—much less to agree upon the meanings or, worse, the implications of our attempted discriminations.

Whatever else our contemporary arrangements and understandings of nature writing may reflect, they attest to an age-old conflict between nominalists and realists; between those, on the one hand, who see human language as the inescapable determiner of the "known" and "knowable" world (whatever may lie beyond or beneath it) and those, on the other hand, who view human language (however inadequate and limiting) as the only tool we have to get at the real, phenomenal, nonlinguistic world, the only tool we have to escape the limitations of our condition. A part of what we are dealing in, then—however haphazardly—is the classical (and still very much current) conflict between those who would argue that we cannot avoid anthropocentricity or anthropomorphism (or, if you will, original sin)—that each is an inescapable given in the condition of what we call the species—and those, on the other hand, who would argue not only that we can avoid them, but that we must, if we are in any sense to be able to comprehend our condition or to understand the other (and especially nonhuman) elements of the environments in which we seek to sustain ourselves. No wonder our collections of "nature books" are so disparate, or the history and criticism of nature writing so loosely organized.

In one of my minds, in fact—the one which says that a deep sense of locality is, finally, almost everything (whatever may happen in the battle between nominalists and realists)—I seriously doubt that the effort to refine and extend our understandings of nature writing is worthwhile, or even healthy. In yet another mind— the one which says that in a Western (and, especially, in an American) world a lasting sense of locality or place may be an impossibility (at least a partial contradiction in cultural terms) or that a sense of Western and American "place" can be attained only with a deep appreciation and acceptance of the inescapable and irresolvable conflicts between nominalism and realism or monism and dualism—I just as seriously assert that we must make some kind of effort to refine and extend our understandings and interpretations of nature writing, even if the effort leads (as it seems it must) to further conflict—in part because nature writing is one of the forms of our literature that openly deals with the intricacies and constraints of place and locality, in part because it is one of a very few contemporary cultural forms in which idealists and realists may seriously engage one another, and in part because the history and criticism of nature writing we have so far developed provide at best a one-sided representation of those classical conflicts—and, hence, a one-sided view of the cultural heritage of nature writing.

In the criticism and history of nature writing, such as we have it, the realists and dualists have so far won not only the day, but the century; and for Western peoples at least, continued health would seem to demand a daily, if not hourly, draw between the parties, an open and mutually appreciative standoff. On the whole, the contributions of social, intellectual, and even political historians to the understanding of nature writing have been far more sustained—in their respective disciplinary ways, more systematic and discriminating—than have the offerings of literary historians and critics, particularly in the United States. In terms consistent with contemporary historical method and historiography, the former have generally done a creditable (and even extensive) job of placing the concerns of nature writers and nature writing in social, political, and even economic contexts.[1] Literary historians and critics, on the other hand, have contributed comparatively little to the developing canon of a commensurate disciplinary quality—little other than names, titles, and an occasional study of an individual figure or work—little, that is, to balance the philosophic scales by and in which nature writing is read and interpreted.[2]

For the most part, in fact, the history and criticism of nature writing as form and style have languished in modes of understanding that have changed only slightly since the 1950s, and little more since the 1890s—modes of conceiving language and reality or fable and fact which, despite their apparent dedication to the study of literary and linguistic form, have characteristically recited the logical and rhetorical litany of popular scientific culture with greater (and less questioning) faith than have the philosophic writings of scientists or the more reflective writings of nature writers themselves. As a result, the fairly extensive studies of nature writers and nature books undertaken by social, political, and intellectual historians have yet to be refined or amplified by the kinds of additional (and sometimes intricately contrary) understandings that might derive from close, comparative readings of individual texts—from the search for (and the comparative study of) the kinds of stylistic patterns and persuasions that have enabled us to relate changing rhetorical strategies and forms in narrative fiction, for example, or verse to the broader designs of social, economic, and intellectual history. With very few exceptions, the small number of literary historians and critics who have taken an interest in nature writing have treated it in much the same way it has been treated by popular audiences, as a source of phenomenal and factual security (if not harmony and hope)—the kind of security, ironically, that has become harder and harder to attain in contemporary literary studies of fiction, verse, or dramatic literature, if not indeed in the philosophy and historiography of science and a good deal of contemporary nature writing itself. In short, while the broad cultural history of nature writing and related matters has continued to develop, the history and criticism of nature writing as form and style have remained essentially static—reassuring, perhaps, but superannuated—and this despite the increasing popularity and sophistication of nature writing that have grown out of the heightened "ecological" and "environmental" awareness of the last twenty years or so.

By the 1950s, at least, most serious readers of nature writing had heard the names of John Muir's literary predecessors. Most were at least vaguely aware that what Muir and Mary Austin and Dallas Lore Sharp had written—what Henry Beston, Sigurd Olson, and Edwin Way Teale were writing—was rooted not just in Thoreau's *Walden* or W. H. Hudson's *Green Mansions* but also in the writings of William Bartram and Gilbert White, in the development of systematic biology and in eighteenth-century notions of the sublime and picturesque, in the literature of biotic and geographic discovery, in the works of the seventeenth-century clergyman-naturalist John Ray, in the natural histories of Aristotle and Pliny the Elder, and perhaps even in medieval herbals and bestiaries. If they weren't aware, if they hadn't read John Burroughs on "The Literary Treatment of Nature," "Nature in Literature," "Henry D. Thoreau,"

"Gilbert White's Book," or "The True Test of Good Nature Literature"—if they hadn't read Francis Halsey's "The Rise of Nature
Writers" (1902), Norman Foerster's *Nature in American Literature*
(1923), Philip Marshall Hicks's *The Development of the Natural
History Essay in American Literature* (1924), Henry Chester Tracy's *American Naturists* (1930), or N. Bryllion Fagin's *William
Bartram: Interpreter of the American Landscape* (1933)—they
could readily turn to Joseph Wood Krutch's ninety-three-page "Prologue" to *Great American Nature Writing* (1950), the first substantial anthology of its kind, and certainly the first notable attempt by
an established literary critic to declare nature writing a distinct
genre and to account for its history.[3]

Though it has long since been all but forgotten—neglected, one
suspects, largely because its conceptions of nature, literature, history, science, and their relations have been absorbed in popularly
received knowledge of English and American literature—Krutch's
"Prologue" to *Great American Nature Writing* sets out the essential critical and historiographic terms—the underlying categorical
distinctions and the view of history—that for the most part still control the discussion of nature writing as a literary form. Though they
may no longer recognize their debts to the nature writer–cum–
critic-historian who put together this first serious effort to account
for the genre, most literary historians and critics still follow the
broad outline of his "Prologue" when they think of the history and
characteristics of nature writing. Thus, it is still almost entirely customary for students of nature writing to begin their disquisitions by
considering the problems of generic classification posed by Thoreau's writings (particularly *Walden*) and then to work their way
back to William Bartram and Gilbert White, from White to John
Ray's *The Wisdom of God Manifest in the Works of His Creation*
(1691), and from Ray to occasional and carefully selected passages
of earlier natural history—a few in medieval herbals and bestiaries
perhaps, but most in the natural histories of Pliny and, especially, of
Aristotle.

In this still widely accepted view of the literary history of nature
writing, medieval times were distinctly Dark Ages, when a writer
not only had "fewer facts at his disposal" than we do (or Thoreau
did), but when writers (and Western peoples generally) were "apparently less aware of what a fact was or why it was important." As
the still prevailing story goes, these were at best quaintly nonscientific times when writers and thinkers had "relatively little respect"
for the "power of observation," times, unlike our own, when observation was deemed a "crude instrument," and people had no proper
sense that some things, at least, were their "own excuse for being,"

that they "existed" and "ought to exist" in their own rights, or that their "most important meanings" were themselves, and not the "useful" meanings humans derived from or imposed upon them, "either directly or as an allegory"—all in all, dark, backward, unenlightened times when people (or at least writers) insisted "upon some absolute uniqueness in man" and were unable to look at nature "from some point of view common to all its creatures." These were times and people whose writings about "nature" seem to us not only "remote" but "absurd" or, worse, dangerously wrongheaded—"not primarily because their compilers knew so much that was not true and so little that was, but because the whole tendency of their thinking was anthropocentric and teleological" (Krutch, 6–10).*

With this view of the Dark Ages in mind—and supplementing it with our understanding both of modern man's ever-increasing observational knowledge of the natural world and of the new aesthetic "appreciations of nature" that grew out of the Renaissance and developed with the Enlightenment and Romanticism—the conventional literary history of nature writing works its way forward from Thoreau as well, not only to Hudson and Burroughs and Muir but beyond them to Mary Austin, William Beebe, Sigurd Olson, and John Hay. Along the way, the empathetic literary historian and critic (here Krutch) begins to discover an attitudinal and conceptual common denominator that seems distinct to nature writing, a "new feeling for nature," a "sense of oneness" and "intimacy," in which Western man (though, in point of literary fact, only the British and, later, the Americans), sometime in the late seventeenth century, begins to feel a bond "between himself and all creatures," an attitude utterly new to the Western world, a post-Renaissance and truly modern conception of a "*life in nature*," an ostensibly anti-Cartesian way of thinking, an idea and a motivation related to, but finally distinct from, both the classical pastoral impulse to "retreat" from civilization and the popular Romantic "desire to celebrate the soothing or inspirational effects of natural scenery"—an entirely new notion that nature is "one vast fellowship," a "sense of kinship" that cannot be said to derive simply from an interest in natural history (because "natural history was already a science in Aristotle's time," and this sense of being "a part of nature" was not present then), but a historically novel notion of a "fellowship defined by protoplasm itself," a notion no more scientific than it is pastoral or Romantic (Krutch, 6, 24–26, 72, 87).

---

*All references to Krutch in the text refer to his "Prologue" to *Great American Nature Writing* (New York: Wm. Sloane, 1950).

This is the notion, the "sense of identity, material as well as spiritual," still often said, in one phrasing or another, to characterize nature writing as a genre. Its origins are to be found "not in the history of science itself, but in the development of a certain emotional attitude toward the world that science reveals" (Krutch, 15)—an attitude that attains its first significant Western expression in *The Wisdom* of John Ray and then slowly develops in other literary forms—with Shaftesbury, Pope, Burke, Burns, Cowper, Gray, and Wordsworth—until it begins to take specific generic shape in the writings of Gilbert White and William Bartram, and finally comes to full modern fruition in the works of Thoreau and W. H. Hudson. Finally, it is this "sense of identity" that defines nature writing and distinguishes it not only from the literature of travel and exploration, or natural history, but also from various literary forms of "nature appreciation," in prose or in verse, and apparently from the nature poetry of Wordsworth or Frost as well.[4]

With the development of this sense and the coordinate emergence of nature writing as a "recognizable genre of belles lettres," "man now has his being," in Krutch's words, "not in the center of a vast machine, but simply as a member of a society every other member of which is, like him, alive, sentient, and capable to some extent of participating in experiences like his own" (Krutch, 4, 26). In this one particular literary form, at least, man is now, in mind as in body, "a part of nature"—as he was not (and could not be) in the Middle Ages or at any prior time in Western history. The underlying assumption of nature writing, that "man's place is *in* nature rather than apart from it," has created an apparently distinguishing kind of pantheism, "a kind of pantheism in which the symbol of unity of all living things is not an elusive spirit, but a definable material thing," a "definable material thing" which is also "a symbol, and hence does not necessarily imply any thoroughgoing materialistic philosophy," a sense of identity which "implies merely that life itself rather than something still more mysterious called the 'cause of life' is the bond between fellow creatures" (Krutch, 19, 73).

In this still very much conventional view of its literary history, nature writing is a product of the Renaissance, the rise (or rebirth) of natural science, and the more or less coincident development of a "feeling for nature" that grew with the Enlightenment and Romanticism. It is an almost entirely modern literary form embodying a thoroughly modern way of thinking, a way of thinking unknown in the West before the late seventeenth century. Its preeminently modern qualities and persuasions are illustrated first by contrasting the sense of a kinship with nature one finds in Thoreau's writings with the apparent absence of such a sense one finds in the views of "orthodox Christianity" (in this case, the views primarily of Saint Thomas and, after him, of Descartes)—by noting, for example, that

> Thoreau could feel as he did, not so much because he was tender toward inferior creatures as because he did not think of them as inferior; because he had none of that sense of superiority or even separateness which is the inevitable result of any philosophy or religion which attributes to man a qualitative uniqueness, and therefore inevitably suggests that all other living things exist for him. St. Francis preached to the birds; many moderns have hoped, on the contrary, that the birds would preach to them. (Krutch, 6)

Having established this initial and essential contrast, the progressive critic-historian of nature writing seeks to underscore it further with illustrations from medieval theology—by noting, for example, that though Saint Thomas found cruelty to animals a sin, he did so "not because it results in pain to the animals (which have no souls), but because it may lead to similar cruelty toward men" (Krutch, 12).

With such by now conventional distinctions between moderns (or, at any rate, modern nature writers) and ancients (or, in any case, "orthodox Christians") well cemented, the critic-historian sets out to reinforce still further his sense of the originality of nature writing, by contrasting exemplary passages from a medieval bestiary with the kinds of descriptive and observational writing familiar to readers of *Walden* and *The Natural History of Selborne*, in this case by taking on the encyclopedia, *De Proprieteribus*, of a medieval monk named Bartholomew Anglicanus. In doing so, the critic notes that medieval bestiaries are comprised almost exclusively not of records of "original observation" but of recountings of what their authors have read in "other equally ill-informed books," accounts of a crocodile that weeps, for example, or of an elephant captured when humans cut down the tree against which it has leaned to sleep (Krutch, 10). Only very rarely does the critic run across something of the "observational" kind for which he is looking, something akin to Gilbert White's affectionate account of his garden tortoise, for example; but even in the medieval bestiary, once in a while, the critic discovers something incipiently "modern," some small indication that, even in the Middle Ages, affectionate and accurate personal observation could survive—something like Bartholomew's account of the cat:

> Of The Cat: He is a full lecherous beast in youth, swift, pliant,
> and merry, and leapeth and rusheth on everything that is to fore
> him: and is led by a straw, and playeth therewith: and is a right
> heavy beast in age and full sleepy, and lieth slyly in wait for
> mice: and is aware where they be more by smell than by sight,
> and hunteth and rusheth on them in privy places: and when he
> taketh a mouse, he playeth therewith, and eateth him after the
> play. In time of love is hard fighting for wives, and one scratch-
> eth and rendeth the other grievously with biting and with claws.
> And he maketh a ruthful noise and ghastful, when one prof-
> fereth to fight with another: and unneth is hurt when he is
> thrown down off an high place. And when he hath a fair skin, he
> is as it were proud thereof, and goeth fast about: and when his
> skin is burnt, then he bideth at home, and is oft for his fair skin
> taken of the skinner, and slain and flayed. (Krutch, 10-11)

As Krutch (and numerous others after him) would have it, "obviously Bartholomew knew cats," as he just as obviously did not
know crocodiles or elephants. A sense of Thoreauvian or Hudsonian
"wonder" might be "largely absent" from his rendition of the cat
(perhaps he had "no sense that the cat is as wonderful as the dragon—to which he devoted a fuller account—would be if the dragon
had ever existed"), but knowledge (personal, observational knowledge) and, most tellingly, love "shine through his lines" in a way
familiar to readers of Gilbert White and Thoreau, a way "which
every good modern writer about nature must to some extent ex-
hibit" (Krutch, 11).

Still, such knowing, loving observations are extremely unusual
in Bartholomew's work, as they are generally rare in all premodern
writings about "nature"; and even the few "genuine . . . telling"
accounts one can find, usually of domesticated animals, leave something to be desired when compared to their counterparts in modern
nature writing. Though he was clearly capable of observation, and
even of love, Bartholomew differs from modern nature writers not
simply because he "had fewer facts at his disposal," nor even because he was "apparently less aware of what a fact was or why it
was important," but because, on top of all that, he "could not ration-
alize, or perhaps even respect, the love which went out from him
toward the dog and the cat" (Krutch, 12).

Bartholomew Anglicanus lived, thought, and wrote, then, in an
"orthodox Christian" time when "the natural world could teach
nothing radically new." Worse, perhaps, the "natural world" of his
time was "merely a collection of metaphors and fables ingeniously

repeating in figurative language the truths already known from authority":

> On occasion, to be sure, it might propound riddles to tempt the ingenuity of man, as in the case of the toad and his jewel. But the answer, when found, would always be one consonant with what was already known. Nothing really new would ever be discovered. The meaning of the universe, the proper place of man in it, was already known, completely and finally. (Krutch, 9–10)

In this first serious attempt to explain the history and distinguishing characteristics of nature writing as genre, one can find the essential logical categories and the view of history that for the most part continue to govern discussions of its forms and persuasions. In the premodern and medieval world "nothing really new would ever be discovered." "The meaning of the universe, the proper place of man in it, was already known, completely and finally." By contrast, in the world of the thoroughly modern nature writer new things are being discovered constantly; and all one knows, completely and finally, is that man is a "member of a society every other member of which is, like him, alive, sentient, and capable to some extent of participating in experiences like his own" (Krutch, 10, 26). From this modern persuasion—as from Saint Thomas's or Bartholomew's—there is, apparently, little or no rational or emotional dissent. Man's proper place, however different it may be from the proper place defined by orthodox Christianity, is "already known" with some considerable assurance—and so, by the way, are the proper places of all one's "fellow creatures." Today's "discoveries," however constant and novel they may be, are made under the authority of "kinship." Though they may occasionally propound riddles to us, we know that both we and our discoveries are parts of nature, completely and finally. Constant change and continuously novel experiences in a global society provide the authorizing paradigm—the absolutes or independent variables—which our "observational" and "factual" knowledge confirms and repeats.

The avowed persuasion is not, finally, much different from the persuasion or belief it claims to have supplanted. The explicit view of history—ostensibly antimedieval, anti-Christian, and promodern—places the responsibility for Western man's original alienation from nature squarely upon the awesome, threatening shoulders of "orthodox Christianity"—in much the same way Bartholomew or Saint Thomas might have placed it upon the shoulders of Eve and Adam—upon classical and orthodox modes of thought which are said to have divorced man (or at least Western man) from nature, as they originally divorced man from God and, later, under the influence of Descartes, further separated nature and God, reason and emotion, mind (or soul) and body, man and animal, and, not least, science and art. In the most extreme contemporary phrasings of this view of Western intellectual history (the vast majority of them American), it is not uncommon to find the whole distressing condition of modern man's relations to the nonhuman environment—the tragedy of the commons—the story of pollution, exploitation, and misuse—redounding to the divisive and destructive credits of Descartes, Saint Thomas, Saint Augustine, and the Bible (curiously and perhaps tellingly, little is typically said of Saint Teresa's responsibilities, or of Calvin's or Luther's or Erasmus's, and even less of Plato's or Avicenna's or Maimonides'). The way out of this mess, in turn—the way down or up or back to harmony with nature, the idea (if not the reality) of a new (or renewed) kinship, a fellowship, a synthesis, and perhaps even a marriage (or remarriage)—is to be found not in configurations of Christ or Mary or Krishna, but in nature writing and in the lives of its central exemplary figures, in those modern literary forms and exemplars in which and in whom science and literature are blent and relations between man and nature are mutually supportive rather than disjunctive.

All in all, it is an awkward, struggling view of the history of nature writing and related matters. In Krutch's version of it, one can see the anthologist, practicing nature writer, and everyday reader trying to reconcile first-hand experience and common sense with the convictions of the literary critic and the learning of the intellectual historian. On the one hand, there is the more or less obvious evidence that the writings he has selected (all passages of prose and all commonly recognized as "nature writing") are indeed a distinct literary form—different, if in no other way, at least visually and rhythmically from known forms of nature poetry, for example, and almost as obviously different, in various ways, from the forms of prose with which nature writing might be associated or confused, different—if not in imagery or the explicit use of metaphor, then certainly in narrative structure, point of view, and vocabulary—from natural history, travel literature, and various forms of what the self-acknowledged nature writer is given to calling "purely subjective musing." Even common sense, then, would seem to suggest that the writings he has chosen are too often extensively systematic and "scientific"—reportorial or informational—to be called, say, the "poetry of nature" in prose (whatever might be the inclination of advertisers and commercial publicists). By virtually the same tokens, popular (and even commercial) usage has long ago established that such writings are too "personal," too "subjective," or too "emotional" to be classed as natural history. And even a cursory reading of the anthologized passages reveals that none of them is sufficiently controlled by "movement" in conventional narrative space and time to make it readily alignable with travel literature or the literature of exploration, scientific or otherwise. Their authors are simply far too inclined to confine themselves to the details of local or, at best, regional experience for them to be classed as explorers or discoverers. Their "discoveries," in turn, are most often too intense or, alternatively, too flat (too expository)—psychically too deep or philosophically too expansive or methodologically too exegetical—and their inclinations to "explore" them temporally (and narratively) too inconsistent—for their writings to be classed as conventional narratives of any recognized literary kind. So much, then, for common sense and at least part of the practicing nature writer's first-hand experience.

On the other hand—and, at best, in partial congruence with the evidence of common sense—there are the convictions and the phrasings of the literary critic of 1950 and the knowledge of the erstwhile intellectual historian—the conviction of the critic that distinct literary forms convey distinctive ways of formulating experience, distinctive ways of thinking and feeling (hence, whatever their limitations, the then current critical idioms, "feeling for nature" and "sense of oneness," that are said to distinguish nature writing as a "recognizable genre")—and, running rather intractably against the critic's conviction, especially when it is phrased in such a manner, the knowledge of the historian (both literary and intellectual) that the "sense of oneness" and the "feeling for nature" are hardly distinct to (much less original with) the writers or the writings his anthology represents, however "observational" they may be—that, as every serious student of literature knows, the "sense of oneness" can be found as well in Wordsworth, Emerson, Frost, or Dickinson—as in Rilke, Stevens, and Jeffers, if not indeed in Dante, Petrarch, Hardy, Conrad, or Faulkner—and certainly in a good deal of oriental literature—in short, in several already recognized literary forms, both in prose and in verse, and perhaps even in times and places other than modern Britain or America.

So much, then, too, for the laboring voices of the literary historian and critic of midcentury, both of which tend to direct one's attentions away from form and style. There is another, and still more troublesome, voice here as well, a voice that continues to worry the history and criticism of nature writing as literary and linguistic type. It is the voice, finally, of the moralist and even of the amateur ethicist, the part of the nature writer who would adjudicate Western man's relations to nature, both past and present—the voice of the seriously concerned citizen for whom nature writing is far less literary or cultural form than it is environmental vision or historic hope. For there is a part of this nature writer, this cultural critic and concerned citizen, who would not only account for the historic causes of Western man's conceptions of nature, but who would also establish and expose the moral responsibilities for same—on the one hand, the blame for such misconceptions as continue to exist (and the misuses that follow from them)—on the other hand, the credit for introducing and sustaining such improved attitudes and conceptions as are necessary to a true and lasting fellowship with our fellow creatures. There is, then, a tension between the critic, historian, and nature writer as moralist—who would argue the essential rightness and accuracy of the nature writer's view, and extend the sense of kinship with nature to all dimensions of modern Western culture—and the critic, historian, and nature writer as student of literary and cultural forms—who would argue that this sense of kinship is peculiar and definitive to nature writing, and that it, more than anything else, distinguishes nature writing from other literary forms, both scientific and nonscientific, both ancient and modern.

In something like this fashion, the *nature* writer's concerns for the moral state of mankind's relations to nonhuman environments—his concerns for tortoises and toads as well as human conceptions of them—get in the way of the literary critic's (and perhaps the nature *writer*'s) concerns for and about the status and stature of literary and linguistic form—his concerns to delineate and appreciate the discriminating features of a genre. If I may be permitted the phrasings, the one is fundamentally a concern for tortoises, toads, cacti, and mankind. The other—alternately identical to and radically (ontologically) different from the former—is finally a concern for the forms and shapes of language, a concern not only for nature writing and travel literature but for "toad" and "*Bufo cognatus*," if you will, rather than for toad and *Bufo cognatus*. The conflicts between these two concerns—the inconsistency and incongruity between these two views of language and nature, however implicit— are fundamentally (philosophically and historically) the same conflicts that trouble John Hay's appreciator of the Indian pipe— though the conventional historian-critic of nature writing, like the nature writer devoted exclusively to orthodox modes of conceiving nonhuman phenomena, is not the one to recognize the correspondence or to acknowledge the cultural continuity.

The *underlying* dialectic, then, of Krutch's "Prologue" to *Great*

American Nature Writing—and the dialectic embedded in most historical and critical discussions of the genre—are philosophically
(logically and epistemologically, if not metaphysically) identical to
the underlying conflicts of John Hay's *Nature's Year*, and close kin
as well to the defining conflicts of *Walden* or *A Sand County Almanac*. What distinguishes the former from the latter—the conventional history and criticism of nature writing from nature writing
itself (or at least the most sophisticated forms of it)—is partly, of
course, the difference between criticism or history and that which it
seeks to explicate or historicize—partly, that is, a difference in the
psychology and implicit epistemology of their respective genres.
Finally, however, the dramatic extremes of *Walden*, and even the
milder fluctuations of *Nature's Year* or *A Sand County Almanac*,
are distinguished from the essentially unwitting and, therefore,
"nondramatic" conflicts of Krutch's "Prologue" not by the constraints or implications of genre but by the degree of self-consciousness (the breadth and depth of understanding and conception) entertained by their authors—by the extent to which their narrating
and narrative figures are able or willing to consider their subjects as
expressions and configurations of themselves or of their own biotic
and cultural kinds—in much the same way Thoreau's nature writing is distinguished from John Hay's and Hay's, in turn, from Muir's
or Ann Zwinger's or Gilbert White's.

Krutch's "Prologue" thus participates (as it should) in the underlying concerns of its subject—but it does so only unknowingly.
Like the vast majority of its critical and historical successors (and,
for that matter, like orthodox nature writing itself), it partakes of the
cultural heritage—the defining philosophic and dramatic conflicts—
of nature writing, but without openly acknowledging its participation, and in fact by claiming to resolve those conflicts. It takes as
given, for example, the ordinary, normal, modern (and, perhaps especially, post-Cartesian) distinctions not only between literary history (or criticism) and literature, or between history and the historical, but also those between fact and fable, object and subject,
science and literature, among several others—without explicitly
recognizing its own dependence upon those distinctions and, what
is more important, without a hint that any of the nature writers it
considers was in any significant way troubled by them. In fact, it
suggests quite the opposite, that nature writers, with their special
sense of a kinship with nature, have found the various disjunctive
and dualistic categories of classical Western thought and modern
scientific culture rather easy to overcome (easier to overcome, certainly, than did Saint Thomas or Descartes or Darwin or Wittgen-

stein and, if I may hazard the suggestion, easier as well than Thoreau did)—as if a deep sense of identification with nonhuman
creatures did nothing but eliminate or decrease one's sense of being
human, nothing to suggest an estrangement caused by language or
art or human quests for knowledge, nothing to remind one of what
Emily Dickinson once called "the Seal Despair," the despair, occasioned by what we are given (or driven) to calling human consciousness, of ever being able to participate consciously in the apparently
unconscious processes of nonhuman nature.

Thus Krutch (here as literary or cultural critic and historian) is
unwilling (and perhaps unable) openly to consider his version of
history or his view of nature writing (much less his view of crocodiles or Bartholomew or Saint Thomas or even of Thoreau) as in any
sense an extension or expression of himself and his allegiances. In
much the same way, his Bartholomew and Saint Thomas (not to say
his Descartes and even his Thoreau) are disinclined to consider
their renditions of experience as figurative or linguistic extensions
of their own needs. Like his Bartholomew, his Saint Thomas, and
his Descartes—indeed, like his Thoreau and his W. H. Hudson—
Krutch is more concerned with Truth and Rectitude than he is with
renditions or configurations of experience. Like all but a few historians and critics of nature writing (and, indeed, like the majority of
America's nature writers)—of his own and later times—he is after
disinterested knowledge and redeeming moral (or aesthetic) value,
knowledge and value that are functions neither of his own psychobiotic condition nor of his cultural heritage. He is far more concerned to solve the problems posed by Saint Thomas and Descartes—and, hence, the conflicts faced by a Thoreau or a W. H.
Hudson—than he is to characterize or dramatize them.

As moralist and concerned citizen, Krutch is thus not in a position to see (or if he sees, to admit) the similarities between his own
views of Saint Thomas and Bartholomew or Descartes and theirs, in
turn, of Eve or Adam. Because he is finally more concerned with
scientifically informed relationships to land—with right relationships to and for nature—than he is with delineating the forms and
types of nature writing or the conditions of the nature writer, he is
able to muster only the slightest sympathy with Bartholomew as
domestic citizen, and none for Bartholomew's work as natural historian. Because he is as much given to discriminating idea and style
(or concept and grammar, or thing and word, or reality and language) as he is to relating them (or examining their connections)—
because, like Descartes and Saint Thomas, he sees some ideas and
styles as right and others as wrong, some as true and others as
false—because, to use terms consonant with his own, he is finally

more concerned with the persuasions of nature writers (and their ancestors) than he is with the style, grammar, or logic in which those persuasions are cast—because, in the terms of his world, he is finally more committed to crocodiles than he is to configurations of crocodiles (or, more accurately, because he takes as given a clear distinction between crocodiles and configurations *of* them)—because, like Bartholomew, he cannot afford to consider the anthropomorphic in "crocodile"—in short, because (like most of us, most of the time) he cannot afford to undercut his own categorical declaratives and imperatives—he cannot conceive of *De Proprieteribus* as natural history. To do so would undermine both his explicit argument and the implicit "natural world" in (and for) which it is made, the "natural world" in which he seeks to live.

Because, in orthodox modern parlance, natural historians record observed facts rather than fables or figurative confirmations of authority, and because Bartholomew must somehow be different in logical and epistemological kind from Thoreau, Krutch is unable to entertain even the suggestion that Bartholomew was, in his orthodox world and in his and Saint Thomas's orthodox way, writing a natural history and recording the facts, even when he wrote about the weeping crocodile—as we, in our orthodox world and orthodox ways, may likewise be recording the facts, even when we write about the mating rituals of pinnated grouse or the genetic code or prairie dog towns—as we in our way may be figuratively confirming the truths already known from our authorities, or (perish the thought) putting together a natural world that is "merely a collection of metaphors and fables." The point to be made here, of course—a point of some significance to the history and criticism of nature writing—is not that Bartholomew and his contemporaries were ignorant of facts or their importance, but that what we call medieval facts are not what we call modern facts (as modern metaphors are not medieval metaphors), that each orthodoxy has its respective tests of truth and facticity—that in his own natural world, Bartholomew was as much natural historian as Linnaeus or Louis Agassiz were in theirs—and that in his natural world, Krutch was as much literary critic, intellectual historian, nature writer, and concerned citizen as anyone is in ours.

And so it seems to me—in my natural world and in my time— that the critical and historiographic stance embedded in Krutch's "Prologue" (and most subsequent discussions of nature writing) is especially inappropriate to the works of Thoreau or Hudson or Richard Jefferies or John Hay—however adequate it may be to some kinds of theological or philosophic prose. For despite its declared allegiance to the notion that "man is a part of nature," it presents the nature writer, the central figures of nature writing, and their ancestors almost solely as carriers of ideas and attitudes—as philosophers, scientists, and theologues—rather than as human organisms. It treats philosophy, theology, science, art, and (most ironically perhaps) nature writing not as natural expressions of toiling human organisms, not as instances of organic human behavior, but solely as metaorganic (literally meta-physical) truth-claims *about* their subjects (or *by* their authors) rather than *of* them. Not only does it thus presume that the history and criticism of nature writing are exempt from the conflicts of nature writing itself (most importantly, perhaps, from the competing allegiances of individual human organisms), but it presumes as well that the statements of nature writing are to be taken more or less as testable propositions, in much the same way philosophers take philosophy, or biologists biology.

Such a one-sided critical and historiographic stance is especially troublesome applied to nature writing, it seems to me, because nature writing (certainly the best nature writing, the paradigmatic text of *Walden*, for example) takes as *one* of its fundamental assumptions the notion that its author (or its central narrating figure) is a human organism (in the last analysis, little different from—and certainly no better or worse than—other organisms, human or otherwise, of whatever time or place) *and* that its author's *works* (or its narrator's expressions) are products or formulations of human organisms (in the last analysis, little different from—and certainly no better or worse than—the expressions of other organisms, human or nonhuman, of whatever time or place). Krutch was thus approaching one of the distinguishing traits of nature writing when he argued that the discriminating feature of the genre is its author's deep feeling of kinship with other organisms. Without that deep feeling—without both the sense and the idea of identification between human self and nonhuman other—one would not have *Walden*, or any of a number of other accomplished works of nature writing. What Krutch missed, however—and what several others have missed after him—was (and is) the depth to which the feeling and the idea of kinship often go.

However one may attempt to phrase it, a "sense of kinship," a strong inclination to identify and empathize with one's "fellow creatures," is a necessary ideational or attitudinal condition to nature writing as a genre. It is not, however, a sufficient condition. There is more, much more, to nature writing than a sanguine "feeling for nature" or a benign "sense of kinship." In what I have called the "best" nature writing, in *Walden* and *Desert Solitaire* or *Pilgrim at Tinker Creek*, for example, but even on occasion in the works of a

Muir or a Sigurd Olson, there is also (and here precise phrasing begins to matter a good deal) a strong inclination to identify oneself *as* a creature, a disposition and a desire (if not a need) to take one's kinship *with* other organisms very seriously indeed, not only by arguing the abstract proposition that "man is a part of nature" but by examining that proposition and by considering one's action (including, often, one's actions as a writer) in the same terms (or the same kinds of terms) one uses to consider the gatherings of a muskrat or the territorial scent markings of timber wolves. Particularly in the most self-conscious and self-reflexive nature writing, the thought that man is a part of nature, because it is an active or narrative thought, frequently leads the nature writer (or protagonist) to dramatize his or her own endeavors (including even "literary" and "scientific" endeavors) as the efforts of an organism—in Paul Shepard's phrase, a "tender carnivore," perhaps, but a carnivore (or omnivore) nonetheless.

Kinship was, one might say, too much Idea and Ideal for Krutch (and, perhaps, for his audience as well)—as a sense of "oneness with nature" has continued to be too much concept or disembodied spiritual state (and not enough quotidian fact) in subsequent discussions of nature writing—not enough organic effort or sibling rivalry—perhaps not even enough kinship. As literary historian and critic, at least, Krutch was apparently unable to see (or, if able to see, unwilling to say publicly and openly) that if a sense of kinship with nature is taken seriously, then human language and literature—Bartholomew's bestiary, Saint Thomas's *Summa*, Descartes's *Discourse*, Thoreau's *Walden*, Krutch's "Prologue," and this sentence—are thoroughly analogous to the songs of cardinals wafting from the tops of high spring maples, or to the squeaks of mudhens echoing amid marshgrass and cattails on a foggy morning. As moralist and ethicist, if not as nature writer, Krutch was unable to admit that if the sense of organic fellowship is taken seriously, then not only the cat and the crocodile but Bartholomew and Saint Thomas and Descartes as well must be considered and treated as "fellow creatures" (if not as biotically and culturally contingent "figures" of fellow creatures), where the emphasis falls at least as much on "creatures" as it does on "fellow," and where the biotically and culturally contingent is kept fairly constantly in mind.

One of the primary difficulties, then, with the conventional view of the history and motivations of nature writing is that it does not sufficiently recognize or consider Bartholomew or Saint Thomas or Descartes—or, perhaps more significantly, Gilbert White or Thoreau or Muir (much less the historian or the critic)—as laboring human organisms (however they may see themselves). It considers them, rather, as more or less disembodied "authors," "minds," or "figures"—as "figurative" exemplars (or antiexemplars), if you will—rather than as interested organisms, however wrongheaded or rightminded (in much the same way, I should add, as Krutch and Krutch's "Prologue" are considered here). In essentially the same philosophic fashion, the conventional criticism of nature writing does not sufficiently recognize or consider the *writings* of its chosen figures as instances of verbal behavior. In short, it is *too* leery of a "thoroughgoing materialistic philosophy" (Krutch, 73)—too afraid of the apparent implications of such a philosophy—too convinced that modern scientific culture is dangerously positivistic or behavioristic—to be adequate to the thoroughgoing organicism that courses through the works of virtually all nature writers, the deep desires to immerse oneself in geobiotic and biophysical processes that define at least half the work of a Thoreau and a good deal of the work of a Muir or a John Hay.

Because the conventional criticism is so leery of what it takes to be the demeaning qualities of materialism, behaviorism, and now no doubt sociobiology—because it views each of them as somehow depriving humankind of its distinguishing feature (soul or consciousness or thought)—because it takes each of them as a set of truth-claims *about* reality (rather than, in Aldo Leopold's words, another in a series of "successive excursions from a single starting-point, to which man returns again and again to organize yet another search for a durable scale of values" or, one might add, facts)—because, ironically, it cannot see materialism or sociobiology as a complex figure of thought, speech, and need (as itself a material or sociobiotic phenomenon)—because (to be frank) it takes each of these philosophical positions as threats to the stature of *Homo sapiens*—it tends to play right into their logical and epistemological hands—it tends, in fact (and for the most part unknowingly), to replicate the prevailing view of language and reality in modern scientific culture in a way that at least half-betrays the writing and the thought of the best nature writers.[5] Because, ironically, the conventional criticism treats materialism, behaviorism, and sociobiology (as well as Christianity and Cartesian thought before them) less as expressions or configurations of a geocultural branch of *Homo sapiens* than as wrong (or misleading) answers or as false (and even dangerous) ideas—and because it takes nature writing, in turn, as correct or accurate or true idea—it ends (or can easily seem to end) less as a celebration of nature (human and nonhuman), and less as a reasonable representation of nature writing, than as a kind of rearguard defensive reaction of some human thinkers and writers to others, a stance appropriate perhaps to the history and criticism of philosophy (which normally makes no pretense to present itself otherwise), but a stance inappropriate to good nature writing (which takes as one of its fundamental assumptions the notion, and the sense, that all human endeavor, including philosophy and even history or criticism, is biotically contingent).

In something like this fashion, the still largely customary history and criticism of nature writing more or less unknowingly equate language and reality—word and thing, composition and fact, style and idea—both when they consider the works of nature writers and, perhaps a bit ironically, when they consider selected "experiential" or "observational" truths deriving from modern science. On the other hand, when they consider the works of premodern or "prescientific" Western thinkers and writers—writers who have not been graced by the sense of oneness that science (or nature writing or, nowadays, the writing of Basho or the *Tao Te Ching*) reveals— they even more unknowingly dissociate language and reality, and hence divorce word and thing, metaphor (or composition) and fact, subject and object, idea and style, persuasion and grammar. When conventional critics and historians consider the works of a Bartholomew or a Descartes, they unwittingly separate language and nature, human composition and nonhuman phenomena, human organism and human idea—largely because they are so concerned to show that the Bartholomews and the Descartes were (and are) wrong. When they consider the works of a Thoreau or a William Beebe, they do just the opposite, and for the most part just as unwittingly—in large part because they are so concerned to show that Thoreau and Beebe were (and are) right. Bartholomew's and Saint Thomas's writings are thus at radical odds with nature, both descriptively and prescriptively, as if somehow their authors were not parts of nature and their works (if not their ideas) were (and are) unnatural. Thoreau's and Muir's writings, on the other hand, are in tune with nature, and their authors, at least by implication, in tune both with themselves and their surroundings. In the latter case, language and language-user are in organic relationship to each other and to the natural world, though the relationship is singularly noncompetitive and benign. In the former case, both the language-user and the text are somehow inorganic, if not even antiorganic, as if they were somehow independent of their ecosystemic surroundings. In the one case, language bears (as it is supposed to) a one-to-one relationship to an essentially nonlinguistic reality or truth; it reflects (and fully reflects) the natural condition of its author. In the other, it just as clearly (and wrongly) does not.

Part of the difficulty here is a function of the critic's desire to promulgate the experiences and understandings of the nature writer—the concepts and images of nature writing—as an answer to what are now called "environmental problems." Because, almost without exception, interested literary historians and critics have continued to view nature writing as a programmatic (ethical, aesthetic, scientific, and even psychological) solution to such problems, the literary history and criticism of the genre remain at least at partial odds with themselves, at partial odds, at least, both with some of the underpinning ideas of contemporary literary theory and historiography and, more significantly, with some of the central concepts (and much of the focal imagery) of modern biology, concepts and images that continue to engage both the authors of nature writing and their narrative or expository personae. However one may characterize the years of structuralism, deconstructionism, and their aftermaths (along with changing contemporary perspectives in anthropology, biology, psychology, historiography, linguistics, and, in this case especially, biology and ecology), they have yet to have a significant impact on the literary history and criticism of nature writing. In conventional discussions of nature writing, such as we have them, phoebes, crocodiles, and Indian pipes are in no sense conceived or treated as signs, for example. To put things bluntly, pollution, acid rain, and wildlife management are simply not conceived as linguistic, stylistic, or ideational phenomena. In no sense are they semiotic or hermeneutic. In fact, no critic has as yet considered them even as psycholinguistic or sociolinguistic events. In short, the literary history and criticism of nature writing continue to exemplify only the most popular, most conventional, and least knowing conceptions of modern scientific culture, a popular culture that (at least a bit ironically) itself continues to exemplify fundamentally Cartesian, if not Thomistic, ways of thinking. Not only do pollution, toad, and Indian pipe thus continue to be unquestioned facts—as the weeping crocodile no doubt was for Bartholomew—but in conventional dualistic fashion, rhetoric and reality, word and thing, language and experience continue to be at least half at categorical and ontological odds with one and other (except, of course, when the critic or historian is dealing with "scientific," "experiential," or "observational" statements; for such statements are at best only marginally "rhetorical" or stylistic; they are, as Descartes or even Saint Thomas might have said, "true to nature").

In such a naively realistic fashion (a fashion many nature writers themselves have long since questioned) the criticism and history of nature writing continue to be characterized largely by views of language and reality in which science and the "scientific" parts of nature writing deal in definable material things, while poetry and the "poetic" parts of nature writing deal in rhetoric or symbols. In a

strong sense, critics and historians of nature writing continue to
view the genre less as literature, if you will, than as the truth-claims
of the philosopher or the observations of the scientist, with a little
"poetry" or "rhetoric" thrown in for moral or aesthetic measure.
Because their discussions of nature writing deal largely in NATURE
or nature rather than "nature"—because they simply do not conceive "environmental problems" as in any sense stylistic or linguistic issues—because they are finally more concerned to change or
improve our attitudes toward nature and land than they are to comprehend them—in short, because they tend to idealize and moralize
ideas, conceptions, and attitudes—language, phrasing, and style
come perilously close to being divorced entirely not only from idea
and attitude but from the environments in which they grow and
from the conditions (especially perhaps the psychobiotic conditions)
they express. Word and idea, sign and environment, and even organism and expression are thus distinct, at least half the time—as
word and thing are clearly distinct and separable when Bartholomew's version of the crocodile is compared to the observed truth
about crocodiles. Or, alternatively, word and thing, language and
attitude, reason and emotion, are clearly and wondrously unified
when Thoreau's view of the phoebe or the goose is compared to
what one might call "the phoebe or the goose itself."

Part of the difficulty, then, with conventional discussions of nature writing is a matter of confounding conceptions of word and
thing, shifting unknowingly between mutually exclusive views of
language and experience—and shifting between them in such a way
that one cannot reasonably account for significant segments of the
most sophisticated forms of the genre, nor even occasionally for
some of the "senses" that define its simplest expressions. Another,
and closely related, part of the difficulty is the critic's consequent
disposition (however understandable) to confound "is" and
"ought"—or, more accurately, to shift unknowingly among incompatible conceptions of "is" and "ought." It is thus quite common to
find the critic-historian, like Krutch, declaring in one paragraph
that man and, by extension, man's artifacts are parts of nature—
and, then, in the next paragraph, declaring Descartes and Descartes's ideas unnatural, treating them as if they were somehow not
parts of nature. It is quite common, in other words, to find the critic
of nature writing unknowingly transposing mutually exclusive conceptions of nature: on the one hand, a conception in which nature is
synonymous with universe or planet earth and, on the other hand, a
conception in which nature is synonymous only with those parts of
earth or universe that are not urban, technological, industrial, "homocentric," or "historical." In the first instance, of course, history

(all history) is natural, inseparable from the workings of geobiotic processes. In the second, history is built upon and juxtaposed with the natural; at best only the "earliest" or most "primitive" forms of humankind are (or were) natural; and nature is that which goes before or after history. Thus the critic declares in one committed voice the inescapable fact that man or woman is a part of nature and, then, in another and no less committed voice, laments the historical "fact" that modern (and especially urban) peoples have forgotten the prior fact, that they neglect their relations to nature— and all without acknowledging that if the first fact holds true, then it simply is not possible for people to forget or neglect their relations to nature—that all humankind (urban or rural, "primitive" or "modern") can do, that all humankind has ever been able to do, is to deal in or change those relations. If the first fact holds true, in other words, then the second is natural. Modern man's apparent neglectfulness, the instances of his "forgetting," and even his various declarations of independence from (or superiority to) nature are parts of nature, quite natural expressions of his ecosystemic conditions, however lamentable they may be. Or, to take another fairly common instance, in one breath the critic-historian will embed the proposition that man is part of nature in a discussion of "early" or "primitive" peoples and cultures—peoples still devoted to mythic modes of understanding (more or less as Adam, Eve, and Pandora once were)—and, then, in a second breath will declare that modern peoples are no longer fully parts of nature, because they have turned away from myth (and by implication at least, toward history and fact), and hence that they are at odds both with themselves and their surroundings—all without acknowledging, and most often even without noticing, that if the first somewhat hidden premise is true (that man is a part of nature), then the condition of so-called modern peoples, however disjunctive, is itself an expression of man's natural condition, an ineluctible part of nature.

The cultural legacies implicit in the critic's shifting stances run deep in the Western world, of course. A part (perhaps a large part) of what the critic and his readers are dealing in is the age-old conflict between free-will and determinism, wanting on the one hand to accept one's fate (if not indeed to celebrate one's condition), wanting to immerse oneself in nature (or to lose one's inherited sense of isolated self and estranged species), and wanting on the other hand to escape or redeem or improve one's condition, to comprehend it if not to transcend it. In this manner, the inherited divisions of classical Western thought (and especially those exacerbated forms of it that seem to have followed from Descartes) live on in the criticism and history of nature writing (as one might expect they would), but generally unbeknownst to the critic and most often unrecognized by readers as well. There is little sense here of T. S. Eliot's self-conscious and self-reflexive "spitting from the mouth the withered appleseed"—and little sense as well of one of the last declamations from *Walden* on Western man's condition: "For the most part, we are not where we are, but in a false position. Through an infirmity of our natures, we suppose a case, and put ourselves into it, and hence are in two cases at the same time, and it is doubly difficult to get out."[6] There is little sense, in other words, that the critic recognizes the conflicting fealties of his inheritance. The popular, Romantic, saving graces and restorative powers of Nature—as birds, trees, and unpolluted waters—and the senses that seem to go with them—that language is an innocent, inexpensive, transparent medium (or, alternatively, an encumbering interference in our relations to a fundamentally nonlinguistic reality)—clearly continue to dominate the history and criticism of nature writing. No wonder the fruit was originally forbidden.

Because the conventional critical approach to nature writing does not seriously consider the nature *writer* as an organism (or nature *writing* as organic phenomenon)—because it basically conceives language to be *about* its subjects or surroundings rather than *of* them—because its essential view of history, science, and even literature is progressive (for all its avowed complaints about Bartholomew's or Saint Thomas's teleological ways of thinking)—because it deals finally in lines of progression or regression rather than in circles, cycles, and circuits—it reflects (and can adequately represent) only that part of nature writing (and only that version of ecological thought and evolutionary theory) that envisions uninterrupted processes or systems moving to states of climax and final equilibrium. It can account adequately only for that version of ecology called Clementsian—and only for that part of nature writing which views "succession," uninterrupted by "outside" influences, fundamentally as progression—in short, as a teleological process. Because this conventional critical stance is dedicated so staunchly to advancing our knowledge of nature—because (against the underlying dictates of evolutionary theory and ecology) it is dedicated so firmly to avoiding or escaping "anthropocentrism" and "anthropomorphism"—it ends by presenting nature writing less as the configuration of natural human impulses or desires, less as the outgrowth of ecosystemic conditions, than as the blueprint for the reformation or redemption of our inherited attitudes and patterns of land use.

Because it is so much given to the party of hope and harmony, and so very much opposed to the party of resignation or acceptance (which, in America at least, remains identical to the party of despair), the still conventional criticism of nature writing tends not only to confuse conceptions of "is" and "ought" but to cross them as well with antipathetic notions of historical, ecological, and evolutionary time. What "is" (and ought not to be) the case in modern man's relations to nature is thus set off against what "is" or "is not" the case in nature writing (an acknowledged *modern* form of thinking and writing). What was (and ought not to have been) the case in earlier Western writings about nature gets crossed with an age-old desire to recover past, unpolluted environments, to return to earlier symbiotic states of existence. What, unfortunately, has been, is, and ought not to be the case in Western man's relations with nature gets all mucked up with what, by contrast, is the case in nature writing (and ought to be the case in our daily lives)—as if nature writers and nature writing do not participate in Western man's relations to nature, whatever they may be—as if nature writers and nature writing can somehow escape or transcend the biotic, historic, and cultural conditions in which they exist. What might have been the case, if we had done (or thought) otherwise, gets crossed with notions of what we are no matter what we do. Nature as ethical and aesthetic norm gets unwittingly tied up with nature as given system or process, whatever may happen to individual species or the relationships among them, in whatever time or place. Nature as something to be preserved or conserved gets crossed with nature as something to be accepted, something to be taken as it changes. And at least some of the terms of Cartesian thought and orthodox Christianity are, as it were, turned in upon themselves—as that which once was immoral becomes unnatural, a sin not against God or God's creation but against Nature. What for Bartholomew or Saint Thomas had been immoral (though by no means unnatural) becomes unnatural and, hence, immoral. Nature tends to become synonymous with The Divine, The Good, and The Beautiful; and nature writers tend to become saintly figures, philosopher kings perhaps (though without the commitment to governing necessarily imperfect states)—not the modern equivalent of a despairing Saint John of the Cross or Saint Teresa certainly, but something more like a Western Buddhist monk. Sometimes it seems to make little difference, as long as nature writers can be imagined free of our guilt-ridden ancestry, the ancestry ultimately responsible for the tragic fate of the entire earth.

As alternative conceptions of "is" and "ought" are crossed with one and other, as the natural becomes the moral (and ceases to include or comprehend the immoral), as false statements (and even fables) cease to be natural events, so what we, in our time, call "observation" gets confused with what we might call "the written impression of observation." The observed and the observable, the verified and the verifiable, get confused (and even identified) with the language and rhetoric of observation, the rhetorical stance of observation, and the rhetoric of verifiability—all in a manner that suggests we have learned considerably less from Descartes and Hume than we might have, and in a fashion that (for all our increased modern knowledge) proves us no more self-conscious, no more aware of the limitations of our conceptions, our language, or habits of usage than we say Bartholomew and Saint Thomas were. In a manner that betrays (and misrepresents) many a nature writer's deep sense of the inadequacies and limitations of human language and formulation, the written expression of desire gets all mucked up with our conceptions of unwritten reality and truth. The analytic phrasing of the linguistic medium—the desire, for example, to "be a part of nature"—gets all mucked up with (in fact, gets identified with) the synthetic dream of what we call the message. The substance of nature and the style of the nature writer—content and form, experience and language, thing and word—are unintentionally and unwittingly identified; and the message that comes through is a lingering expression of the same apparent naiveté, the very separation from nature, the critic otherwise professes to reject. It is, after all, man who wishes to be "a part of nature" (as Bartholomew and Saint Thomas no doubt wished to be "a part of God"); and not nature, presumably, which (and certainly not who) wishes to be a part of humanity.

The story is an old one in the Western world. Few, if any, of us are free of its constraints, confusions, and ambiguities (certainly not Krutch and certainly not the author of this book): responsibility and guilt (or pride), evolution as change and evolution as development, participation and estrangement, contemplation and action, existence and essence, point and counterpoint, analysis and synthesis, nature and Nature, history and myth, fact and fable, analogy and metaphor, object and subject, literature and literary criticism, self and other, division and unity, reason and imagination, deduction and induction, economic harmony and spendthrift profligacy, art and nature, a priori and a posteriori, science and poetry, meaningful and meaningless, human and nonhuman, consciousness or reason or understanding and instinct or impulse or need, linguistic and (paradoxically) "nonlinguistic," equilibrium and disequilibrium, entropy and negentropy, both-and and either-or, language as referent and language as phenomenon, order and disorder, hope and despair, predator and prey, the circular or the cyclical (nitrogen cycles, for example) and the linear (edges and the edge-effect), centers and peripheries, the bounded and the boundless, civilization and wilderness, recognizing that one is inescapably a creature of one's culture and yet striving to knowledge and experience that avoid ethnocentricism, being and becoming (or, worse, overcoming), hyperbola (and hyperbole) and parabola (and the parabolic, or worse, perhaps, the elliptical and the ellipsoid), centrifugal and centripetal, space and place, the dualism of monism and dualism, the nominalism (or is it realism?) of realism and nominalism—all in all, no doubt, the dancer and the dance.

The issues and the drama are as old as the Western hills, one might say; and we would do better, or so it seems to me, to acknowledge more often these ethno-, etho-, and ecocentric facts. We would do a better job of representing nature writing, and perhaps come a bit closer to comprehending our own and the nature writer's conditions, if we spent a bit less time trying to solve the problems or resolve the contradictions, and a bit more time exploring them, not with an eye to resolution but with an eye and an ear to comprehension. Our understanding of the various disjunctions of classical (and modern) Western thought might be a bit more conjunctive, as it were, if we spent more time consciously assuming them, taking them as given, and acknowledging our dependencies upon them, rather than attempting to declare our independence from them or trying to find third (or fourth or fifth) terms to bridge the gaps among them. Heretical—self-contradictory and even hypocritical—as it may be to say so (especially perhaps in America), we would do better by nature writers and nature writing, if not by ourselves, to acknowledge, tolerate, and perhaps even to celebrate ambiguity than we would (knowingly or unknowingly) to continue to run from it or to try to transcend or escape it. For by trying to transcend or escape contradiction, by constantly seeking to redeem ourselves, or to rectify what *we* have done to *our* environments, we appear far less as creatures finally coming to terms with their surroundings or (against their destructive heritage) finally settling in to their ecosystemic places than we do as unwitting supplicants to the very "homocentric," "ethnocentric," and "dualistic" culture we claim to be overcoming. "Homocentric," "ethnocentric," and "dualistic," particularly in their contemporary pejorative senses, are especially Western concepts, after all. So are "disinterested knowledge" and "observational statements." And so, of course, are their opposites. "We shall overcome," in whatever shape or form, is simply not consonant, after all, with settling in or settling down. Increasing one's knowledge of one's surroundings, *comprehending* one's place, is simply not consonant with "letting it be."

Finally, then, the signal deficiency with the conventional history and criticism of nature writing is that it does not sufficiently consider language or writing as a biotic or ecological phenomenon. In other words, it does not recognize one of the central ideas of the most self-conscious nature writers—Thoreau, Eiseley, Hay, Abbey, Janovy, Dillard, and even Leopold, for example—and hence cannot account for one of the central experiences of their protagonists—the sometimes seriously frustrating experience not only of feeling that one's words are utterly inadequate, but of thinking the often consequent thought that language and writing and art inevitably divorce the human from the nonhuman, the woman or the man from nature, and that one is inexorably isolated and estranged in and by one's human (literary and scientific) endeavors—because language and writing and art are devoted to *capturing* the Indian pipe or to *understanding* the crocodile, because they are devices to stop time, as it were, to comprehend or appreciate a passing moment, and because the passing moment, the deceptively subtle movement of the crocodile, or, for that matter, its seemingly concentrated stasis, seems to pass as one tries to comprehend it, because in one's efforts to understand or picture, one seems to be left behind, or to be forced outside, the constantly shifting reflections on leaves and stamen, because you can't write and observe at the same time, because wording and seeing, word and thing, are at quite immediate, practical, and emotional odds with one and other.

Because it does not sufficiently consider the biotic or ecological functions and contexts of language, neither can the conventional history and criticism of nature writing account adequately for the backside of isolation and estrangement—the sense of being a part of nature, as we say, or even the sense of kinship with one's fellow creatures. Because it simply does not recognize the psychobiotic functions of style and grammar, for nature writer or protagonist, because it does not consider language or nature writing as natural (physical and organic) phenomenon, the conventional history and criticism of the genre cannot adequately represent nature writing as participation or the nature writer as participant. It cannot account for the sometimes reassuring, and even on occasion exhilarating, thought that—no matter the limitations of one's language, or the feeling that art and science divorce the erstwhile human appreciator of late-summer cricket-songs from the passing season those songs seem to memorialize, no matter the seemingly passing moment, or the apparent strictures imposed on participation and observation by wording, writing, and thought (quite literally, by paper and pen)—wording and writing and thought (writer and thinker) cannot but participate in (and express) the moment and the season—the recognition (however self-effacing) that the feeling of being left behind is as much a part of the natural, changing seasons and time as the songs of the crickets themselves, that indeed one's "inadequate" statements (however frequently one may need to think of them as statements *about* organic or climatological change—and however they may seem to artificialize, misrepresent, and anthropomorphize what we apparently need to call the nonhuman) are late-summer songs in their own rights—are fundamentally and finally akin to the songs of the crickets—that for all one's sense of isolation and estrangement, one's sense of being left behind with one's human consciousness (or the "awareness" of death and passing time that is said to distinguish our species from others), for all one's inherited sense that writing and observation or thought and instinct are at categorical and (hence) practical odds with one and other, that wording and seeing, or writing and being, cannot finally be divorced from one another, indeed that "thought" and "articulate consciousness" and "the awareness of death" are instinctive and impulsive mechanisms, rhythmic refrains in humanoid "songs" repeated again and again whenever (like the late-summer crickets) the species (or at least the Western branch thereof) feels threatened by waning seasons or (perish the thought) the notion that we are not so distinct or special as we seem to need to think we are.

Because it does not sufficiently consider what we call the biological and ecological contexts of the nature writer's words—in short, because it does not extend one of the central ideas or senses of the best and most self-conscious nature writers to nature writing itself—the conventional criticism of the genre cannot deal adequately with those parts or versions of nature writing which are, intentionally or otherwise, self-reflexive and biotically or ecologically self-referential and circular. By the same philosophic token, neither can it deal adequately with those parts or versions of nature writing that, knowingly or otherwise, are straightforwardly representational and, hence, given to maintaining the distance of *scientia* (historical, scientific, or even autobiographical) upon self-consciousness and style.

Science, after all—like representational art and history—is a means of controlling the often unsettling effects of self-consciousness. Well-practiced and well-formulated, it enables one to establish and maintain a disciplined distance both from one's interested, active self and upon the immediacy and singularity of what we call the Indian pipe or the cat. Science, *scientia*, absorbs and effaces self and self-consciousness in the method and the psychology of understanding and representing the other. It attempts to keep subject and object, self and other, clear and distinct, by repressing or sublimating all awareness of subject and self (as interested human organism,

as what we call political being, and as product of a particular culture). Though *scientia*—in scientific, artistic, theological, mythological, historical, and even anthropological form—may seem to absorb
one entirely in the other—to engross one entirely in its object, or to
immerse one in nature—it does so at the cost of a sense of one's own
particular and immediate circumstances and impulses (one's organic and anthropological, physiological and psychological, historical and linguistic conditions and needs)—at the cost, one might say,
of a sense of one's particular, active, and very much interested place
in nature. In short, *scientia* (in science and art, as in nature writing
and literary criticism) seeks to separate human consciousness from
the objects of human consciousness—to divorce man from nature, if
you will—and the psychological state it expresses and creates is at
least as familiar to nature writers—and the assumption behind it at
least as central to nature writing—as the assumption that "man is a
part of nature" or the "sense of kinship" with one's "fellow creatures" one is said to gather from a "feeling for nature." Read closely,
in fact, each of these phrases is at least as much an expression of
Western man's desire to comprehend (and thus transcend) the limitations of the human condition as it is an expression of "man's
place in nature." Like that last phrase, each depends upon and
maintains a not-so-subtle (and quite classical) categorical distinction between man and nature—between oneself and one's fellow
creatures, between kinship and estrangement—and each thus repeats and reinforces a quite traditional set of logical, syntactic, psychological, and anthropological discriminations at the core of Western thought and civilization, even (or perhaps especially) when its
citizens scck (or need) to deny them.

Without at least an occasional glance in the direction of the
sociobiologist or the ecolinguist, without at least an occasional recognition of the psycho- and sociobiotic functions of the nature writer's language (for author, protagonist, and reader), I doubt very
much that the history and criticism of nature writing can account
adequately either for the development of the genre or for its distinguishing features (much less for its continuing popularity, especially in America). Without some such recognition, "orthodox
Christianity" or, for that matter, any other philosophy or religion or
science—indeed any text—can only be seen as an extrasystemic
theory of life, a commentary *upon* conditions, and not as an integral
part of the environments in which it receives expression. Without
giving at least an occasional thought to the physical, biological, and
psychological status and functions of human linguistic forms,
without at least occasionally taking seriously the notion that language and text and even thought are physical, biological, and eco-

logical phenomena, we are unlikely either to understand Thoreau or to comprehend *Walden*, and unlikely as well to see more conventional nature writing as anything other than sources of information, attitudes, or ideas. We are unlikely, in other words, to understand either the history of nature writing or its internal dynamics, much less the motivations of its authors or their narrative and expository personae.

Without some such recognition, without seriously (and humorously) entertaining such suggestions, I doubt that we will ever adequately understand or explain *Walden*, much less its affinities to the Bible or Aristotle's natural history or Saint Augustine's *Confessions* or Bartholomew's bestiary or the works of Darwin and the writings of John Muir or John Hay. Without some such occasional recognition, we are unlikely to consider as parts of nature writing those passages in *Walden* or *Nature's Year* or *Pilgrim at Tinker Creek* that call explicit attention to their own words or phrases or "sounds." We are unlikely, in other words, to consider the word or the pun as a part of nature. Worse than that, perhaps, in our devotion to a disembodied sense of oneness or kinship—in our dedication and sensitivity to Nature (and, hence, our neglect of language and human *nature*), we are likely to ignore or slight (as "unnatural" lapses) those passages in *Walden* in which Thoreau casts sharp aspersions upon Irishmen and icemen, or that little, seemingly innocent note in *Pilgrim at Tinker Creek* in which Annie Dillard declares "the Law of the Wild"—"Carry Kleenex." Not only are we unlikely to consider Kleenex natural (or "the Wild" civilized), but we are unlikely to consider human desires for such things as natural, and unlikely as well to consider natural any human configurations of those desires. In our neglect of the human organism and the organism's language, we are likely, in other words, to skip over indications of the natural desires and products of human organisms, to neglect Thoreau's or Dillard's fairly frequent (and quite natural) bouts with egoism, and to bracket out not only passages of humor or wit but anything that might suggest "that sense of superiority or even separateness which is the inevitable result of any philosophy or any religion [or any biology or psychology or language] which attributes to man [or "man"] a qualitative [or quantitative or even semiotic] uniqueness" (Krutch, 6, amended).

Without some occasional acknowledgment of the nature writer as organism and of the psychobiotic functions of language, we are unlikely to recognize (or if we recognize, to admit publicly) that one of the results of a deep sense of kinship with nature may well be (as it frequently is in *Walden* and at least a few other works of nature writing) a sense that all organisms and all species regularly need to feel (and even *be*) distinct or separate, and on occasion even superior—that, however, antithetical a sense of superiority may seem to "a sense of kinship" or a "feeling for nature," one of the necessary conditions of being (and continuing to be) an organism or a species may well be (as modern genetics and biology would indicate) the sense of feeling and being superior or separate—as Thoreau stands superior to his battling ants and Irishmen, and indeed to all those who lead lives of "quiet desperation," as John Hay's appreciator of the Indian pipe stands momentarily superior to his botanists and Alice O. Albertson, as Joseph Wood Krutch stands (or tries to stand) superior to Saint Thomas and Bartholomew, and as I, however sympathetically, am trying to stand superior to Krutch (among many others).

To consider orthodox Christian thought or Cartesian philosophy (or, for that matter, "Kleenex") unnatural is, of course, to neglect what one might call the natural functions (the ecological costs and benefits) of language and books. It is to be unable to account for the places of language, books, and other expressions or products of the human species in biotic and ecological systems. It is to leave them unaccounted for in "nature's economy," to leave them out of one's conception of nature, and to divorce the apparently distinguishing traits of humankind, the essential medium of the species and its products, from "the natural world." In short, it is unknowingly to repeat and reinforce the underlying discriminations and schisms of classical, Western thought. In this case, it is to parrot one's heritage by professing to escape or transcend it—all in a fashion that Thoreau and several other nature writers would find at least mildly appalling (however understandable) and certainly ironic—all in a manner that tellingly and unconsciously mimics what we traditionally see (and apparently very much need to see) as the unconscious, instinctive behavior of the insectivorous crickets and the vegetative Indian pipe, a manner at least partially inimical to substantial segments of *Walden* and even to portions of *The Natural History of Selborne*.[7]

For these reasons, and for several others implied above, I wish to suggest an alternative view of the history and forms of nature writing, a view I will here attempt to outline briefly and then in subsequent chapters begin to elaborate and refine. Because the subject is vast, potentially at least as vast as "nature"—and because I am attempting, as it were, to recultivate a substantial tract of literary, philosophic, and historical ground—I beg the indulgence and tolerance of my readers, including especially those critics and historians who will come after me. I apologize at the outset for the crudity of the diagrams below and for the unfinished history and criticism of the subsequent essays.

Because I have wished to provide the essentials of a revised historical overview of nature writing (at least the outline for a revised literary historiography), and because that revised historiography has seemed to depend more than anything else on the close reading and detailed analysis of exemplary, individual texts, I have been forced to compromise my interests in (and my representation of) the extensive history of nature writing with intensive readings of several exemplary tests. The result is a rather awkward amalgam by contemporary standards of literary history and criticism, a book double inadequate: incomplete both as a running account of the history of nature writing and as a series of critical essays on representative works. My concerns with and for the broader history of the genre have kept me from considering in detail many individual texts that ought to be discussed in a book such as this. My concerns, on the other hand, to demonstrate in some detail the underlying psychology—the drama or dialectic—of nature writing have kept me as well from a more complete rendering of the genre's history (its forms, its authors, and its specific occasions). To fill the gaps, as it were, in the history of nature writing—and in an attempt to establish connections between those works I have discussed in detail and the many others which I should have—I have made loosely passing reference throughout the book to many authors and, by implication at least, many works that, though familiar to those few (like myself) obsessed with nature writing, are no doubt unknown to more casual readers, and even to many who consider themselves devotees of the genre. My hope, of course, is that by carefully dropping enough names and titles, I will touch enough comparative and contrastive nerves—and, hence, sound sufficiently resonant cords—that those who have not read John Hay's *Nature's Year* will have read Robert Finch's *The Primal Place*, that those who do not know Sigurd Olson's *The Singing Wilderness* or Josephine Johnson's *The Inland Island* will know John Muir's *My First Summer in the Sierra* or Mary Austin's *The Land of Little Rain*, that those who have not read Gilbert White's *Selborne* will have read Hal Borland's *Countryman* or Peter Matson's *A Place in the Country*, and that those who do not know Richard Jefferies' *The Gamekeeper at Home* will know W. H. Hudson's *Hampshire Days*.

It is a crude strategy at best; and at times it seems an almost impossible task. The effort will inevitably frustrate the expectations and experiences of my readers—and frequently no doubt provoke their anger as well—for, given the nature of the works and the occasions on which they are frequently read, each reader will have a favorite whose name I have not mentioned or whose work I have not covered in sufficient, loving detail. In lieu of standard bibliographies, however—in the absence of established curricula, and in the presence of a literary history and criticism at best superficially popular—I have been able to do little else. Under the circumstances, about all I can ask is that advocates of those works and authors I have slighted pick up the critical and historical gavel and call to order further meetings of concerned minds.

These essays, then, are but the slightest and most suggestive beginnings to the history and critical appreciation of nature writing. There is a vast nature-writing territory that remains to be mapped and gardened, and an even vaster territory of so-called nonfictional prose to which the history and forms of nature writing must be related in formal and historical detail.

Like Krutch and most others who have written on the subject, I have begun by positing *Walden* (and, coincidentally, a good deal of the rest of Thoreau's writing, including the largest part of the journals) as my paradigm text for nature writing, my testcase both for any reasonable definition of the genre and for any sensible account of its history. It seems to me, as it has obviously seemed in different ways to others, that any discussion of the history of what we have come to call "nature writing" (however loosely)—and, hence, any attempt to characterize nature writing as a genre—must be able to account for the several stylistic modes of *Walden*, for its philosophy as well as its science, for the idiosyncracies as well as the conventionalities of its often highly personal narrative and exposition, for its wit as well as its sentiment and its discipline. For if a historical and critical theory of nature writing cannot account for *Walden*, it cannot stand the test of the text most commonly associated with the term.

Walden is thus to be imagined at the center of the Synchronic Diagram of Nature Writing and Associated Literary Forms and Types (see Fig 2.1). With *Walden* in the inner, paradigmatic circle one is to imagine as well other works (presently but a few) that bear extensive stylistic, philosophic, and tonal affinities to *Walden*—*Pilgrim at Tinker Creek*, for example, or Abbey's *Desert Solitaire* or Leopold's *A Sand County Almanac*, but not Hay's *Nature's Year* or Muir's *The Mountains of California*; Janovy's *Keith County Journal*, perhaps, but not Zwinger's *Beyond the Aspen Grove* or Olson's *Listening Point*; Eiseley's *The Immense Journey* or Lopez's *River Notes*, probably, but not Burroughs's *Riverby* or *The Natural History of Selborne* or Teale's *Wandering through Winter* or Jefferies' *Wildlife in a Southern County* (and certainly not Basho's *The Narrow Road to the Deep North* or the *Tao Te Ching*).

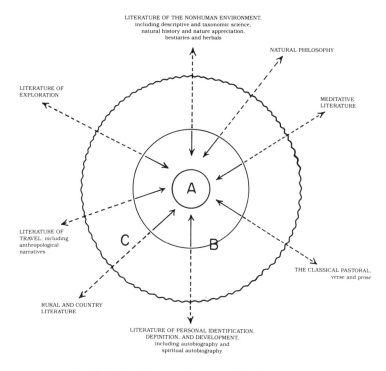

LITERATURE OF THE NONHUMAN ENVIRONMENT,
including descriptive and taxonomic science,
natural history and nature appreciation,
bestiaries and herbals

NATURAL PHILOSOPHY

LITERATURE OF
EXPLORATION

MEDITATIVE
LITERATURE

LITERATURE OF
TRAVEL, including
anthropological
narratives

THE CLASSICAL PASTORAL,
verse and prose

RURAL AND COUNTRY
LITERATURE

LITERATURE OF PERSONAL IDENTIFICATION,
DEFINITION, AND DEVELOPMENT,
including autobiography and
spiritual autobiography

*Fig. 2.1. Synchronic diagram of nature writing
and associated literary forms and types*

With this diagram, then, I suggest that *Walden* and a few other
works be imagined to stand at the exemplary center (within the
circle A) of the literary class called nature writing, in something like
the fashion a particular organism (or a select set of organisms)
might be (and, in practice, often is) conceived to typify or define a
species (or subspecies) and then used both to test the conception or
definition of its morphological type and to aid in delineating its morphology from the morphology of associated types. Surrounding the
exemplary set of organisms, the type or archetype of the type, so to
speak, are—in closest proximity (within the circle B, but outside
A)—those individual phenomena, in this case those particular
works, that upon detailed examination and analysis seem to bear
substantial (particular and fairly extensive) formal resemblance to
those through the analysis of which the type is initially defined.
Here, in the inner range of the second circle, one might locate such
works as *Nature's Year* (and, for that matter, most of the rest of
John Hay's writings), or Louis Halle's *Spring in Washington*,

Krutch's *The Twelve Seasons*, Olson's *The Singing Wilderness*, Johnson's *The Inland Island*, or David Wallace's *The Klamath Knot*, or Kappel-Smith's *Wintering*. In the outer range of the second circle, one might imagine, in turn, the works of Muir and Zwinger and some of the writings of Burroughs, or the writings of Teale and Beebe and Henry Beston, and perhaps (but only perhaps) some of the writings of Hal Borland (his *Book of Days*, for example), Mikhail Prishvin's *Nature's Diary*, *The Natural History of Selborne*, and a few other works of so-called British nature writing. Finally, in the extreme outer reaches of my diagram (in the region C, outside the circle B) are works that, though they bear some formal and substantive similarity to the type exemplified by *Walden*, also bear extensive (and inescapable) similarities to other associated, and previously identified, literary types of at least roughly comparable conceptual orders and historical significance.

Here (in the outer reaches of the diagram) the literary class nature writing begins to break down and to overlap with other recognized literary genres. The description and analysis (and, hence, the classification) of individual works begins to demand terms and vocabularies, modes of conceiving and styling experience, at best of partial relevance to the analysis and description of *Walden* or *Pilgrim at Tinker Creek* or *Desert Solitaire*, and in some cases completely misleading. None of the works in or near the paradigmatic center of the class, for example—neither *Walden* nor *Pilgrim at Tinker Creek* nor Kappel-Smith's *Wintering*—is in any formal way "developmental." None of them is structured in the narrative way of conventional travel literature or the literature of exploration. None is an account of a spatial or temporal journey, and none as a result depends (except in brief interludes) upon the kinds of temporal and spatial connectives—the kinds of stylistic (grammatical and logical) orders—that control conventional narrative literature (whether novel or romance or history or excursion). All may be related to (indeed each may derive from) a kind of journal; but it is not—psychologically or logically—the kind of journal kept by Lewis and Clark or Darwin or Audubon. If each is a journal, each is a journal of a particular place (more diary than journal, perhaps). Neither does any of the works at the exemplary center of the class recount the developmental story of traditional autobiography, the movement from innocence to maturity (or from state of sin to state of grace). Though each is much concerned with psychic or spiritual condition, with personal identification and its implications, in the manner of spiritual autobiography and confession, all of them convey such concerns to some substantial degree in the impersonal terms of science, through "scientific" description, measurement, and analysis. (This dedication to science and *scientia*, by the way—especially when it is accompanied by an intensive concern for self—is finally what distinguishes Western nature writing from the writings of Basho and the *Tao Te Ching*.) Though each paradigmatic work of nature writing is frequently philosophical, though each regularly raises epistemological or metaphysical questions, all of them are far too dedicated to extended (and even unanalyzed) description and explication for them to be called natural philosophy. And though all of them are formally akin to natural history in their extended delineations and explications of nonhuman phenomena, each is also far too personal, far too meditative and philosophic, to be adequately characterized in the terms one might use to represent the natural histories of Aristotle, Buffon, or Agassiz (much less the bestiary of Bartholomew Anglicanus or the modern literature of systematic biology and ecology).

In the simplest, most primitive terms, then, those works at the exemplary center of my diagram—and the genre they may be said to typify—are distinguished from works that might be located on or near its ragged circumference—and from other literary genres (including many of those frequently associated with nature writing)—by a rather unusual combination of intense personal "narrative," a dialectic amalgam of self-analysis and self-reflection (if not self-celebration), on the one hand, and extensive, impersonal scientific description and explication, on the other—a combination that characteristically accompanies (and no doubt at least partly provokes) a distinct philosophical (epistemological and metaphysical) bent—a disposition to delve into the philosophic implications both of "autobiography" and of impersonal geobiotic science, a tendency to push each toward its philosophical (and even its practical) extremes.

Works in the outer range of the circle B of the diagram—the outer edge, as it were, of the class of nature writing—are distinguished, in turn, by their tendencies to emphasize one or another of the exemplary traits of the genre to the exclusion (or near exclusion) of the others—to subdue the first-person singular, for example—either by emphasizing the impersonality (or through personification, the personality) of nonhuman, biological and geological, others, or (as in works that invite comparison with rural literature and the literature of exploration) by turning toward the "we" of community, family, and expedition or team (and even on occasion by developing fully fledged, speaking characters)—in both cases, by muting and chastening the self—by giving it, so to speak, to the other. In Teale's seasonal series (*North with the Spring, Journey into Summer, Autumn across America,* and *Wandering through*

Winter), for example, the singular (and most often isolated) self of Thoreau or Dillard or John Hay gives way for the most part to a "we" of marital and professional association, and nature writing becomes a kind of communal and even "country" literature on the move. The nature writer becomes a kind of traveling naturalist whose primary identity is a function of loosely related, transregional affiliations. In Muir's *The Mountains of California*, to cite another and quite different variant, semblances and memories of the communal, human "we" are hard to come by, though the sometimes strident Thoreauvian self is no less muted than it is in the works of Teale, as both "I" and "we" tend to give way to a scientific and inspirational "it"—whether glacial moraines or dwarf pine (*Pinus albicaulis*)—and on occasion to a generic "you." In Muir's case, self and self-doubt are tamed and quieted for the most part by a science far more specific (and "technical") than Thoreau's and by fairly conventional expressions of religious, "aesthetic," and even "moral" rapture. The self, far less driven than Thoreau's or Dillard's or Janovy's or Eiseley's by epistemological and metaphysical questions or doubts—far less open in its expressions of self-doubt and its declarations of identity or significance—is given rather to enthusiasms and inspirations, rhapsodies deriving largely from technical identifications, descriptions, and extended explications— so that sermonic inspiration and scientific exposition subjugate philosophy and humble the self, and nature writing tends to become a combination of geobiotic science and what is sometimes called nature appreciation.

In something like this fashion, many works less easily alignable with *Walden* than the works of Muir (or even the works of Teale)— many works popularly identified as (and loosely associated with) "nature writing"—depart so significantly from the paradigmatic features of the genre, or so emphasize and highlight one of those features, that it is finally impossible to consider them as nature writing. However much they may increase our knowledge of nature or confirm a "sense of kinship" with our "fellow creatures," however they may ratify our conceptions of Nature or enhance our appreciations of NATURE, such works can only be said to fall outside the class typified by *Walden*. Some such works (Jefferies' *The Story of My Heart* might serve as an illustration) so accent the self (and considerations of self) that the nonhuman other tends to lose its otherness, and so ceases to be a working (logical and dramatic) opposite. What in *The Mountains of California* (and, to a lesser extent, in *Walden*) would be the *object* of scientific identification and extended exposition (whatever else it might be) appears almost solely as self-reflection, as a metaphor of and for a self meditating upon its own condition. Though such works may be written by "nature writers," they are not nature writing, but spiritual autobiography, works in which the primary (and, finally, the sole) object of concern is not the state of nature—not the condition of the dwarf pine or the precise depth of a pond—but the condition of a psyche and the state of a soul, here measured not against God or Christ or Mary (nor in terms of traditional conceptions of true or false "religious" experience), but against (and in terms of) true and false experiences and understandings of mornings, clouds, rivers, and mists—each of which is wed not to detailed microbes or insects, but to "spirit" and "goodness" and "evil" and "inner consciousness" (and even, in Jefferies' case, to something "immeasurably superior" both to immortality and extinction)—the whole and the parts no less religious or sacred for their being what we like to call "secular."

In works such as these, the first-person singular both governs and prevails. Concerns of and for "I" eclipse concerns for "it" and "they" as well as "we." In other works—many of them likewise frequently associated with nature writing—the elements of the exemplary Thoreauvian equation are rewritten in still different forms, most commonly perhaps so that a nonhuman "it" or "they" almost entirely subsumes the personal voice of "I"—or, as in the case of so much British nature writing (more appropriately called rural or country literature), so that both the nonhuman "it" and the singular (and especially American) "I" are absorbed in a communal and historical "we," a "we" replete with quite human "he's" and "she's"—all in all, a perspective in which both the "I" and the object of scientific observation (or aesthetic appreciation) are functions of what "we" customarily make of them.

These, then, are works that might be said to fall well beyond the circle B of my diagram, works that, lacking one or more of the central features of *Walden* and its paradigmatic counterparts, are dominated and finally controlled by at least one of the defining traits of at least one of the associated genres. *The Voyage of the Beagle*, for example, might be said to fall in the outer range of my diagram somewhere between the literature of exploration and the literature of geobiotic science. Jefferies' *The Story of My Heart*, with its striking formal similarities to the likes of Jonathan Edwards's "Personal Narrative," would appear clearly at the nether edge of the diagram, in the region occupied by spiritual autobiography—and so would Wordsworth's "Tintern Abbey" and *The Prelude*; for each is an interior monologue, a work concerned finally not with grasses or skies, but with psyche, soul, and self. Jefferies' *Wildlife in a Southern County*, in turn, might be imagined to fall on the extreme outer edge of my diagram (were that diagram three-dimensional) in the area where rural and country literature might be thought to overlap with the literature of geobiotic science—and so might most of Hal Borland's writings and Wendell Berry's *The Long-Legged House*, or Gretel Ehrlich's *The Solace of Open Spaces* and Carol Bly's *Letters from the Country*, along with *The Natural History of Selborne* and most subsequent works of British nature writing—from William Cobbett's *Rural Rides*, through the best known works of Jefferies and W. H. Hudson, to John Stewart Collis's *The Worm Forgives the Plough*. Each of these works—and many another commonly associated with nature writing—is simply too literally agricultural, too given to institutional mediations between isolated self and scientifically fixed environment, to be accurately or sensibly aligned with *Walden* or John Hay's *Nature's Year* or the best known writings of Muir or Annie Dillard. Works like John Hay's *In Defense of Nature* and Edward Lueders's *The Clam Lake Papers*, in turn, for all their popular reputations as nature writing, might be imagined to fall in the outer reaches of the right-hand side of the diagram, somewhere between natural philosophy and meditative literature, partaking slightly of autobiographical forms, but finally controlled by considerations of epistemology, metaphysics, and even stylistics. Like Emerson's *Nature*, they are far too abstract (and far too little concrete) to be classed with *Walden* or *The Mountains of California* as nature writing.

It may indeed be—as Krutch and several other critics have said, and as numerous popular commentators have implied—that some sense of a "kinship with nature" underlies the works of all these figures, that some common "sense of oneness" unites *Walden* and *The Voyage of the Beagle* and the *Tao Te Ching*. At some point, however, critics and devotees of nature writing must begin to make their appeals not to loosely phrased senses of oneness or kinship but to the forms and styles in which those senses are fashioned and formulated—to the significant differences both among the many forms of writing about nature and among the thoughts and experiences to which they give shape, for readers as well as for what we call authors. Even if, like Krutch, one avows a sense of kinship with one's fellow creatures, one must begin to discriminate (and, hence, to appreciate) the several forms in which that sense is (and has been) conveyed and the psychobiotic and psycholinguistic conditions they express. One must begin to recognize, in other words, that, whatever their rapport—whatever their shared "feeling for nature" or their common "sense of oneness"—these works so often lumped together as nature writing convey that feeling and that sense in formally and logically different types, substantially different styles and forms. Neither Basho's *Narrow Road* nor the *Tao Te Ching* is in any sense given to the logical and stylistic forms of modern biological science, in the way of a Thoreau or a Muir or a Jefferies or a Teale. Neither Muir's writing nor Hudson's nor Basho's nor Teale's nor the *Tao* is in any way driven by or to the self or ego (much less to the extremities of self-consciousness) in the way of *Walden* or *Pilgrim at Tinker Creek* or Janovy's *Yellowlegs*.

At some point in this process of writing about nature writing, it seems to me—at some point in the process of sharing enthusiasms and concerns—we must begin, at least, to discriminate among the forms of those concerns, if not among their implications and potential consequences. My own preference, obviously, would be to restrict the term "nature writing" to those works (almost entirely American) that bear substantial affinities to *Walden*—to identify those associated kinds of writing from which *Walden* and its American successors seem to have derived—to explain their historical occasions and their psychological (if not social) functions—and, hence, to concentrate the history and criticism of nature writing upon that literary tradition that seems so far to be peculiarly American.

For many years now, it has struck me both that there is a form of nature writing peculiar to America and that only literary critics and historians of the United States have been much concerned with the form (or for that matter, with the term "nature writing")—and apparently with good reason. For in technical terms, the kind of writing an educated American refers to as "nature writing" is virtually unknown on the European continent, and generally unknown as well in Asia, Africa, and South America. England, in fact—and, by association, Australia and Canada—are virtually the only places to which the American devotee of "nature writing" (as writer, reader, or critic) can turn for the succor of cultural and artistic affiliation, and even that desired affiliation (as I hope to show) is at least partially misplaced or misconceived.

Recognizing the substantial risks of literary and cultural chauvinism involved in such suggestions, I nonetheless wish to argue that American nature writing is at least broadly distinguishable from other literary forms and types (in both prose and verse) by its dedication to impersonal geological or biological (and now ecological) science and by its concentration on the peculiarities of personal condition and experience—by its coordinate obsessions, in other words, with self and with a scientifically rendered nonhuman nature—all in a largely nonsocial (and frequently even antisocial) "environment" or setting that is readily distinguishable both from its British, Canadian, and Australian counterparts and from the settings of the nature writers, so-called, of other nations and cultures.

For reasons that have much to do with the history of early America, it seems to me that the literary forms and types most relevant to an account of the development and subsequent history of this American form of nature writing—this genre or subgenre—are those that might be said to have played a significant role in enabling early, landed Americans to come to terms with their biotic, psychic, and social conditions. Of the several forms and types represented in the accompanying diagrams, two seem especially (and almost equally) significant. On the one hand, there is what might be called the literature of the nonhuman environment, those forms and types meant impersonally and methodically to codify (and in other ways to appreciate) our nonhuman surroundings. In my conception, the literature of the nonhuman environment includes not only works of taxonomic biology, natural history, geography, geology, biology, and ecology, but bestiaries and herbals and field guides and works of impersonal nature appreciation and promotion. On the other hand—and of almost equal significance to the formative years of the United States—there is what might be called the literature of personal identification, diaries and personal journals as well as more finished forms of autobiography, including spiritual autobiography and the "confession." Arranged between these two most significant forms of writing in early America are those other forms and types that seem to me most closely related (both formally and historically) to what we have come to call nature writing: natural philosophy and theology, the literature of meditation (in both prose and verse), the classical pastoral, rural and country literature, travel literature, and the literature of exploration (including, especially, the literature of scientific exploration).

Like all operative, testable definitions of a class, this one breaks down at its circumference. The criteria that define its center, so to speak, begin to dissipate as one approaches its boundaries. And the same may be said of the classes with which it is most closely and comparatively associated. An individual work that might be considered and classed as meditative literature, for example, begins to look more and more like a form of nature writing as its "objects" of meditation become more and more biotic or ecological, as what students of meditative literature call "the composition of place" is defined and delineated by figures of biological speech and thought. Conversely, what might be considered a meditative piece of nature writing begins to look more and more like conventional meditative literature as it turns toward classically religious imagery and symbols. A personal narrative that might be considered autobiography begins to appear less and less "autobiographical" as its central, narrating figure turns more and more to biotic and ecological models for self-definition, as the largely psychosocial terms of conventional autobiography give way to the psychobiotic terms of nature writing, and as the essentially linear figures of personal development become the circular and cyclical figures of seasonal or systemic repetition. A piece of what might be classed as travel literature begins to approach the terms and concerns of nature writing as the temporal and spatial orders of travel give way to extended reflections upon the biotic, geological, or ecological elements of restricted (and restricting), individual places, as the condition of the "traveler" becomes more and more a function of psychobiotic meditation in place.

In this way, variants of each of the associated genres may (and do) take on the characteristics of nature writing (and vice versa)—as works of what might be considered pastoral verse or prose assume the terms and figures of natural science, or consider the state of the narrating and expository self (rather than some distant, "rural" figure or custom)—as works of natural philosophy or theology become more descriptive (and simultaneously more personal)—as works of natural history and nature appreciation become openly personal and philosophic—as the literature of exploration becomes geographically less extensive and psychologically (and biotically) more intensive, as "exploration" becomes more psychic, biotic, and philosophic—and as rural or country literature turns away from the characters, figures, and customs of local community toward the psychobiotic condition of the individual self.

In a synchronic nutshell, these seem to me the formal and substantive relationships between the literary class exemplified by *Walden* and the literary types most commonly and closely associated with it. In the Diachronic View of Nature Writing (see Fig. 2.2), I very crudely attempt to diagram the history of these related genres and to suggest that several of their logical and stylistic features converged in mid-nineteenth-century America to produce *Walden* and nature writing.

With this second diagram I attempt to suggest that nature writing, in its peculiarly American and Thoreauvian form, be viewed as a product of the historical convergence of several literary types, including especially those types dedicated to the identification and codification of what we call the nonhuman environment, as well as those types primarily concerned with the identification of what we call the human individual. For reasons that have everything to do with my view of the quotidian life of early, landed Americans, I suggest that those literary types designed to answer the question "What is it?" or "How shall it be named and explained?" and those

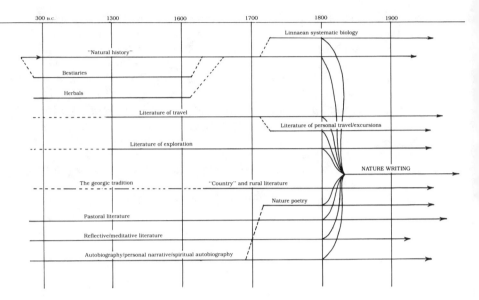

Fig. 2.2. Diachronic view of nature writing

types aimed at the question "Who (or what) am I?" or "How am I to characterize my condition?" came together with particular force in early nineteenth-century America, as "landed Americans" (the phrase is tautologous in more than one sense) sought forms and types of writing to account for the peculiarities of their experience, including not only their experience of a vaunted American land, but their daily experiences (psychological, biological, and ideological) of particular American places, and their experiences as well of "history," "art," and "literature" (not to say "beauty," "goodness," "harmony," and "truth"—or "wildness," "falsehood," and "chaos").

Basic to this view of the history of nature writing is my conviction that the needs satisfied by semantic and syntactic traits of these several literary forms and types—the genres that led to *Walden*—were (and to a great degree still are) sufficiently immediate and pressing to bring those traits together in the thinking and writing of many people of the United States, not simply in Thoreau, and not just in *Walden* or Thoreau's journals, but in many another person and work, however less accomplished or articulate. Basic to this view of the history of nature writing, in other words, is the notion that though Thoreau's "mind-prints" may seem to have been "ahead of their times," as we say, or utterly "original and unique," they are less unique and considerably less ahead of their times, or outside their places, than we, in *our* quests for uniqueness, like (or need) to think they are (or were)—and, indeed, that that manner of critical thinking which speaks naively of Thoreau's mental tracks in terms of "uniqueness" (or, worse, "transcendence") is at least half at odds with the tracks it professes to identify and follow. Better, it seems to me, to view Thoreau's mind-prints—especially in their quests for originality, uniqueness, and transcendence—as the archetypal formulations and expressions of what we call their times and places—the tip of a cultural (and psychobiotic) iceberg, if you will—the exemplification of a species, perhaps, but a member of the species nonetheless—in short, as natural outgrowths of their contexts, and certainly not as maladaptive variants doomed to extinction.

In the history and criticism of nature writing, at least—if not with other literary forms and types—it would seem sensible to take a lesson and a model from evolutionary biology and genetics, to think less of "new" ideas or attitudes somehow springing spontaneously from the soil, and to search less for the "novel" forms that embody them, than to think of variations, refinements, combinations, and recombinations of evolving forms—to seek, in other words, patterns of stylistic and linguistic mutation, extinction, and survival and then to track their relationships. This is not to say that what we might call "original" literary and artistic forms never *appear*, but it is to say that they are best looked on not as creations ex nihilo, but as radical mutations for which we are presently unable to account; and it is to suggest, as strongly as possible, the values implicit both in our current, essentially antibiotic and antihistorical views of artistic "originality" and in the alternative view I am attempting to sketch. It is to suggest, in other words, that "truly original" artistic and literary forms are considerably less common than many critics and artists like (and apparently need) to believe—that perhaps especially in the "modern" world such "original" forms are less "original" than they appear to be—that what we call "originality" is more often a function of mutation, adaptation, and natural selection than it is of creation ex nihilo.

In my view, then, nature writing—as typified by *Walden*—is a modern literary form, unknown except incipiently, before the late eighteenth century and unrecognizable as a fully developed literary type before the midnineteenth. (To this extent, Joseph Wood Krutch was quite right.) Whatever its distinguishing features, whatever one may be able to make of its logics and allegiances, it is a particularly modern response to a particularly modern set of conditions, conditions both cultural and linguistic as well as philosophic and environmental. Its roots, however—its logical and stylistic traits—go back at least as far as Aristotle and Saint Augustine; and it is best viewed not as a herald of the spiritual future, but as one among several literary forms in which modern, Western (and, as it seems to me, especially American) people attempt to codify their experiences and, hence, to deal with their conditions. In some of its specific incarnations, it may be a response to Descartes or Saint Thomas, an attempted solution to the particularly modern (and extreme) schisms of Cartesian thought, especially as they take shape in America. It might even be said to blend (or, more accurately, to attempt to blend) reason and emotion, observation and appreciation, science and poetry, nature and man, in a peculiarly modern manner; but in doing so, it is less a redemption of our continuing sins against nature and ourselves than it is a variant expression of the perennial categories that make such hopes and worries possible. As I see it, nature writing is an especially (though not too especially) American elaboration upon classical, Western ways of conceiving and formulating human experience. In the later twentieth century, it is not to be confused with travel literature or autobiography or natural history or the literature of conservation and preservation. It is to be viewed rather as a literary form that concentrates upon a single, restricted place (or region) while simultaneously concerning itself primarily with the state of an individual (who is its narrator and expositor) and with the disciplined, detailed, "scientific" description or exposition of what we call the nonhuman environment—all in all, and initially at least, the product of the convergence and coalescence in early America of the several antecedent literary types from which it seems to have derived and to which it continues to bear some essential and original affinities. If it is "new," it is new only in one sense, as a complex mutant is new, in the previously unknown morphological combinations it provides both of ancient linguistic forms and of more recent variations upon them.

In presenting this view of the history of nature writing, by no means do I wish to deny the significance or the development of the British "country" tradition (sometimes identified as nature writing), much less the "rural" tradition that has continued to develop (at least in part) in response to it. Neither do I wish to suggest that the country tradition of Britain or its rural antagonist has somehow been absent from America or without influence on American nature writing. Few statements could be further from the truth. Both traditions were well represented in American literary and artistic culture of the nineteenth century, and both are, if anything, even better represented in American writing and art of the late twentieth. I do wish to suggest, however, that in *Walden* and its many successors, the United States have produced yet another (and distinct) kind of writing about human and nonhuman nature—a literary type whose orders and concerns are as much formally scientific and personal as they are rural or expeditionary, and whose allegiances are as much seriously wild as they are civilized or countried—a form whose essential psychobiotic configuration is rooted not so much in *The Wisdom* of John Ray, nor even in *The Natural History of Selborne* (despite Thoreau's reading), but in the likes of William Byrd's histories of "the Dividing Line" and in William Bartram's *Travels*, or in *Jonathan Dickinson's Journal* and *The Journal of Madam Knight*—she it was who wrote of "Company next to none, Going I knew not whither, and encompased with Terrifying darkness"—as well as in Edwards's "Personal Narrative" and Jefferson's *Notes on the State of Virginia* and Audubon's journals and the touching (because so often pretentious) notes of those many early Americans who aspired to be gentlemen-naturalists or sought their identities as recognized contributors to the growth of systematic biology and geology.

In presenting this view of the history of nature writing, neither do I wish to disagree with those who, having come to Thoreau's writings with different concerns than mine, have suggested other genres as appropriate analogues for (and influences upon) *Walden* or *Cape Cod* or *A Week*.[8] Certainly the catalogue, the diary, the literary excursion, the classical pastoral, and the natural history essay are fruitful types to have in mind when one is reading and analyzing the writings of Thoreau. If one is interested, however—as I am—as much in *Walden*'s numerous successors as one is in *Walden* itself or its antecedents and contemporaries, one is virtually driven to look for broader generic patterns in literary and cultural history.

In the final analysis, then, I present this view of the history of nature writing as literary and linguistic type because, despite my rather serious reservations about the philosophic underpinnings of his position, I nonetheless wish to cast a large portion of my lot with that reader and writer in Joseph Wood Krutch who sensed and sought the contours of a "recognizable genre"—because, in other words, I view the seeming idiosyncracies of *Walden* and *Cape Cod* or *A week* less as the extraordinary elements of an isolated literary case study than as parts of what has become a fairly significant literary tradition—because, following in Krutch's tracks, I seek to account not only for *Walden* but for *Pilgrim at Tinker Creek* and *A Sand County Almanac*—and because I wish to suggest, at least, how others might conceive and later account for the nature writings of Burroughs, Muir, Hudson, Jefferies, Mary Austin, William Beebe,

Loren Eiseley, Sigurd Olson, Krutch himself, Edwin Way Teale,
Henry Beston, Paul Errington, Donald Culross Peattie, Louis Halle,
John Kieran, Leonard Hall, Helen Hoover, Gavin Maxwell, John
Terres, Fredric Klees, Hal Borland, Paul Brooks, Irving Petite, Jo-
sephine Johnson, John Hay, John Stewart Collis, Allan Eckert, and
Sally Carrighar—and, more recently, the writings of Edward Abbey,
Ann Zwinger, Raymond Cowles, Alexander Skutch, Dwight Smith,
Robert Arbib, Christopher Rand, Elizabeth Arthur, Barry Lopez,
John Janovy, Anne LaBastille, David Rains Wallace, Paul Lehm-
berg, Robert Finch, Rob Schultheis, Diana Kappel-Smith, John
Nichols, Gretel Ehrlich, and John Hanson Mitchell, among many
many others.

Theoretical and philosophic criticisms aside, Krutch had
several things to say almost in passing about the formal characteristics of nature writing—and, at least implicitly, about their history—
that need to be remembered and acknowledged in any attempt to
refine and elaborate the history and criticism of the genre. Though
the tenor of his critical and historiographic times led him to seek the
development of an "attitude" or an "idea" as the distinguishing
feature of nature writing—to accent moral and scientific "content"
rather than logical or psychological "form," if you will—and indeed
to distinguish clearly between the two (as he just as clearly distinguished between the subjective and the objective, or imagination
and observation), in a way that later twentieth-century philosophy
and literary theory simply do not permit—as a practicing nature
writer and avid reader he made note along the way of some of the
essential features of nature writing and their history. He noted, for
example (though he never elaborated upon the thought) that the
works represented in his anthology—and, hence, the "emergent literary form" he sought to define—excluded "accounts of discovery,
exploration, and adventure, insofar as they are that and nothing
more." He noted as well that his collection excluded "both purely
subjective musing on one hand, and purely objective scientific observation on the other." In other words, he marked, however
roughly, several of the obvious logical and stylistic traits that distinguish nature writing from the literary forms with which it is commonly associated (and, hence, with which it may easily be confused). Though he consistently neglected to elaborate upon terms
and categories that might have led him to extended considerations
of form, style, and logic—though he saw "subjective" and "objective" not as stylistic and psychological kinds, but rather as ontological categories ("subjective" synonymous with mind, imagination,
and poetry, and "objective" identical to reality, fact, observation,
and science)—he nonetheless distinguished between nature writing

and "the literature of travel and adventure" as well as between nature writing and poetry or "other traditional forms of belles lettres" devoted to "the appreciation of nature" (Krutch, 4–5).[9]

While recognizing the "vast body of scholarly writings" devoted to the analysis of nature in literature, especially those concerned with the eighteenth-century shift in Anglo-American attitudes toward natural scenery—and while acknowledging the considerable influence upon nature writing of "the concept of wild nature as sublime"—Krutch nonetheless sought to distinguish the fashionable literature of landscape appreciation (sublime or picturesque) from nature writing. As he put it, "both the Romantic poet and the Romantic prose writer were moving away from the student of natural history, instead of converging with him toward some common ground," as the nature writer was (Krutch, 38, 42). Neither Thoreau nor Gilbert White, nor any of their nature-writing successors, was thus comparable to Wordsworth. In fact, the works of Thoreau and William Beebe were better aligned with *The Origin of Species* and *The Descent of Man* than they were with *The Prelude*. Gilbert White, in turn, was not quite Thoreau, but "a kind of Thoreau—if it is possible to imagine an eighteenth-century gentleman being at all like Thoreau" (Krutch, 53). The "almost purely aesthetic" promotional excursions of the popular William Gilpin were entirely unlike anything Thoreau had written, and different, too, from *The Natural History of Selborne*. If one had to compare Gilpin to an American writer, perhaps he was best compared to John Muir, though Krutch was clearly less comfortable with this comparison than he was with the correlation of Thoreau and White (Krutch, 60, 53). In short, though the terms of his comparisons went almost entirely undeveloped, Krutch was noting some of the essential differences between nature writing and the forms with which it was (and too often still is) loosely allied; and he was attempting to discriminate as well, if even more sketchily, among some of the specific variants of nature writing itself.

Like John Burroughs before him, Krutch was struggling to bring the critical and historiographic terms and categories of his time into coherent relationship with the commonsense evidence of the writings he had selected. He was unwilling (and perhaps unable) to give up the popular moral and aesthetic associations that (despite Darwin and Tennyson and the social Darwinists) had been inseparable from the term "Nature" since at least the early eighteenth century. On the other hand, he was instinctively suspicious of the sanguine sensibilities—the undisciplined warm feelings and warmed-over clichés—those associations continued to produce. Nature writing was thus more "scientific" and less "aesthetic" or "poetic," more tough-minded and less tender-minded, more "rational" and "observational" and less "emotive," than the literature of nature appreciation or nature poetry. And yet the nature writer had to be "something of a poet"—though never at the expense of "the facts." Melville was, thus, "neither a scientist" nor, like Thoreau, one who believed "that the key to the meaning of man may possibly be found in the larger world of nature." Melville was not a "nature writer"—not even when he wrote about tortoises—but a moralist and a metaphysician, because to him tortoises were "more emblems than natural facts," were "almost what Emerson called hieroglyphics" (Krutch, 80). And yet the genre of nature writing could only be created by artists who, determined "to communicate the personal experience of living in contact with the natural world," had previously absorbed "part of what the scientist and philosopher were teaching" (Krutch, 27).

In just this way, Krutch came close to sensing the interplay in nature writing among the forms of impersonal science, autobiography, and philosophy. When he admitted that his selections for the anthology occasionally stretched his definition of nature writing "to its limit," he came close as well to speaking openly of the genre not as a fixed form, but as a flexible literary genus whose peripheral subspecies are difficult to sort out from the subspecies of other genera. There are even suggestions in Krutch's ruminations, though almost entirely subliminal, that he may have begun to suspect that "Thoreau and the Thoreauists," as he called them—and, hence, American nature writing—were more distinctly and peculiarly American than he was first inclined to suggest—that Thoreau and Muir might bear greater affinity to William Bartram and Alexander Wilson than they did to Gilbert White or William Gilpin or Darwin. Though in a prefatory note he insisted he was interested "in a genre which is quite international"—and though he neglected entirely to point out that the kind of writing (and indeed the taste for "nature") with which he was concerned is (and has been) almost exclusively confined to Britain and her cultural offshoots—toward the end of his "Prologue," he also hinted that the explanation of American nature writing might alternatively begin "at the beginning—with the discovery of America"—not, in other words, by seeking the ideational analogues and ancestors of Thoreau in Gilbert White and John Ray, but by turning to Sir Walter Raleigh and Thomas Hariot, to Captain John Smith's *Map of Virginia* and William Wood's *New England's Prospect*, and later to the likes of Audubon's journals (Krutch, 88–95).

By way of acknowledging the anxiety of influence, then—and despite (and in light of) my earlier disparagements of many of his pronouncements—my own efforts to come to terms with nature writing owe much to Krutch's "Prologue." In both synchronic and diachronic nutshells, the seeds of a more elaborate history and criticism of nature writing, including especially American nature writing, are almost all present in Krutch's concerned and committed ponderings—except for that one crucial component, that one essential conception that influences (and radically changes) one's view of all the others—and the obverse of which Krutch could simply not give up—the fact that a fact (or what appears as a fact) is sometimes (and frequently in *Walden*) not a fact—or that facts (as Krutch would say, "natural facts") are often in the best nature writing both natural facts and natural hieroglyphs—that in the most self-conscious and self-reflexive nature writing "what nature was really like" is often not what nature was really like (or, for that matter, what it is)—or worse, perhaps, that "the facts of nature" are (or become) what the erstwhile critic can only see as categorically different kinds of facts—that in the best nature writing, words are sometimes synonymous with what we call things, and sometimes quite antonymous, though at the same time quite natural and factual—that in the best nature writing, language is sometimes identical to what we call experience, and sometimes quite at odds with it, though by no means unnaturally.

The inability to see and consider emblems and symbols and words as natural facts—and, conversely, the unwillingness to see or consider the nuthatch or the grosbeak as words and emblems—are the kinds of conceptual obstructions that kept Krutch (and still keep most devotees of nature writing) from admitting the Melville and the Wallace Stevens in the Thoreauvian nature writer. They are also the kinds of philosophical impediments that continue to keep the history and criticism of nature writing (as they kept Krutch) from the underlying psychology (and even from the biology) of more ordinary nature writing, from the unwilling assumptions of belief that attend the reading and writing of less "extra-vagant" writers than Thoreau or Dillard or Eiseley. Without an occasional glance at the grosbeak as emblem, and at the emblem as a natural fact (however human and "artificial")—without some willing suspension of belief in "the facts of nature," some willingness to consider what we call the unreal and even the fictional as quite real and natural—one can only conclude with Krutch, as most literary critics and historians have, that nature writing bears little instructive resemblance, on the one hand, to the literature of Romantic landscape appreciation, and only a little more resemblance to natural history, on the other— and then be left without means to account for combinations of the two, much less their logical and psychological relations or the implications following from them.

If one's final allegiances are to "the larger world of nature," as distinguished from "the meaning of man"—if one is disposed (as Krutch was) to preserve "the facts of nature" at all costs—the discrepancies between nature writing and nature appreciation or nature poetry will seem obviously enough to reside in the nature writer's dedication to scientific description and the observation of "natural facts." The discrepancies between nature writing and good natural history or philosophic biology, on the other hand, will be far less easy to explain without embarrassment, because one is so shy of "poetic nature," so convinced that nature must not be conceived or treated as hieroglyph.

For Krutch, the distinction between natural history and poetry, between natural fact and metaphor or symbol—as between science and literature or body and mind—was far too much a matter of "either . . . or" and not nearly enough of "both . . . and" to be adequate either to Thoreau and his self-conscious associates or to an understanding account of more conventional nature writing. And the same can be said for virtually all subsequent discussions of the genre.

Where the conventional history and criticism of nature writing fails, then, it fails (at least a bit ironically) because it does not conceive of science and scientific writing in the same kinds of terms it conceives poetry and belles lettres. Ironically, it conceives scientific writing (and the scientific parts of nature writing) as working scientists conceive them, neither as rhetorical or logical forms nor as the expressions of interested organisms—neither as "literature," if you will, nor as organic phenomena—and in either case in ways alien to the thoughts and writings of the most self-conscious nature writers, in ways that make it virtually impossible to account for nature writing and nature writers as literary and organic types.

What is required for a reasonable account of nature writing, it seems to me, is a set of critical and historiographic conceptions that are kin to the conceptions (and, hence, the experiences) of the best nature writers. For if one cannot account for the exemplary works of a genre, one cannot be said to have accounted for the genre as a whole; and the mind-set central to a full account of the best nature writing seems clearly to be one in which both language and science, both nature writing and nature writer, both fact and fable, must frequently be considered as natural (biotic) phenomena. In short, the history and criticism of nature writing demand a shift in our views of writing and an extension of our conceptions of nature—a revision, if you will, in the ways we conventionally conceive both literature and science.

Part Two

Philosophical Considerations
and Historical Conditions

Chapter Three

Science and Our Declarations of Dependence:
A Prolegomenon to the Study of
Nature Writing

he male crayfish differs from the female. In the female the first foot is bifurcated, in the male it is single. In the female the fins on the underside are large and overlap on the "neck"; in the male they are smaller and do not overlap. Further, in the male there are on the last feet large sharp projections like spurs: in the female these are small and smooth.

ARISTOTLE, Historia Animalium

PELICANUS the Pelican is a bird which lives in the solitude of the River Nile, whence it takes its name. The point is that, in Greek, Egypt is called *Canopos*. The Pelican is excessively devoted to its children. But when these have been born and begin to grow up, they flap their parents in the face with their wings, and the parents, striking back, kill them. Three days afterward the mother pierces her breast, opens her side, and lays herself across her young, pouring out her blood over the dead bodies. This brings them to life again.

From a twelfth-century bestiary

. . . discovered a Village of Small animals that burrow in the grown (those animals are Called by the french Petite Chien) Killed one and Caught one a live by poreing a great quantity of Water in his hole we attempted to dig to the beds of one of those animals, after diging 6 feet, found by running a pole down that we were not half way to his Lodge, we found 2 frogs in the hole, and Killed a Dark rattle Snake near with a Ground rat in him, (those rats are numerous) the Village of those animals Cov.^d about 4 acres of Ground on a gradual decent of a hill and Contains great numbers of holes on the top of which those little animals Set erect make a Whistleing noise and whin allarmed

91

Step into their hole. . . . Those animals are about the Size of a Small Squ[ir]rel Shorter & thicker, the head much resembling a Squirel in every respect, except the ears which is Shorter, his tail like a ground squirel which they shake & whistle when allarm.^d the toe nails long, they have fine fur & the longer hairs is gray.

Journals of Lewis and Clark
September 7, Friday, 1804

Plains Prairie "Dog" (*Cynomys ludovicianus*)
PRAIRIE "DOGS," BARKING SQUIRRELS: PETITS CHIENS: PRÄRIEHUNDE: PERROS LIANEROS, PERRITOS.

The five species with their four subspecies inhabit most of North and South Dakota, Nebraska, Kansas, Oklahoma, Texas, Montana, Wyoming, Colorado, New Mexico, Utah, Arizona, and a small area in northern Mexico.

They are not dogs but are stout, short-tailed, short-legged, burrowing squirrels which inhabit open plains and plateaus. The length of the head and body of adults is about 300 mm.; the tail is about 87 mm. long; and they weigh from .9 to 1.4 kg. . . .

Prairie "dogs" show a high degree of social organization. Their "towns," often containing several thousand individuals, are divided into "wards," the boundaries of which are generally determined by the structure of the country. Each ward contains several "coteries"; each coterie is headed by a male that won the coterie by feats of strength, one to four females, and the young of the last two years. When there is quarreling among neighbors about boundaries, the decisions are made by the dominant males and they expel all invaders.

E. P. WALKER ET AL.,
Mammals of the World, volume 2

WOODCOCK. *Philohela minor.*
Field marks: — 10–12. A large, chunky, almost neckless, warm-brown bird with a 'dead-leaf pattern'; a little larger than a Bob-white, with an *extremely long bill*. It is usually flushed from a woodland swamp or leafy thicket, and makes away on a straight course, often producing a whistling sound with its short, *rounded* wings.

ROGER TORY PETERSON,
A Field Guide to the Birds

All groups operate by means of phantasy. The type of *experience* a group gives us is one of the main reasons, if not for some people the only reason, for being in a group. . . . Our perception of 'reality' is the perfectly achieved accomplishment of our civilization.

R. D. LAING. *Self and Others*

It is true that we instinctively recoil from seeing an object to which our emotions and affections are committed handled by the intellect as any other object is handled. The first thing the intellect does with an object is to class it along with something else. But any object that is infinitely important to us and awakens our devotion feels to us also as if it must be *sui generis* and unique. Probably a crab would be filled with a sense of personal outrage if it could hear us class it without ado or apology as a crustacean, and thus dispose of it. "I am no such thing," it would say; "I am MYSELF, MYSELF alone."

WILLIAM JAMES,
The Varieties of Religious Experience

he heritage of *scientia*, in both its humanistic and scientific forms, runs naturally and necessarily deep in the Western world. It is a rightly honored heritage; for, among other things, it provides us with what is by now perhaps our major means of assuring ourselves that we can transcend the limitations of being human and, for even hours at a time—in the laboratory, the library, and the field—escape the limitations of our psychobiotic conditions. To know, for example, that "the male crayfish differs from the female," however tautologous the statement, is, among other things, to be taken out of one's self and, in that sense at least, to escape one's anthropo-logical motivations. It is to concentrate neither on the forms and functions of language, nor on the personal drives behind them, but on the impersonal and, in this case, nonhuman "things" to which language is said to refer.

To concentrate further on the differences among crayfish, or between crayfish and woodcock—even to the point of seriously disagreeing with one another about them—is to be taken even further out of ourselves and away from the potentially deleterious condition in which we may recognize that our quest for knowledge is not (and has not been) so much a process of acquiring further information as it is (and has been) an ongoing effort to construct psychological "others," an effort to erect and sustain ever more detailed psycho- and sociolinguistic orders as a stay against confusion, chaos, and potentially maddening self-consciousness. To go even further and render mathematical or classically Latinate what we have previously been able to couch only in ordinary language is to erect a wonderfully and terribly intricate sociolinguistic scaffolding that, if we can keep from viewing it as such, may provide sustaining psychosocial orders and, hence, help to ensure not only personal sanity but also sociopolitical stability, and perhaps even the survival of our part of the species.

The heritage of *scientia*, then, is not to be undervalued, especially not in the twentieth century, when few if any such scaffoldings show much promise at all of being able to sustain such fundamentally critical orders. In a world of often bewildering differences among human languages and cultures, the conventions and logic of *scientia* continue to succeed where others do not in establishing a world of psychologically and psychosocially inviolable "others," a world of impregnably "other" phenomena, a world impressively intercultural in its ability to fix and ratify "other" times, "other" places, and "other" things. In short, the metaphysics and conventions of *scientia* give us our current best handle on the critical "not-me" we must have both for self-definition and for continuing communication.

Certainly, no form of *scientia* is (or has been) any more critical in this regard than geobiotic science; for it has aided us in fixing perhaps the most other of psychic others, not simply an impersonal other, but a nonhumanly impersonal other, the crucial psychic function of which is, finally, to isolate—and, by negation or falsification, to define—the human individual and the human community. From its inception in the caves and camps of early humankind—through the natural histories of Aristotle, Pliny, and Buffon—to the intricate and specialized taxonomics of modern biology and geology, geobiotic science has served admirably in our ongoing quest to name and, hence, fix a nonhuman element in our experience. And it continues to serve—in those taxonomies themselves, in catalogues of local lore held in oral tradition by landed peoples throughout the world, and in the field guides of urbanized, modern people seeking a quick fix on things they otherwise all too often forget or of which they no longer have extended experience.

Even in medieval and early Renaissance bestiaries and herbals—now so often characterized simply as unscientific—one can sense the age-old human need to get perspective on the human, to delineate and establish, if not comprehend, relations among the nonhuman elements of our experience, including, in this case, relations among the geobiotic and the nonhuman divine. The authors and readers of early bestiaries and herbals were, after all, merely doing what we today do with our taxonomies and field guides—and what Lewis and Clark sought to do with their journals—attempting to sort out and, at least initially, substantiate those critical distinctions between the human and the nonhuman which we need for personal stability as well as sociopolitical coherence.

From a literary, psychological, and anthropological point of view, the discriminations to be drawn between a twelfth-century bestiary and Walker's *Mammals of the World* are not a matter of relative "accuracy." They are, rather, a matter of types and forms of accuracy. One takes as given a need on the part of the authors of each to be accurate, in the terms of accuracy appropriate to what we call the times and places of each. The point is not, finally, that one set of authors is more accurate or more experienced than the other, or that one knows more than the other, or has more information than the other. The point is, rather, that each set of authors seeks in its own grammar and logic to establish and then to reinforce those psychically and socially critical distinctions between "me" and the nonhuman "not-me," between "my kind" and "*other* kinds," between "I" and "It."

Geobiotic science, then—in its bestiarial and herbal forms no less than its modern morphological styles—has served us well and critically in isolating and circumscribing major categories of our experience. It has enabled us to substantiate and to reinforce the substantiation of a large part of what we have come to call the "external world," which phrase itself is a part of the theoretical underpinning we have sought to provide for the nonhuman "It" we have sought to erect and maintain. The rhetoric and logic of geobiotic science are well designed to establish and maintain inviolate distinctions between our phrasings of things and what we call the things themselves, to deflect our attention from our own basic needs to externalize the major elements of our experience. That rhetoric and that logic are (and have been) designed to make us assume that the nonhuman world is phenomenal rather than assertional, that its status as nonhuman other is neither a function of our figural phrasings nor of our needs to phrase.

The assertion of such a phenomenal nonhuman other is, of course, psychologically and culturally essential. So, too, is the utter need to believe and act as if it is not an assertion. For if the assertion is to be successful, if it is to perform its functions, and if we are to be successful in our efforts to restate and reinforce it, we must not be reminded too often of its basically figural character. We utterly need, in other words—and for all kinds of quite natural reasons—to believe that a large part of our experience is phenomenal, that we can ourselves comprehend or transcend it, and that the fruit of the tree of knowledge about it is inexhaustible.

But if we are to be more than unconscious slaves to our own

necessary fictions, if we are to be knowing representatives of our entire cultural heritage, we need also to remember that we are no longer in the garden, that the fruit was forbidden, and that it is inexhaustible only to innocents. We need always to remember, in other words, that the distinctions we and other humans draw between "our kind" and "*other* kinds," between "the human" and "the nonhuman," are human distinctions at best, serving human functions and satisfying human needs.

To say as much is not to belittle or undermine the theoretical, experimental, and technological achievements of the geobiotic sciences. In fact, one might argue that to say as much is to celebrate them. It is, however, to ground those achievements in the psychobiotic needs of humankind and to call attention to their functions as psychological and sociological stabilizers.

To emphasize the stabilizing functions of geobiotic science, in turn, is to remind us that we too often read such seemingly unpretentious statements as Aristotle's on crayfish or Roger Tory Peterson's on woodcock as nothing more than so-called straightforward propositions to be confirmed, denied, or refined by what we have come too easily and too innocently to call "further observation," as if further observation itself were not—like the instinctual behaviors of crayfish and woodcock—a natural response on the part of humans trying—like crayfish and woodcock—to maintain a grip on their environments and their definitions of same. To accent the psychobiotic functions of geobiotic science, then, is to ground even our most systematic and cerebral endeavors in animal behavior. It is to call attention not to the progress we have made since Aristotle's time but to the common psychic denominators in his efforts and our own. It is to remind us that, in our scientific endeavors at least, we all too often forget "the withered appleseed."

The heritage of *scientia*, then, is not to be overvalued any more than it is to be undervalued, especially not in its geobiotic forms, and especially not in the late twentieth-century West, where it may all too easily blind us to our anthropoid limitations and to many of the underlying continuities of Western culture. Even as we value the capacity of geobiotic science to substantiate the elements of our experience, and even as we use its methods to order and control our environments, we must also remember that its rhetoric and logic are designed to ignore—and, in that sense, to forget—the anthropological origins of geobiotic science and its basic psychobiotic foundations.

The telling trouble with our usual response to the conventions of geobiotic science is that it satisfies only one of two critical psychobiotic needs. It overtly satisfies only our need to be apart, to transcend or rise above the limitations of our condition, and then only unconsciously. It does not satisfy, or it satisfies only indirectly, our complementary need to be a part, to see ourselves as undistinguished and undistinguishable parts of a nonhuman other. It only takes us out of ourselves. It does not return us to self or to the needs of our kind, and it all too easily blinds us to our roles as geobiotic participants and psychobiotic beings.

The telling irony in our usual response to the conventions of geobiotic science is not that those conventions, in their claims to disinterested knowledge, take us outside ourselves or separate us from our environments and interests—for these are perfectly natural drives—but, rather, that we, in our continuing quest for gratification, tend to reify the rhetoric and logic of those conventions and to take their discriminations as given rather than composed. The irony is not, as some sociologists of knowledge would apparently have us believe, that the conventions of geobiotic science may veil from us our vested political or economic interests. The bottom line, after all, is psychobiotic rather than political or economic. The irony is, rather, that in responding to the conventions of geobiotic science we too often innocently act and speak as if we have somehow literally escaped our vested psychobiotic interests and that, in doing so, we too frequently appear only as the unwitting dupes of our own desires to escape the human condition—*la comédie humaine.*

The further and, perhaps, final irony, I suppose, is that in our innocent pursuit of disinterested knowledge we end appearing only as unknowing anthropoids, enacting (rather than comprehending) the culture and civilization in which we live and which, willy-nilly, we represent. Though, at our theoretical best, we may know that "crayfish" and "woodcock"—like "male," "female," and "differs"— are human constructs, and human constructs only, we too often speak as if they were interest-free terms given to us (and through us, to the world) on a long-term loan, the principle of which we may ultimately have to repay but which, for the duration of our business here, we may simply invest (and reinvest) in a most innocent and apparently economical quest for ever more accurate knowledge.

The desire to secure such a loan is, of course, eminently understandable. So, too, are the drive to renew it continually and the need to believe it is interest-free. In the human comedy of the West, we do not enjoy being reminded that we thrive, when we thrive, on a kind of geobiotic lien or that our endeavors (especially not our cerebral endeavors of "articulate consciousness") are psychobiotically entailed. We wish and need to believe, rather, that our most cerebral endeavors, at least, can partake of the gods, the godlike, and the angelic—that if mind can't triumph over matter, it can, at least, comprehend it. And the rhetoric and logic of geobiotic science are nicely suited to reinforce these natural drives, these needs to believe. Its grammar and its implicit theory of knowledge are precisely adapted to underwriting our need to believe that human endeavor is special in some peculiar way, and not to be explained (or explained away) in the same terms we use to explain the behavior of other species or the thermodynamic states of other phenomena.

Still, in our responses to geobiotic science, we too often end— scientists and nonscientists alike—at unknowing odds with ourselves. In large part, no doubt, because of the passion of our quest for disinterested knowledge, we appear (or run the risk of appearing) less as the conscious beings we might at moments be, and more as the unconscious and instinctual animals we naturally and traditionally insist we are not. Like most animals, we find it more comfortable to be unknowing, unthinking participants than to be self-conscious beings aware of our participation. Though, at our theoretical best, we may know (and need to know) that what we name and categorize as "crayfish" is not so named and categorized by what we likewise name "mergansers," "smallmouth bass," or "blue herons"—each of which apparently has a more intimate and regular experience of crayfish than we—we too often naively speak and act not only as if we can know what a merganser *is* (in some sense other than the one we ourselves predicate) but also as if we can know what true health and happiness for a merganser and its crayfish associates would be. Though, in our theoretical moments, we may know (and need to know) that a merganser swallowing a crayfish does not say (or even think) to itself the merganser equivalent of "Aha, I got myself a crayfish" or even "Aha, I got myself what humans call a 'crayfish,' " we do not like to allow even the conjecture that our manner of mechanizing or dehumanizing the animal may be nothing more than a psychobiotic defense mechanism that keeps us feeling special and, simultaneously, blinds us to one of our most basic needs. All species, after all, need to behave as if they are distinct. Were it not so, the world's genetic resources would be considerably less diverse than they are.

In our opposition to anthropomorphism, we too often end by ignoring one of the major lessons of our own investigations into the geobiotic world, the lesson that even our scientific endeavors are not so fundamentally different from our poetic efforts—or from plain animal behavior—as we would like to believe. We continue unwittingly to desire escape from the limitations of our conditions, just as we do when we attempt to free Aristotle's statement on crayfish from its psychobiotic contexts.

The desire, of course, is natural and necessary, perhaps especially in the Western world; but our expressions of it are too often unthinking. As we seek to distinguish those styles which are rightly anthropoid from others which are not, we prove, more than anything else, our need to be distinct, our need to believe that, in one style at least, we can surmount our anthropo-logical limitations. Though we may know (and insist) both that nonhuman animals do not think as we do and that it is illegitimate to see them as doing so, we too often forget that we must imagine them doing so in order to create the laughable situation in which we can vicariously prove to ourselves that they do not. The merganser could, perhaps, care less about our proof.

Perhaps, too, our modern opposition to the so-called anthropomorphic is a sign of increasing insecurity in the face of increasing indications that we are neither so special, nor so capable, nor so much at home in the world as we would like to be. Certainly we in the post-Renaissance West have become far too unconscious of our own psychobiotic limitations—too unconscious because, in continually insisting on the cerebral distinctions of humankind, we have, in reverse fashion, proved ourselves less than human. We have appeared more as innocent animals proclaiming their own special status than as human beings capable of acknowledging our needs for same.

The trouble, the irony, and the difficulty lie not in the attempt to dehumanize the nonhuman that goes with geobiotic science but in the implicit dehumanization of the human that has gone with it, the tendency of all of us—scientists and nonscientists alike—to view geobiotic science as somehow free of our vested psycho-and sociobiotic interests. If the rhetoric of geobiotic science has led us to be less than human, it is not because that rhetoric dehumanizes what we need to call the nonhuman, but, rather, because we, in our responses to it, have not been able to keep it in perspective. We have been unable to see and unwilling to admit what ought to be obvious, that the process of dehumanizing is a human, and *humanizing*, process, expressing human needs and satisfying human desires.

The telling irony, then, lies not in or with the conventions of geobiotic science themselves. They are, in fact, no more or less than terribly significant and well-established conventions which can help us get and keep a grip on our experience; and they sustain that part of our cultural heritage which aids us in getting a distance on our otherwise all-too-interested lives. No, the telling irony lies in our responses to those conventions and in the manner by which we attempt to hide from that other part of our cultural heritage, that part that would remind us of our origins, our limitations, and our utter dependence on the "other."

Our responses to the rhetoric and logic of geobiotic science are too often simply unwitting, unconscious, and un-self-conscious. The irony is not that we clutch or grab at the assertions implicit in the grammar of geobiotic science, but rather that we too seldom step back and reflect on our needs to do so. In our responses to field guides and taxonomical treatises, we too often act like early springtime avians responding instinctively to the calls of our kind overhead. But even that analogy does not sufficiently capture the irony. The irony is, rather, that we too seldom think of ourselves in such terms. We do not think often enough of our pronouncements—written and spoken, scientific and nonscientific—as territorial claims loudly declared or quietly asserted by questing organisms seeking to establish and maintain some control over their environments. We are reluctant to acknowledge the linguistic dimension of our environments and even more reluctant to consider it as we consider what we call "the distress signals" of a dying rabbit or a beached whale. We would, however understandably, exempt human language and linguistic endeavor—or, at least, experimentally confirmable propositions—from our considerations and theories of ecosystemic interaction. In short, we are uneasy—except perhaps in poetry—about applying the major metaphors of geobiotic science to human endeavor, and especially uneasy about applying those metaphors to geobiotic science itself. We are reluctant to see them for what they are, figural expressions of the human condition.

In our driving quest for disinterested knowledge, we do not like to allow that the author of a book or article—especially not a scientific book or article—is trying to stake a claim to disputed, or potentially disputable, territory. And yet our knowledge of biology itself certainly allows by now that the author of a book or lecture is—in this book and in this sentence—making a set of pronouncements directly analogous to the pronouncements made by singing robins on the worm-rich ground of rain-drenched lawns.

What we call the circadian rhythms of the two species may be different—and we may need to see them as such. Their life spans and metabolic systems may be different—and we may need to see them as such. But there are as many fundamental similarities between them as there are differences—and these similarities, too, we need to view as such, even if (and perhaps especially because) the human user of language then becomes nothing more (or less) than an organism declaring its particular orders—and even if human language then becomes nothing more (or less) than a negentropic song composed against chaos. If anything distinguishes the human being from the nonhuman, it is not "articulate consciousness" but, rather, the capacity for articulate and inarticulate self-consciousness. As Jonathan Swift might have said, the human at its best is an animal capable of seeing itself as an animal while simultaneously acting as an animal.

No, the trouble with our usual response to the conventions of geobiotic science is that it encourages us to ignore or misrepresent the geobiotic and psychobiotic functions of language, especially the language of geobiotic science itself. The telling irony is neither that we—scientists and nonscientists alike—have sought to escape the limitations of our anthropoid conditions through such science, nor that, in attempting to do so, we have constructed a rhetoric and a logic dedicated to separating the human and the nonhuman, the figurative and the literal, the poetic and the scientific, or even the linguistic and the nonlinguistic. Each of these distinctions is, after all, a means of coming to terms with one's experience; and the drive to establish them is completely understandable and highly admirable—but admirable, finally, in the same way the dam-building of a diligent beaver is admirable.

The telling irony is, rather, that, in our nonscientific moments—when we are neither practicing scientists nor simple souls seeking a fix on our environments—we do not more often self-consciously consider our scientific endeavors for what they are, complex codes established and reinforced by a set of organisms seeking a stay against disorder. In fact, we often seem so insecurely dedicated to the logic of our scientific codifications that we cannot easily tolerate the suggestion that they constitute a world composed out of simple and continuous psycho- and sociobiotic need. As R. D. Laing has said, "our culture, while allowing certain marginal license, comes down very sharply on people who do not draw the inner/outer, real/unreal, me/not-me, private/public lines where it is thought to be healthy, right, and normal to do so."[1]

To Laing's list of critical distinctions of Western culture, one must add, in the present context, both the distinction between the human and the nonhuman and its all-too-frequent modern analogue, the discrimination we have attempted to establish, particularly in the post-Renaissance West, between the unnatural or artificial and the natural. For, generally speaking, we allow no more license to persons who do not draw these "healthy" distinctions than we allow to persons—often the same—who do not readily and appropriately discriminate between the real and the unreal, fact and fiction, public and private, or reality and language. What license we do allow is, indeed, marginal, and has been since at least the early Renaissance. We have come to call it "poetic license," by that phrase meaning to say that, like problems or phrases which are "merely rhetorical," poetry and poetic license are nice, perhaps, but, finally, inessential. At the very least, we wish poetry and poetic license clearly segregated from our normal lives, in which the business and science of fixing our environments and our experience can go on unexamined. It is, perhaps, no accident that we often hear poetic license associated with at least mild neurosis and "creative" instability. For we characteristically reserve our vicarious indulgence in such creative license for special, leisure occasions on which we can safely give free rein to our "imaginations," implying by the term that our normal lives are unimaginative and artless.

The specific license to confuse, expose, and identify the human and the nonhuman we characteristically reserve to poets, nature writers, authors of children's books, "primitive" peoples, and perhaps an occasional sociobiologist. And yet, our disposition to grant such license only under special, segregated circumstances and only in clearly defined leisurely situations is itself a telling dramatization of the basic dilemmas of Western thought. By not allowing ourselves to reflect upon the distinctions we draw between the human and the nonhuman, or by considering the psychobiotic basis of geobiotic science only when we read the poetry of A. R. Ammons, we betray our alienation both from a large part of our own heritage and from the geobiotic environments we would otherwise comprehend.

Some of us, at least, would claim, for example, that "man is a part of nature," but without recognizing that the logic and grammar of the claim are at radical odds with its content, or that to make the claim we must distinguish between "man" and "nature," or that if the claim were believed without doubt it would go without saying. We feel no comparable need to claim, for example, that "the crayfish or the woodcock is a part of nature." Our modernly conventional definitions of "nature" and "the natural" are, in fact, a telling commentary not on our sapience but on our desire to avoid self-consciousness, our need to have our nature while simultaneously eating it, and without thinking too much about it. We speak, for example, of a developing "appreciation for nature" in the post-Renaissance West, most often pointedly excluding the human. We speak, following Hobbes, of how things are in a "state of nature" and profess to mean by the phrase how things are when we're not around, or how they were before we got some civilization and somehow left our geobiotic environments. We speak, similarly, of "getting back to nature," a nature which, since we have left it, includes, more often than not, only such things as the antics of feeding birds, the movement of airborne leaves, and the reflective powers of clear, blue waters. We would know and experience "the wilderness," but without remembering that "wilderness" is a highly civilized notion and that "the wilderness experience" is nothing if not civilized, except perhaps to people who do not know it as "wilderness." We speak, after Leopold, of wilderness giving "definition and meaning to the human enterprise," but we neglect to mention that the opposite is also true. We forget that Leopold also said and knew that "all conservation of wildness is self-defeating, for to cherish we must see and fondle, and when enough have seen and fondled, there is no wilderness left to cherish."[2]

Worse, perhaps, we forget that all *knowledge* of such wildness—like all knowledge of nature unconceived or unobserved—is likewise self-defeating and even self-contradictory (unless we define knowledge and the process of acquiring it as something other than civilized, human, and artificial, in which case knowledge of nature is simply tautologous and redundant). As long as we define the wild or the natural as prehuman or nonhuman—phenomena as they stand or processes as they work prior to human observation and conception—the wild and the natural, like God and the philosophical ding an sich, are beyond human ken. By our own logic, and through our own needs to distinguish ourselves, we put the wild and the natural beyond human knowledge and beyond human experience.

Any knowledge of nature or the wild so defined is, of course, logically impossible. For to know we must observe, and to observe we must be present—as actors in or influences on the very "undisturbed" ecosystems we would observe. Being in our own terms a major species—a large omnivore—we can do nothing but alter or "disturb" the "natural" workings of the ecosystems we enter to know or experience in their "natural" states. Not only must we perceive to acquire such knowledge or experience and, hence, by our own acknowledgment, impose artificial, species-specific, and human orders upon the nature and wildness we would observe in their natural, nonhuman states; but we must also conceive such "natural states" and such "wildness" even as (or before) we "experience" them and, hence, by our own logical acknowledgments, pollute such experience of the natural and the wild with human compositions and conceptions. Under such definitions, all knowledge of wildness and "the natural" is self-defeating, for to know we must perceive and conceive, and as each of us perceives and conceives, "the natural" and "the wild" are no longer natural or wild.

In this regard, as in so many others, we would have our natural cake and eat it too, without thinking too much about it. We desire, at least covertly, both that nature and the wild be utterly beyond human ken and that they be open to full human knowledge and complete human participation. The psychology and social psychology of the situation are tellingly familiar. We would fix and maintain in our individual and culturally collective psyches an utterly inviolable, unknowable "other," while simultaneously allowing ourselves to know that other exhaustively, to participate in it totally, and to see ourselves deriving from it intricately, whenever the psychic or psychosocial occasion demands.

The dilemma is, of course, classical, and inevitable, at least for self-conscious people of the Western world. But we are far too often unaware of its workings in our quests for disinterested knowledge and in our programmatic solutions to "environmental problems." Even in ecology and biology we far too often innocently differentiate between what happens, as we say, "in nature" and what happens in the laboratory or the computer center—as if laboratories, computer centers, and the human investigators working in them were somehow unnatural. It is far from uncommon to find an ecologist or biologist drawing the same naively realistic distinctions between man and nature that dominate the popular press on such subjects: "One is impressed with the many mechanisms in nature that control or reduce grazing, just as one is unimpressed with man's past ability to control his own grazing animals."[3] Ecologists and biologists are, after all, creatures of their cultures; and we should expect them to replicate and reinforce the controlling discriminations of their inherited cultural traditions.

Still, those traditional discriminations, presented in logical and rhetorical isolation and viewed uncritically, are the very distinctions that continue to blind us to the limitations of our own anthropological conditions and to a part, at least, of our cultural heritage, even as they are said to "alienate" us from our "natural" environments. Our fixation on the logic of "either . . . or"—either the wild or the civilized, either nonhuman nature or human artifice, either real nature or unreal mathematical model, either body or mind—particularly when it is combined with our modern emphasis on the first terms in each of these dichotomies, not only keeps us from acknowledging the kinds of perspective that can be gained from a logic of "both . . . and," but also undermines many (if not all) of our most honest efforts to see the human in what we call nonhuman nature, and vice versa. Even those who profess to be most sympathetic to the view that man is a part of nature continue to speak of what humans have done *to* nature rather than of what we have done (and are doing) *in* it. The basic persuasion, at least half ironically, remains the same both with the so-called exploitive engineer and with the advocate of so-called nonexploitive preservation. When a chemist speaks of the ninety-odd elements that exist "in nature," as if the elements existing or created in the laboratory are unnatural, he is reinforcing the same basic dualism—the same basic isolation of man and nature—reinforced by the advocate of wilderness areas who quotes Thoreau's famous "in Wildness is the preservation of the World" as if Thoreau meant by "Wildness" only what we popularly mean by wilderness.

Thoreau, like Leopold and many a thinking ecologist after him, knew better and meant much more. He spoke figuratively, as we say, as well as literally. He meant by "Wildness" not only what we popularly mean by literal wilderness, but also what we might call literal human wildness, wild behavior, eccentricity, and even abnormality. He also meant what we might call figurative wildness, the notion, the idea, the conception, and the figure of wildness, in or for both human and nonhuman phenomena. He spoke primarily not of the preservation, and certainly not of the legislation, of the wild; but of the preservation of the "World." He meant by "preservation" not simply literal preservation within geolegal boundaries—not simply preservation in a glass bottle—but also figurative preservation, preservation in mind, language, and figura. He meant by "World" not simply literal planet earth, but also figurative "world" or "universe"—an idea or configuration held in human mind and framed in human language so long as human mind and language survive. He did not even insist on the literal survival of the human species, and he would have found our efforts to legislate the wild at least mildly ironic.[4]

And yet, his statements and his position have been almost inevitably misconstrued as we have sought to politicize and publicize his thoughts and to contain the wild and the natural in programmatic solution:

> Somehow, we must make the transition to a society where growth of technology, growth of resource demand, growth of population and growth of materialistic economic greed are supplanted by a focus on developing and sustaining a new dynamic equilibrium between human society and the biosphere that supports it. The assumption that we must continue increasing production in order to accommodate more and more people at higher and higher economic levels must be replaced by a concern for the long-term quality of living for man both as an individual and as a species inextricably bound up in the health of the biosphere. Unless we can succeed in this, all of life—including man—is threatened with extinction or severe degradation.[5]

The underlying persuasion is clear and quite traditional, whether you are engineering to increase our gross national product or attempting to engineer a change in our definition of same. Both kinds of engineer are singing the same underlying song. Both share the fundamental assumption that humans can overcome their psychobiotic limitations and escape their historic conditions. Both share as well the traditional Western belief that mankind is uniquely and solely responsible for the state of the earth. In a nearly direct echo of seventeenth-century jeremiads, the state of the earth, if not the universe, hinges on human action alone, as if mankind existed in geobiotic isolation, as if humans acted without biological consorts, and as if human pronouncements were somehow geologically and biologically contextless. Worse, perhaps—and even more tellingly— the state of the globe seems to hinge on the actions of Western, and even American, people alone.

The call to change our assumptions and attitudes is, of course, honest; but it is also logically and rhetorically naive. One does not change traditional attitudes or assumptions (or even put them in reasonable perspective) without changing the traditional formulations of those attitudes and assumptions. To call, however honestly and earnestly, for humans to consider themselves—as both individuals and species—"inextricably bound up in the health of the biosphere" without simultaneously considering the psycho- and sociobiotic interests in one's own statement is either to defeat one's argument or to appear as un-self-consciously innocent as one's chosen opponents. To say, however earnestly and honestly, that we must create "a new dynamic equilibrium between human society and the biosphere that supports it" is, ironically, to reinforce the very separation of humankind and the biosphere, the very isolation of man and nature, which the argument is intended to change. It is to reinforce as well that inadequately extrapolated reading of Genesis in which man is the only moral agent on earth. The "new dynamic equilibrium" is, thus, undermined from the outset by formulations and phrasings that, far from being new, are fundamentally and classically old, phrasings that not so subtly present humankind and the biosphere as coequals.

In one sense, of course, the dilemma is inescapable. We are the prisoners of our inherited logical and metaphysical traditions. But we need not be entirely unwitting or unknowing prisoners. We could more often recognize that "to feed the people of the world" or "to upgrade the standard of living of all the peoples of earth" is, in one very important sense, the same fundamental and classically Western persuasion implicit in seemingly contrary efforts "to control the world's population" or "to clean up the biosphere." Both positions, however different programmatically, are classically evangelistic. Both betray a desire to save the world and a deep-seated conviction that we (humans, Western humans, and especially Americans) are uniquely responsible for doing so—alone if need be.

As we quote Thoreau, Leopold, and Eiseley in support of our programmatic efforts to create "new" dynamic equilibria, we could as well remember that Thoreau, Leopold, and Eiseley spoke literally and programmatically no more than half the time. We could as well remember that, on more than one occasion, each of them considered such efforts to redeem the world and regain paradise the height of unknowing human pride. We might even remind ourselves that each of them—like Edward Abbey and Annie Dillard after them— frequently considered his own actions, including his own written actions, as nothing more or less than the actions of an organism. In fact, to understand fully the disjunctive drama of individual human and nonhuman nature in the Western world, we could do much worse than to turn to their works and the American environments that spawned them. For in those works—in the likes of *Walden, Desert Solitaire,* and *Pilgrim at Tinker Creek*—the competing allegiances of that drama are most fully and self-consciously played out in all their dimensions.

Chapter Four

The Musquito in My Garden:
Early American Selves
and Their Nonhuman Environments

ne of the joys in building a backwater dwelling lies
            Not only in the satisfying
                      Of an instinct old as fear,

But in the hope that you can make it
            What you want—I'm not sure how much I'm after
                  Just pleasant protection

Though: if I log my shack up tight
            & caulk it sound, the copperheads won't hole-up
                  Where my hands & feet are likely

To abound; but if a dwelling's where you stay, &
            I keep out alot more than I keep in,
                  I'll be staying in a poverty that won't

Be comfy. I don't think I'll want to be a bar
            To berry bushes waxwings & rose-crested
                  Cardinals grosbeak with battening

In July, & windows are classy mediations cowsparsnip
            & raspberries can't grow through—I don't
                  Think I'll want to shut

Out mayflies, deerflies, ticks, spiders, mosquitos, leopard
            Frogs, wasps, woodmice, hornets & bees,
                  For such distractions may keep me

From the ornery speculation that what I'm mucking up
            Was made especially for me: if a lake
                  Below the welt my easynook is on

Gets cranberry bogged & mineral rich
            With decayed lamprey, duck bones, musselshells
                 & carp—& willows assert themselves

In the ooze the water's recession gives rise to,
   I'll let the events such altercation ventures
     As to my praising be

My study—I'll take it
   For granted the common place we have's
     Embrangly enough for wonder

To nest & feed & cry in, & dabble in the scum the wind
   Swings shoreward: watch the galaxies
     Of guppies shifting round

The pickerelweed; touch the unkindredly whorls
   Of the driftwood's grain; smell
     In the smoke

Risen dew the skunk's musk,
   & let the wind that's so high
     Today it's turned all

The brush & trees into limbwagging prophets shouting over
   & over again, The wind is high
     Today, blow through my home
        JERALD BULLIS, "Homestead Act"

   Now I understand why I am so envious of the snail king
[*Stagnicola elodes*]. It has nothing to do with being in a serene
place, a calm and warm place. It has everything to do with being
in your own place, the place that is for you at the time that is for
you. It has everything to do with a built-in device, a built-in
inherited mechanism, for finding one's place in the world, regardless of how calm or serene, regardless of a maelstrom in the
center of that place. . . . I will be a pioneer. I will try things I've
never tried before. I will gamble some stuff, maybe I don't know
just what yet; but if the snail king can gamble trillions of eggs, I
also can gamble some things to find my place and time.
       JOHN JANOVY, *Keith County Journal*

owhere are the disjunctive relations of "man" and "nature" in the Western world any more apparent than they are in America. Nowhere so much as in America have Western peoples been so dedicated to the ascendance of the human, the perfection of human society, or the redemption of history and, yet, simultaneously so continuously struck with the imminence of human animality, the insignificance of being human, and the imperfections of human institutions compared with the mystery, sublimity, and deep evolutionary power of nonhuman nature. Nowhere have Western peoples been so committed to the pragmatics of shaping their environments and, yet, simultaneously so taken by those environments themselves, so convinced that those environments are simply to be engaged rather than shaped. Nowhere, in fact, have the peoples of the West been simultaneously so absorbed by the state of nonhuman nature and, yet, so determined to save it, redeem it, or reclaim it.

Those critics and historians of American culture are far from wrong who define America and the American in terms of the largely unmediated, radical antipodes of Western thought. For nowhere so much as in America have the peoples of the West been dedicated to separating the human and the nonhuman—the individual human self and its nonhuman others, the orders or burdens of civilization and the chaos or freedoms of wilderness, the pragmatics of engineering nonhuman environments and the aesthetics or ontology of being part of nature. And, yet, nowhere so much as in America have those people found themselves confronted with so consistent a set of inducements to do away with those very classical distinctions, nowhere more often faced with experiential threats to the classical discriminations of Western thought, and nowhere more frequently tempted to reject them and to declare their complete inadequacy and utter artificiality.

Nowhere in the world, in fact—West *or* East—has the drive to fix the geobiotic environment, to erect and maintain that impersonal, nonhuman "other," been any stronger or any more consistently urgent than it has in historic America. That drive began, of course, long before the "actual discovery" of American lands. It began in the earliest European attempts to create and imaginatively explore those promised mythic countries to the West—Elysium, Atlantis, El Dorado, Vinland, and Eden—those sacred, original (and aboriginal) places of innocence and perfection which, when later transferred to the land to be known as America, have proved a futuristic legacy of newness, rectitude, reform, and redemption which no American has been able to resist or, for that matter, to adjust happily to his or her first-hand experiences of America's geobiotic environments.

Though there was little specific to the ecosystems of later America in the original statements of such sacred places, there was much to condition and precondition the American settler's response to those ecosystems; and there was much in later reconfigurations of such places, from the fifteenth to the twentieth centuries, to specify further how the details of those ecosystems might be rendered paradisal, much to reinforce the efforts, however paradoxical, of a recently landed settler to adjust the terms of those dreamlands to the realities of daily psychobiotic life. Each of these later reconfigurations and much (if not all) of American literature is, in fact, an attempt to save the original mythic place, while simultaneously adjusting and modifying its terms to fit the detailed and often troublesome exigencies of daily psycho- and sociobiotic life. And the reconfigurations—classic and contemporary—have seldom been satisfying; for the thinking American settler has typically been all too aware that each adjustment and modification entails both a compromise of original Edenic vision and a civilized imposition on the original wildness of America.

None of the original European explorers, discoverers, or settlers of America was able to observe America's ecosystems without preconceptions conditioned by such visions; and no European ever became American without so preconceiving the American land, or without more or less continuously attempting to modify the terms of original, landed American dreams to accommodate the novelties and vagaries of daily experience. For not to so dream, and not to be confronted by the often radical odds between Edenic vision and mosquito-filled environment, between real rhetorical unity or synthesis and real ecological diversity or competition, is not to be American.

The classic American self, then, is—from the beginning—a self divided, a self divided by its allegiances to its dream visions of the American land and its allegiances to the elements of that land once experienced—once discovered, named, and substantiated. It is a self of radically competing allegiances, a disjunctive and disjointed self, because it has always and forever believed that, finally, in America the experience of human self, human society, and nonhuman nature will be conjunctive—that in America self, society, and nature will be conjoined in a mutually supportive harmony, if not of the spheres, then of nutrient cycles, energy circuits, and uptake loops.

This divided, dreaming self was thrust untimely from the womb of European history to begin its life in the persons of early explorers who, carrying with them such visions of perpetual harmony be-

tween man and land in America, were left without the means to
report adequately, much less accurately, what they found in this
wondrous land. Caught as their settling heirs would later be between their dream visions and the "realities" of American environments, they found themselves without grammars or vocabularies to
shape their experiences of this "unknown" land, this land known
only in the vocabularies and styles of epic, romance, and pastoral,
this land made of elements for which there was no published language other than the language of medieval bestiaries and Renaissance herbals.

The American self began, then, in what one might call a radical
conflict between rhetoric and reality—or, perhaps more accurately,
between rhetoric and rhetoric—in an essentially unknown land.
The vocabularies, the grammar, and the rhetoric later used by an
Amundsen, a Cook, and a Darwin were unavailable to the early
American self; for America was initially explored, discovered, settled, and reported before the rise of disinterested geobiotic science
and, what may be more telling, before the development of representational landscape art. The only vocabularies, the only styles, for
landscape, watershed, or ecosystem available to the early American
self as it wished to shape and share its experiences with a more than
local public were the very vocabularies and styles of romance, epic,
and pastoral which that self was awkwardly trying to adjust to its
first-hand experiences of the American land. There were no mosquitoes in Virgil's *Eclogues*, no utter tangles of blackberries on
Circe's island, no cedar swamps in David's psalms, and few rac-
coons in either *Tristan and Iseult* or *The Song of Roland*.

And the botanical and zoological lore held in local colloquial
phrasing from the early American's European home region could
hardly do anything but further confuse the issue. It could hardly
help an early American self if, for example, the only word it had for
what most of us today still call *myrtle warbler*—that flitting, yellow-
rumped, but otherwise black and white, occupant of high spring
canopy—was the Dutch word *Tjiftjaf*. It could hardly help even if a
sympathetic British neighbor agreed to call it *chiffchaff*; for both
would be using names, however akin, for a much less colorful, Old
World phenomenon that characteristically occupies much lower
reaches of much different vegetational communities "back home."
The Dutch-speaking, early American self would be even more confused if, as might well happen, its British neighbor had only the
word "warbler" for the pine- and maple-topping yellow-rump or for
any of its seeming kind. For the modern Dutch word *wervel*, though
it once meant "harp" and, along with the likes of Old French
werbler and Old High German *werbel*, apparently helped give

shape to the English *warbler*, now meant "vertebra." In any case, both English- and Dutch-speaking early American selves were attempting to order their experiences of often colorful New World *warblers* in the only way they could, by naming them in terms previously applied to drab, inconspicuous Old World counterparts.

The effort and the result are both poignant and familiar, though hardly as familiar as they ought to be. If the bird an early American self would nostalgically call *robin* was twice as large as the one named *robin* back home, and if this New World robin inhabited not hedgerows but moist, open understories and clearings in fairly aged forests, then the classic American self, if it thought at all, was bound to be a bit troubled by its own nostalgia, by the power of memory and habit in this enlarging, engrossing land dedicated to the redemption of the past and the reformation of historic civilization. If, on the other hand, the seemingly identical birds called *woodcock* here as there—and brought by gun to hand in an evening of what used to be called "dusking"—were never as large here as the early American self remembered them being there, then what was one to make of dusking in this seemingly engrossing land where some said that things were larger, grander, and more colorful than they were (or are) at home?

If the effort to fix the geobiotic environments of America is both poignant and familiar—even in the case of so-called economically inessential species and their relationships—it is also definitive, both to the American self and to American culture, definitive both in its visionary attempts to wed Old World hope and New World fact (in whatever vocabulary) and in its implicitly honest self-doubts about the possibility (or even the virtue) of such a wedding. Awkwardly, and tellingly, it began not only before locally consistent "common" names could be developed but also before the rise of *Philohela minor* (or even *Scolopax rusticola*), before *Turdus migratorius* (or *Erithacus rubecula*), before *Phylloscopus collybita* (or *Dendroica coronata*), and well before a Dutch- or English-speaking settler could be assured that the Old World chiffchaff and all its kind (*Sylviidae*) are of a different family than the New World Myrtle and its kind (*Parulidae*), and yet each of the same order (*Passeriformes*), no matter what language you and your neighbors might speak.[1] The initial attempts to make sense of the nonhuman others of America were undertaken before Western peoples had created the so-called metalinguistic mediators of Linnaean science and systematic biology, and long before those mediators were institutionalized. In fact, the exploration, discovery, and settlement of America— along with the growth of the classic American self—go hand in historical hand with the development and institutionalization of such mediators, and by no means always happily.

Though we may note the sometimes almost obsessive drive to systematize the geobiotic environment which arose among educated Europeans in the late Renaissance, and continued unabated throughout the Enlightenment and beyond, and though we may likewise note that the rise of geobiotic science coincided with the breakdown of traditional theological and sociopolitical orders, as educated Europeans sought alternative formulations of their nonhuman others, we cannot help but note as well that the early American's need for such alternatively ordered others was far greater than his European counterpart's. If the Renaissance European's ecclesiastical and sociopolitical orders were breaking up—and if, as one result, his essential nonhuman others were becoming less "supernatural" and more "natural," less "sacred" and more "secular"— the institutions which supported such changing discriminations and definitions nonetheless continued to survive, even if only in substantially altered form. Though "Thou" might be giving way to "It," and "I" might be on the rise, in modern Europe, national churches, established legal institutions, and national languages still provided securing frameworks and traditions in which to attempt revised formulations of self, society, and nonhuman others. Dominant educational institutions and the socioeconomic establishments to support them continued to protect attempted rephrasings of self, society, and nature even in times of seeming social and intellectual upheaval.

The early American self, on the other hand—having begun its trek by reacting to these same upheavals, these same dislocations of its traditional categories of experience—not only lacked such established institutional mediators, but was driven and dedicated to erecting reformed or idealized versions of the very institutions now seeming to disassemble in Europe—all in a set of New World environments which themselves seemed only to threaten those traditional categories and the institutions which had grown up upon them. Even the seventeenth- and eighteenth-century American self, then, lacked what a reader of de Tocqueville might call a coherent, established "middle ground," the psychosocial scaffolding (the word is Tony Tanner's) provided by established institutions to aid in mediating the elements of one's experience, to aid in shaping one's conceptions of relations between "I" and "It" (or "Thou") as well as "I" and "We." And in no part of the life of early America does the absence of such psychosocial scaffolding prove any more apparent, any more troublesome, or, finally, any more definitive than in the efforts of early American selves to come to terms with their nonhuman environments.

A good deal of the unsung literature of sixteenth-, seventeenth-, and eighteenth-century America is, in fact, a dramatization of colonial American attempts to erect such a scaffolding, a study in the detailed linguistic and stylistic adjustments colonial American selves attempted to make between their all-too-often generic preconceptions, on the one hand, and the biological and geological minutiae of their experiences, on the other. Many an early American self—exploring, discovering, traveling, and attempting to settle both its environments and itself—was, in the words of Wayne Franklin,

> painfully aware of the many problems which language posed for people separated as they were from their own world. There was the almost universal issue of native languages, to begin with, and hence the constant need for translation (and guesswork) as well as for some conceptual grasp of the proliferation of tongues in the New World. . . . Likewise, the profusion of unknown natural objects in America placed an extra burden on the traveler's mind and language, as did the frequently tangled web of European events in this hemisphere of strange peoples and strange sights. Wherever he turned, the New World traveler seemed to be faced with strains on the one cultural tool by which he might hope to organize his life and explain it to others who had not shared in it.[2]

Many an early American self was, in other words, all too aware of the dilemmas, stylistic and psychic (not to say social, economic, or political), involved in trying to fix the elements of New World environments in the orders of Old World knowledge, not only the dilemmas of trying to identify those New World things that *would* fit in Old World orders, but especially the dilemmas encountered in attempting to name "things" for which no Old World terms (or even cognates) were available. Each such early American self was driven, often desperately, to seek or create such terms and to fit the "things" they referred to into the orders of Old World knowledge. Each such self sought to give existence—linguistic status and stasis—to the particulars, especially, of its geobiotic experiences, because each knew from awkward daily experience what it was to be faced with the unnamed and at least presently unnameable—in short, the unknown and seemingly unknowable.

There is, of course, a strong sense, psychological if not logical, in which a phenomenon does not exist until it is named, until one has a name for it, a name on which the naming self can depend and which it can then share with others of its kind. There is also a sense, an even stronger sense, in which generic terms such as "thing," "phenomenon," "bird," "plant," or "marsupial" are, at best, of secondary aid in coming to terms with one's environment or in building the crucial lower rungs of the kinds of psychosocial scaffolding so imperative, and yet so unavailable, to the early American self. When a "thing" is not a part of the known, named universe, or when it is a part only generically—only as "bird," say, or "plant"—it is bound to create difficulties for the person seeking to deal with it in detail on a daily basis, especially if the previously known universe is itself undergoing significant change *and* if knowing (or coming to know) this new "thing" will itself substantially alter that universe.

Franklin is, thus, quite right both in saying that "more than anything else, the West became an epistemological problem for Europe" and in suggesting that the simple fact "of 'another' world . . . thoroughly deranged the received order of European life," if not also, and more pointedly, the personal orders of those who, being European, confronted it or, worse, sought to define (or redefine) themselves to include its "terms." In analyzing a statement from the letter of Columbus's fourth voyage (1502–1504)—"On the day of Epiphany I reached Veragua, completely broken in spirit"— Franklin has done a masterfully suggestive job of showing how Columbus's attempts to relate Epiphany, Veragua, and his own depressed condition provide an almost archetypal dramatization of the early American's awkward efforts to connect self, society, and nonhuman nature in a sustainably coherent pattern of kinship. Franklin has not only revealed the barely covert, internal drama of such efforts—the agony of Columbus's realization "that if he really was at Veragua, it was *not* Epiphany," in more senses than one—but he has also convincingly shown that "the juxtaposition of 'Epiphany' and 'Veragua' becomes a model of the [near?] loss of control to which so many American travelers found themselves subjected." Having shown as much, Franklin has rightly concluded that Columbus's statement powerfully "suggests the degree to which the tensions between word and thing, art and fact, self and experience, were to become the heart of future New World life, and future American writing."[3]

Franklin is only half right, however, in saying that "what is almost inexpressible for Columbus" or, by implication, for any other such early American self "is not the phenomenal surface of America but the spiritual depths of his own being. The question no longer concerns what the new lands are; it centers instead on who the voyager is, on how his experience has altered his essential nature. His location thus matters only as a sign of his identity."[4] Identity and location, "phenomenal surfaces" and "spiritual depths," are hardly so easily separable, unless one admits or contends as well that a self's identity matters *only* as a sign of its location. A self's "essential nature" is not separable from its experience or, what is the same thing, its knowledge or conception of that experience. To say that Columbus's (or anybody else's) "location thus matters only as a sign of his identity" is, ironically, to belittle the "essential nature" of the self—in this case the early American self— with which Franklin is otherwise so concerned. What else but identity, firstly and finally, might location matter to? What else might it be a *sign* of? The essential (and even inessential) nature of a self is not separable from that self's ability to fix and comprehend both its experiences and its place (or places) and to relate them coherently. To be unable to fix one's self is to be unable to fix one's location, and vice versa. To be unable to identify one's location is to be unable to identify one's self. And this inability, as Franklin otherwise seems almost fully to sense, is the special and definitive dilemma of the classic American self, in the Renaissance as well as in the eighteenth, nineteenth, and even twentieth centuries.

Columbus was, indeed, unsure of himself; but his uncertainty about who he was cannot, finally, be separated from his uncertainty about where he was or from his inability to account coherently for the elements of the environments in which he "found" himself. He was unsure of who he was because he had no developed methods of determining where he was, nor any even half-adequate means of identifying and correlating the elements of his experiences, past and present, "imaginary" and "real," human and nonhuman. Though he could not have known it beforehand, he had come unprepared to determine in any reasonable detail what the elements of this "new" environment were. Beyond creating and repeating place-names, beyond creating rough prosaic accounts and awkward cartographic diagrams of where he thought he found himself and how he had gotten from there to here, he could do little to identify further the elements of his environments and much less to fix those elements in coherent definitions of place or self-in-place. Because he could not adequately determine *where* he was, or what *it* was, or what *they* (the elements of his environment) were, he came perilously close to finding himself lost. Reminded daily, if not hourly, of his own basic animal needs to survive, he was confused by the *ecos* of this land which, in preconceived *typos* and *mythos*, was supposed to redeem or, at least, to minimize such needs. Confronted on his third voyage, along the coast of what we now call Venezuela, with the outlet of one of the four rivers of paradise or, if not that, a

"marvel . . . still greater"—where survival was to be assured
without significant effort, competition, or predation—he was almost
bound to doubt himself and his society. Driven continuously to attempt to fix his environment, at Veragua as elsewhere, he was constantly taken out of himself by these "new" environments; but he
was just as constantly thrown back upon himself, by his inability to
make sense of those environments and by daily reminders of primitive drives to survive—in short by his only barely successful efforts
to relate self, society (or received societal notions), and nonhuman
nature—in active practice as in active prose.[5]

Columbus's American experience and his written attempts to
deal with its elements were (and are) definitive indeed, if not archetypal, both for the individual American and for American culture as
a whole. That fundamentally paradoxical experience and its disjointing codifications were repeated again and again in the lives and
writings of later sixteenth-, seventeenth-, eighteenth-, nineteenth-,
and twentieth-century European-Americans who sought to erect
the scaffolding in which America might be defined and upon which
they in America might, then, depend. Under the circumstances, it is
hardly surprising that so many of them turned to writing and reading diaries, journals, personal narratives, and spiritual autobiographies—or that their histories, sermons, and even political statements so often seem bound by personal cause and condition. To
many, if not all of them, the ancestral institutions that defined,
sponsored, and celebrated the resolutions of Epiphany and paradise
seemed at best inadequate to this "new," entangling land; and yet
this land itself had been (and was yet to be) heralded in the traditional terms of those very institutions as an epiphanic place of redemption and salvation for those institutions themselves and for
the ancestral conceptions of places and times upon which they were
founded. Place-names deriving from those ancestral conceptions,
and applied naturally to harbors, bays, rivers, and points of land in
this presumed epiphanic world seemed at best out of place. The
detailed elements of these "New" World places seemed only defec-
tively named by terms deriving from one's ancestral home, much
less from the varying languages of "New" World peoples, who,
themselves seeming to derive from times way past, were apparently
unconcerned with standardizing terms for the elements of the book
of nature.

For Captain John Smith as for Columbus—for William Bradford, Mary Rowlandson, or William Byrd—the drama of the experience and the attempt to shape its components were fundamentally the same. Though a Smith, a Rowlandson, and a Byrd might
be said to have had at their disposal more fully fledged means of

flying among the seasons of the lingering European past and the not yet fully American present, they were also more aware than Columbus of the difficulties of mediating the as yet unwritten American past and the increasingly less immediate European present. They were, in other words, even more aware than Columbus of the depths of opposition among their competing allegiances. They were heirs to the amplifications and expansions of Columbus's agony and uncertainty which had been produced over more than a century. As Smith sought to make sense of the "glistering tinctures," which were said to make Virginia's hills seem "guilded," he repeated in an only slightly more refined style the insecurity of Columbus at Veragua. As Bradford lamented the absence of a Pisgah among the moist, low-lying, scrub-oak coastlands of southern New England, he sought with broken spirit to explain the identity of himself and his kind at Plymouth. And the same can be said of Jonathan Dickinson recalling a struggle to survive on the cold, wind- and water-swept sands of Daytona Beach by eating "a sort of shellfish called Water-Soldiers" because "the land yielded nothing."[6]

As Jonathan Edwards recalled building prayer booths in swamps with his schoolmates or meditating alone in his father's altarless pasture—as John Woolman curled on damp ground beneath an oak near Goose Creek, Virginia, on a mosquitoed night to contemplate "the condition of our first parents when they were sent forth from the garden"—each repeated, if only in slightly more refined terms, the uncertainty of Columbus at Veragua. So, of course, did Thomas Jefferson at the "Natural Bridge" over Cedar Creek; and so did Nathaniel Hawthorne on that July day in 1844 when he worried over his inability to compose an America pastoral that would coherently blend not only the oaks, white pine, and "pyramidal" chestnuts edging the village of Sleepy Hollow—not only the "tinkling of a cow-bell" and the "long shriek, harsh, above all other harshness" of the whistling locomotive herald of the westward (and urban) course of history—but also a fly, "two little round white fungi," the "intense hum of a musquito" (whose "grim and grisly," crushed corpse was the "ugliest object in nature"), and, by no means least, both his own motives in attempting to unify the elements of the scene and his own "malevolent" responses to the mosquito and an anthill, responses which did nothing but undermine desired pastoral composure:[7]

> To sit down in a solitary place (or a busy and bustling one, if you please) and await such little events as may happen, or observe such noticeable points as the eyes fall upon around you.

For instance, I sat down to-day—July 27th, 1844, at about ten
o'clock in the forenoon—in Sleepy Hollow, a shallow space
scooped out among the woods, which surround it on all sides, it
being pretty nearly circular, or oval, and two or three hundred
yards—perhaps four or five hundred—in diameter. The present
season, a thriving field of Indian corn, now in its most perfect
growth, and tasselled out, occupies nearly half of the hollow; and
it is like the lap of bounteous Nature, filled with bread stuff. On
one verge of this hollow, skirting it, is a terraced pathway, broad
enough for a wheeltrack, overshadowed with oaks, stretching
their long, knotted, rude, rough arms between earth and sky;
the gray skeletons, as you look upward, are strikingly prominent
amid the green foliage; likewise, there are chestnuts, growing up
in a more regular and pyramidal shape; white pines, also; and a
shrubbery composed of the shoots of all these trees, overspread-
ing and softening the bank on which the parent stems are growing;—these latter being intermingled with coarse grass. Observe
the pathway; it is strewn over with little bits of dry twigs and
decayed branches, and the sear and brown oak-leaves of last
year, that have been moistened by snow and rain, and whirled
about by harsh [75] and gentle winds, since their departed ver-
dure; the needle-like leaves of the pine, that are never noticed in
falling—that fall, yet never leave the tree bare—are likewise on
the paths; and with these are pebbles, the remains of what was
once a gravelled surface, but which the soil accumulating from
the decay of leaves, and washing down from the bank, has now
almost covered. The sunshine comes down on the pathway with
the bright glow of noon, at certain points; in other places, there
is a shadow as deep as the glow; but along the greater portion,
sunshine glimmers through shadow, and shadow effaces sunshine, imaging that pleasant mood of mind where gaiety and
pensiveness intermingle. A bird is chirping overhead, among
the branches, but exactly whereabout, you seek in vain to determine; indeed you hear the rustle of the leaves, as he continually
changes his position. A little sparrow, indeed, hops into view,
alighting on the slenderest twigs, and seemingly delighting in
the swinging and heaving motion which his slight substance
communicates to them; but he is not the loquacious bird, whose
voice still comes, eager and busy, from his hidden whereabout.
Insects are fluttering about. The cheerful, sunny hum of the flies
is altogether summerlike, and so gladsome that you pardon
them their intrusiveness and impertinence, which continually
impels them to fly against your face, to alight upon your hands,
and to buzz in your very ear, as if they wished to get into your
head [76] among your most secret thoughts. In truth, a fly is the
most impertinent and indelicate thing in creation, the very type
and moral of human spirits whom one occasionally meets with,
and who perhaps, after an existence troublesome and vexatious

to all with whom they come in contact, have been doomed to reappear in this congenial shape. Here is one intent upon alighting on my nose. In a room, now—in a human habitation—I could find in my conscience to put him to death; but here we have intruded upon his own domain, which he holds in common with all other children of earth and air—and we have no right to slay him on his own ground. Now we look about us more minutely, and observe that the acorn-cups of last year are strewn plentifully on the bank, and on the path; there is always pleasure in examining an acorn-cup, perhaps associated with fairy banquets, where they were said to compose the table-service. Here, too, are those balls which grow as excrescences on the leaves of the oak, and which young kittens love so well to play with, rolling them on the carpet. We see mosses, likewise, growing on the banks, in as great variety as the trees of the wood. And how strange is the gradual process with which we detect objects that are right before the eyes; here now are whortleberries, ripe and black, growing actually within reach of my hand, yet unseen till this moment. Were we to sit here all day, a week, a month, and doubt [77] less a lifetime, objects would thus still be presenting themselves as new, though there would seem to be no reason why we should not have detected them all at the first moment.

Now a cat-bird is mewing at no great distance. Then the shadow of a bird flitted across a sunny spot; there is a peculiar impressiveness in this mode of being made acquainted with the flight of a bird; it affects the mind more than if the eye had actually seen it. As we look round to catch a glimpse of the winged creature, we behold the living blue of the sky, and the brilliant disk of the sun, broken and made tolerable to the eye by the intervening foliage. Now, when you are not thinking of it, the fragrance of the white pines is suddenly wafted to you by a slight, almost imperceptible breeze, which has begun to stir. Now the breeze is the gentlest sigh imaginable, yet with a spiritual potency, insomuch that it seems to penetrate, with its mild, ethereal coolness, through the outward clay, and breathe upon the spirit itself, which shivers with gentle delight; now the breeze strengthens so much as to shake all the leaves, making them rustle sharply, but has lost its most ethereal power. And now, again, the shadows of the boughs lie as motionless as if they were painted on the pathway. Now, in this stillness, is heard the long, melancholy note of a bird, complaining alone, of some wrong or sorrow, that worm, or her own kind, or the immitigable [78] doom of human affairs has inflicted upon her. A complaining, but unresisting sufferer. And now, all of a sudden, we hear the sharp, shrill chirrup of a red squirrel, angry, it seems, with somebody, perhaps with ourselves for having intruded into what he is pleased to consider as his own domain. And hark, terrible to the ear, here is the minute but intense hum

of a musquito. Instinct prevails over all the nonsense of sentiment; we crush him at once, and there is his grim and grisly
corpse, the ugliest object in nature. This incident has disturbed
our tranquillity. In truth, the whole insect tribe, so far as we can
judge, are made more for themselves, and less for man, than any
other portion of creation. With such reflections, we look at a
swarm of them, peopling, indeed, the whole air, but only visible
when they flash into the sunshine; and annihilated out of visible
existence, when they dart into a region of shadow, to be again re-
produced as suddenly. Now we hear the striking of the village-
clock, distant, but yet so near that each stroke is distinctly impressed upon the air. This is a sound that does not disturb the
repose of the scene; it does not break our Sabbath; for like a
Sabbath seems this place, and the more so on account of the
cornfield rustling at our feet. It tells of human labor, but being so
solitary now, it seems as if it were on account of the sacredness
of the Sabbath. Yet it is not so, for we hear at a distance,
mow[79]ers whetting their scythes; but these sounds of labor,
when at a proper remoteness, do but increase the quiet of one
who lies at his ease, all in a mist of his own musings. There is the
tinkling of a cow-bell—a noise how peevishly dissonant, were it
close at hand, but even musical now. But, hark! There is the
whistle of the locomotive—the long shriek, harsh, above all
other harshness, for the space of a mile cannot mollify it into
harmony. It tells a story of busy men, citizens, from the hot
street, who have come to spend a day in a country village; men
of business; in short of all unquietness; and no wonder that it
gives such a startling shriek, since it brings the noisy world into
the midst of our slumbrous peace. As our thoughts repose again,
after this interruption, we find ourselves gazing up at the leaves,
and comparing their different aspect, the beautiful diversity of
green, as the sunlight is diffused through them as a medium, or
reflected from their glossy surface. You see, too, here and there,
dead, leafless branches, which you had no more been aware of
before, than if they had assumed this old and dry decay since
you sat down upon the bank. Look at our feet; and here likewise
are objects as good as new. There are two little round white
fungi, which probably sprung from the ground in the course of
last night, curious productions of the mushroom tribe, and
which by and by will be those little things, with smoke in them,
which children call puff-balls. [80] Is there nothing else? Yes;
here is a whole colony of little ant-hills, a real village of them;
they are small, round hillocks, formed of minute particles of
gravel, with an entrance in the centre; and through some of
them blades of grass or small shrubs have sprouted up, producing an effect not unlike that of trees overshadowing a homestead. Here is a type of domestic industry—perhaps, too, something of municipal institutions—perhaps, likewise (who knows)

the very model of a community, which Fourierites and others are
stumbling in pursuit of. Possibly, the student of such philos-
ophies should go to the ant, and find that nature has given him
his lesson there. Meantime, like a malevolent genius, I drop a
few grains of sand into the entrance of one of these dwellings,
and thus quite obliterate it. And, behold, here comes one of the
inhabitants, who has been abroad upon some public or private
business, or perhaps to enjoy a fantastic walk—and cannot any
longer find his own door. What surprise, what hurry, what confusion of mind, are expressed in all his movements! How inexplicable to him must be the agency that has effected this mischief.
The incident will probably be long remembered in the annals of
the ant-colony, and be talked of in the winter days, when they
are making merry over their hoarded provisions. But come, it is
time to move. The sun has shifted his position, and has found a
vacant space through the branches, by means of which he levels
his rays [81] full upon my head. Yet now, as I arise, a cloud has
come across him, and makes everything gently sombre in an
instant. Many clouds, voluminous and heavy, are scattered
about the sky, like the shattered ruins of a dreamer's Utopia; but
we will not send our thought thitherward now, nor take one of
them into our present observations. The clouds of any one day,
are material enough, alone, for the observation either of an idle
man or a philosopher.

And now how narrow, scanty, and meagre, is this record of
observation, compared with the immensity that was to be observed, within the bounds which I prescribed to myself. How
shallow and scanty a stream of thought, too,—of distinct and
expressed thought—compared with the broad tide of dim emotions, ideas, associations, which were flowing through the
haunted regions of imagination, intellect, and sentiment, sometimes excited by what was around me, sometimes with no per-
ceptible connection with them. When we see how little we can
express, it is a wonder that any man ever takes up a pen a second time.

Like William Byrd or William Bartram before him—like Thoreau, John Muir, Edward Abbey, and Annie Dillard after him—
Hawthorne at Sleepy Hollow was agonizing over much more than
the machine in the garden, much more even than the simple odds
between pastoral vision and technological reality, or between the
rural and the urban. He was, of course, seeking to make coherent,
pleasant, pastoral sense of a scene; and, unquestionably, the "startling shriek" of the locomotive broke his attempted concentration;
but so, prior to the appearance of the locomotive, did a fly and a
mosquito, and, after its appearance, the "two little round white

fungi," "a whole colony of little ant-hills," and, perhaps most troublesomely, his own obliterating responses to them.

It is misleading (and far too anthropocentric) to suggest that the drama of this passage from Hawthorne's American notebooks turns solely (or even primarily) on the shrieking whistle of the locomotive. For throughout the passage, the composing self is caught not between rural nature and urban technology but between its desire to lose itself in its environment and its composition, on the one hand, and its all too frequent awareness of self (both as competing animal and as self-conscious human composer), on the other. This classic American self is caught between its need to get out of itself, to divest itself of its competitive and composing predaciousness, and its contrary need to assert itself, to declare (through language and action) its ascendant superiority over flies, mosquitoes, and ants, if not over entire landscapes.

This self, then, seeks, constantly, to "fix" its environment and, yet, just as constantly doubts the motives and presumed "virtues" involved in attempting to do so. In fact, this is the kind of self which asks seriously whether its efforts to compose itself and its environment are finally any different from the songs of birds overhead—the kind of early American self which, having answered its own question with an affirmative and declarative, conscious, human "yes," seriously worries that its efforts and its answer, however natural, have taken it outside the environment of which it so much wishes to be an unthinking, representative part. This self, in other words, is all too aware of the final, fundamental psychobiotic similarities between the composer of artistic pastorals, the inventors and users of locomotives, the confused and homeless ant, the melancholy bird, the angry squirrel, and the human "mowers whetting their scythes" in the seeming quiet of civilized distance.

For reasons both positive and negative that have more than a little to do with its American heritage, this self begins by seeking to compose both its environment and its self in pastoral, Edenic contentment. For the same reasons, however, it very soon loses its initial contented composure, and long before the locomotive's whistle blasts its way to attention. Perhaps the first sign of anxiety appears with a bird "chirping overhead" which the composing self can neither locate nor name, a bird "among the branches, but exactly whereabout, you seek in vain to determine; indeed you hear the rustle of the leaves, as he continually changes his position." In at least half-frustrated association, this unlocatable, unidentifiable bird gives rise to "a little sparrow" that "hops into view, alighting on the slenderest twigs, and seemingly delighted in the swinging and heaving motion which his slight substance communicates to them." With this slight, delighting sparrow, the observing, composing self seeks to regain its initial repose. But this sparrow is *not* "the loquacious bird," which continues to trouble the attempted composition, and "whose voice still comes, eager and busy, from his hidden whereabout."

This early American self, like so many others, would know its environment; but, like so many others, it can only be momentarily satisfied in its "knowledge"—because it seeks, finally, not only knowledge but participation as well. It seeks, finally, not only to know its place but to be of it; and it is constantly reminded what it is to be of a place.

If this self can only partially fix the bird overhead, perhaps the seemingly more apparent insects will provide a more satisfying object of composition and composure:

> Insects are fluttering about. The cheerful, sunny hum of the flies is altogether summerlike, and so gladsome that you pardon them their intrusiveness and impertinence, which continually impels them to fly against your face, to alight upon your hands, and to buzz in your very ear, as if they wished to get into your head among your most secret thoughts. In truth, a fly is the most impertinent and indelicate thing in creation, the very type and moral of human spirits whom one occasionally meets with, and who perhaps, after an existence troublesome and vexatious to all with whom they come in contact, have been doomed to reappear in this congenial shape. Here is one intent upon alighting on my nose. In a room, now—in a human habitation—I could find in my conscience to put him to death; but here we have intruded upon his own domain, which he holds in common with all other children of earth and air—and we have no right to slay him on his own ground.

Throughout this "pastoral" scene, the composing self moves alternately in and out of itself, alternately in and out of the "human" in itself, and in and out of the irascible animal in itself and "nonhuman" nature. Now driven to explore the overlapping boundaries of the human and the nonhuman, it attempts to blend the hum of flies into a "cheerful," "sunny," "summerlike," "gladsome" scene of mutual pleasantry and, to that end, even magnanimously seeks to pardon their "intrusiveness and impertinence"; but the effort undermines itself as the attempt at congeniality (however magnanimous) with the impertinent and intrusive finally gives the lie to the initially desired contentment and drives the self back on its own psycho- and sociobiotic condition in near-thoughts of maggots on the brain. More than half troubled by its own irascible disposition, it attempts once again to save its humanity by respecting the "domain" of the irritant, no more than half subtly trumpeting its human ability to rise above base irritation, to forgo raw self-interest, and to keep from descending to the level of animal fly-swatter.

And for the most part it succeeds, recovering its original "pastoral" composure for another twelve sentences or so—by shifting its own identification and point of view from "you" and "I" to the more communal "we" (thus gaining some distance on personal irritants and irascibility) and by isolating a series of nonhuman phenomena which do not so easily disturb repose. It loses itself in "acorn-cups," "mosses," and "whortleberries" and in the "shadow of a bird" flitting "across a sunny spot" to bring the mind's eye to the blue of sky and the "brilliant disk of the sun, broken and made tolerable" by "intervening foliage," *until*—until it hears "the long, melancholy note of a bird, complaining alone, of some wrong or sorrow, that worm, or her own kind, or the immitigable doom of human affairs has inflicted upon her. A complaining, but unresisting sufferer"— until "the sharp, shrill chirrup" of an angry squirrel answers for the bird's suffering, and "the minute but intense hum" of the mosquito leads "instinct" to prevail "over all the nonsense of sentiment" as "we," with all our now combined communal power, "crush him at once" into a "grim and grisly corpse."

"This incident has disturbed our tranquillity," and it has provoked serious thoughts both about man's relations to nonhuman nature and about the assumptions and motivations underlying the human and personal effort to seek noncompetitive, pastoral composure:

> In truth, the whole insect tribe, so far as we can judge, are made more for themselves, and less for man, than any other portion of creation. With such reflections, we look at a swarm of them, peopling, indeed, the whole air, but only visible when they flash into the sunshine; and annihilated out of visible existence, when they dart into a region of shadow, to be again re-produced as suddenly.

Even the initial segments of Hawthorne's meditations at Sleepy Hollow are more, much more, than simple "descriptions of contentment." They are, in fact, a dramatization of a self's attempts to come to coherent terms both with itself and with its surroundings, especially its nonhuman surroundings. And geobiotic phenomena are no less unsettling than man-made wonders, harsh or otherwise.

Both the tone and the mood of this self's meditations change frequently, even before the vaunted locomotive whistle thrusts itself upon the composer's attention. Indeed, the composing self takes no longer to regain its initial composure, or the initial terms of its composition, after being interrupted by the harshness of the locomotive than it does after being disturbed by the mosquito or the fly. In fact, the locomotive itself is far from simply harsh and antipastoral. While it brings to the mind's eye "dead, leafless branches, which you had no more been aware of before, than if they had assumed this old and dry decay since you sat down upon the bank," it also— by its "startling," sudden appearance—calls to the composing mind other "objects as good as new," specifically the "two little round white fungi, which probably sprung from the ground in the course of last night, curious productions of the mushroom tribe, and which by and by will be those little things, with smoke in them, which children call puff-balls."

But "is there nothing else?" Is there nothing else as similarly "new" to eye or ear to take one out of one's self, away from thoughts on the innocent exploitations of childhood, away from fungi, or decay, or the harshness of the locomotive?

> Yes; here is a whole colony of little ant-hills, a real village of them; they are small, round hillocks, formed of minute particles of gravel, with an entrance in the centre; and through some of them blades of grass or small shrubs have sprouted up, producing an effect not unlike that of trees overshadowing a homestead.

Driving out of itself momentarily in its concentrations on nonhuman others, briefly losing its sense of psychobiotic self in nonhuman nature, the composing, human self cannot for long escape its kind, or thoughts on same—hence, the effect of "trees overshadowing a homestead":

> Here is a type of domestic industry—perhaps, too, something of municipal institutions—perhaps, likewise (who knows) the very model of a community, which Fourierites and others are stumbling in pursuit of. Possibly, the student of such philosophies should go to the ant, and find that nature has given him his lesson there.

"Meantime, like a malevolent genius," the self drops "a few grains of sand into the entrance" of one of the "dwellings" of this community and, thus, quite discomposes it—both the "figurative" community of the Fourierites and the "literal" community of ants. Both of these communities compete, of course, with the self and its preferred conceptions of nature, human as well as nonhuman; and both, like the mosquito and the locomotive, prompt competitive and self-preserving response.

It is difficult, if not impossible, for the American self to compose a pastoral, partly because the American self—like the Fourierites (and the ants?)—is always and forever seeking programmatic, practical harmony among itself, its kind, and the nonhuman environment; partly because the true American can never rest content with mere metaphoric or "rhetorical" harmony; but largely because the programmatic harmonies sought are noncompetitive, while the competitive relations among species (and, within the human individual, between the need to be a part and the drive to be apart) are all too apparent in American environments. It is painful to realize that if you really *are* at Sleepy Hollow, then neither self nor scene can be harmonious, except in brief, unconscious moments between mosquitoes, flies, or locomotives. No wonder the movements of the now homeless ant express not only dislocated surprise but "confusion of mind." No wonder the "clouds, voluminous and heavy, are scattered about the sky, like the shattered ruins of a dreamer's Utopia," or that the communal speaker concludes: "When we see how little we can express, it is a wonder that any man ever takes up a pen a second time." The experience of nonhuman nature in America, the effort to fix it in language, naturally leads to serious doubts both about the efficacy of human mediators and about their capacities to do anything other than take one out of one's "place in nature."

The sense of dislocation is there in the attempted composition from the beginning. The conflicts between self and other, human and nonhuman, are present from the start, and nowhere more than in the attempts of early Americans to substantiate the "phenomenal surfaces" of their environments and to relate them coherently to their senses of self and society, mythic and actual, promised and present. If even Hawthorne could not compose himself and his environments satisfactorily, it is hardly any wonder that so many early Americans, turning away from pastoral meditation, politics, theology, or law, sought instead to establish their own identities and the identities of their American places by learning to identify the "loquacious" bird by its song and habitat.

If, like Columbus at Veragua, Hawthorne found his experience at Sleepy Hollow almost completely discomposing, if Captain John Smith on the shores of the Chesapeake found his ancestral institutions almost completely unsettling, if William Bradford at Plymouth could find but "little solace or content" either in the old conceptions he sought to substantiate in this New World or "in respect of any outward objects," it is nothing but natural that so many early Americans turned to the business of identifying, describing, and explaining those very "outward objects" in their efforts to make sense of themselves, their preconceptions, and their American places.

If the conflicts among Epiphany (or paradise or Canaan), Veragua (or Sleepy Hollow or New Canaan), and one's own spiritual condition proved almost completely uprooting to any thinking early American, it is nothing but natural that so many, many early Americans turned to detailing, modifying, and amplifying the geobiotic elements of their Veraguas. It is nothing but natural that so many turned away from meditative journals, spiritual autobiographies, and secret diaries—away even from histories, political tracts, and election day sermons—to the seemingly much more hopeful and apparently much less troublesome business of systematic biology, the business of naming and learning to name the features of the American land, the business of collecting, examining, and conversing about the nonhuman elements of their adopted places.

America, after all—or Veragua or New Canaan or Cairo (Illinois)—was little if not a landed phenomenon, both in original mythic vision and in often awkward daily experience; and if seeking to adapt inherited European conceptions and terms to American places only created a despairing sense of displacement, one might naturally assume that the cause of despair lay in one's ignorance of the details of those places. The other routes, the ways of Epiphany and private meditation, had been tried for centuries. If solutions were to be found, they would be found in the land. If identity was to be secured, it would be secured with knowledge of the land, or so it seemed.

If one's grand, inherited, visionary terms only disconcerted one's sense of self and place, one might naturally seek to work from the ground up, from the skies down, and from the hills over to place one's self coherently. One might seek a way out of confusion and insecurity by turning to daily, detailed experience of soils, outcroppings, and the particulars of flora and fauna for some of the primary terms of one's identity.

Considering the agonies not only of Columbus and Hawthorne, but also of Cotton Mather, William Byrd, and Mary Rowlandson—considering the landed identity given to America and the American in both New World and Old—and considering as well the utter need to know the land for personal and familial survival—it is nothing but natural not only that so many Americans were pushed or driven to the land in their quests for security and identity but also that so many of their compatriots turned to natural history and the incipient sciences of geology and systematic biology for the primary terms of their identifications with, and in, America.

Diaries, secret diaries, and spiritual autobiographies, though natural expressions of the early American's condition, finally tended only to accent self-consciousness and to remind the self of its inherent instability. Spiritual autobiography and secret diary, however common, were, in fact, psychologically risky genres in which to seek or examine one's identity as an American. Classically genres in which familial, social, educational, religious, or political institutions provided frames in which the self could be defined, in America such genres could only remind the self that its life was institutionally destitute, that institutions in America were less conspicuously American than they were inconspicuously European, and that institutions in America were considerably less perfect than they had been promised to be. Unalloyed, spiritual autobiography and secret diary drove the self inward, forced it in upon itself; and few early American selves could stand the sustained pressure of such self-consciousness.

Despite—and in part, at least, because of—Romantic, protestant, and democratic affirmations of the individual and individualism, the classic American self needed more than anything else to erect and detail coherently sustainable psychic others that would be simultaneously *American* (rather than European) and yet not so amorphous or abstractly vague that they satisfied only one's intellectual or philosophic curiosity. The early American self needed, then—and often desperately—to fill de Tocqueville's "middle ground," the void experienced in America between one's own, "insignificant" self and "the huge apparition of society or the even larger form of the human race" or Nature.[8] And few, if any, existing institutional frames could satisfactorily perform that crucial psychic function.

Though the institutional furniture then in existence in America—its churches, its legal codes, its political forums, its architecture, and its art—could obviously provide the kinds of mediating structures needed to erect and sustain such a psychosocial scaffolding between one's paltry self and Mankind or Democracy or History or God or Nature, it could not do so without violating, dissatisfying, or undermining one's coordinate demand that the details of such scaffolding be distinctly and distinguishably American. As R. W. B. Lewis has noted, and many others have confirmed, no observer of early America could have failed to note "dotted across the Ameri-

can scene, many signs of the continuing power of the past: institutions, social practices, literary forms, and religious doctrines—
carry-overs from an earlier age and a far country and irrelevant
obstructions (as it seemed) to the fresh creative task at hand."⁹ For
various reasons, all closely connected with America's and the individual American's drive to escape or redeem the past, the half-fash-
ioned and all-too-European surface of institutional life in America
could not and did not satisfy the early American's need for a coherently sustainable identity. Most institutions in America seemed
frankly inadequate, in fact—both as projections of their European
counterparts, historic or contemporary, and as expressions of the
promising novelties that were or were supposed to be America.

To a thinking early American—and there were many, many
upon whom thinking was thrust by the force of psychobiotic and
psychosocial circumstance—the quest for institutionally sanctioned
psychic others could be, at best, unsatisfactory and, at worst, completely unsettling. If, for example, one's church on the treeless
grasslands of Nebraska or North Dakota was, as it was likely to be, a
conspicuous copy of the church of memory in the fjorded, half-
forested valley of southwestern Norway—and if the language of both
sabbath conversation and service was, say, Norwegian—together
they could do little more than reinforce the awkwardness of one's
situation, little more than periodically introduce reminders of one's
psychic discomposure. Though both church and language might
periodically introduce a comforting nostalgia, it was, finally, a discomposing nostalgia. For both language and church seemed per-
ceptually, stylistically, and conceptually out of American place.

Though one might be intellectually persuaded that God and
Christ—what the altar and the stained-glass windows represented—
transcended the distinctions of immediate times and places, one
could not help being struck by the odds between the well-intended
nostalgia of the transcendent message and the psycho- and sociobiotic immanence (and imminence) of the ride home through a
landscape whose elements one couldn't even name, much less explain. One couldn't help being struck by the unsettling odds between the kaleidoscope of stained glass and the seemingly feature-
less monotones of American prairie winters or springs or falls. One
couldn't help but be struck not simply by the incongruities among
message, medium, and place but also by the clashes between medium and medium in the as yet unknown place. The single apple
tree on what there was of a church lawn, or the lonely cedar so
worshipfully nurtured through the year by the Ladies Aid, seemed
(no, *was*) completely out of long- or short-stemmed grassy place. If
it *was* Easter, it would not be easy to prove to yourself that you were

at Bergen (N. Dakota) or Gilead (Nebraska). And much the same
kinds of things might be said about the likes of Paris (Maine), Al-
hambra (California), Rome (Pennsylvania), Pembroke (Georgia),
Versailles (Ohio), or Genoa (Colorado).

At times, perhaps, such an early American self might be reluctantly convinced that to be in America (or, worse, to be American)
was to be in just this divided condition, at odds with one's self and
one's environment. But such conviction, however accurate, was
seldom satisfying for long and, in any case, at considerable additional odds with the publicly pronounced identity of America and
the American appearing even in Norwegian-language newspapers.

If many early American selves turned, then, to the land, to the
elements of their geobiotic environments, for some of the primary
terms of their identities, they did so partly out of desperation, partly
because there seemed nowhere else to turn for a coherent and yet
distinct conception of self and America, but largely and basically
because the dominant logic and metaphysic of the post-Medieval
West seemed to ensure that the identification of America and the
American through the geobiotic environment—through knowledge
of a "Nature" increasingly conceived to exclude humankind—could
be accomplished without raising the kinds of vexing self-doubts occasioned by attempts to identify one's American self or one's American kind in political, legal, or theological terms.[10]

If Hawthorne was almost completely discomposed in his attempted pastoral meditation at Sleepy Hollow, he was so in large
part because he had no satisfactory means of identifying or
otherwise explaining the "loquacious" bird overhead, no appropriate method of explaining his own utterly basic desire to name the
bird, nor any reasonably satisfying means of fitting his own desires
for order into the scene he sought to compose. Committed to and
trained in the vocabulary, the style, and the tone of the traditional
literary pastoral, he had no personally satisfying method of modifying that pastoral to include and amplify not only that bird but also
the flies, the mosquitoes, the locomotive, the ants, and, most importantly, his own basic reactions to them. He lacked, then, someone
might say, the kind of understanding of complete biotic systems
that might have enabled him to shape his experience coherently. In
particular, he lacked a vocabulary and an environment, cultural as
well as geobiotic, that might have enabled him to get outside himself, to distinguish coherently among the "phenomenal surfaces" of
his location, his own responses to the elements of those "surfaces,"
and the difficulty he was experiencing in trying to capture both in
conceptually coherent prose.

Full-blooded heir to a deeply ancestral dream, he sought in immediate personal experience and in private journal the synthesis of self, social custom, and nonhuman environment that was both the transcending end of classic pastoral art and the imminent "promise of America." But simultaneously heir to a modern metaphysic in which human and nonhuman, artificial and natural, art and nature, were inviolably distinct, he sought as well to avoid the discomforting psychobiotic self-consciousness that would identify his own attempted pastoral song with the song of the nameless bird overhead, his own frustration with the anger of a red squirrel, or his own confusion with the confusion of a suddenly homeless ant.

Faced with an environment in which basic personal needs and fairly primitive animalian habits were all-too-immediate and all-too-apparently kin to the habits of both human and nonhuman organisms around him, he found it exceedingly difficult to separate pastoral vision from his own basic needs to create such a vision. In short, he found it next to impossible to distinguish clearly between himself and his actions (verbal and nonverbal) and the elements of his environment, between himself and the phenomenal surfaces of his location.

His environment, both geobiotic and cultural, and his own needs for distinction inevitably forced self-consciousness upon him, so much so that he sought, quite naturally, to escape it in pastoral synthesis. At the same time, however, his environment, again both geobiotic and cultural, forced upon him an extreme consciousness of others, perhaps especially nonhuman others; and his just as natural self-defense was to celebrate the self (however humbly), to accent self-consciousness, and to avoid any account of others (human or nonhuman) that would undermine his all-too-tentatively established sense of personal security. He may never have celebrated himself and sung himself overtly. He may never have sounded his own particular "yawp" over the rooftops of Sleepy Hollow, but then neither did he overtly declare his desire to be absorbed by them. He certainly would never have said that "nothing . . . is greater to one than one's self is," and he never found himself incorporating "gneiss, coal, long-threaded moss, fruits, grains, or esculent roots"—never saw (or wished to see) himself "stucco'd with quadrupeds and birds all over"—but, then, neither did he ever overtly enjoy the thought of being incorporated or stucco'd by them. He never enjoyed Whitman's egotism because he never enjoyed the self-consumption implicit in Whitman's mystic vision. He never attempted overtly to possess the universe because he knew that the contrary wish—to be dispossessed by it—was to be dispossessed of both it and one's sense of self—to be reft and ripped from it as a living, individual organism.

For the same reasons, he could never finally accept the kind of understanding of "complete biotic systems" that some say can shape experience coherently, because he also knew that such an "understanding" is but another form of mystic, pastoral vision, a vision of universal homeostasis or symbiosis that can only lead to the dispossession of self and, hence, explain the self by explaining it away. As he sought to unify the elements of his experience in a coherent account of the others of Sleepy Hollow, as he sought to immerse himself in the scene, he simultaneously fought the self-denying implications of such a unifying immersion. In his own way, he knew that to understand or shape one's experience, however coherently, in the terms of "complete biotic systems" was to deny the self and to divest himself of his own ego.

Others among Hawthorne's compatriots were either less deeply committed to ancestral dreams of American synthesis, or, what is more probable, less able to tolerate the ambiguities of American self-consciousness. Most early American selves, confronted by the insecurities, implicit and explicit, in the works of Columbus and Hawthorne, were much more readily convinced by the logic and metaphysic of modern Western thought, the kind of "disinterested" and apparently "nonsectarian" logic or metaphysic that, because it insisted on clean distinctions between self and other, subject and object, human and nonhuman, and art or science and nature, might provide the means to escape the throes of self-consciousness and self-doubt. With and for most "early" Americans, in fact—those of the twentieth as well as the seventeenth century—the business of attempting to identify America and the American went hand in hand with the quests of modern Western culture to separate clearly the all too apparently interested propositions and institutions of politics, theology, law, and poetry from the disinterested and objective knowledge of nonhuman nature provided by geobiotic science.

In this sense, and for this reason, America and the American are born as much of Cartesian dualism and Baconian classification as they are of ancestral visions of paradise regained or history redeemed. As the insecurities of Columbus and Hawthorne ought to make clear, much of America and the individual American self are born of the postmedieval drive to distinguish categorically—logically, psychologically, sociologically, and ontologically—between objective, scientific, verifiable, nonnormative, "meaningful" knowledge free of the vested interests of political parties, personal preference, and established institutions, on the one hand, and the value-laden, unconfirmable, and even "meaningless" declarations of political prejudice, religious persuasion, and vested human interest, on the other. In fact, nowhere in the Western world has the drive to secure such disinterested knowledge and to keep it and its sponsoring institutions free of the taint of sectarian interest been stronger or more insistent, or more desperately needed and sought, than in America; because nowhere have personal preference and individual interest been more highly accented and nowhere have the historically established institutions that might otherwise mediate among such interests been more pointedly suspect. Nowhere have such vested social, economic, political, and religious interests been viewed with more suspicion; and, hence, nowhere has such "objective," "empirically confirmable," interest-free knowledge been more valued or more essential, or more difficult to come by.

Nowhere in the Western world, in fact, has the drive to secure consistent names and coherent configurations for the elements of the nonhuman environment been any more insistent or any more definitive than in America. Nowhere has the demand for the transcendingly impersonal and "international" language of systematic science been any greater, and nowhere has the need to accumulate rapidly and record a comprehensive knowledge of one's geobiotic environments been any more personally or culturally defining. Nowhere have so many writers of what might simply be called "nature appreciation" sought to prove their mettle and transcend the details of local and personal experience by providing in telling parentheses the Latinate binomials of Linnaean science for plants and animals of private backyards, sequestered lakeshores, or solitary wilderness experiences. Nowhere have field guides to birds, flowers, trees, and even insects been more marketable; and nowhere has the kind of nature writing that simply recounts observations been more popular.

The motivations to fix and refix one's environment in the terms of systematic biology run deep in America, as deep certainly as the divided efforts of the seventeenth-century Virginian and transplanted Oxonian, the Reverend John Banister, whose efforts to account for the cockroach in his manuscript "Collectio insectorum" tell much of the story of the early American's attempt to locate self and escape self-consciousness in impersonal identification of the elements of America's biotic systems.

> Blatta alis curtis forte molendineris Mouf. These Cockaroaches (for so I suppose ye Natives taught us to call them) are one of ye Plagues of this country. I have gon at night with a Candle, into our Larder & Kitchin, & seen ye Shelves & dressers, & whatever has been thereon, coverd with them; but as soon as ye Light approaches, they all vanish. Moufet (p. 139) therfore certainly guest right that < <these certainly are> > those mischavous

Insects ye Peruvians call Araners or (according to Lerius, after is quote a Angl. (Dm C)) Aravers are not Papiliones but Blattae (Clus. in his notes on Monardes, C.X.) & also that Cardan's Animal Scarabeo similis non foetens is some such kind of Creature (Mouf. 69, 70).[11]

There is no overestimating Banister's commitment to the early taxonomic system of Oxford's first significant zoologist, Edward Wotton, no overestimating his desire to learn and repeat the method of Wotton's categories, to contribute, as we say, to the growth of scientific knowledge, and to establish a name for himself and for his American surroundings in the respected circles of international science. There is, in short, no exaggerating his desire to transcend purely personal experience of local Virginian environments, to provide phenomenal surfaces (that is, systematic names and comparative descriptions or explanations) for the features of his location, and to shape the surfaces of that location in something more than the terms of isolate, individual experience.

Like his contemporary scientific counterparts, like every zoologist or botanist after him, and like almost every landed American settler, Banister sought to make his nonhuman others as distinctly other as possible. He sought to make the nonhuman elements of his surroundings, in this case "Cockaroaches," into something distinctly other than a phenomenon of personal experiences with the night, the kitchen, the larder, and a candle—something even more than a plague of "this country." He sought to tie his cockroaches and, hence, his own experience of them not only to the sixteenth-century British naturalist Thomas Mouffet, but also to Mouffet's French contemporaries (explorer Jean de Léry and botanist Charles de L'Escluse), to the Italian mathematician and physician Girolamo Cardano, and to what he (Banister) could make of what the Peruvians called these nighttime, "kitchin" creatures. He sought, in other words, to render his nonhuman others placeless and generic and, in the process, to give the phenomena of American places (as well as himself) an institutionally sanctioned, international identity.

His motivations in this regard he shared not only with his scientific contemporaries but also with almost every recently landed American settler, of the seventeenth century as well as the twentieth. His desires to establish a name for himself by substantiating the elements of his nonhuman surroundings in Latinate phrasings were repeated again and again in the lives of his successors—in the Bartrams, the Catesbys, the Audubons, and the Agassiz—and the basic drama of his works and theirs, and many others like them, exemplifies the drive of virtually every early American self to sort out the elements of its location and, hence, to define a crucial part of its American psyche. In fact, the life and works of Banister and Agassiz, or Henry Rowe Schoolcraft and John Wesley Powell, are less special cases of the scientist in America than they are specialized expressions of the effort of every landed American self to fix coherently that part of its experience to be called nonhuman nature.[12]

Because the effort to identify the nonhuman others of America was fraught with difficulty from the start, because it was closely tied to the identification of the American self, and because it was laced with paradox— with as much melancholy as hope—the drive to succeed and the dedication to systematic identification were all the stronger. For many in America, there was precious little to go on if one could not successfully delineate and then systematically corroborate the nonhuman elements of one's American places. Thus, when William Bartram attempted to catalogue the montane vegetation around Clayton, Georgia, and then to lend it landscapetual configuration, he not only repeated John Banister's motivations but he also amplified and extended their methods:

> At this rural retirement were assembled a charming circle of mountain vegetable beauties, Magnolia auriculata, Rhododendron ferruginium, Kalmia latifolia, Robinia montana, Azalia flammula, Rosa paniculata, Calycanthus Floridus, Philadelphus inodorus, perfumed Convalaria majalis, Anemone thalictroides, Anemone hepatica, Erythronium maculatum, Leontice thalictroides, Trillium sessile, Trillium cesnum, Cypripedium, Arethuza, Ophrys, Sanguinaria, Viola, uvularia, Epigea, Mitchella repens, Stewartia, Halesia, Styrax, Lonicera, &c. some of these roving beauties are strolling over the mossy, shelving, humid rocks, or from off the expansive wavy boughs of trees, bending over the floods, salute their delusive shades, playing on the surface, some plunge their perfumed heads and bathe their flexile limbs in the silver stream, whilst others by the mountain breezes are tossed about, their blooming tufts bespangled with pearly and crystalline dewdrops collected from the falling mists, glisten in the rain bow arch. Having collected some valuable specimens at this friendly retreat, I continued my lonesome pilgrimage. My road for a considerable time led me winding and turning about the steep rocky hills; the descent of some of which was very rough and troublesome, by means of fragments of rocks, slippery clay and talc; but after this I entered a spacious forest, the land having gradually acquired a more level surface; a pretty grassy vale appears on my right, through which my wandering path led me, close by the banks of a delightful creek, which sometimes falling over steps of rocks, glides gently with serpentine meanders through the meadows.[13]

Like Banister, Bartram was dedicated to escaping the depths of self-doubt and self-consciousness. Like Banister, he sought to establish a name for himself and the features of his surroundings in the respected circles of international science; and, even more than Banister, he sought to free his nonhuman others, his American environments, from the insignificance of isolate, personal experience—first, no doubt, through extended systematic descriptions and lengthy Latinate catalogues of the characteristic species of an area, but also through the shades, limbs, and "crystalline dewdrops" of sublime and picturesque landscapes. Like Banister, he knew that without the kinds of institutional sanctions provided by systematic science, however imperfectly understood, or sublime and picturesque landscapes, however unevenly composed, his experiences of flora, fauna, and outcroppings would amount to little or nothing—because he knew as well that, unshaped and unconfirmed, William Bartram's places (and William Bartram) amounted to little, if anything. Like Banister before him, and Audubon and Agassiz after him, he sought, often desperately and almost always pretentiously, to codify and then to ratify the generic patterns especially of his geobiotic environments. Like Catesby, Schoolcraft, and even Powell, he sought, for fundamentally personal reasons, to authenticate what would be (but was not yet) a set of fundamentally impersonal environments, a set of largely geobiotic environments, that, once authenticated, would lend him personally a secure and sensible identity, a personal sense of national, if not regional and local, place.

Try as he might, then, he could no more escape self-consciousness and self-doubt than John Banister could. He could not help blowing the trumpet of his own isolate, personal experience, most often, paradoxically, in distinctly European terms that undermined, if not denied, his own needs for personal distinction.

Just as Banister could not free his attempt to classify Virginia's cockroaches from his terribly ordinary and utterly personal experiences of nighttime kitchens and larders, so Bartram, finally, could not free his magnolias and hepaticas, or even his "delusive shades" and "serpentine meanders," from his belief (or his need to believe) that his "lonesome pilgrimage"—indeed, his loneliness—like Banister's candlelit perception of flitting, nocturnal insects—was significant, and even distinct. He could not free his attempts to ratify his geobiotic environments from his all-too-obvious needs to make a name for his lonely and otherwise insignificant self; and he ended, ironically and tellingly, by making his loneliness less than exceptional, by portraying himself as the isolated, diminutive, formulaic figure of Romantic landscape art. Seeking personal distinction, he became not individual but figural. Seeking to escape his loneliness and to publicize his isolation, he made his oft-imperiled, nature-loving American self into the formulaic traveler of Romantic art, and so lost a crucial part of the individuality and locality he so much desired.

For all his desire to objectify his American environments, to distinguish them from the minutiae of daily psychobiotic experience, he could not satisfactorily separate his environments from his personal experience of them, or, finally, from his own special needs to shape and order them. If he wanted—very much wanted—to distinguish self and other, to free his environments from his personal experience of them, or to subdue personal impression in favor of impersonal knowledge, he also wanted to find some way of blending the two, some way of declaring their utter inseparability and, hence, the special non-European significance of *his* experience in *his* environments. And he could not succeed, in part because the scientific identities he sought demanded that he separate personal impression from impersonal knowledge and systematic codification; and in part because the aesthetic blend he sought, though it argued the interdependence of self and other, allowed only an unfamiliar, European persona, a highly civilized, formulaic poseur who seemed only to pretend the kinds of insecurity he himself knew all too well in troublesome daily experience.

Like Banister, he was torn between his need to declare his identity, to shout from the tangles of Georgia's mountains and Florida's wetlands the significance of his own experience, and his logically contrary (but psychologically complementary) need to declare the significance of his surroundings, to trumpet to an international audience the wonders of those mountains and wetlands. In either case, his efforts were undermined (except for brief moments) both by his inability to make his declarations in terms other than the terms of Linnaean science or full-blown, Romantic landscape art, and by his own divided attitude toward those terms and the institutions from which they derived.

As he sought to construct a part of de Tocqueville's middle ground, to fill the void between his own insignificant self and Nature (not to say Mankind), in the only terms he knew, in the abstract and generic terms of systematic biology and the even more generic terms of the formulaic sublime and picturesque, he did little more than deepen the void, because the terms he used were at best impersonal and nonlocal and at worst abstractly specialized and singularly "un-American."

Like Banister, he gave crystal-clear evidence of wanting to separate personal narrative and impersonal description. A large part of his *Travels* and the manuscript journal that preceded it is built upon a stylistic strategy that alternates passages of impersonal

description or classification with bits of personal narration or reflection. The dominant logical and rhetorical habit of his work is, thus,
to distinguish as far as possible in conventional late eighteenth- and
early nineteenth-century fashion between personal story and impression and the impersonal delineation of landscape, between the
interested human observer and the apparently disinterested observation, especially, of the nonhuman environment:

> This exalted peak I named mount Magnolia*, from a new
> and beautiful species of that celebrated family of flowering trees,
> which here, at the cascades of Falling Creek, grows in a high
> degree of perfection, for although I had noticed this curious tree
> several times before, particularly on the high ridges betwixt
> Sinica and Keowe, and on ascending the first mountain after
> leaving Keowe, when I observed it in flower, but here it flour-
> ishes and commands our attention.
> This tree, or perhaps rather a shrub, rises eighteen to thirty
> feet in height, there are usually many stems from a root or
> source, which lean a little, or slightly diverge from each other, in
> this respect imitating the Magnolia tripetala; the crooked
> wreathing branches arising and subdividing from the main stem
> without order or uniformity, their [340] extremities turn up-
> wards, producing a very large rosaceous, perfectly white, double
> or polypetalous flower, which is of a most fragrant scent; this
> fine flower sits in the center of a radius of very large leaves,
> which are of a singular figure, somewhat lanceolate, but broad
> towards their extremities, terminating with an acuminated
> point, and backwards they attenuate and become very narrow
> towards their bases, terminating that way with two long, narrow
> ears or lappets, one on each side of the insertion of the petiole;
> the leaves have only short footstalks, sitting very near each
> other, at the extremities of the floriferous branches, from
> whence they spread themselves after a regular order, like the
> spokes of a wheel, their margins touching or lightly lapping
> upon each other, form an expansive umbrella superbly crowned
> or crested with the fragrant flower, representing a white plume;
> the blossom is succeeded by a very large crimson cone or strob-
> ile, containing a great number of scarlet berries, which, when
> ripe, spring from their cells and are for a time suspended by a
> white silky web or thread. The leaves of these trees which grow
> in a rich, light, humid soil, when fully expanded and at maturity,
> are frequently above two feet in length and six or eight inches
> where broadest. I discovered in the maritime parts of Georgia,
> particularly on the banks of the Alatamaha, another new species

---

*Magnolia auriculata

of Magnolia, whose leaves were nearly of the figure of those of
this tree, but they were much less in size, not more than six or
seven inches in length, and the strobile very small, oblong,
sharp pointed and of a fine deep crimson colour, but I never saw
the flower. These trees grow strait and erect, thirty feet or more
in height, and of a sharp conical form, much resembling the
Cucumber tree (Mag. acuminata) in figure.

[341] This day being remarkably warm and sultry, which,
together with the labour and fatigue of ascending the mountains, made me very thirsty and in some degree sunk my spirits.
Now past mid-day, I sought a cool shaded retreat, where was
water for refreshment and grazing for my horse, my faithful
slave and only companion. After proceeding a little farther, descending the other side of the mountain, I perceived at some
distance before me, on my right hand, a level plain supporting a
grand high forest and groves; the nearer I approach my steps are
the more accelerated from the flattering prospect opening to
view; I now enter upon the verge of the dark forest, charming
solitude! as I advanced through the animating shades, observed
on the farther grassy verge a shady grove, thither I directed my
steps; on approaching these shades, between the stately columns of the superb forest trees, presented to view, rushing from
rocky precipices under the shade of the pensile hills, the unparalleled cascade of Falling Creek, rolling and leaping off the
rocks, which uniting below, spread a broad, glittering sheet of
crystal waters, over a vast convex elevation of plain, smooth
rocks, and are immediately received by a spacious bason, where,
trembling in the centre through hurry and agitation, they gently
subside, encircling the painted still verge, from whence gliding
swiftly, they soon form a delightful little river, which continuing
to flow more moderately, is restrained for a moment, gently un-
dulating in a little lake, they then pass on rapidly to a high per-
pendicular steep of rocks, from whence these delightful waters
are hurried down with irresistible rapidity. I here seated myself
on the moss clad rocks, under the shade of spreading trees and
floriferous fragrant shrubs, in full view of the cascades.[14]

The method of separating and alternating impersonal description or exposition and personal narration or reflection is, of course,
far from uncommon in late eighteenth- and early nineteenth-century prose. Without the distinctly personal note, it is the method in
fiction of Sir Walter Scott and James Fenimore Cooper. With the
occasional, narrating "I," it is the method of much early modern
geological and biological science, sciences that, because they often
involved travel and the keeping of a daily notebook or journal, almost inevitably engaged at least a residual personal voice.

Brought to America, however, and amplified by the rhetorics of the sublime and picturesque, the method betrays a need for personal recognition—a begging for attention—and, hence, it seriously qualifies the scientific desire to subdue the self and self-interest. Worse, it separates, or seeks to separate, personal narrative (and, hence, personal experience and development) from knowledge of nonhuman environments, in a manner and style quite out of place in a country where the two were utterly inseparable, and would be for some time to come.

In the *Travels*, then, one can see William Bartram—an early American self—attempting to separate personal experience from impersonal "knowledge" of his environments. The attempt is an expression of a perfectly natural drive, of course, especially in a land so poorly known; but it is also a drive doomed to frustration and an attempt doomed to failure as long as the erstwhile composer of self and scene hides from himself or seeks to veil his own motives and insecurities in the vocabularies and styles, scientific or aesthetic, of the secure European interpreter of scenes long-established and locally well known.

Thus, in the two parts of the extended passage quoted above one can also see an early American self torn between its desire to establish detailed identities in ordinary language for at least some of the phenomenal features of its local or regional American places and its contrary desire to establish generically placeless identities in a specialized language for those same phenomenal features—a self torn between its needs for an international and institutionally sanctioned identity for itself and its surroundings, on the one hand, and its contrary needs to define itself and its surroundings in the common language of extended personal experience of local and regional place, on the other hand. This self wishes to establish for "this tree" [*Magnolia auriculata*] an extended local identity, an extended description of it that will provide for detailed personal acquaintance; and yet he is uneasy about claiming it for his own, hesitant about pinning it too closely to the ordinary language of its American places. He is caught among his awareness that few of the features of American lands have established local identities, his knowledge that such local identities grow very slowly indeed, his deep desire to contribute to their growth, and his at least half-contrary need to provide such identifications and to extend their acquaintance as quickly and rapidly as possible in the international, impersonal, and essentially placeless terms of sanctioned geobiotic science. He is torn between the highly European languages of Linnaean science and developed landscape art—the kinds of languages that can provide rapid recognition, however superficial, both for himself and for his surroundings—and the more ordinary (and, hence, more "American") language of extended description and detailed definition—the kind of language that might help contribute to a lastingly local identity for those surroundings, if not indeed for their composer.

If modern, European conventions of systematic science demanded that the gentleman scientist subdue the self as much as possible, and if most of Bartram's European contemporaries succeeded admirably in doing so, Bartram, the American, was considerably less successful. Like many of his American contemporaries, he was unable to sustain the separation of self and nonhuman other for more than a paragraph or two, because in his world the two were nowhere as easily distinguishable as they were for his European counterparts. His personal identity depended, in more ways than one, on his ability to identify the elements of his nonhuman surroundings; and, to make matters worse, a large part of his European audience was as much interested in him as a "child of nature" (or as untutored "natural" botanist) as it was in the elements of his surroundings. In fact, he might reasonably have guessed that few, if any, Europeans would have been willing to publish his efforts, much less read them, if he hadn't appeared in one or another of the guises for the "natural" progeny of America then popular in Europe.

In one sense, then, he was caught between the conventions of early modern science, which demanded that he subdue self and self-reflection (in favor of a disinterested knowledge of nature), and the conventions of Romantic literature, which demanded, quite to the contrary, that he accent self and celebrate self-reflection (if need be, at the expense of a disinterested account of his surroundings). In another and much more fundamental sense he was simply caught between his need to declare or establish a case for himself (and his personal experiences of New World places) and his contrary need to render himself significant by rendering his environments impersonally significant. He was caught between his desire to synthesize self and other in the only contemporaneously synthesizing figures of thought and language he knew (European as they were) and his contrary desire to distinguish clearly self and other in the interest of contributing to systematic knowledge of his environments.

Torn between his needs to be a part—a part of established, institutionally sanctioned human communities as well as the land communities of the southeastern United States—and his need to be apart—apart from the human communities of Europe, from their ill-defined counterparts in America, and (not least) from the some-

times engulfing environments of Florida, Georgia, and Alabama—
he was torn as well between his competing allegiances to concrete,
local or regional places—places still undefined—and his allegiances
to the all-too-apparently defined identities proffered by the impersonal and disinterested science of systematic biology, a science dedicated to transcending the limitations (and awkwardness) of local,
personal experience.

Where, in Europe, systematic biology was aimed at mediating
among centuries-old variations in local and dialectal bestiaries and
herbals (and, hence, could be said to be building upon historically
secure local or regional conventions and names), in America, of
course, no such secure conventions or names were available (and,
hence, the international language of systematic biology served not
so much as mediator among long-established dialectal variants as a
largely esoteric set of abstract, generic, and basically placeless
terms to guide initial identification of many of the elements of one's
immediate surroundings). In Bartram's case, as in many others, the
business of finding out what "x" was in early America as often
meant determining (or creating) names for it, including its scientific
names, as it meant asking citizens of local communities to supply
common names and information about it.

In early America, such generic terms as Linnaean science provided did not, of course, derive from extended personal experience
of a locale. As parts of an international quest for disinterested
knowledge, moreover, they were meant (as they still are) to subdue
or comprehend the variants and idiosyncracies of local and personal
experience. They were aimed at surmounting, escaping, or transcending the vagaries of strictly local or regional convention and
prejudice. For quite honorable causes, they were dedicated to denying one of the things an early American self needed most, and yet
found most difficult to establish—extended, intimate, and local codifications for the phenomenal surfaces of its daily environments.

Similarly, the vocabularies and stylistic conventions of sublime
and picturesque landscapes were meant (as they still are) to take
one beyond and above normal, daily psychobiotic experience toward something approaching transcendental appreciation or insight. Like systematic biology, they were designed to take one away
from mundane psychobiotic consciousness and self-consciousness,
to immerse the self in consciousness of others, especially nonhuman others. And, like systematic biology, they could provide some
considerable solace and content to any early American self who
could, however briefly, adopt them without thinking too much
about them or about their basic psycho- and sociobiotic functions.

For such a self, both Romantic landscape art and systematic

biology could provide institutionally sanctioned refuges from the almost daily uncertainties of personal experience of one's nonhuman surroundings. Both could provide institutionally sanctioned objectifications of nonhuman nature which, if and when one could get over the feeling that they were too clearly European, might offer at least momentary or periodic escape from the ambiguities of being (or seeking to be) American. But neither could provide—without substantial qualification or modification—the kinds of extended local intimacy with one's surroundings which Bartram sought implicitly throughout his travels, and Hawthorne sought more explicitly in his broken meditations at Sleepy Hollow.

In fact, both landscape art and systematic biology served fundamentally different functions in early America than they served in contemporaneous Europe. To the early American self, transcending or comprehending one's environment—escaping one's normal psychobiotic condition—meant something quite different than it meant to a European contemporary. The European appreciator of landscape and nature, like the European systematic biologist, sought escape from (or disinterested knowledge of) geobiotic phenomena (and psycho- and sociobiotic experiences) that had been known for centuries. The early American, if and when he could, sought escape from (or disinterested knowledge of) phenomena and experiences essentially unknown or barely understood. The European could, moreover, return at will from sublime giddiness, binomial classification, or picturesque appreciation to the familiar and safely mundane affairs of everyday psychobiotic life. The early American had no such previously established psycho- or sociobiotic base to return to.

To know, as William Bartram wanted much to know, that one's nonhuman environment is sublime or picturesque is, no doubt, elevating when you and your kind have known their opposites for centuries, and can return safely to the comforting inanities of daily life whenever necessary. To know, as Nathaniel Hawthorne would have been at least momentarily happy to know, that the loquacious bird overhead is really an instance of *Icterus galbula* is undoubtedly reassuring when you and your kind have known it for centuries as the Baltimore Oriole, and can return comfortably to calling it such whenever necessary (even if the field guides have dropped the colorful "Baltimore" for the utterly uninteresting "Northern"). When you have known it not at all, however, when you have not even a common name for it, or when you do not recognize its song, "*Icterus galbula*" may easily seem the height of civilized pretense. When the landscapes you would know as sublime or picturesque provide you—despite yourself—with little more than spirits sunken by labor, fatigue, humidity, and thirst, landscape appreciation and landscape art may easily seem the height of cloistered innocence, or plain and simple inexperience.

It is much easier to discriminate between self and other, between personal narration and impersonal description or classification, when your personal identity, stature, and significance do not depend so completely on the new, beautiful shrub you and your father first observed in 1765 and then named, in almost overt sociopolitical gesture, *Frankliniana alatamaha*, long before it became known colloquially as the Franklin tree. In fact, the history of the naming of that new, beautiful shrub itself demonstrates the basic insecurities of many early Americans, their desires to be (or become) part of history, on the one hand, and their utter inability to be (or become) such a part in normal historical process. To derive the common name for an organism from a prior, scientific binomial—rather than to impose a scientific binomial on a multitude of prior common names—is, after all, to reverse the normal, and generally inductive, historical process by which humans have elsewhere come to fix and know their geographic and biotic environments.

It is much easier to discriminate between one's own so-called subjective states and the state of so-called objective knowledge if one can readily and willingly distinguish between one's own words and actions in location, on the one hand, and consistent public understandings both of one's locations and of one's condition in location, on the other hand. When, however, one's own words and actions determine the only public understanding there is of the location one is attempting to identify, one may come perilously close to identifying the two—either by reducing the self to such public understandings as one imagines might be attractive, by formulating one's personal experience solely in the most clichéd public terms available, or by overaccenting the self, by reducing public understanding to an expression of personal condition and desire.

It is much easier to take honest personal pride in one's "original" discoveries if one is something other than a self-trained amateur in a country of amateurs and if one can depend on established public understandings of one's self and one's environments. The satisfaction gained by being *the* original discoverer of "x" is less than satisfying if one cannot depend on established methods of confirming both one's self and one's discoveries. To be the first, the very first, to name or describe or experience "x" is but small consolation to persons who, like William Bartram and many of his compatriots, needed as much to know (or to prove that they knew) *the* publicly established name for "x." It is, in short, much easier to distinguish self and other effectively—and then to relate them in meaningful phrasings of kinship—if one has inherited a coherently sustainable sense both of one's self and of one's others—in early America a sense, especially, of one's nonhuman others.

The early American self—from Columbus through Bradford and Byrd to Banister, Bartram, and Hawthorne—had, of course, inherited neither; and because, particularly after the Revolution, the nation was publicly dedicated to denying such inheritances, that self often stood (and wrote) in desperate need of both. Like numbers of his "scientific" compatriots—and not a few of his unscientific ones—William Bartram would have written an American version of Aristotle's *Historia Animalium* had he been able to. But his own insecurities, his own lack of stature, and his own consequent desires for recognition, when coupled with the inadequacies of the grammars and styles available to him, prevented him from doing so. Nathaniel Hawthorne—like many another self-conscious early American composer—would have written an American's version of Saint Augustine's *Confessions* had he been able to. But he was prevented from doing so by his own extreme self-consciousness, his self-consciously admitted inadequacies in the face of his environment, and his implicit fears of losing the independence and freedom that come with such self-consciousness. Unlike Saint Augustine, he was unable to compose or to put his faith in any coherently sustainable set of nonhuman others.

Hawthorne and Bartram—though they can hardly be said to encompass the totality of relations among selves and their nonhuman surroundings in early America—nonetheless exemplify together most of the disjunctive consequences that follow from a situation in which the drive to identify the human person is inseparable from the drive to identify the nonhuman environment. Together, and before the time of *Walden*, the attempted pastoral meditation of the one and the *Travels* of the other comprehend quite adequately that range of experience and genre so characteristic of the early American's attempts to come to terms with his or her surroundings, that range between personal definition sought through landscapetual composition and impersonal scientific (or aesthetic) identification sought in a running account of personal experience. In barely implicit desire, the weakness of each seeks the strength of the other.

Hawthorne's concern for and about the unidentifiable, loquacious bird, his worries about his own malevolent actions, and his nearly self-defeating doubts about the efficacy of writing and composition are answered in Bartram's obsession with the systematically impersonal identification of species and in his coordinate desire to minimize (or subdue entirely) his memories of occasionally sunken spirits. The proof in the pudding of Bartram's flitting moments of depression, the nearly obsessive drive behind his hyperbolic dilations and overextended Latinate catalogues, is supplied, in turn, by Hawthorne's openly phrased self-doubts. Bartram's quest for an un-self-conscious synthesis of self and surroundings, his ultimate desire to immerse himself in unconscious identifications of his environments, is answered by Hawthorne's final inability (and unwillingness) to leave self-consciousness behind, his final disposition to assert, if only indirectly, the primacy of the questing, ordering human psyche.

If Bartram could secure nothing else, he would secure an impersonal understanding of his nonhuman surroundings; and, if need be, he would sacrifice all options on self-analysis and all prospects of self-knowledge to such an understanding. If Hawthorne could secure little of the comprehending (and comprehensive) pastoral synthesis he sought between self and other, between the human and nonhuman, he would secure, and preserve at all costs, his options on self-analysis and his prospects for self-knowledge, however unsettling they might be. If Hawthorne needed Bartram's unquestioning technical ability to name the bird, his unconscious assurance that this shrub was, and forever would be, an instance of *Magnolia auriculata*—if Hawthorne needed Saint Augustine's assurance that the pear tree had been (and was) forever tempting—Bartram needed Hawthorne's capacity to face his own needs for order openly, to admit and confront his obsessions with fixing in name and, hence, in nature the elements of his geobiotic surroundings.

Each lacked what the other had. Each had, at times in excess, what the other lacked. And yet both faced the same combination of basic needs, the need to know (and accent) the self and the need to know and codify the nonhuman environment. Hawthorne had the capacity to raise openly the essential, if inevitably discomposing, questions and to admit not only that he didn't have the tools to answer them but also that they might well be unanswerable. Bartram had the ability to repress those questions and to dedicate himself to the tools and methods of securing their just-as-essential answers. Hawthorne had the ability to repress (or redirect) his desires to know his surroundings and to restrict himself to such codifications as would be consistent with preserving his options on self-consciousness and self-knowledge. Bartram had the capacity to pursue openly his need to know his nonhuman surroundings in detail and to restrict himself to such phrasings as would be consistent with his options on systematically impersonal understandings of his environments. Hawthorne lacked Bartram's dedication to establishing conventional codifications for our nonhuman others.

Bartram lacked Hawthorne's commitment to the ambiguities of self-consciousness, his dedication to the desiring human (and animal) self.

William Bartram and his kind—the Catesbys, the Alexander Wilsons, and the Audubons—were, then, little more successful finally, than Hawthorne and his kind—the Cotton Mathers, the William Byrds, and the Edgar Allan Poes—in their attempts to secure their relations with their American environments. Bartram and his kind sought basically to subdue the self in favor of what they and others thought (or needed to think) of as disinterested knowledge of nonhuman nature. Their underlying motivations were to separate self and other and, in the process, to seek a selfless knowledge of their nonhuman surroundings. To the extent they succeeded, and under the circumstances their success was considerable, they far outdid Hawthorne (or Mather or Byrd) both in escaping the throes of self-consciousness in America and in coming to terms with their nonhuman environments. By the same token, however, or through the same methodological motivations, they were far less successful than Hawthorne and his kind in openly confronting their own basic needs and in dramatizing the inward nature of the human and American self.

Hawthorne and his kind—natively more skeptical, perhaps, but no less insecure—sought fundamentally to assert the priority of the knowing, human self, even at the expense of the unity of knowing self and known other, which they otherwise so much desired. Their underlying motivations were to seek above all a self-fulfilling knowledge of their nonhuman others and to reject, finally, any understanding, any persuasion, or any method that would threaten their notions of self-knowledge, self-determination, and individual freedom. As a result they were far more successful than Bartram (or Catesby or Audubon) in keeping their nonhuman others, their geobiotic environments, at a self-controlling distance. They avoided being overwhelmed by their surroundings or by the self-consuming business of continually attempting to codify them; and they were far more successful than Bartram and his kind in coming to know themselves and their most basic human needs.

For the early American self, then, neither natural history nor spiritual autobiography—neither systematic biology nor pastoral meditation—would finally suffice to secure its relations with its geobiotic surroundings. The one—natural history—threatened to subdue or absorb the interested human self in unconscious identifications of (and with) its nonhuman surroundings, a threat all too familiar in struggling daily experience of the new land. The other—spiritual autobiography—threatened to concentrate the state of the universe in consciousness of one's puny self, a threat that, though it might be momentarily satisfying to egomaniacs, was somewhat less than satisfying to persons already too often concerned with their individual states of being.

All in all, it seems fair to say that the early (and classic) American self was truly a divided being. Taken out of itself almost constantly by its efforts to fix its nonhuman surroundings—for psychological security if not plain biotic survival—this self was just as constantly thrown back upon itself and its own resources, both psychic and biotic. Forced to concentrate its attentions on its nonhuman others, it was simultaneously (and consequently) driven to reflect on its own severely limited condition, and without the comforting psychosocial insulation provided by consistent, established institutional mediators between itself and its nonhuman environments.

If conditions of daily personal life were, at best, disjunctive, the public and institutional face of America, such as it was, did little but underscore and amplify their disjointing effects. Ironic as it must have seemed to both Bartram and Hawthorne, a self-fulfilling condition, a liberation of the human individual from the institutional and environmental confinements of the past, was, of course, one of the public promises of America, particularly after the Revolution. Individual self-consciousness, self-knowledge, and self-determination were premier, published causes of America and the American. But so, too, were the perfection of human history; an original, absorbing experience of nonhuman nature; and the rediscovered synthesis of self, society, and nature that had been the aboriginal and prelapsarian soul of Judeo-Christian thought.

The early (and classic) American, then, sought not only a new experience of and with its own kind, but also—and simultaneously—a new experience of self and a new, absorbing experience of and with nonhuman nature—all in an environment (cultural as well as geobotic) as yet barely known and in which the terms or categories of human experience were anything but new or original. Driven by the force of circumstances and heritage to fix, substantiate, and control its nonhuman environment, this self was simultaneously suspicious (for reasons deriving from the same circumstances and the same heritage) of human and historically civilized attempts to fix it, substantiate it, or control it—in part because such categorical fixings as this American knew were the very decadent and disproven ones it was trying to escape, and in part because any such categorical fixings seemed only to interfere with its original, unmediated relation to nature.

On the one side, this American's search for paradise and its coordinate suspicions of the sinning historical past led it to seek escape from all the trappings of historic civilization, including language—anything that would interfere with its primordial relation to nature. Reinforced by bits of Reformation theology, the shades of Rousseau, and much of Romanticism, it would have no mediators between itself and nonhuman nature; and it held this position as often and as long as it could hold a sanguine view of itself and NATURE. On the other side, faced as it often was by nature in the raw (both in itself and in its environment), this American also sought to guard its own chances, to perfect human history, and to secure in historical reality and personal achievement what Europeans had been able to secure, if at all, only in fast-fading remembrances of mythic places past. Its daily psychobiotic condition and its drive to perfect human history led it naturally not only to seek the comforting mediations of civilization but also to exploit them for basic personal causes and to identify their most current formulations with the modernity of America. Reinforced by the Renaissance, by the historical promise of the Reformation, by the rise of geobiotic science, and not least by a frequently Hobbesian experience of both human and nonhuman nature, this American saw the categories of modern Western thought being consummated in a final, historical harmony of which it itself would be an assertive exemplum.

Driven both by America's original identification with paradise and by a natural and national pride in the seeming uniqueness of its unmediated relation to nature (both human and nonhuman), this American was sorely tempted to celebrate the conjunctions of its American experience, to identify the human and the nonhuman, if not the sacred and the profane, and to glorify the unification (or reunification) of name and nature, self and other, myth and reality, in America and the American. But driven as well both by its own daily psychobiotic circumstances and by its natural dependence on the categories of experience and knowledge then current in Europe, it was also sorely tempted to deny its own inherited notions of America and the American. It was forced both by circumstances and heritage to draw the very distinctions—between self and other, private and public, or subject and object; between human and nonhuman, artificial and natural, or myth and reality—which its devotion to the ideals of America and the American had convinced it were the original troublers of Western history, if not its own life.

Chapter Five

Nature Writing and America

Why didn't someone hand those newly sighted people paints
and brushes from the start, when they still didn't know what
anything was? Then maybe we all could see color-patches too,
the world unraveled from reason, Eden before Adam gave
names.

ANNIE DILLARD, Pilgrim at Tinker Creek

ut of the attempts of early Americans to com-
pose themselves and their nonhuman environ-
ments, out of their efforts to settle both themselves and the phenomenal surfaces of their
locations, has come, among other things, the
American version of what most people today
call nature writing. At its most characteristically American, it captures and reflects the peculiarly deep and detailed, if often troublesome,
relationship between ego and ecos, or psyche and bios, in American
history and culture. In its distinctive combination of pointedly personal narrative and pointedly impersonal, "scientific" description
or exposition, it derives directly from the experience of those early
American settlers who found themselves caught, quite unwillingly,
between their needs to account for personal experience and their
needs to account impersonally for the features of their nonhuman
surroundings—to begin with, at least, without the reassuring inter-
polations of historically established social, economic, or political
customs and institutions, much less the comforting intercessions of
a nationally sanctioned ecclesiastical polity.

In its special, attempted blend of spiritual autobiography and
systematic biology, ecology, or natural history, American nature
writing plays the deep self-doubts of a Nathaniel Hawthorne off

153

against the taxonomical assertions of a William Bartram; and, in so doing, comprehends the early and classic American's desire to fill the empty psychic space not only between an insignificant self and "the huge apparition of society" or "the even larger form of the human race," but also between that self and the still larger form of NATURE as a whole.

American nature writing contains, then, the early and classic American's quest both for a coherent sense of self and a coherent sense of place. It dramatizes as does no other form of writing the intimate and largely unmediated engagement of individual human self and nonhuman other that is classically, if not definitively, American. It captures and explores the radically different modes of ordering experience that first attained full expression in Aristotle's *Historia Animalium* and Saint Augustine's *Confessions* and that later came together with particular force in early America. It is, in fact, largely the product of these two traditional modes of thought. It is likewise the largely unarbitrated expression of the two—geobiotic science and autobiography—which has arisen from the early experience of what Seymour Martin Lipset has called "The First New Nation," that America born of rebellion in which an uprooted individual attempts to deal with the details of an unsettled land while simultaneously setting out to redeem history, human nature, and the traditional institutions that might aid him in coming to terms with himself and his nonhuman surroundings.

At its best and most characteristic, in fact, American nature writing is quite unlike the "nature writing" of any other nation or culture. Indeed, were we to apply the term "nature writing" solely to works that address themselves both to intense self-assertion or self-analysis and to insistently intricate, systematic delineations of geobiotic others, we would find ourselves referring almost exclusively to an American form of writing. Under such a restricted (if accurate) definition, to read nature writing would be to read almost entirely in the tradition of Thoreau, Leopold, Dillard, and Janovy.

In one sense, of course, all so-called nature writing—in prose or poetry, in Chinese or English—is concerned primarily with relations between "I" and "It," relations between the human self of its author or narrator and the stuff of the geobiotic other, which, in English at least, is nonhuman nature. The best and most characteristic American nature writers, however, have been more concerned than their British or Chinese counterparts both with the isolate human self and with the systematic identification and exposition of what we call the nonhuman environment.

For what are by now, perhaps, obvious reasons, the best American nature writers have been more dedicated (or driven) than the "nature writers" of other cultures to the causes and needs of the solitary human self. The most characteristically American among them have been more inclined than their counterparts in Europe or South America or the Orient to celebrate or accentuate the idiosyncrasies of individual behavior and conception and, in general, far more inclined to separate the human individual—the narrating perceiver, actor, and appreciator—both from others of its psycho- and sociobiotic kind and from the kinds of historically established systems of thought or organization—religious or metaphysical, political or economic—that would associate them with such human others.

By some of the same tokens of American ideology and history, American nature writers have been far more dedicated than their counterparts in other nations to the disinterested and nonsectarian codification of their geobiotic surroundings. On the whole, they have found it far easier to "free" their explanations of their environments from the kinds of deep associations with coherent mythological traditions or long-established connections among castes and classes that have inevitably characterized the works of their counterparts in other countries. Conversely, they have found it far more difficult (when they have so desired) to connect their observations of phoebes, ants, or cheat grass to meaningful religious, social, or political traditions. They have had to press hard, much harder even than their Australian or Canadian cousins, to lend the elements of their geobiotic environments extended metaphoric or spiritual meaning. To create working American bestiaries, if indeed they have succeeded, they have had to deal in often strained hyperbole, if not in the bombast which de Tocqueville years ago predicted would typify their efforts; for they have been unable to assume even a regional communality of tradition and experience in themselves or in their audiences.

As a result, the best and most characteristic of them have been much less inclined than their counterparts elsewhere to define the self in humanly communal terms, whether historic, political, economic, or broadly cultural. Concomitantly, they have been far more inclined to define that self in terms of its relations to a basically nonhuman community, to what they have wanted to view as an apolitical and noneconomic community of flora and fauna whose relationships have ranged from the openly predatory and even violent to the spiritually symbiotic. The self of the best American nature writing has been far more inclined than its counterpart elsewhere to consider, assert, and even celebrate its own predatory instincts. Similarly, it has been much more disposed to ponder and even to accentuate the whimsical and profligate, the improvident and rapacious, the recondite and enigmatic in nonhuman nature.

The works of the best and most characteristic American nature writers have tended, then, to purify or, in a mathematical sense, to radicalize the relations among self and nonhuman other which in the "nature writing" of other cultures have been moderated by sociopolitical custom and habit, by economic considerations, or by long-established mythological and theological tradition. The best of America's nature writers and their narrators have been far more self-conscious than their counterparts elsewhere. The worst have been far less self-conscious. By the same reasoning, the best and most characteristic American nature writing has been far less secure psychologically and philosophically, far less inclined to absorb or portray the self in humanly communal relations, and far less disposed to compromise either personal eccentricity or the singular, prodigious, and inscrutable in nonhuman nature by subsuming them in a peace-seeking human community. Indeed, in the literatures of many nations of the world, one is hard-pressed to find anything even vaguely similar to *The Desert Year* of Joseph Wood Krutch or *The Singing Wilderness* of Sigurd Olson, much less to *Walden* or *Pilgrim at Tinker Creek*.

Except momentarily, the best and most characteristic American nature writing has lacked the equanimity and contentment, the solid normalcy, if not the spiritual quietude, of the "nature writing" of other cultures. And the reasons for the differences are not difficult to discover. As Raymond Williams and W. J. Keith have recently demonstrated, what has often been loosely called the nature writing of England is not nature writing at all in the sense that *Walden* and *A Sand County Almanac* are. As both Keith and Williams have shown, and with quite different commitments, the writings of the Gilbert Whites, William Cobbetts, Richard Jefferies, and W. H. Hudsons of Britain (writings popularly associated with the American works of Thoreau, Burroughs, Muir, and Teale) compose not a tradition of nature writing in the American sense but, rather, a tradition of rural writing, a tradition perhaps as distinctly or originally British as nature writing of the Thoreauvian kind seems to be distinctly American.

As Keith's *The Rural Tradition* amply illustrates, the "nature writers" of Britain have traditionally been concerned with the countryside and the habits and customs of countrymen as much, if not more, than they have with their own psychic and spiritual states or the strictly geobiotic states of their nonhuman surroundings. In fact, as Keith has indicated, both implicitly and explicitly, it has been virtually impossible for so-called British nature writers to separate the consideration of their own psychic states from the psychic and social (as well as political and economic) states of their fellow countrymen—villagers, shopkeepers, farmers, or country laborers. Concomitantly, it has been just as difficult for them to separate the historically coordinated condition of themselves and their rural kind, permanent or transient, from the condition of the nonhuman environment. As a result, British "nature writing"—like almost all the "nature writing" of other Western nations, and a good deal of the literature wrongly labeled "nature writing" in the United States—has traditionally contained and depended upon a socioeconomic or broadly sociological commitment to the states, both past and present, of a country life defined largely not by the interactions of self and nonhuman nature but by the historic practices and causes of rural human society. As Williams, especially, makes clear, the literature of the rural tradition in Britain is characterized not by the opposition of individual person and nonhuman nature but, rather, by the historical and, finally, psychosocial or socioeconomic opposition of town or city and country. As Keith, in turn, has reminded us, such a literature is georgic rather than pastoral in its motivations, concerns, and persuasions.[1]

The literary tradition of which Keith and Williams speak has, of course, had its crucial place in American history and culture, as it has in the histories and cultures of Australia and Canada. In fact, it has been at least as significant to the history and culture of the United States as has the tradition of nature writing; and historians and critics would do well to heed the example of Williams and Keith by following the rural tradition in literature to America, by discriminating its forms and analyzing its persuasions, and by tracing its patterns from Susan Fenimore Cooper's *Rural Hours* through the writings of Hamlin Garland to the essays of Wendell Berry, from Henry Beston's *Northern Farm* through Vance Bourjaily's *Country Matters* and Noel Perrin's persons rural to the likes of Peter Matson's *A Place in the Country* and Sue Hubbell's *A Country Year*. Indeed, it is hard to imagine how any critic or historian can reasonably claim to understand modern American literature or culture without having some minimal acquaintance with the revival of the rural tradition in the second half of the twentieth century. At the same time, critics and historians, as well as publishers and readers, would be well advised to avoid confusing the rural tradition in literature with the tradition of American nature writing; for though the two traditions obviously influence each other, they are fundamentally different in literary kind, if not in broadly cultural function and place.

Unlike their British counterparts, and unlike writers of the rural tradition everywhere, American nature writers have been unable to create, and at least half unwilling to seek, the kinds of coherent normative views of self, society, and nonhuman nature that have typified the literature of the countryside. Except in the generic terms of a "land ethic," or the even more abstract terms of metaphysics or theology, they have been reluctant to seek the historic equanimity or communal commitment of the rural tradition; for they have most often viewed any and all developed human relations as violations of (or interferences in) their special, original, and prehistoric relations to nonhuman nature. In short, they have been unable to resolve their competing allegiances toward human history and the human community, rural or urban.

While they have shared with writers of the rural tradition a georgic disposition to reject urbane civilization, they have not sought its historic and moral alternative in the farm or the village. Their relations to farmers and villagers, like their relations to urban visitors and institutions, have characteristically been distant and far less detailed than their relations to rattlesnakes, chickadees, or muskrats. At the same time, though they have shared with writers of the rural tradition a disposition to retreat from "society" and to separate themselves from developed human relations, their perspectives on their surroundings have been only partially pastoral; for they have as often been possessing actors and even questing predators (if not angry moralists) as they have been disembodied meditators or dispossessed appreciators. Their causes, then, have not been to detailed, dramatized visions of sociobiotic harmony, at least not among humans; for they have always suspected that such human relations are, by their very nature, disharmonious. Their fealty and homage they have paid not to the Ceres and Hermes of harvest, marketplace, and commercial conversation—not to the Vesta or the Penates of hearth and home, nor even, except momentarily, to the dancing figure of Pan—but rather to the lonely, chaste huntress, Artemis, and, perhaps, to Orion. Their overwhelming dedication has been to the psychobiotic relations of a self segregated from its human kind and seeking, at least half uneasily, integration with (or meaningful segregation from) its aboriginal nonhuman kind.

In this regard, and in several others, the best and most characteristic American nature writing has been much closer in broad persuasion—if not also in style and point of view—to the classic American novel (and a good deal of American poetry) than it has been to literature of the rural tradition, in either England or

America. In fact, the most characteristic American nature writing has borne a relation to literature of the rural tradition strikingly similar to the relation between classic American fiction and fiction of the great British tradition; and the salient characteristics of the best American nature writing have been much closer in form, type, style, and tone to the classic American novel than they have been to traditional rural writing.

Though Thoreau and Janovy, or Leopold and Dillard, may not have created fabulous or melodramatic "worlds elsewhere" in the manner of Cooper and Melville, or Hawthorne and Faulkner, they certainly have come close, much closer than Cobbett and Hudson, or Jefferies and Collis. Though their nature writings—like the nature writings of Burroughs, Muir, Krutch, and Olson—have been dedicated in substantial part to the detailed delineation of intimately local places, the places they have detailed and codified have, on the whole, been far removed from the normal daily life of their surrounding human communities. More often than not they have rendered the phenomenal surfaces of their locations in scientific or near-scientific terms, in the vocabularies of geology, ecology, and natural history rather than the vocabulary of local folklore or everyday colloquial usage. Typically, their narrators have been (or have wanted to be) at least amateur scientists—botanists, ecologists, or ornithologists; and, hence, their identifications of and with their surroundings have almost invariably been in some fundamental way scientific. Typically, too, they have occupied a large part of their time in the supposedly simple business of identifying and codifying the elements of their nonhuman surroundings. At times, in fact, they have seemed almost to reify the processes of taxonomical categorization and scientifically systematic exposition. In short, they have been far more concerned than writers of the rural tradition with the business of fixing in mind and language their geobiotic environments.

At the same time, they have tended to view and present that business as a fundamentally personal (rather than institutional) endeavor; and characteristically their relations to their nonhuman environments have been as personally (if not privately) intense as they have been scientific—as intense, certainly, as Ahab's relations to Moby Dick or Nick Adams's to the grasshoppers and trout of the Big Two-Hearted River—and far more intense than anything which has yet surfaced in the literature of the rural tradition.

Nothing in the literature of the rural tradition, British or American, can rival the intensity of Aldo Leopold's relation to the sandhill crane or Thoreau's to the surfaces and depths of Walden Pond. Not even Gilbert White's celebrated tortoise can rival in concentrated energy John Hay's absorption with the alewife or Annie Dillard's with and in the giant water bug:

> A couple of summers ago I was walking along the edge of the island to see what I could see in the water, and mainly to scare frogs. Frogs have an inelegant way of taking off from invisible positions on the bank just ahead of your feet, in dire panic, emitting a froggy "Yike!" and splashing into the water. Incredibly, this amused me, and, incredibly, it amuses me still. As I walked along the grassy edge of the island, I got better and better at seeing frogs both in and out of the water. I learned to recognize, slowing down, the difference in texture of the light reflected from mudbank, water, grass, or frog. Frogs were flying all around me. At the end of the island I noticed a small green frog. He was exactly half in and half out of the water, looking like a schematic diagram of an amphibian, and he didn't jump.
>
> He didn't jump; I crept closer. At last I knelt on the island's winterkilled grass, lost, dumbstruck, staring at the frog in the creek just four feet away. He was a very small frog with wide, dull eyes. And just as I looked at him, he slowly crumpled and began to sag. The spirit vanished from his eyes as if snuffed. His skin emptied and drooped; his very skull seemed to collapse and settle like a kicked tent. He was shrinking before my eyes like a deflating football. I watched the taut, glistening skin on his shoulders ruck, and rumple, and fall. Soon, part of his skin, formless as a pricked balloon, lay in floating folds like bright scum on top of the water: it was a monstrous and terrifying thing. I gaped bewildered, appalled. An oval shadow hung in the water behind the drained frog; then the shadow glided away. The frog skin bag started to sink.
>
> I had read about the giant water bug, but never seen one. "Giant water bug" is really the name of the creature, which is an enormous, heavy-bodied brown beetle. It eats insects, tadpoles, fish, and frogs. Its grasping forelegs are mighty and hooked inward. It seizes a victim with these legs, hugs it tight, and paralyzes it with enzymes injected during a vicious bite. That one bite is the only bite it ever takes. Through the puncture shoot the poisons that dissolve the victim's muscles and bones and organs—all but the skin—and through it the giant water bug sucks out the victim's body, reduced to a juice. This event is quite common in warm fresh water. The frog I saw was being sucked by a giant water bug. I had been kneeling on the island grass; when the unrecognizable flap of frog skin settled on the creek bottom, swaying, I stood up and brushed the knees of my pants. I couldn't catch my breath.[2]

A writer of the rural tradition would undoubtedly accuse Dillard of being too "het up," of reading too much into (or out of) her experience with a common bug. And that, of course, is just the point.

Dillard's giant water bug bears more similarities to Ike Mc-Caslin's bear than it does to the garden tortoise of Gilbert White. It is alternately to be respected and feared, respected to the point of being enthralled, feared to the point of all but losing control. Where White literally befriends his tortoise by rendering its unfamiliarity familiar, by granting it neighborly citizenship, and by absorbing it into the moral center of domestic and communal life, the pilgrim at Tinker Creek moves or shies away from the domestically and communally familiar. She seeks beneath and beyond ordinary friendship and social familiarity. Like Thoreau, she seeks "to drive life into a corner" or, conversely, to be driven herself into a corner. Like Thoreau, she seeks to reduce life to its lowest, or to uncover its highest, terms and conditions. Going before or after the normal and conventional, she seeks the essentials of life to find them, at once, spellbinding beyond citizenship and overwhelming beyond easy moral control.

In just such a fashion, the best and most characteristic American nature writing—like the classic American novel—has moved "among extreme ranges of experience" (the phrase belongs to Richard Chase) rather than working the solid middle ground which has traditionally characterized rural writing. From *Walden* through *A Sand County Almanac* to *Desert Solitare* and *Keith County Journal*, American nature writing has ranged from minute observation and straightforward classification to metaphysical and theological questioning, from extreme self-consciousness to anthropological reflection, from intense self-analysis and personal reaction to unconscious identification of the elements of the geobiotic environment.[3]

In fact, virtually all of the characteristics Chase has pointed to in distinguishing the classic American novel from its British counterpart can be applied as well, with but slight modifications, to classic American nature writing. Thus, the best and most characteristic American nature writing not only "moves among extreme ranges of experience," but, as I hope the essays to follow will demonstrate, it also tends "to rest in contradictions" rather than attempt to resolve them. It tends to rest in paradoxical tensions and in the irreconcilable competing allegiances of the early (and classic) American self: in the basic need of that self to fix with certainty the elements of its environment, particularly its nonhuman environment, and in its contrary need to unfix previous codifications of its environment as it attempts to create and explore a new relation to Nature, whatever the risks to its own desired stability.

If and when American nature writing attempts to resolve contradictions, it may not quite do so "in oblique, morally equivocal ways," but it certainly does do so in ways that do not fully engage characters other than an ever-present narrator, and in styles and fashions that do not enlist the aid of the social or political institutions of historic human communities. If and when it does seek to reconcile the competing allegiances of "I" and "It," it may not do so in the extreme melodramatic manner of *Moby-Dick*—though melodrama is far from foreign to the texture of its narrator's relations to nonhuman nature—but it certainly does do so in snatches of "pastoral idyl."

Even the pastoral moments of American nature writing, however, are curious constructions when placed beside the eclogues of Virgil or Milton or Wordsworth; for the singular pastoral figure of American nature writing is almost invariably part scientist and part metaphysician, part poet and part autobiographer, part botanist and part philosopher. More often than not, in fact, the narrator of American nature writing cannot rest content in idyllic pastoral. More often than not it seems, he or she must go on to question the motives of traditional pastoralism, either its presumed quietude or its high-flown urbanity—on all counts its conspicuous lack of familiarity with giant water bugs, sandhill cranes, alewives, glaciers, and their engaged human perceivers.

Perhaps the most conspicuous trait of American nature writing—other than its dedication to geobiotic science and metaphysics or epistemology—is its narrator, the prototypical "I" of so much American literature, an Ishmael-like figure ranging the gamut of philosophical stances and psychological states, constantly (and unpredictably) shifting its point of view (both grammatical and philosophic), continually changing its tenses, its vocabulary, and its stylistic techniques—in almost every way indicating both the basic instability of its positions or perspectives and its final reluctance to bring conventional, "civilized" order to an experience best lived and understood in a continual series of situational surprises or unanticipated discoveries, and best responded to with momentarily brilliant flashes of insight or straightforward instances of recognition, short-lived orders (however penetrating or comforting) that are most genuine because most pointedly occasional.

By contrast with its counterpart in literature of the rural tradition, the almost invariable narrative "I" of American nature writing is a figure alternately possessed, either implicitly or explicitly (or both), by its need to possess or appropriate (to speak of "my" river or "my" raccoon) and by its need to be completely dispossessed (to speak of being released "into an order of timelessness," or simply to concentrate its every attention on the loquacious bird overhead).[4] The narrator of American nature writing would, on the one hand, command or master its environment; and yet it would also lose itself either in the unconscious business of identifying its surroundings or in the more mystical experience of being utterly immersed in them. Unlike its counterpart, when there is one, in literature of the rural tradition, this narrating self would not only assemble but also disassemble—and, what is more, *be* disassembled. Alternately passive and active in both grammatical and psychic mood, it would settle both itself and its environment, and yet simultaneously unsettle them (and, hence, be utterly unsettled *by* them)—all in manners, moods, and styles quite foreign to traditional rural writing.

What American nature writing and its narrators have *not* attempted is what rural writing has always depended upon—a vision of a largely communal life, a life of agricultural seasons and customs which, if rightly conceived and adopted, would resolve the tensions of modern life. In fact, American nature writing has been "rural," if at all, only in the very limited sense that many of its practitioners have written from nonurban areas. Some, of course, have written from what might conventionally be called rural environs; but even they have been less dedicated to the portrayal of local, agrarian character and custom than they have been to the delineation and exposition of the nonhuman environment and to the meanings derivable from intimate personal relations to its elements. More, perhaps, have written from areas of mountaintops, forests, deserts, or lakes which have little if anything directly to do with the agriculture and agronomy of traditional rural writing. Several, in fact, have written from what must be classified as suburban areas, nonagricultural areas on the fringes of urban centers of population; and at least a few have written from pointedly urban environments (see, for example, John Kieran, *Natural History of New York City*).[5] All in all, then, it must be said that American nature writing has been more devoted to natural science, metaphysics, and self-analysis than it has been to the conditions of an agricultural and agronomic community.

Where the causes and occasions of rural writing have consistently been sociobiotic and socioeconomic (if not, on occasion, overtly political), the causes and occasions of American nature writing, like the underlying drama of a good deal of American literature and art, have traditionally been psychobiotic. In a manner consonant with America's "case against history," American nature writing has sought to clear the stage of normal social, economic, and political

life.[6] When it has approached political, economic, or social issues, it
has done so indirectly, if not in oblique ways, then by embedding
such issues in abstract saunterings on ecological balance and imbalance or by embodying them in its narrator's personal meditations on the state of nature or society as a whole. What it has not
done is to dramatize those issues in the speech and daily lives of
fully developed characters.

Unlike writing of the rural tradition, at least in its British forms,
American nature writing has not sought a middle ground, a concili-
ation or reconciliation of the extremes of experience through the
human community, whether village, farm, or family. When it has
dealt with the opposition of town or city and country, American
nature writing has done so only in nondramatic ways, by address-
ing the issue abstractly or by embodying it in the complaints of its
narrator. It has not sought to detail, and certainly not to dramatize
(except perhaps humorously), the sociopolitical or sociobiotic life of
its narrator or his neighbors. In fact, the narrators and major figures
of American nature writing have never been granted a developed
political persuasion of any discernible kind. If anything, they have
tended to view conventional political, social, and economic life with
the eye of a metaphysician or theologue—the eye of an evolutionary
biologist, self-conscious ecologist, or thinking paleontologist—who
can see the "ratiocinative" efforts of *Homo sapiens* for what they
are in evolutionary and ecological perspective, species-specific pre-
tenses to territory (abstract or concrete, conceptual or factual),
semipathetic quests for order and security in a universe dead-set
against the perpetuity of any single species or ecosystem.

The characteristic persuasions of American nature writing have
been evolutionary, metaphysical, and theoretically ecological rather
than political, economic, or sociological. Few, if any, of the narrators
of American nature writing have led normal economic lives, and
none has been seriously engaged in the regular socioeconomic life
of his or her community. The usual daily routines of both author
and narrator of American nature writing have, in fact, been far less
directly presented and far more difficult to derive from the text than
have the routines of their counterparts in writing of the rural tradition. Few, if any, of the narrators of American nature writing have
been blessed with a consistent means of income; and when they
have been, neither their own daily efforts nor the efforts of their
human neighbors have had much to do with their basic substance
or sustenance. More often than not, they have withdrawn from customary socioeconomic life and retired from the usual business of
making a living. Typically, they have presented the illusion of being
engaged in largely noneconomic relations with the nonhuman ele-

ments of a local or regional ecosystem, relations psychic and biotic as well as intellectual—but social only in a very special sense.

Characteristically, and tellingly, the narrators and central figures of American nature writing have most often been propertyless. Typically, the land they have "possessed" they have neither owned nor worked, and never worked for. The possessives they have applied to the features of their nonhuman surroundings have been psychic—figurative, as we say, rather than literal—aesthetic, philosophic, or scientific rather than legal or economic. Typically, too, their lives have been sexless and—in a conventional, human sense—loveless. More often than not, they have had few decent, human acquaintances, and even fewer close friends. At least as tellingly, they have had few specific human dislikes—few concrete aversions to or loathings for things or persons human, other than traits in themselves or trends in society as a whole.

In a sense, then, one might say that American nature writing has been fundamentally pastoral in its motives and manners. Certainly, there has been much in American cultural and intellectual history to encourage such a view.[7] Certainly, too, at least in the abstract, American nature writing has been far more pastoral than georgic—as metaphysical as it has been physical, as passively reflective as it has been actively engaged, and far more antisocial and apolitical than politically concerned or sociologically interested.

The "pastoralism" of American nature writing, however, has been far from conventional. Even as its narrators have withdrawn from normal socioeconomic life, shunning the human community and appreciating the distant prospects of man and nonhuman nature, they have appreciated as well (in more than one sense) their own states; and unlike the central figure of classical pastoral, they have consistently argued, both implicitly and explicitly, the vital activity and even physicality of their intellectual and linguistic pursuits. If they have been so-called aesthetic appreciators, they have also been eager, scientific investigators, wetland seekers of the western grebe, understoried stalkers of the hermit thrush, wet-bellied musers on the surfaces of ice-covered ponds. In quite "unpastoral" relations with their environments, they have scratched and scrambled the canyon walls and rockfaces of the West, and crouched in nose-dripping concentration upon the muskrat's bridges of the East. And while they have consciously sought the somewhat "pastoral" perspectives of evolutionary biology and paleontology (if not, indeed, of Romantic landscape art—the distant prospects of the picturesque and the awe-full conceptions of the sublime), they have also sought and taken the "antipastoral" perspective of the modern poet or novelist, for whom the business of writing and art is all too clearly a matter of gaining and keeping control of one's experience, a far from pastoral control, garnered not in easy, comforting appreciation of distant environments but, rather, in the often discomforting business of attempting, in a primitive sense, to know—to name and detail—the phenomenal surfaces of one's immediate location.

The conventional distinction between the pastoral and the georgic is, in fact, only misleadingly applied to American nature writing. For America's best and most characteristic nature writers have consistently queried both the logic and the metaphysics, if not the sociology and the politics, of that distinction. They have consistently queried both the practical dualism of town and country and the more theoretical dualisms of mind and body or meditation and action so often associated with it. In like manner, they have consistently questioned as well those other dualistic categories of Western experience so often used to explain what is by now nearly an ontological opposition between pastoral appreciation and georgic engagement—subject and object, metaphor and fact, word and thing—emotion and reason, art (or poetry) and science (or reality)—and, above all, man and nature. Perhaps because their narrators have been "isolated" scientists or "idiosyncratic" writers and artists, American nature writers have constantly fought the traditional implication that science and authorship, even when practiced privately, are somehow removed from the customary run of meaningful daily life. They have normally argued, in fact—for their own sakes as well as others'—that the customary run of human, social life, in both town and country, is either benumbing or utterly disillusioning. The meaningful life, in turn (a life prior to both country and town), they have found in relations—intellectual as well as emotional, linguistic as well as nonlinguistic—of individual human self and nonhuman environment.

America's best nature writers, then, have consistently rejected the notion that the lonely seeker's life is either inactive or ideal. Though they may, in one sense, have adopted a "pastoral" mode of existence, they have consistently argued, both implicitly and explicitly, that the supposedly comforting perspectives offered by pastoral living are anything but comforting. Instead, they have been inclined to remind us that "pastoral harmony" is nothing but a potentially unsettling ideal, and so-called pastoral living far more alive (and, hence, active) than either georgic or urban life—far more alive and unsettling because far less subject to the insulations, arbitrations, and conciliations of the organized human community.

On the whole, America's nature writers and their narrators have found the farmer's life no more satisfying that the urban politician's or the suburban salesman's. Again and again, they have argued that the truth of one's relations to nonhuman nature is found, if it is to be found, not in the opposition of town and country, nor even in the conflict of wilderness and civilization, but in the exploration of a relationship (sometimes conflicting, sometimes harmonious) at once far more primitive and far more abstract, far more personal and far more impersonal, than any such easy phrasing can suggest—in the conflict of the civilized and the wild in one's self, in the conflict within one's self between the desire to accept and enhance the orders and distinctions of traditional Western civilization and the desire to reject those distinctions because they misrepresent, if not falsify, the original relation of human individual and nonhuman other.

For reasons that have much to do with their early American heritage, America's nature writers have never been comfortable with the classical categories of Western thought and culture. At their worst, they have parroted those categories (and the classifications that follow from them) with a blind obedience that borders on obsessive need. In such an unthinking frame of mind, they have produced the kind of nature writing that says little more than "today the first redpoll (*Acanthus flammea*) of the season came to the feeder" or "the sandhill cranes (*Grus canadensis*) built a gigantic nest in a low tree overlooking Houge's bog"—terribly primitive identification and reportage which, while reinforcing and reciting the codification of America's environments, nonetheless betrays an insistent need simply to know and record the elements of one's surroundings. At their best, on the other hand, they have done much more than simple recording and classifying, much more than easy meditating. They have disputed the traditional categories of Western experience even as they have used them, and they have continued to be uncomfortable, if not distressed, with conventional understandings of man's relations to nature. Characteristically, they have found the terms of pastoral vision as much frustrating as pacifying, the georgic condition as stultifying as it is amiable, and the classic Western distinction between human and nonhuman as misleading as it is psychobiotically necessary.

At their best, American nature writers have seriously puzzled over the relationship between language and reality, even as they have fussed over the conventional separation of human subject and natural object, and generally doubted the modern distinction between appreciation, aesthetic or otherwise, and action—all because these categorical discriminations, and others like them, have seemed woefully inadequate to their own and their ancestors' experiences as Americans. If there has been much in their literary and intellectual heritage to encourage them to distinguish between the pastoral and the georgic, there has been little in their daily experiences of their environments to cement that distinction, and much in their ideological and political history to incite them to reject it. If there has been much in their European heritage to press upon them discriminations between name and nature, or nature and nurture—between metaphor and fact, or emotion and reason—there has been much in their revolutionary heritage to lead them to disavow such discriminations, and even more perhaps in their daily experience to undermine or seriously qualify them.

Mythic visions of America to the contrary, the central figures of American nature writing, like their ancestors, have traditionally begun their experiences of American environments in a condition somewhat less or more than pastoral; and, like their ancestors, they have typically concluded that experience in a condition more or less than georgic. To a great extent, they have owed and declared their allegiance not to Jefferson's nation of yeomen farmers but to a special version of R. W. B. Lewis's "American Adam," an isolate, independent (and occasionally alienated) figure who, through strength of will and mind, is uncoerced by human society, unrestricted (except by psychobiotic needs and philosophic concerns) and, yet, able to comprehend both social coercion and psychobiotic limitation. The central narrating figures of the best American nature writing have, in fact, borne greater affinity to Ishmael, Huck Finn, and Ike McCaslin than they have to Crevecoeur's farmer or Gilbert White's village curate; and if they have sought to clear the stage of human history, to restore man's original relation to the earth, or to start completely anew in the quest for psychoecological harmony, they have done so not in the spirit of American agrarianism or British country life (which has seemed, at best, an already disproven ideal) but in the spirit and for the cause of the largely self-sufficient American individual in whose life are contained all the essential truths, foreboding or promising, of mankind's relations to nonhuman nature.

In several regards, then, the "stories" and "minds" of American nature writing—like the stories and minds of Ishmael, Huck, and Nick Carraway—have tended to bear out de Tocqueville's and Tony Tanner's comments on the American writer of fiction, who "tends to start from a closely perceived sub-social or non-social reality and attempts to move towards some sort of metaphysical and philosophical generalization."[8] In several other regards, however, the minds of the best American nature writing seem to have gone the classic American novel one better or deeper in the dramatization they have given to American experience. The "sub-social or non-social reality" they may be said to have "started from" has, of course, always been far more pointedly subsocial—and far less easy to presuppose, far harder to come by—than it has been in American fiction. Like America's early explorers, discoverers, and settlers, the central figures of American nature writing have indeed been preoccupied with what Tanner calls the "minutely scrutinized particular," far more preoccupied than Ishmael or Huck—more preoccupied, even, than Nick Adams. And the reasons for their preoccupations with minute detail—the causes of their inabilities to find (or rest content with) the solid middle ground of rural literature—are (or ought to be) immediately clear. The "minutely scrutinized particular" has not been given in their American experience. The name and nature of the loquacious bird overhead have not been (as they could not have been) assumable.

Concomitantly, and understandably, the philosophic generalizations toward which the central figures of the best American nature writing may be said to have moved have as often led to epistemological and ethical ambiguity as they have to Tanner's "vague affirmative generalization." Their vague affirmative generalizations, in turn—when they have occurred—have almost invariably been expressions both of their epistemological incertitude and of their plain, daily insecurity. Their frequent epistemological queries—their doubts even about the status and functions of the minutely scrutinized particular, if not their considerable disquietude about their own roles in scrutinizing the particular—have naturally and inevitably derived, on the one hand, from a nearly obsessive drive to fix, in mind as in language, the elements of their nonhuman surroundings and, on the other hand, from an almost debilitating self-consciousness, an awareness of themselves and their relations to their environments so deep and quite simply primitive that they have always been able to see, however reluctantly, the human and personal interests—psychological as well as sociological, primitively biotic as well as intricately historic—in supposedly impersonal, "disinterested" accounts of their nonhuman surroundings.

Crucial as such disinterested, scientific accounts of their environments and themselves have been to their own sanity and security, their native suspicions of the psychology and sociology—if not the commerce and politics—of impersonal, scientific knowledge have frequently led them to consider such knowledge, including their own acquired expertise, as a fundamentally personal and psychobiotic phenomenon, as a psychobiotic and even poetic quest for working, autobiographical figures of thought and speech, psychoterritorial figures they have been more than willing to see as well in the songs of orioles and cardinals as in the cries of coyotes and cranes. For reasons and causes that have much to do with the intimacy of their daily experiences of their environments, and much to do as well with their desires to accent human kinship with the non-human—to extend democratic empathy from human to nonhuman kind—the central, narrating figures of the best American nature writing have as often drawn lines of affinity between themselves and their nonhuman others as they have drawn lines of distinction—and in that former way, as every Western psychologist knows, lies madness or poetry or mystic vision—anthropomorphism, personification, and the pathetic fallacy.

The best of the minds of American nature writing have, then, consistently ruminated upon the personal and immediate needs served by (and expressed in) scientific identification and explanation. Science, in fact, has always been for them far more (or less) than a simple matter of discovering the facts, naming the phenomenon, or confirming the paradigm. It has always been a process, a matter, and a business of establishing initial and yet somehow simultaneously sanctioned orders for what they have needed to see both as an idiosyncratic, utterly personal, autobiographical experience and as an experience deriving from and participating in— even as it exemplifies and comprehends—the entirety of mankind's relations to nature. They have wanted, on the one hand, to discover, or recover, and portray mankind's original relation to nature. On the other hand, they have wanted to declare their experiences utterly new in history, utterly unique and distinctive—if occasionally all too distinctive, all too original. Like many an early American settler, they have been caught between two competing conceptions of the "original," if not the "aboriginal"—the absolutely new and the protohistorical. They have wanted to have their aboriginal American cake and to eat it, well decorated, at the same time.

If their personal, intimate, and intricate efforts to come to terms with themselves by coming to impersonal terms with their nonhuman environments have led them to far greater than average doubts about the "disinterested" business or science of accounting for the nonhuman environment, their awareness of the interests— personal as well as cultural, psychobiotic as well as sociobiotic— veiled in such "disinterested" terms has, when combined with their native American suspicions of things established and institutional, led them to be even more suspicious—not because they have not needed such established, sanctioned identifications and explanations, but rather because they have needed them so desperately, and because they have been all too aware of their needs. The central figures of the best American nature writing have been all too aware that what T. S. Kuhn calls "normal science" is far too "normal," far too basic and primitive—primordial, if not pristine—to be explained simply by referring to the detailed confirmation of previously established paradigms.[9] Even as they have needed such paradigms and their established taxonomies to get a fix on their environments, even as they have sought the security such paradigms and their vocabularies càn provide, they have suspected them of providing a false sense of security.

Like the early and classic American self attempting to settle, the minds of the best American nature writing have believed, on the one hand, that *their* experiences of *their* surroundings have been (and are) unique and distinctive. Hence, they have always been tempted to remain silent about them, to treasure in private, incommunicable measure their own special, intimate understandings of their sacred, local, and immediately intricate places. On the other hand, they have just as strongly needed to blow the trumpet of their own special, original conditions—especially their aboriginal, prelinguistic relations to nonhuman nature—and that need has, of course, driven them to use the very established, sanctioned, shared, and hence unoriginal language for man's relations to nonhuman nature which they have otherwise sought to avoid or deny. Like the mystic who wishes to capture eternity in language, they have been caught between their desires to have their original, prehistoric, and prelinguistic relations to nonhuman nature and, simultaneously, to have others appreciate them, if not duplicate them—in short, to bring them into history, literature, and culture. They have wanted their relations to nonhuman nature to be both mysterious and original, if not originally wild, and yet also completely comprehensible and generally understood. Under the circumstances, it may be small wonder that Emerson found Thoreau so difficult to read.

Part Three

Three Variations on the Type

H. D. T. sends me a paper with the old fault of unlimited contradiction. The trick of his rhetoric is soon learned: it consists in substituting for the obvious word & thought its diametrical antagonist. He praises wild mountains & winter forests for their domestic air; snow & ice for their warmth; villagers & wood choppers for their urbanity; and the wilderness for resembling Rome & Paris. With the constant inclination to dispraise cities & civilization, he yet can find no way to know woods & woodmen except by paralleling them with towns & townsmen. . . . it makes me nervous and wretched to read it.

EMERSON, Journals

Thoreau is never wholly a man of the transcendental camp. He is, in a sense, a double agent.

LOREN EISELEY, The Star Thrower

We oscillate between wishing we were unreflective animals and wishing we were disembodied spirits, for in either case we should not be problematic to ourselves.

W. H. AUDEN, "Concerning the Unpredictable,"
the introduction to Loren Eiseley's The Star Thrower

Chapter Six

Walden and Paradox:
Thoreau as Self-Conscious
Ecologist

f, from the beginning, in the age of ecology as in the age of transcendentalism, so many Americans have oscillated between wishing they were "unreflective animals" and wishing they were "disembodied spirits" or minds (both conditions being more easily achieved the less they are thought about), and if the best of America's nature writers have known these oscillations in the extreme, then perhaps one can explain something of Emerson's distress with Thoreau by considering *Walden* as a book of three voices—three perspectives, three epistemologies, perhaps even three metaphysical points of view. The first such perspective might be called the perspective of the philosophic environmentalist or naturalist. The second might be called the perspective of the personalist or philosophic idealist. And the third might readily be called the perspective of the self-conscious ecologist, provided, of course, that the terms "ecology" and "ecological" are adequately understood in each of their current meanings: as science, subject matter, and normative point of view; as method, phenomenon, and ideal; as both "is" and "ought," and as the means of relating the two.

If one might isolate these three points of view, momentarily wrenching them from their contexts in *Walden*, one might uncover a good deal of what Stanley Cavell has called *Walden*'s "power of dialectic," and discover coincidentally substantial similarities between the voices and styles of *Walden* and the "unsettling of perspective" that Sharon Cameron has noted not simply as the practice of Thoreau's *Journal* but as its prevailing *subject*.[1]

   The environmentalist's metaphysic is, perhaps, best illustrated in descriptive prose, especially in prose that aims to represent the nonhuman environment—the following passage on Walden Pond, for example:

> It is a clear and deep green well, half a mile long and a mile and three quarters in circumference, and contains about sixty-one and a half acres; a perennial spring in the midst of pine and oak woods, without any visible inlet or outlet except by the clouds and evaporation. The surrounding hills rise abruptly from the water to the height of forty to eighty feet, though on the southeast and east they attain to about one hundred and one hundred and fifty feet respectively, within a quarter and a third of a mile. They are exclusively woodland. (Pp. 175-76)*

   In a passage like this, one can readily detect a commitment to provide accurate information about the physical and biological environment. The effort is to create or represent an environment that persists and subsists without human support; an environment with a significance of its own, whatever people may think about it. The passage as a whole is controlled by (and dedicated to) conventions of public verification. Each sentence is presented in such a way that it can be subjected, at least hypothetically, to conventional, public tests of accuracy and authenticity. Each phrase is primarily denotative in meaning, including the phrases "perennial spring" and "clear and deep green well." The phenomena denoted are set forth impersonally, without the mediating eyes of a human subject. They are to be identified and explained in their extratextual relations to each other—their relations "out there"—not in their relations to an author, and not even in their relations to the language or style in which they are presented. In the perspective of the environmentalist, meaning and identity are functions of nonlinguistic relations. Things are prior to words, objects prior to subjects, and things signified prior to signs.
   Impersonal, public, and nonfigurative though it may be, the environmentalist's perspective is by no means narrowly geobiotic, at least not in *Walden*. Though it is, perhaps, most readily understandable in its application to physical and biological phenomena, it can be (and is in *Walden*) applied to the human environment as well. It can be applied to economic phenomena, for example—to the price of rice, molasses, and rye meal (p. 59); or to historical events—

---

*All page numbers in parentheses refer to J. Lyndon Shanley's edition of *Walden* (Princeton: Princeton University Press, 1971).

to the Jesuits and to Indians burned at the stake (p. 75). It can be applied to groups of men and their behaviors—to Irishmen and Yankee overseers who come from Cambridge to take the ice from Walden Pond (p. 295); or to individual men and their peculiarities—to a farmer, a fox hunter, a fisherman, or a woodchopper. It can even be applied to one's self: "Near the end of March, 1845, I borrowed an axe and went down to the woods by Walden Pond, nearest to where I intended to build my house, and began to cut down some tall arrowy white pines, still in their youth, for timber" (p. 40).

In the world of the environmentalist, even the self is to be identified in its extratextual and essentially nonlinguistic relations to other things. When the environmentalist identifies himself—as he does so often in *Walden*—by speaking in the first person, he presents himself in terms of the public record. His self is the self of public record, an auto*biographical* self—the self who built a cabin, hoed a bean field, caught a fish, and surveyed a pond:

> Every day or two I strolled to the village to hear some of the gossip which is incessantly going on there, circulating either from mouth to mouth, or from newspaper to newspaper, and which, taken in homœopathic doses, was really as refreshing in its way as the rustle of leaves and the peeping of frogs. As I walked in the woods to see the birds and squirrels, so I walked in the village to see the men and boys; instead of the wind among the pines I heard the carts rattle. (P. 167)

Though the environmental style may be autobiographical, the environmentalist is not an *auto*biographer. He is not a self-conscious stylist or rhetorician. He does not take personal or idiosyncratic liberties with the public record. Rather he presents himself in much the same way he presents physical, biological, and cultural phenomena—with primary attention to public criteria of meaning. He typically keeps his distance from his materials, sacrificing himself to his environment, or at least to the public record of it. His function in *Walden*, as in other nature writing, is to put things (whether rocks, water, people, or himself) "out there," to separate them from the times and places of their conception and composition, to distinguish them (and free them) from the prose forms in which they appear. The total complex of what he presents, or what is presented from his point of view, is what might be called the environmental component of *Walden*, the component that conservationists emphasize and literary critics tend to ignore.

To the extent that the materials of *Walden* are rendered independent of their writer, the processes and occasions of writing, and the prose forms in which they appear—to that extent *Walden* is an environmentalist's book, controlled by an empiricist's logic and dedicated to a rhetoric of public verification. To that extent the self in *Walden* is the self of public record. The narrator (qua narrator) keeps his distance from the materials being presented. And empirical models or well-established public metaphors supersede idiosyncratic figures of speech.

When, however, the self in *Walden* becomes the writer, the author of himself, environments, and figures of speech, then *Walden* ceases to be an environmentalist's book. When the self in *Walden* becomes, as he so often does, the self-conscious stylist, then highly personal figures of speech take over from public metaphors and empirical models. The latter tend to become metaphors, and public metaphors tend to become idiosyncratic figures of speech and thought. No longer strictly the self of public record, the narrator becomes an *auto*biographer, a manipulator of the public record, in process of creating his own story. The public facts of the environmentalist's world are no longer rendered independent of the writer, the occasion of writing, or the forms in which they appear. Rather, the writer and his writing are rendered independent of the public environment. Publicly verifiable fact and the public historical record are sacrificed to a prior and often defiantly independent, personal style. *Walden* becomes a personalist's book, controlled by a logic of analogies and antiempirical suggestions, and dedicated to a rhetoric of idiosyncratic formulation and fabrication.

Often in *Walden* the narrator pointedly does *not* keep his distance from his materials. Much of the time, in fact, he seems concerned to minimize the distance between himself as writer and the subject matter of his writing, to destroy the environmentalist's distinctions between things and the prose forms or styles in which those things appear. In his most extreme personalism, he indulges himself at the expense of his environment, in utter defiance of public criteria of meaning:

> I long ago lost a hound, a bay horse, and a turtle-dove, and am still on their trail. Many are the travellers I have spoken concerning them, describing their tracks and what calls they answered to. I have met one or two who had heard the hound, and the tramp of the horse, and even seen the dove disappear behind a cloud, and they seemed as anxious to recover them as if they had lost them themselves. (P. 17)

In passages like this one the narrator of *Walden* goes as far, perhaps, as one reasonably can in asserting the priority of the writer and his language; in openly denying the primacy of the public environment (physical, biological, or cultural); in mocking, exposing, and exploiting conventional notions of denotation and verification. Though the passage is presented in a straightforward autobiographical *manner*, though it takes the same stylistic *form* as other discernibly autobiographical parts of *Walden*, the "events" it "denotes" (so far as generations of scholars have been able to tell) simply are not there to be denoted; the "facts" it "represents" never have been there to be verified. The hound, the horse, the turtledove, the self, and his peers are, perhaps, figures of speech. But figures for what—other than the narrator's thoughts? They are meaningful or significant *because* they do not meet conventional tests of meaning and significance, or at the very least because they provoke questions about the whole concept of public criteria for meaning.

If, at its most extreme, the personalist's perspective in *Walden* leads to the utter rejection of public theories of meaning and identity, most often (obviously) it is not presented so radically. Most often the personalist narrator in *Walden* simply personalizes and personifies his environment. Speaking idiosyncratically, he turns the environmentalist's world around by crossing conventional, logical categories at will; by pointedly authoring comparisons among radically different kinds of phenomena; by drawing unconventional analogies; by playing up aconventional figures of speech; and by playing down empirical models and conventional public metaphors:

> Nevertheless, of all the characters I have known, perhaps Walden wears best, and best preserves its purity. Many men have been likened to it, but few deserve that honor. Though the woodchoppers have laid bare first this shore and then that, and the Irish have built their sties by it, and the railroad has infringed on its border, and the ice-men have skimmed it once, it is itself unchanged, the same water which my youthful eyes fell on; all the change is in me. (Pp. 192–93)

"All the change is in me"—that, perhaps, is the basic postulate of the personalist's metaphysic. Few statements could be further from the environmentalist's truth—where all the change is environmental; where even changes in "me" are functions of changes in what is not me; where "I" am measured and identified by ponds and their shores, the Irish and the railroad, the ice-men and the ice; where change is conceived as publicly testable physical, biological, and cultural change.

If, for the personalist, "all the change is in me," so, of course, at any point in the process of change, are the things changing—to the extent they are distinguishable from other things, to the extent they are different from (or the same as) what they have been or will be. If Walden Pond is unchanged, it is unchanged from what "*my* youthful eyes fell on." It is unchanged in "*my*" terms, as "*I*" am unchanged, as "*my* eyes" are unchanged, as "*my*" conception and perception of it are unchanged—or so the personalist would have it. The constant, the unchanging element, in the personalist's epistemology is not the pond but "me." "I" am the norm against which ponds and water are measured and in terms of which they are to be identified. Sometimes Walden Pond may be a character, sometimes a crystal, and sometimes a "perennial spring" or a "deep green well." But its status as "perennial spring" or "deep green well" is no more fundamental than (nor really any different from) its status as character or crystal. From the personalist's point of view the status or state of things is a function of his conception or formulation of them. What the environmentalist sees as constant geobiotic change, the personalist views as one among several shifting ideational constants.

Philosophic idealist that he is, the personalist in *Walden* places idiosyncratic configuration above the public impersonality of things figured. In the personalist's style the process of configuration and disposition subsumes things being disposed or figured. An owl becomes a pessimist: "*Oh-o-o-o-o that I never had been Bor-r-r-r-n!*" (p. 125). Sensual man becomes the reptile who "attacked at one mouth of his burrow . . . shows himself at another" (p. 220). A locomotive becomes a snorting, fire-breathing dragon. So pervasive is the personalist's style in *Walden* that all major elements of the environment are subjected to it in one way or another. Physical and biological phenomena are presented in cultural terms, as ants become republicans and imperialists, and their conflict an Austerlitz or Dresden; as pines become old acquaintances; and the skin of a woodchuck the trophy of Col. Quoil's last Waterloo. Cultural phenomena are rendered in geobiotic terms, as Mill-dam sportsmen become autumn leaves, rustling through the woods; as Fenda, the wife of Brister Freeman, becomes the duskiest orb that ever rose on Concord; and meat-eating men become gross feeders in a larval stage of development. Abstractions—time, nature, and commerce, for example—are personified. Thoughts become shingles and fishes, thinkers become carvers and fishermen, and discourse becomes whittling and fishing:

> Having each some shingles of thought well dried, we sat and whittled them, trying our knives, and admiring the clear yellowish grain of the pumpkin pine. We waded so gently and reverent-

ly, or we pulled together so smoothly, that the fishes of thought
were not scared from the stream, nor feared any angler on the
bank, but came and went grandly, like the clouds which float
through the western sky, and the mother-o'-pearl flocks which
sometimes form and dissolve there. (P. 269)

Figures of speech—similes, metaphors, and mixed metaphors—
come to command considerably more attention than the things
they figure.

The personalist in *Walden* is the self-conscious rhetorician, the
narrator whose words demand rhetorical attention, and who, far
from sacrificing himself to his environment, calls explicit attention
to his own rendering of it—"By the words, *necessary of life*, I
mean" (p. 12), "I hesitate to say these things" (p. 221), "I do not
say," etc. He speaks of himself in the present tense—"I think," "I
cannot believe," "I will not deny"—concentrating attention not on a
nonhuman environment, nor on his own past experience, but on
himself as thinker-writer and on his own prose. He casts impersonal
description, narration, and exposition into present, personal perspective by openly considering them in stylistic—that is, logical and
linguistic—terms. Unlike the environmentalist, he places words before things, himself as subject before objects, and signs before
things signified. About the only time his words do not call attention
to themselves is when he speaks about words or language: "There
are probably words addressed to our condition exactly, which, if we
could really hear and understand, would be more salutary than the
morning or the spring to our lives, and possibly put a new aspect on
the face of things for us" (p. 107). The author of this statement is the
self in *Walden* whom conservationists ignore and literary critics accentuate, the self who would put words (his *own* words) before bud-
ding beeches and migrating geese. For him, metaphors and symbols are significant because they *cannot* be translated into what we
call extralinguistic terms. Indeed "extralinguistic" is itself a metaphor. Language (especially his language) is more than a means to
meaning, a transparent medium, or a dependent variable to be
measured against extratextual phenomena. Language *is* meaning,
the primary form of meaning, an independent variable against
which extratextual events are to be measured and in terms of which
they are constructed. Text (his text or, better, "*my*" text) is primary.

The difference between the personalist's perspective and the
environmentalist's perspective is the difference between, on the one
hand, a highly personal point of view in which all or nearly all environmental factors are accounted for and given meaning by a person and, on the other hand, a kind of species-general point of view

in which the person attains meaning only in public and impersonal environmental context. The environmental point of view gives meaning to the man by placing him in an environment. The personalist point of view gives meaning to the environment by conveying its significance to and through a man, a self-conscious rhetorician.

To the extent that these two perspectives can be considered separate in *Walden*, to that extent, perhaps, the conflicts between them can be considered implicit and covert, and *Walden* can be seen as a book of two styles. To the extent, however, that the personalist and the environmentalist cannot be separated in *Walden*, to that extent *Walden* is a book of three styles and three perspectives. When the personalist and the environmentalist come together—as they do so often in *Walden*—when their respective points of view are brought into close proximity—as they must be if both are taken seriously—then distinctions between them blur, and together they form a third style—a stylistic hybrid containing inextricable elements of both originals, but reducible to neither alone.

Often in *Walden*, publicly verifiable statements and idiosyncratic figures of speech are so closely interwoven that they form a dialectic combination, a stylistic alloy, of which not even extended analysis can provide a guaranteed refinement. The "Conclusion" to *Walden*, for example, begins with what seems like an environmentalist's paragraph, a series of apparently straightforward literal statements ending in the readily testable proposition "The universe is wider than our views of it":

> To the sick the doctors wisely recommend a change of air and scenery. Thank Heaven, here is not all the world. The buckeye does not grow in New England, and the mocking-bird is rarely heard here. The wild-goose is more of a cosmopolite than we; he breaks his fast in Canada, takes a luncheon in the Ohio, and plumes himself for the night in a southern bayou. Even the bison, to some extent, keeps pace with the seasons, cropping the pastures of the Colorado only till a greener and sweeter grass awaits him by the Yellowstone. Yet we think that if rail-fences are pulled down, and stone-walls piled up on our farms, bounds are henceforth set to our lives and our fates decided. If you are chosen town-clerk, forsooth, you cannot go to Tierra del Fuego this summer: but you may go to the land of infernal fire nevertheless. The universe is wider than our views of it. (P. 320)

In this paragraph the world of geese, bison, and stone walls is primary—both descriptively and prescriptively, both for what is the case and for what ought (or ought not) to be the case. Human thoughts and habits are juxtaposed with, and measured by, the non-human environment. Meaning and significance reside in a publicly testable universe. Our views improve as we experience and absorb the world outside ourselves—as we, quite literally, travel and become cosmopolites.

In the second paragraph of the "Conclusion" the environmentalist's world is turned virtually outside in. The paragraph begins unobtrusively enough with what may, at first glance, appear as a figurative elaboration of the previous paragraph: "Yet we should oftener look over the tafferel of our craft, like curious passengers, and not make the voyage like stupid sailors picking oakum. The other side of the globe is but the home of our correspondent." By at least the third sentence, however, it is clear that neither of the first two sentences is simply a figurative expression of the need for travel: "Our voyaging is only great-circle sailing, and the doctors prescribe for diseases of the skin merely." With the third sentence, at least, it is clear that the second paragraph is written *against* the norms and the terms of the first. Voyaging is primarily figurative, rather than literal, "great-circle sailing," primarily psychic, rather than spatio-temporal. Travel ends where it begins, and vice versa. Departure and arrival are of personal, rather than public, significance.

"Doctors prescribe for diseases of the skin merely"—the second paragraph of the "Conclusion" to *Walden* is antithetical to the first. A taffrail is no longer a taffrail, but rather a psychic fence or wall. A correspondent is no longer a correspondent, but rather a psycho-metaphysical equivalent. To recognize that "the other side of the globe is but the home of our correspondent" is not, as it might have been in the first paragraph, to go traveling. It is rather to stay at home, to stay at a home itself metaphoric, to stay at home to oneself—the philosophic idealist's way of saying that the world "out there" is a projected reflection of the world "in here."

Like so many other paragraphs in *Walden*, the second paragraph of the "Conclusion" exploits the terms of the paragraph preceding it. In this case, the stylistic strategy is to *use* the environmentalist's terms to destroy (in a sense, to falsify) the primary fabric of the environmentalist's world—to take, for example, three quite innocently literal statements and work them over into a prior and antithetical figurative construction—

> One hastens to Southern Africa to chase the giraffe; but surely that is not the game he would be after. How long, pray, would a man hunt giraffes if he could? Snipes and woodcocks also may afford rare sport; but I trust it would be nobler game to shoot one's self. (P. 320)

—to bring Africa and giraffes back to New England and woodcock; to bring New England and woodcock, in turn, back to oneself; to work literal hunting into a prior, figurative shooting; and shooting, in turn, toward still other figurative expressions, such as "Explore thyself." To travel is now to "direct your eye sight inward." To be a cosmopolite is to become "expert in home-cosmography."

> What does Africa,—what does the West stand for? Is not our own interior white on the chart? black though it may prove, like the coast, when discovered. Is it the source of the Nile, or the Niger, or the Mississippi, or a North-West Passage around this continent, that we would find? . . . Nay, be a Columbus to whole new continents and worlds within you. . . . Every man is the lord of a realm beside which the earthly empire of the Czar is but a petty state, a hummock left by the ice. . . . What was the meaning of that South-Sea Exploring Expedition . . . but an indirect recognition of the fact that there are continents and seas in the moral world, to which every man is an isthmus or an inlet, yet unexplored by him. . . . (P. 321)

In the world of this paragraph, subjects are prior to objects. Africa and the West are psychic configurations before they are geobiotic phenomena. The geobiotic environment is presented in the terms of philosophic idealism.

Still, the paragraph does not belong to a philosophic idealist, and the falsification of the environmentalist's persuasion is only partial. Though subjects are prior to objects, signs are not prior to things signified. Idiosyncratic formulation and fabrication do not precede the record of publicly confirmable "facts." Rather, publicly confirmable facts suffer a metaphysical or ontological change in status. The psychic regions to which the external environment stands as a sign (of which it is an "indirect recognition") are themselves facts. However internal, they are presented as publicly confirmable phenomena, shared psychic possibilities mutually discoverable in a common process of exploration. If, in the course of the paragraph, the environmentalist's facts are rendered figurative, so are the personalist's figures rendered public and impersonal, so is the personalist's basic persuasion rendered communal. The paragraph as a whole is written from a point of view (second-person and first-person plural) less impersonal than the environmentalist's and less idiosyncratic than the personalist's. The result is a world in which both original perspectives are blurred and the conflicts between them seemingly muted, a world in which both the environmentalist's facts and the personalist's singular designs become particular functions of a collective psyche, if only momentarily.

Taken together, the first and the second paragraphs of the "Conclusion" to *Walden*—like so many other closely related paragraphs in the book—offer two mutually exclusive propositions—that the universe is wider than our views of it *and* that the universe (the significant universe) is no wider than our views. In the first case, human conceptions are meaningful as they match the geobiotic environment. In the second case, the geobiotic environment is significant as it matches or expresses human conceptions. Literal and figurative statements are so closely interwoven that, in conventional terms, it is difficult to distinguish between them. One can even say that the terms "literal" and "figurative" change meaning in the course of two pages, "literal" coming to mean psychic as well as geobiotic, and "figurative," in turn, coming to mean geobiotic as well as psychic. In two paragraphs man becomes both an explorer of environments "out there," and a discoverer of environments "in here." Environments "out there" become the environment "in here." Man is a lamentably limited part of the universe, and the universe a limited part of man's collective psyche, a part of what "we" are (or may be). But who or what are "we" in this sense, a public sense, if not reflections or "indirect recognitions" of our own common psyche? To know oneself and one's environment is both to travel and not to travel—with very little in the way of a happy medium other than the expression that we may all be on the same ship (or in the same home). But is the ship a public fact or a personal design? A personal fact or a public design?

Much of *Walden* is written in a style appropriate neither to an external environment nor to an idiosyncratic rhetorician but rather to the relationships between them, and to the exploration of those relationships. Much of *Walden* is written from what one might call the perspective of the self-conscious ecologist, the perspective of a man who consciously seeks both holistic vision and operational sense but who knows, at the same time, that holistic vision cannot be attained in language and that the demand for operational sense (not to say operational sense itself) is only an expression of greater synthetic processes in a holistic universe.

The self-conscious ecologist is the dialectician in *Walden*. He views and identifies himself and other people as functioning parts of a geobiotic environment. But he also looks on the geobiotic environment as a linguistic and conceptual phenomenon, a cultural paradigm, a formal creation of humans, a figure of speech that (in the last analysis) expresses the geobiotic condition of its human authors, a figure of thought conducive to human survival. He identifies himself as a member of his species, and he views his own behavior (even his most idiosyncratic behavior) as an expression of needs common to his species. But he also, knowingly, seeks to distinguish himself from other humans *and* from the nonhuman components of his environment, to declare his own identity and the uniqueness of his own particular experience. He often *insists* on his own uniqueness or, at the very least, on the uniqueness of his own thought and writing, the singularity of his own special formulation of experience. But he also, and just as often, considers his own thought and writing in cultural and geobiotic context, recognizing his egotistic insistence as a trait common to all organisms. In short, the self-conscious ecologist assumes a variety of views toward himself and his environment. He not only appreciates variety and diversity, but he puts them to stylistic use, even to the point of juxtaposing mutually exclusive conceptions, even to the point of contradicting himself.

Designed to explore the competing claims of the environmentalist and the personalist, the style of the self-conscious ecologist is dialectic, in the fullest sense. At the very least, it is a style of unresolved tension and ambiguity. At worst (or best), it is a dissonant style, a style of alternating points of view and competing conceptions, a style that (pursued too seriously) can easily lead to cognitive dissonance—the kind of style utterly appropriate to a writer who would fully explore the competitive relationships between the individual and his or her environment, the individual and his species, species (including species possessed by language and logic) and their environments.

The self-conscious ecologist in *Walden* is the man-writer who, having identified himself with others of his species in one paragraph, will, in the next paragraph, write impersonally of Mirabeau and the individual's relationship to society—the man who, having written in the third-person of Mirabeau, will, in the ensuing paragraph, return to writing solely of himself and his past experience: "I left the woods for as good a reason as I went there. Perhaps it seemed to me that I had several more lives to live, and could not spare any more time for that one." Having appealed to a collective human psyche in one paragraph, having converted geobiotic exploration into a communal psychic exploration, he will, in the next paragraph but one, fear that others have fallen into the path he trod:

> It is remarkable how easily and insensibly we fall into a particular route, and make a beaten track for ourselves. I had not lived there a week before my feet wore a path from my door to the pond-side; and though it is five or six years since I trod it, it is still quite distinct. It is true, I fear that others may have fallen

> into it, and so helped to keep it open. The surface of the earth is soft and impressible by the feet of men; and so with the paths which the mind travels. How worn and dusty, then, must be the highways of the world, how deep the ruts of tradition and conformity! I did not wish to take a cabin passage, but rather to go before the mast and on the deck of the world, for there I could best see the moonlight amid the mountains. I do not wish to go below now. (P. 323)

"I do not wish to go below now"—is that to say merely that he does not wish to be buried? Or is it to say that the psychic exploration of two paragraphs past is no longer viable?

Proud of his path—"it is still quite distinct"—the self-conscious ecologist worries that it may become less distinct as others make it more distinct. Paradox is the hallmark of his style. His chapter on "Solitude" is, in part, about visitors; his chapter on "Visitors," in part, about solitude—each the falsification as well as the antithesis of the other: "I never found the companion that was so companionable as solitude" (p. 135); "I have a great deal of company in my house; especially in the morning, when nobody calls" (p. 137). The book he writes is structurally and logically complex, convoluted and uneconomical. Yet perhaps its primary theme is simplicity and economy: "In proportion as" a person "simplifies his life, the laws of the universe will appear less complex, and solitude will not be solitude, nor poverty poverty, nor weakness weakness" (p. 324).

The self-conscious ecologist is a man of extremes as well as multiple perspectives. He enjoys pursuing each of his adopted perspectives to its conceptual limits. If, for example, he loves to see "Nature carried out" in the fisherman—"The perch swallows the grub-worm, the pickerel swallows the perch, and the fisherman swallows the pickerel; and so all the chinks in the scale of being are filled" (p. 284)—he also loves "to see that Nature is so rife with life that myriads can be afforded to be sacrificed and suffered to prey on one another; that tender organizations can be so serenely squashed out of existence like pulp,—tadpoles which herons gobble up, and tortoises and toads run over in the road; and that sometimes it has rained flesh and blood!" If, as a disinterested environmentalist, he appreciates and affirms a food-chain view of life, as an interested human organism he explores its ethical and logical implications, he presses it toward its ethical and logical limits: "The impression made on a wise man is that of universal innocence. Poison is not poisonous after all, nor are any wounds fatal" (p. 318).

Though multiple meanings are essential to the self-conscious ecologist, his style is not simply a style of multiple meanings. It is also a style in which *theories* of meaning are juxtaposed with one another. The self-conscious ecologist knows full well that poison is poisonous, that poverty is poverty, that weakness is weakness, and that solitude is solitude—and that it makes no sense to speak otherwise. He knows that statements like "poison is not poisonous after all" are senseless, meaningless, and even false—that neither he nor others who use the word "poison" can know the "after all" or explain the holistic vision. He seeks to explore the dissonant relation of analytic medium and synthetic message, the necessary and inevitable conflict of form and content in phrases like "holistic vision," "synthetic whole," "non-linguistic," and "Nature's unity." He feels that the statement "poison is not poisonous after all" makes sense, but he knows that it makes sense only because conventional concepts of meaning make good, solid sense. He knows, in other words, that the truth or meaning of the statement is a function of its utter and commonsensical falsehood, that the statement is true *because* it is so patently false, that it is meaningful *because* it is so distinguishably meaningless.

Though he knows that subscripts can help to clarify such cognitive dissonance, the self-conscious ecologist steadfastly refuses to introduce them. Though he knows that he is speaking of at least two different kinds of meaning, he refuses to distinguish between sense or meaning "sub-one" and sense or meaning "sub-two," between sense$_1$ and sense$_2$. He refuses to distinguish between analytic statements and synthetic statements, between a priori statements and a posteriori statements, because he is concerned with their relations, because he knows that they are as dependent on one another as they are distinct, because he knows that distinctions among kinds of meaning only produce further tests of meaning—a course of explanation that leads either toward an infinite series of distinctions or back toward what is sometimes called "ordinary language."

The self-conscious ecologist in *Walden* is a dialectician par excellence. He is the self in *Walden* who knows that "Nature" can support many orders of understanding (p. 324), one of which is the conception that nature can support many orders of understanding. He is dedicated to the logic of "both-and" as well as the logic of "either-or." He is a personalist writing a personal book, a book of necessarily and inevitably personal truths, a book in which all statements may be projections of a particular "I"—his idiosyncratic habits in ordering, his peculiar needs for order:

> In most books, the *I*, or first person, is omitted; in this it will be retained; that, in respect to egotism, is the main difference. We commonly do not remember that it is, after all, always the first

> person that is speaking. I should not talk so much about myself
> if there were any body else whom I knew as well. Unfortunately,
> I am confined to this theme by the narrowness of my experience.
> (P. 3)

But he is also, and knowingly, an environmentalist. Hence the irony
in his opening remarks, their utter dependence on what is the case
with "most books" and on "what *we* commonly do not remember"—"that it is, after all, always the first person that is speaking"—their only slightly veiled suggestion that every "I" needs an
other, an other that is sometimes "It" and sometimes "We." Hence,
at the end of his book of personal statements, the statement "We
need to witness our own limits transgressed, and some life pas-
turing freely where we never wander" (p. 318). And the fear "lest
my expression may not be *extra- vagant* enough," the fear lest his
book "may not wander far enough beyond the narrow limits of my
daily experience, so as to be adequate to the truth of which I have
been convinced"—an impersonal truth (p. 324).

To present an environmentalist's point of view in a personal
voice. To immerse the person, the personal voice, in an environment. To deny the self and affirm the environment. To deny the
environment and celebrate the self. To view the self as a product of
its environment and the environment as a product of the self. To
view the self as a metaphor for the environment and the environment as a metaphor of or for the self. Such is the habit and the
strategy of the self-conscious ecologist, the man at Walden. Difficult
though it may be to get what we call reasonable answers or intelli-
gent programs from him, perhaps there is profit in what he says
about man and the environment after all:

> For the most part, we are not where we are, but in a false
> position. Through an infirmity of our natures, we suppose a
> case, and put ourselves into it, and hence are in two cases at the
> same time, and it is doubly difficult to get out. (P. 327)

If ecology is the science of the relation of organisms to their environment, including, of course, the *interactions* between the environment and the organism, and if man himself is an organism, then the relations of interaction between plants and animals on the one hand, and man on the other, are parts of ecology.

STEPHEN A. FORBES, presidential address to
the Ecological Society of America, Toronto,
December 28, 1921

Ecology is the science of all the relations of all organisms to all their environment.

W. P. TAYLOR, presidential address to the
Ecological Society of America, St. Louis,
December 31, 1935

Nature is a word that must have arisen with man. It is part of his otherness, his humanity. Other beasts live within nature. Only man has ceaselessly turned the abstraction around and around upon his tongue and found fault with every definition, found himself looking ceaselessly outside of nature toward something invisible to any eye but his own and indeed not surely to be glimpsed by him.

LOREN EISELEY, *The Star Thrower*

Maybe I only see the wilderness because I am convinced it is there; maybe that wilderness is only in my mind. Maybe a wilderness of the mind can also be that avenue into the future.

JOHN JANOVY, *Yellowlegs*

Chapter Seven

A Sand County Almanac
and the Conflicts of
Ecological Conscience

 f reasonable answers and intelligent programs are hard to come by in Thoreau's *Walden*, in the last analysis they are just as difficult to discover in Aldo Leopold's *A Sand County Almanac*—which is not to say that tens of thousands of Americans haven't found them, as they have found them in *Walden* for at least a century. If *Walden* is dedicated finally to a kind of perpetual dislocation, to the stirring instabilities of distorting and distorted perspectives, the underlying devotion of *A Sand County Almanac* is no less dialectic, though the methods and tones of worship are less extreme, the shifts in perspective less radical and less explicit, the self-assertions and self-doubts less open, and the antitheses to an ostensibly programmatic thesis less pointed and more subdued. If *Sand County* is less agitated than *Walden*, and ostensibly more schematic—more settled, perhaps—a good part of the differences between the two can be explained by noting the rather rapid "professionalization" of natural resource management that occurred in the United States between the time of Thoreau and the time of Aldo Leopold—and the commercialization and politicization (indeed, the legislation or regulation) of "nature" that accompanied it.

Less intense than *Walden* though it is—and more schematic though it may seem—no book does as much as *Sand County*, in itself and in the history of its publication and reception, to illustrate the continuing complexities of mankind's relations to "nature" in America and, in the terms of the twentieth century, to sustain the heritage of Bartram and Thoreau. No book illustrates so well the complications and convolutions of "ecology" as it developed through the first few decades of the century and then blossomed in the popular American garden of the late 1960s and early 1970s. No book has come so close to containing the several meanings of ecology that then became current—ecology as science, ecology as subject matter, ecology as ethical and aesthetic point of view, and even ecology as preferred environment.

Ecology and the ecology movement, however, are plainly insufficient to explain the popularity and by now the reasonable longevity of *Sand County*, and certainly not to explain the substantial coterie—by now almost a subculture—of historians, philosophers, legislators, citizen scientists, lawyers, environmental activists and educators, social commentators, landscape planners, architects, and even occasional literary critics who have occupied themselves in quoting, analyzing, summarizing, refining, and even amplifying its major terms and conceptions.[1] There is clearly much more to *Sand County* than meets the usual popular eye—much more, in fact, than its many readers, both professional and popular, have generally suspected—enough, surely, to make one think one is dealing with an American classic, a classic of the kind that captures the basic drama of a culture.

Whatever else it may be, *Sand County* is a quintessentially American book, quintessentially American because, in its twentieth-century vocabulary, in its commitment to the science of ecology, it dramatizes—however subtly and unobtrusively—the traditional competing allegiances of historic America—and, in so doing, proves the vitality of that paradoxical American determination, on the one hand, to reform or redeem history (in the process, restoring or reclaiming an original harmony with nature) and, on the other hand, to escape history entirely, by turning (or returning) to nature, as we say, by letting nature take its course, by leaving nature to its own devices, or by simply appreciating nature and its workings in all their deep evolutionary power and ecological complexity.

Like several other American classics—like Cooper's *The Pioneers*, or *Moby-Dick*, or Faulkner's *The Bear—Sand County* is defined in part by a deep, abiding commitment to a programmatic—scientific, ethical, and finally social—solution to the problems and disharmonies of mankind's historic relations to nonhuman nature. Like *The Great Gatsby*, *Walden*, and *My Ántonia*, *Sand County* is devoted in part to that perennially Western and especially American dream of perpetual harmony among self, society, and nonhuman surroundings. At the same time, and like each of those other American classics, *Sand County* is bound to and by a conviction, just as deeply held and at least as abiding, that, finally, historic time—the time of programmatic solutions and ethical axioms—is not the time that matters, that all human endeavors and all human history must be held and kept in long-term perspective, that all human history ends in paradox rather than solution or resolution.

Appearances and popular responses to the contrary, *Sand County* is a surprisingly complex and intricate work, rewarding to anyone who would examine closely its overt argument, its many covert questions and counterarguments, the relationships among them, and the methods used to present them. Its primary argument, the argument which has served its author in much the way Thoreau's declared quest for simplicity has served him, is a twofold statement: a descriptive illustration and explanation of land communities—what they are, how they work, and how they change— and a closely related, prescriptive declaration of needs served by maintaining certain kinds of land communities.

As the book develops, its overt and primary argument moves logically from images of the land community as empirical fact, through the recognition of man's place in land communities, to a plea for ethical standards of land use.* The argument progresses inductively: from one restricted land community; through a set of more loosely structured and less detailed land communities; to a discussion of the concept of land community—from detailed description and narration of a single land community; through description, narration, and exposition of several diverse land communities; to a largely expository discourse on the aesthetics, ethics, science, and culture of land communities. In essence, the relation of *Sand County*'s Part I, "A Sand County Almanac," to Part II, "Sketches Here and There," to Part III, "The Upshot," is the relation of percept to generalized observation to concept.

Part I establishes the land community as an empirical (descriptive and narrative certainty). It presents a series of essentially mundane facts in the life of a Wisconsin landowner. It speaks of pasque-flowers, geese, chickadees, mice, grouse, deer, cornfields, high waters, and old boards, among other things. It is noticeably lacking in conceptual terms. Conceptions and concepts, when they appear, are colored, qualified, and finally overshadowed by perceptual terms. The whole is broken into what might be called perceptual situations. Even individual chapters are occasionally fragmented. "October," for example, begins and ends with grouse hunting but

---

*In this chapter I have frequently used "man" and the masculine pronoun "he" as synonyms for humankind. Where I have done so, I have done so because such usage has seemed truer to the text and the narrating figure of *Sand County* than other available alternatives.

presents, in between, a deer, a chickadee, some geese, some ducks, and a marsh. "December" begins with a canine rabbit hunt and then jumps to more chickadees, deer tracks, grouse, pine trees, and finally to chickadee 65290. Through such a perceptual conglomeration, the members of a land community are introduced, and along with them another significant member of the community—a man perceiving, digesting, and pondering a set of basic materials and relationships in a restricted environment.

Of first importance to the methods and meanings of Part I are the perceptual raw materials that form the substance of the man's surroundings. Without meadow mice, old boards, and chickadees, the man would amount to very little. Meadow mice, grouse, and deer tracks substantiate the man's experience, not to say his identity. Pine trees, high waters, and woodcock corroborate the existence of the land community. But the man and his reflections are also central to the environment, as they are to the primary argument of the book as a whole. Without the man and his reflections, neither meadow mice, nor old boards, nor chickadees would amount to much.

Part I is made of more than perceptual raw materials, however crucial they may be to the major statement of *Sand County*. The simple sense experiences of the man are occasionally crossed and complicated by symbolic reflections and interpretive analogies. Trout, as they rise to the man's brown miller and eventually land in his creel, call to his mind a similar human disposition—perhaps even his own—"to seize upon" gilded morsels containing hooks (p. 39).* Grouse that thunder across narrow openings in tamarack swamps suggest to the man that "many thoughts, like flying grouse, leave no trace of their passing, but some leave clues that outlast the decades" (p. 57). And the long growth of pines in 1941 leads him to wonder whether these pines "saw the shadow of things to come" and "made a special effort to show the world that pines still know where they are going, even though men do not" (p. 83).

Sometimes the man in Sand County reads the book of nature rather heavily. At other times he only suggests symbolic intricacies

---

*All page numbers in parentheses refer to the original edition of *Sand County* (New York: Oxford University Press, 1949). The pagination of the original edition is identical to that of the first paperback edition (Oxford University Press, 1968); and, except for the pages (xv–xxviii) devoted to Robert Finch's introduction and a brief biographical endnote about Leopold, identical as well to the Special Commemorative Edition (Oxford University Press, 1987). The pagination and the text of two other "editions," however, vary considerably from the original. The "Enlarged Edition" of 1966 (New York: Oxford University Press) and the second paperback edition (New York: Ballantine Books, 1970) both include eight essays from *Round River* (New York: Oxford University Press, 1953) and substantial rearrangements of the text of the original *Sand County*.

to a perceptual situation. In "January," for example, a meadow mouse "darts damply" across a skunk track, leading the man to wonder:

> Why is he abroad in daylight? Probably because he feels grieved about the thaw. Today his maze of secret tunnels, laboriously chewed through the matted grass under the snow, are tunnels no more, but only paths exposed to public view and ridicule. Indeed the thawing sun has mocked the basic premises of the microtine economic system!
>
> The mouse is a sober citizen who knows that grass grows in order that mice may store it as underground haystacks, and that snow falls in order that mice may build subways from stack to stack: supply, demand, and transport all neatly organized. To the mouse, snow means freedom from want and fear. (P. 4)

In situations like this one, the basic perceptual substance of the land community momentarily recedes into the background, as the narrator becomes a symbolist, in this case perhaps a satiric symbolist. The mouse becomes an analogue for the narrator's conception of economic man, and mouse tunnels become metaphors for the inroads civilized man makes on the land. A midwinter thaw may be equivalent to the passage of time that exposes man's economic determinism. It may be that man, like the mouse, is a sober citizen who will continue to believe that grass grows to make haystacks (which may be fed to cattle, which may profitably be sold to other men)—"supply, demand, and transport all neatly organized." Sometimes the man in *Sand County* reads the book of nature so suggestively that his readings can only be said to have multiple meanings. At still other times, he does not seem to read the book of nature at all, but simply to present it, without interpretation.

As Part I develops, the Sand County land community and the personality of the man in that community develop coordinately. Through his symbolic interpretations of seemingly mundane events, he becomes more than a recorder of details or a personifier of plants and animals. With the meadow mouse he becomes a socioeconomic critic of sorts. When he makes wood in "February" he becomes a historiographer—saw, wedge, and axe, in turn, becoming three distinct, if complementary, approaches to the past. When he interprets the "December" pine (which has its own "constitution" prescribing terms of office for its needles), he becomes yet another kind of ironist, a commentator on the relations of human language and the so-called nonhuman environment.

The episodes of Part I have the quality of developed perceptions.

Their denotative and connotative impression is cumulative rather than progressive. The prose is basically descriptive, narrative, and dramatic (rather than expository or imperative). The voice, the point of view, is fundamentally personal rather than collective or impersonal.

If Part I of *Sand County* validates the land community, Part II extends that validation, taking it beyond personal experience and carrying it across conventional geobiotic and cultural boundaries. Where Part I concentrates attention on a single psychobiotic locus, Part II covers several loci in a much broader field of reference. Where, in Part I, explanations are the dramatized thoughts of narrating or narrative character, in Part II they are also (and often) rendered independent of specific narrative occasions. The narrative "I," "my," and "me" of Part I often become, in Part II, expository "we," "our," and "us"; or generic "you" and "your." The largely psychobiotic drama of Sand County becomes, in substantial part, the sociobiotic exposition of Wisconsin, Illinois, Iowa, Arizona, New Mexico, Chihuahua, Sonora, Oregon, Utah, and Manitoba. The largely personal and local history of Sand County tends to become generic—regional, American, and even Western. In more senses than one, "Sketches Here and There" is an expansion of "A Sand County Almanac."

In fact, the second part of *Sand County* is a hybrid of the styles that define the first and third parts, a stylistic amalgam of the concrete and the abstract, personal narrative and impersonal exposition, idiosyncratic perception and generalized conception. As it extends the style of "A Sand County Almanac" it also leads into "The Upshot."

In "Manitoba," for example, one reads not only a past-tense personal narrative about grebe-watching, but also an impersonal, present-tense interpretation of grebes and grebe-watchers:

> I was starting to doze in the sun when there emerged from the open pool a wild red eye, glaring from the head of a bird. Finding all quiet, the silver body emerged: big as a goose, with the lines of a slim torpedo. Before I was aware of when or whence, a second grebe was there, and on her broad back rode two pearly-silver young, neatly enclosed in a corral of humped-up wings. All rounded a bend before I recovered my breath. And now I heard the bell, clear and derisive, behind the curtain of the reeds.
>
> A sense of history should be the most precious gift of science and of the arts, but I suspect that the grebe, who has neither, knows more history than we do. . . . If the race of men were as

old as the race of grebes, we might better grasp the import of his
call. Think what traditions, prides, disdains, and wisdoms even
a few self-conscious generations bring to us! What pride of continuity, then, impels this bird, who was a grebe eons before there
was a man. (Pp. 160–61)

Specific, narrative grebes become the archetypal grebe. The events
of personal, narrative experience are rendered exemplary and set in
expository and collective context. Past-tense personal narrative
leads to self-reflection, and reflection leads to what "we" characteristically do, to what "we" might be, to a shared human condition. Personal narrative is explained and subsumed by impersonal
exposition.

Of the six chapters in Part II, only the short chapter "Illinois
and Iowa" maintains the unbroken personal narrative prose of Part
I. In the other five, personal experience of and in land communities
is rendered collective, generically human, and increasingly abstract. The chapter "Wisconsin" is almost entirely discursive and
impersonal. Even its most personal and narrative segment, "Flambeau," ends in a brief historical account of the REA, the Conservation Commission, and the Legislature. In "Arizona and New Mexico" the nonhuman environment is identified primarily in its
relations to "*Homo texanus*," and the narrator becomes a horse-
man, an "undistinguished" member of a sociohistorical and human
community of cowmen, sheepmen, foresters, and trappers. "Oregon and Utah" is dedicated to an explanation of cheat grass and its
effects on the American West, an explanation interrupted only once
by a personal narrative that illustrates and corroborates prior, impersonal exposition.

As personal experience of land communities is generalized, so,
of course, are the detailed events of the geobiotic environment. As
the first-person singular gives way to the first-person plural (or the
second-person), so it also gives way to the even less personal third-
person:

High horns, low horns, silence, and finally a pandemonium
of trumpets, rattles, croaks, and cries that almost shakes the bog
with its nearness, but without yet disclosing whence it comes.
At last a glint of sun reveals the approach of a great echelon of
birds. On motionless wing they emerge from the lifting mists,
sweep a final arc of sky, and settle in clangorous descending
spirals to their feeding grounds. A new day has begun on the
crane marsh. (P. 95)

The descent of sandhill cranes in "Wisconsin" gives rise to a discussion of their historicity; to notes and comments on a Holy Roman emperor, Marco Polo, and Kublai Khan; and, finally, to historiographical ponderings: "Thus always does history, whether of marsh or market place, end in paradox" (p. 101).

The stylistic strategy of Part II of *Sand County* is to take the quotidian details of a man's relations to land communities and to generalize them, to lead them toward the major concepts and arguments of "The Upshot"—to gradually withdraw the personal voice of the monthly "Almanac" and to turn increasingly toward the materials and concerns of history, if not indeed to outright socioeconomic criticism.

Arguments at best only implicit in Part I become increasingly explicit in Part II. Judgments at best tentative in Part I become increasingly overt: "That the good life on any river may likewise depend on the perception of its music, and the preservation of some music to perceive, is a form of doubt not yet entertained by science" (p. 154). As personal experience is generalized, as social and economic events become primary subjects of concern, so the apparently unassuming personal observations and reflections of Part I tend to become discrimination and adjudication. Prescriptive terms, such as "overgrazing" and "misuse," multiply. Cheat grass is "inferior," and research is a "process of dismemberment."

As adjudication increases, so, appropriately, does ratiocination—the formation and explanation of conceptions necessary to support normative judgment. The notion of the land pyramid, for example, becomes in Part II something more than the unnamed thought of a Sand County landowner, and yet something less than the "mental image" it will be in "The Upshot":

> Food is the continuum in the Song of the Gavilan. I mean, of course, not only your food, but food for the oak which feeds the buck who feeds the cougar who dies under an oak and goes back into acorns for his erstwhile prey. This is one of many food cycles starting from and returning to oaks, for the oak also feeds the jay who feeds the goshawk who named your river, the bear whose grease made your gravy, the quail who taught you a lesson in botany, and the turkey who daily gives you the slip. And the common end of all is to help the headwater trickles of the Gavilan split one more grain of soil off the broad hulk of the Sierra Madre to make another oak. (Pp. 152–53)

As the details of personal experience are rendered collective and abstract, as prescription and explanation take over from description and narration, so the unsifted percepts of Part I are gradually built into conceptions, conceptions that will become concepts in Part III.

If Part I of *Sand County* is about things like a meadow mouse, a Wisconsin landowner, and chickadee 65290; and Part II about things like horsemen, government trappers, and sandhill cranes; Part III is about things like wilderness, recreation, science, wildlife, conscience, aesthetics, conservation, ethics, land health, the A-B cleavage, and the community concept. "The land pyramid"—a complex of oak, buck, cougar, and goshawk in Part II—becomes in Part III a "symbol of land," an "image," and "a figure of speech":

> Plants absorb energy from the sun. This energy flows through a circuit called the biota, which may be represented by a pyramid consisting of layers. The bottom layer is the soil. A plant layer rests on the soil, an insect layer on the plants, a bird and rodent layer on the insects, and so on up through various animal groups to the apex layer, which consists of the larger carnivores.
>
> The species of a layer are alike not in where they came from, or in what they look like, but rather in what they eat. Each successive layer depends on those below it for food and often for other services, and each in turn furnishes food and services to those above. Proceeding upward, each successive layer decreases in numerical abundance. Thus, for every carnivore there are hundreds of his prey, thousands of their prey, millions of insects, uncountable plants. The pyramidal form of the system reflects this numerical progression from apex to base. Man shares an intermediate layer with the bears, raccoons, and squirrels which eat both meat and vegetables. (P. 215)

The oaks, jays, and bucks of Part II become more abstract plants, birds, and animals—logical components of "the biotic pyramid" rather than characteristic members of regional ecosystems. The individualized actors of Part I—the dog, the meadow mouse, and the landowner—give way to carnivores, herbivores, and mankind.

In more ways than one, Part III is the upshot to *Sand County*. In formal terms, it is the ideational conclusion to a logical and stylistic order that moves inductively from the narrative raw materials of Part I through the generalized observations of Part II. As the land community of Part I and the regional communities of Part II become the concept of land community in Part III, so the landowner of Part I and the community member of Part II become the ethicist and moralist of Part III. Thoughts, impressions, and preferences that are functions of a first-person narrative and narrating character in Part

I become theoretical constructs in Part III. Judgments and criticisms that are expressions of shared experiences in Part II become in Part III the reasoned end products of a formal normative system, a moral code for man's relations to nonhuman environments.

As "The Upshot" to *Sand County* develops, "mental images" and concepts become primary subjects of concern. Figures of speech—"the land community" and "the land pyramid"—become the philosophic cornerposts to a land ethic. Symbols—"the biotic pyramid" and "the pyramid of life"—become necessary psychosocial conditions to developing an ecological conscience. In short, the primary argument of *Sand County* is made explicit—the argument from ecosystem as fact and concept to the need for maintaining certain kinds of ecosystems.

In one sense, it is an easy argument to follow. Its descriptive and nomothetic elements are easy to understand, and its prescriptive or normative components seem to grow logically from systematic premises and historical evidence: Land is, and for a long time has been, a complex organism, a "highly organized structure" of interlocking food chains and energy circuits. The continuous functioning of land depends, and for a long time has depended, on "the co-operation and competition of its diverse parts," of which man is simply one among many. "The trend of evolution is to elaborate and diversify the biota." "Evolution has added layer after layer, link after link" to the pyramid of life; and man is but "one of thousands of accretions" to its height and complexity (pp. 215–16). Man, however, has often behaved as if he were an overlord rather than a citizen of the land community. Modern man especially has simplified (or oversimplified) the land pyramid. He has, in fact, been a counterevolutionary force in the biota. He has had counterevolutionary effects on the environments he has occupied. He has depleted soils and deranged the circuits of energy–flow that sustain the land. He has upset the capacity of land for self-renewal. He has thought of land as property and of himself as property owner. He has applied to land a narrow system of strictly economic priorities and values. He has thought of himself as possessing the land rather than being possessed by it. As a result, both he and the land are in need of a new system of concepts and values; a system that will assure the continued existence of empirical norms for healthy land through the preservation, conservation, and restoration of lands that have not suffered the most disruptive inroads of civilization; a system of values and images that will restore, and then maintain, harmonious relationships between man and land.

To many people it is a satisfying, if not compelling, argument— the argument from land community as fact and concept to the land community as value. It derives not only from the intimate narrative experiences and personal preferences of Part I but also from the generalized observations and collective experiences of Part II. At the same time, it contains or encompasses its logical components. It explains the relations of man to land, both the relations of the individual man as they appear in "A Sand County Almanac," and the relations of historic, human communities as they are expressed in "Sketches Here and There." It calls for "an internal change in our intellectual emphasis, loyalties, affections, and convictions"; an "extension of the social conscience from people to land." And it rests finally on the proposition that *Homo sapiens* must begin to think of itself as "plain member and citizen" of the land community rather than as "conqueror" of it: "A thing is right when it tends to preserve the integrity, stability, and beauty of the biotic community. It is wrong when it tends otherwise" (pp. 210, 209, 204, 224–25).

Compelling and satisfying though it may be, direct though it may appear, the primary argument of *Sand County* is far more complex than any simple summary of its development can suggest—in part because its descriptive and prescriptive components are at stylistic and conceptual odds with one another; in part because the dialectic of their relationship is typically covert; and in part because that dialectic changes form as point of view and prose style change.

Like virtually all American nature writing—and much of classical American literature—*Sand County* is dedicated to and defined by two mutually exclusive conceptions of man's relations to nature: one basically descriptive, synthetic, and holistic; the other essentially prescriptive, analytic, and dualistic. Man in *Sand County* is, and ought to be, a plain member and citizen of the land community. But he is also an exploiter and subverter of land communities, and ought not to be. He is, whether he likes it or not, an overseer and guiding force in the biotic community, "a King . . . one / Of the time-tested few that leave the world, / When they are gone, not the same place it was" (p. 223). Yet he is also but "one of thousands of accretions" to the pyramid of life, and cannot be otherwise. Nature, analogously, is the self-sustaining system of energy circuits that contains and absorbs all humans and their artifacts. But it is also that which humans naturally attempt (and must attempt) to contain and absorb, if not in supermarkets and power plants then in "mental images" and symbols. The land pyramid is a "mental image" in terms of which humans must conceive their actions. Yet it is also the contextual system, the "revolving fund of life," in which all those actions are taken, including actions leading to the creation of "mental images."

To be a part, yet to be apart; to be a part of the land community, yet to *view* or *see* one's self as a part of that community (and, thus, to remain apart from it)—that is the dilemma. And these are the classical desires—to be a part of the biotic pyramid, yet to know the pyramid and the terms of one's position in it; to identify man in terms of his environment, yet to know the terms of that environment and the terms of man's place in it; to present the land pyramid as an accurate description of man's relations to the environment, yet to present the land pyramid as a "symbol" for land, a symbolic key to an ethical system created and held by humans, and not very many humans at that. Both conceptions are as conventional in American nature writing, both as traditional in classic American literature, as they are definitive in *Sand County*. So, too, are the impulses they express and the needs they seek to satisfy. The one—a holistic conception of man's place in nature—aspires to a nonnormative theory of the development and operation of the geobiotic environment, a disinterested account of the relations of organisms (including humans) and their surroundings. The other—a dualistic conception—aims at an at least partially normative theory of man and nature; a bilateral and at least partially adjudicative account of man's relations to the geobiotic environment; a conception of man and nature based on fundamental distinctions between the natural (that is, geobiotic and, therefore, appropriate) actions of man and at least some of his civilized (that is, social and economic) habits.

The holistic conception of man's place in nature is dedicated to the proposition that human behavior—however distinctive, however cultural, however linguistic—is finally, and fully, explainable in the same basic terms as the behavior of other organisms. The holistic perspective draws no fundamental distinctions between natural and civilized human actions. It identifies man as an integral part of the land community, and other members of that community as integral parts of man and man's environments. It explains the actions of man, whatever their form, as functions in and of ecosystems. So, too, it explains ecosystems (and the behavior of their constituents) as functions in and of human communities. It represents evolution as a process subsuming human history and containing man, even as man foreshortens food chains and "deranges" the "normal" succession of nonhuman ecosystems. It emphasizes an integral, ongoing connection of man and land, even as man "destroys" land, even as changing lands provoke changes in man—the whole to be traced through time. And it, therefore, expresses, and no doubt satisfies, that deep human desire to be immersed in one's surroundings.

The dualistic view of man and nature, by contrast, presupposes that some of man's relations to land are integral, and that some are not; that some members of the land community have integral relations to man, and that some do not. Resting on the proposition that "man-made changes" in the biotic pyramid "are of a different order than evolutionary changes," it represents evolution as a process in which humans participate only imperfectly, a process in which they may early have participated but now, very often, do not. Taking essentially nonhuman biotic communities as norms, it explains human actions as functions in and of evolving ecosystems only when those actions are consonant with the needs of other elements in such systems, where "consonant" means conducive to the continued, healthy existence of all present species—as defined and determined by humans and human science. The dualistic perspective, then, identifies man as an integral part of the land community only as human actions perpetuate and sustain that community's component food chains and energy circuits. At the same time, this perspective identifies man as *Homo sapiens,* as a knowing creature capable of altering or directing the course of evolution, a creature whose behavior can only be partially explained in geobiotic or ecological terms. As a complex of ideas and impulses, the dualistic perspective is, thus, biosocial rather than geobiotic, disjunctive rather than conjunctive. It assumes that humans can do (and have done) inimitable things to the pyramid of life, but it also assumes that humans have the capacity (unique among organisms on earth) to rectify their misdeeds, to become (or once again become) plain members and citizens of the land community—only this time knowing, self-conscious citizens. And it, therefore, effectively expresses, and perhaps satisfies, that classical and continuing need in humans (or at least Western and American humans) to be on top of their environments, to transcend (or at least to comprehend) their surroundings and their conditions.

Taken together, these two conceptions of man's relations to nature are not only the logical antipodes to the world of *Sand County;* they are also its warp and woof, its constant stylistic threads. They intersect each other on almost every page of every chapter, and they make the book as a whole a composition of opposites, a fabric of coordinates converging from two radically different directions, a fabric of ironies, ambiguities, and paradoxes. Together they account not only for the frontside of *Sand County*—the overt argument from land community to land ethic—but also for its backside—the covert pattern of questions, doubts, and contrary impulses that runs just behind the primary surface and upon which its overt statements depend.

In Part III, of course, the dialectic cloth of *Sand County,* the web of relationships between holist and dualist, is more abstract and more open than it is in either of the first two parts. In two or three short pages of "The Land Pyramid," for example, one hears both holist and critical dualist: Man is "one of thousands of accretions to the height and complexity" of the pyramid of life, and "the trend of evolution is to elaborate and diversity the biota." In short, man is a plain member and citizen of the evolving land community. "Evolution is a long series of self-induced changes" in the circuit of life, "the net result of which has been to elaborate the flow mechanism and to lengthen the circuit." And yet "man's invention of tools has enabled him to make changes of unprecedented violence, rapidity, and scope" in the biotic pyramid. He has simplified its flow mechanisms and shortened its circuits. His agriculture, industry, and transportation have produced an "almost world-wide display of disorganization in the land," a disorganization that "seems to be similar to disease in an animal, except that it never culminates in complete disorganization or death" (pp. 216, 217, 219).

Loosely interwoven as they are in Part III, the perspectives of the monist and the dualist are comparatively easy to separate, and the contradictions between them are readily apparent and inescapable. If man *is* a plain member and citizen of the land community, one of thousands of accretions to the pyramid of life, then he *cannot* be a nonmember or conqueror of it; and his actions (like the actions of other organisms) *cannot* but express and affect his position within the pyramid of life. If the trend of evolution *is* "to elaborate and diversify the biota," and man is an inextricable part of the process, then man *cannot* be simplifying its flow mechanisms or shortening its circuits. If evolution *is* "a long series of self-induced changes" in the circuit of life, and man's actions are inseparable parts of evolution, then "man's invention of tools" cannot logically be said to have enabled *man* to make changes of "unprecedented violence, rapidity, and scope" in that circuit. Conversely, if man's technology *has* enabled man to make unprecedented changes in the circuit of life, then evolution is *not* simply a long series of self-induced changes in that circuit. It is in recent earth history, at least in part, a series of man-induced changes. If man *is* simplifying the flow mechanisms and shortening the circuits of the biotic pyramid, then the trend of evolution is *not* to elaborate and diversify the biota, at least not so long as man is a functioning member of it. If man is an exploiter and conqueror of the land community, then he is not a plain member and citizen of it, or at least he is a citizen only part of the time.

Because its composition is bold, direct, and expository—because its alternative conceptions and arguments are unmediated by narrative occasions or shared experiences—Part III of *Sand County* raises almost as many questions as it seems to answer: Is man a plain member and citizen of the land community? Or is he a conqueror and exploiter of land communities? Or is he both? Is man a citizen of the land community only part of the time? If so, when? Under what conditions? Is he a citizen of the land community when he *thinks* of himself as such, when he consciously seeks to understand his place in the biotic pyramid? Do man's thoughts and language take him outside the land community? Or are his thoughts, conceptions, and ethics (like his search for shelter, food, and sex) simply expressions of his place in the pyramid of life? And, if so, can any fundamental distinction be drawn between his "land ethic" and any other ethic he may apply to land? Is evolution a long series of self-induced changes in the circuit of life? Or is it also man-induced? And, if so, to what extent, when, and under what conditions? If at least some man-made changes in the land are of a different order than evolutionary changes, how is *man* to tell whether or not such a change (say the adoption of a land ethic) is evolutionary?

Questions such as these, lying just behind the surface of "The Upshot," produce a series of critical uncertainties for the serious reader of *Sand County*. Deriving, as they do, from the clash of disinterested science and interested criticism, they create a pattern of critical doubts and ambiguities, a pattern that surrounds almost every important statement in the final, abstract section of the book. If, for example, "an ethic, ecologically, is a limitation on freedom of action in the struggle for existence" (p. 202), then an ethic (any ethic) is very much like a water supply, a windstorm, or a wheat field; like money, cancer, or language. Are any of man's ethics more than expressions of man's geobiotic condition? Have they ever been? Can they ever be? In what sense is a "land ethic" or an "ecological conscience" more than an ecological or evolutionary event, to be understood (as are other such "ethics" and "consciences") as another in the series of "successive excursions from a single starting-point, to which man returns again and again to organize yet another search for a durable scale of values" (p. 200)? Does all history consist of "successive excursions from a single starting-point," successive searches after a durable scale of values? Or is history progressive? Can man find in the land ethic a *final*, durable scale of values? *Have* we learned "that the conqueror role is eventually self-defeating," because "the conqueror knows, *ex cathedra*, just what makes the community clock tick, and just what and who is valuable, and what and who is worthless, in community life" (p. 204)? Can, or should, we learn?—"A thing is right when it tends to preserve the integrity, stability, and beauty of the biotic community. It is wrong when it tends otherwise." Is man to determine when the biotic community is stable and beautiful? Or must man take counsel from other citizens of the community—not only pines, deer, and wolves but cheat grass, algae, gypsy moths, and rats? Can man take anything more than *human* counsel with the other members of the land community? Can such counsel ever express more than the ecological interests of humans and the species they most closely identify with? Is the problem *we* face simply a matter of extending "social conscience from people to land"? Are *we* willing to extend to other members of the land pyramid the conscience and the consciousness that would make the notion of land community a working analogy? Or would that simply be another human imposition on the pyramid of life, another example of exploitive anthropocentrism?

Virtually every key word in "The Upshot" has two mutually exclusive meanings—one descriptive, the other prescriptive. "Evolution," for example, is the process of change that occurs over time in the geobiotic environment. But "evolution" is also the process by which the land sustains itself, the purpose of which is to preserve the life of *the* biotic pyramid. "Ecological situations," similarly, are networks of organisms and environments changing over time. But "ecological situations" are also the kinds of situations that men ought to seek, the kinds of relations among organisms and environments that must not be violated and which evolution is designed to foster. "The land pyramid" is both fact and value. So are "the pyramid of life," "the land community," and even "the land."

The conflicts between fact and value in Part III of *Sand County* are both radical and unconditional, more radical and less conditional than they are in either Part I or II. Neither shared regional experiences nor personal narrative occasions are present to relieve or moderate the tension between them. "The biotic pyramid" both "is" and "ought to be." An "ecological conscience" involves both a conscious understanding of the biotic pyramid, a cosmogonic sense of what it is and how it changes, *and* a desire to discriminate its healthy and unhealthy states, a teleological need to indicate where it ought or ought not to go: "In all of these cleavages, we see repeated the same basic paradoxes: man the conqueror *versus* man the biotic citizen; science the sharpener of his sword *versus* science the searchlight on his universe; land the slave and servant *versus* land the collective organism" (p. 223). But is not man a conqueror when he thinks of himself as conqueror? Or even when he *writes* of himself as a plain citizen? Is not science (*scientia*) the sharpener of his sword even when he *styles* it a searchlight? Is not land a slave and servant even when, or perhaps especially when, humans call it a collective organism? Is not man indeed a king, "one / Of the time-tested few that leave the world, / . . . not the same place it was" (p. 223)? Does any organism leave the world the same place that it was?

Logical and philosophical questions arise easily in "The Upshot" to *Sand County*. One might even say "The Upshot" is designed to raise such questions—by alternating conceptions of man and nature, by juxtaposing competing theories of history, by rotating "is" and "ought," by interlacing fact and value. At the same time, however, "The Upshot" exposes the basic threads of the book as a whole, the elements that make up its imperative primary surface as well as its interrogative subsurface, in Parts I and II no less than in Part III.

Though they are less obvious in either of the first two parts than in the third, the ambiguities and uncertainties that underlie "The Upshot" are no less central to "Sketches Here and There" or "A Sand County Almanac." In both Parts I and II, the fabric woven of holism and dualism, fact and value, NATURE and nature, is tighter than it is in Part III (though considerably more open in the second than in the first).

In "Wisconsin" of Part II, "a new day has begun on the crane marsh":

> A sense of time lies thick and heavy on such a place. Yearly since the ice age it has awakened each spring to the clangor of cranes. The peat layers that comprise the bog are laid down in the basin of an ancient lake. The cranes stand, as it were, upon the sodden pages of their own history. These peats are the compressed remains of the mosses that clogged the pools, of the tamaracks that spread over the moss, of the cranes that bugled over the tamaracks since the retreat of the ice sheet. An endless caravan of generations has built of its own bones this bridge into the future, this habitat where the oncoming host again may live and breed and die.
>
> To what end? Out on the bog a crane, gulping some luckless frog, springs his ungainly hulk into the air and flails the morning sun with mighty wings. The tamaracks re-echo with his bugled certitude. He seems to know.
>
>   *   *   *
>
> Our ability to perceive quality in nature begins, as in art, with the pretty. It expands through successive stages of the beautiful to values as yet uncaptured by language. The quality of cranes lies, I think, in this higher gamut, as yet beyond the reach of words. (P. 96)

This passage, like so many others in *Sand County*, presents a divided picture of the natural world. On the one hand, it suggests that man is not a part of nature, that nature—the crane marsh and the events that make it up—is an essentially nonhuman phenomenon, a set of processes that man participates in only vicariously, however much he may wish otherwise. On the other hand, it also suggests quite the opposite, that man is indeed a part of nature, that nature—insofar as it is *known* and *appreciated*—is at least as human as it is nonhuman, at least as much the product of human ingenuity as it is the conditioner of man's "creative" impulses—an expression of his science, his language, and his needs for order as much as it is their underlying substance.

Perhaps the greater part of the passage implies that nature is foreign to humankind, that nature is never more than inadequately understood by humans. "A sense of time lies thick and heavy" on crane marshes, as it typically does not on human farms and cities. "The cranes stand, as it were, upon the sodden pages of their own history." Humans, by implied contrast, often seem to stand on the pages of a history not their own, their own history being, too frequently, thin and dry. A time, not human time, is the time of the crane marsh. And while humans may, in one sense, know that time—know that lake, mosses, tamaracks, cranes, and peat have built the crane marsh, "this bridge into the future, this habitat"— humans do not know, perhaps cannot know, "to what end," however much they may wish to. The crane, on the other hand, flailing "the morning sun with mighty wings" and bugling his certitude, "seems to know"—not only where he has come from but also where he and his marshes are going—a quality of knowledge man can perceive perhaps, but which he cannot capture in language.

In such a world (at least half the world of *Sand County*), man is a stranger to nature, a questing perceiver of natural processes, an outside observer attempting with little success to encompass and comprehend cranes, crane marshes, and their relations. As outside observer, man only learns slowly to perceive quality in nature. His efforts to capture such quality in language are a never-ending, and seldom successful, struggle to reconcile his own needs and his own terms with the nonhuman world around him. His dilemmas are not the crane's dilemma. He tries to write and understand, while the crane simply goes on living. There is a world of difference between cranes and the man who seeks to know them.

Tellingly, ironically, and inevitably, man's desires to know—his needs to order, explain, and understand (to the extent they are realized)—set him apart from the very things he would know. In his questing, ordering hands, a complex of sounds and silence, cries and mists, arcs and spirals, becomes a crane marsh. The crane marsh, in turn, becomes a product of ecological succession—mosses, tamaracks, cranes, and peat, "all neatly organized"—and more than that, even. For the differences between man and marsh are apparent not only in his scientific propositions but also in his "poetic" figures of speech. Ecological succession becomes "an endless caravan of generations" building futuristic bridges, and the crane in his habitat becomes a phoenix, what some humans call a mythic being, with a capacity for self-renewal and a certitude (if not a determination) that man can only envy.

In man's hands, the crane becomes considerably more than a plain member and citizen of the land community, more than a crane perhaps. For to be a crane in man's ordering hands is not just to be named. It is to be compared with other named things. It is to become a member of complex systems—energetic, genetic, morphological, and ecological—systems in which the thing you are swallowing (what humans call a frog) is no longer a primary term, systems in which "frogs" are replaced by "heat," "waste," "structure," "energy," and "time." To be a "crane" is to be vested with man's hopes and doubts, with man's particular kinds of order.

Strangers though they may be in one sense, crane and man are, in another and no less significant sense, not strangers at all, but acquaintances of the most intimate kind. As stylized products of ecological succession and evolutionary change, cranes and crane marshes express man's needs to know even as they pattern man's knowledge. The crane marsh—the "bridge into the future," the "habitat" for the "oncoming host"—is a method for coming to terms with living, breeding, and dying—for man no less than for the crane. The crane, in turn—the bugling phoenix—is an assurance that life is self-renewing, a means to knowing or imagining that something or someone can answer the question "To what end?" even if man cannot.

Despite apparent differences in their respective media, perhaps the crane's dilemma *is* man's dilemma. Still, it is no doubt only in man's power to say in words, while trying to capture the quality of cranes in words, that "the quality of cranes lies . . . as yet beyond the reach of words." It is no doubt only in man's power to conclude with paradox and yet, paradoxically, continue to seek resolutions to paradox—to say in quite civilized words, in sentences far from "wilderness incarnate,"

> Thus always does history, whether of marsh or market place, end in paradox. The ultimate value in these marshes is wildness, and the crane is wildness incarnate. But all conserva-

tion of wildness is self-defeating, for to cherish we must see and
fondle, and when enough have seen and fondled, there is no
wilderness left to cherish. (P. 101)

Mutually exclusive views of history and evolution, alternating
notions of man's relations to nature, are no less central to Part II of
Sand County than they are to Part III. In Part II, however, history
and evolution are only infrequently presented as theoretical constructs. Divergent views of man and nature are only occasionally
treated as concepts or "mental images." And the conflicts among
the dialectic elements of *Sand County* are only inadequately explained in logico-philosophic terms.

In "Sketches Here and There," as one might expect, logico-
philosophical problems—ethical, metaphysical, and even scientific
questions—are raised in contexts of regional economics, national
politics, and cultural traditions. History and evolution are
embedded in regional development and ecosystemic change, in the
details of cranes and crane marshes, or coyotes and abandoned log-
ging camps. Man's relations to nature are the crane-watcher's relations to cranes, or the government trapper's relations to the mountain Escudilla. By the same token, the crane-watcher's inability to
capture the quality of cranes in words is less an epistemological
dilemma than it is a shared, cultural difficulty. The paradoxes of
wilderness preservation are less logical problems than they are
communal concerns. And problems generated by competing ideas
of conservation are less theoretical difficulties than they are "our"
problems—emblematic problems that express "our" needs, national problems that "we" have created, regional problems that
"we" must solve, if any solutions are to be found.

As one returns from "The Upshot" to "Sketches Here and
There," the dialectic cloth of *Sand County* becomes, in one sense,
more dramatic and familiar. As farmers and cornfields replace concepts and symbols, philosophic doubts become geohistorical ironies, logical dilemmas become biocultural ambiguities. The basic
elements of *Sand County* are held constant, while the patterns they
form vary.

As one moves, in turn, from "Sketches Here and There" back to
"A Sand County Almanac," the fabric of *Sand County* is further
compressed; its dialectic threads are even more closely interwoven
than they are in Part II. As the voice of collective experience—regional and historical experience—becomes a personal voice, the
voice of the Sand County landowner, so sociobiotic ironies become
psychobiotic uncertainties. As the historical time and space of

geocultural regions become the personal narrative time and space of a Sand County farm, so logical dilemmas become psychological dilemmas, and philosophical problems become personal problems. Alternative notions of man and nature are absorbed in personal narrative. Competing conceptions of history and evolution are embedded in autobiographical experience. What had been "our" traditions and desires become "my" personal habits and needs, and "our" disagreement becomes "my" uncertainty. What ought to be the case is what "I" wish for; what is the case is what "I" see, and need to see; and any differences between the two are facets of "my" personality.

In "A Sand County Almanac" the dialectic elements of the book as a whole are fully dramatized. Both cultural traditions and philosophic questions are functions of an individual man's relations to his land:

> I find it disconcerting to analyze, *ex post facto*, the reasons behind my own axe-in-hand decisions. I find, first of all, that not all trees are created free and equal. Where a white pine and a red birch are crowding each other, I have an *a priori* bias; I always cut the birch to favor the pine. Why?
>
> Well, first of all, I planted the pine with my shovel, whereas the birch crawled in under the fence and planted itself. My bias is thus to some extent paternal, but this cannot be the whole story, for if the pine were a natural seedling like the birch, I would value it even more. So I must dig deeper for the logic, if any, behind my bias.
>
> The birch is an abundant tree in my township and becoming more so, whereas pine is scarce and becoming scarcer; perhaps my bias is for the underdog. But what would I do if my farm were further north, where pine is abundant and red birch is scarce? I confess I don't know. My farm is here.
>
> The pine will live for a century, the birch for half that; do I fear that my signature will fade? My neighbors have planted no pines but all have many birches; am I snobbish about having a woodlot of distinction? The pine stays green all winter, the birch punches the clock in October; do I favor the tree that, like myself, braves the winter wind? The pine will shelter a grouse but the birch will feed him; do I consider bed more important than board? The pine will ultimately bring ten dollars a thousand, the birch two dollars; have I an eye on the bank? All of these possible reasons for my bias seem to carry some weight, but none of them carries very much.
>
> So I try again, and here perhaps is something; under this pine will ultimately grow a trailing arbutus, an Indian pipe, a

pyrola, or a twin flower, whereas under the birch a bottle gentian is about the best to be hoped for. In this pine a pileated wood-pecker will ultimately chisel out a nest; in the birch a hairy will have to suffice. In this pine the wind will sing for me in April, at which time the birch is only rattling naked twigs. These possible reasons for my bias carry weight, but why? Does the pine stimu-late my imagination and my hopes more deeply than the birch does? If so, is the difference in the trees, or in me? (Pp. 68–70)

"Is the difference in the trees, or in me?"—with that question the Sand County landowner gives the dialectic of *Sand County* as a whole perhaps its purest expression. On a November day, he poses the question implicit in virtually all the logico-philosophical dilem-mas and sociobiotic inconsistencies of "The Upshot" and "Sketches Here and There." Is man a plain member and citizen of the land community? Or is he its conqueror? Or is he both? Why do I find man as plain member more attractive than man as conqueror? Does the notion of man as biotic citizen stimulate my imagination more than the notion of man as conqueror? If so, is the difference in man's actions, or is it in me and my notions? Am I a citizen, or conqueror, or both? Is the biotic pyramid a fact? Or is it a figure of thought and value? Is the difference between fact and figure, or fact and value, a function of things in the pyramid of life? Or is it a function of needs in man, and in me? Is there a difference between what man knows and what the crane on the Wisconsin marsh knows? And, if so, is the difference in what each knows, or in me? Are man and nature both inextricable parts of a unified natural whole? Or are man and nature distinct? And, if so, are the distinc-tions in man and nature, in man, or in me?

Crucial though such questions (and their answers) are to the formulation of a land ethic in "The Upshot"; central though they are to the conception of regions in "Sketches Here and There"; in "A Sand County Almanac" they concentrate in one fleeting, reflec-tive November moment of a self-conscious landowner's life; they come back to earth, as it were, to the relations of an organism and its environment, the personal relations of a man and his surround-ings.

In the landowner's almanac of Part I, the dialectic threads of *Sand County* produce an autobiographical cloth, a closely woven pattern of personal perceptions, individualized arbitrations, and self-conscious reflections. As one might expect, in Part I of *Sand County* epistemological and metaphysical dilemmas become mat-ters of momentary self-interrogation, passing rhetorical queries of a man "wasting" his November weekends "axe-in-hand." Alternative approaches to history become idiosyncratic analogies for "saw, wedge, and axe" as the man makes wood in February. The events of history—a federal law prohibiting spring duck shooting, for example—become personalized analogues for the growth-rings on the oak he is cutting. Members of the human community—neighbors, tourists, and speeding grouse hunters—become the substance of occasional, and often self-gratifying, thoughts. And nonhuman elements of the geobiotic environment become configurations of singularly personal ideas and impressions.

A meadow mouse "darts damply" across a skunk track, provoking questions and reflections, complex figures of speech and developed conceptions, perhaps even concepts and mental images:

> Why is he abroad in daylight? Probably because he feels grieved about the thaw. Today his maze of secret tunnels, laboriously chewed through the matted grass under the snow, are tunnels no more, but only paths exposed to public view and ridicule. Indeed the thawing sun has mocked the basic premises of the microtine economic system! (P. 4)

Perhaps the mouse *does* suggest man in his current relationships to land, and perhaps some thaw will expose man's habits of land use:

> The mouse is a sober citizen who knows that grass grows in order that mice may store it as underground haystacks, and that snow falls in order that mice may build subways from stack to stack: supply, demand, and transport all neatly organized. (P. 4)

But there is also a strong possibility that the mouse and his tunnels represent each member of the land community, each member of the land community (humankind included) soberly and unconsciously pursuing the mouse-eat-grass, hawk-eat-mouse pattern that prevails in all ecosystems: "To the mouse, snow means freedom from want and fear." To the hawk, in the next paragraph, "a thaw means freedom from want and fear" (p. 4).

Perhaps the mouse, the hawk, and every other member of the land community (man included) will continue to see snows, thaws, and bioeconomic organizations as meaning freedom from want and fear. Maybe it is natural for man, mouse, and hawk to use their surroundings to be free from want and fear. Perhaps it is necessary that man, mouse, and hawk attack and exploit other members of the land community—if not with underground haystacks and eco-

nomic systems, then with scientific explanations and ethical judgments, with language and figures of speech. In short, just as there is
evidence to support an ironic and satiric reading of the meadow
mouse episode, so there is evidence to suggest that the episode is
nothing more or less than a *picture* of the actions and habits of *one
diminutive member* of the land community. Or, to put it another
way, just as there is evidence for a prescriptive reading of the situation, so there is evidence to support a descriptive reading.

Such are the ways of analogies and analogues that both the
figure and the thing figured are brought to the same end. Only the
maker of figures, perhaps, is provided momentary freedom from
want and fear, and even that kind of freedom seems terribly fleeting
to the self-conscious ecologist. In the end, then, we return to the
man in Sand County, to a man in a land community.

We had been traversing a level tract, which we had supposed lay rather low than high. In a few minutes, we found ourselves on the very verge of a miniature precipice; a bluff which overhung what must certainly have been originally a lake, though it is now a long oval-shaped valley of several miles in extent, beautifully diversified with wood and prairie, and having a lazy, quiet stream winding through it, like—like—"like a snake in a bottle of spirits;" or like a long strip of apple-paring, when you have thrown it over your head to try what letter it will make on the carpet; or like the course of a certain great politician whom we all know. My third attempt hits it exactly, neither of the others was crooked enough. . . .

One must come quite away from the conveniences and refined indulgences of civilized life to know any thing about them.

CAROLINE M. KIRKLAND, *A New Home—*
Who'll Follow?

. . . I admit I have to do a sort of vanishing act just to begin to see. I have to go over to another side, passing through walls of human presumption.

JOHN HAY, *In Defense of Nature*

Like the bear who went over the mountain, I went out to see what I could see. And, I might as well warn you, like the bear, all that I could see was the other side of the mountain: more of same.

ANNIE DILLARD, *Pilgrim at Tinker Creek*

At the same time that we are earnest to explore and learn all things, we require that all things be mysterious and unexplorable, that land and sea be infinitely wild, unsurveyed and unfathomed by us because unfathomable.

THOREAU, *Walden*

. . . the uncertainty of vision, the horror of the fixed, the dissolution of the present, the intricacy of beauty, the pressure of fecundity, the elusiveness of the free, and the flawed nature of perfection.

ANNIE DILLARD, *Pilgrim at Tinker Creek*

Chapter Eight

Composition and Decomposition
at Tinker Creek

ore of same"—the certainty of "the uncertainty of vision," the well-fixed "horror of the fixed," the resolution in and of "the dissolution of the present" (and, coincidentally, of the past), the unwieldy "intricacy of beauty," the pressure of "the pressure of fecundity," the easily graspable "elusiveness of the free," the flawless comprehension of "the flawed nature of perfection." The permanence and persistence, the immutability, of mutability. The absoluticity of relativity and probability. The determinacy of The Principle of Indeterminacy. The presumption that one can (much less than one must) "go over to another side"—that one can pass through "walls of human presumption"— or worse, perhaps, that the "other" side of the mountain is "more of same."

The quite civilized, indulgent, and much-refined dream that one can (and must) "come quite away from the conveniences and refined indulgences of civilized life" in order to comprehend them— or that to write about them is not to indulge and refine them. Perhaps, as the American pilgrim says, "we need to start all over again, on a new continent, learning the strange syllables one by one" (p. 107).*

The dreamed content (not to say the continent) and the linguis-

---

*All page numbers in parentheses in this chapter refer to the original edition of *Pilgrim at Tinker Creek* (New York: Harper's Magazine Press, 1974). As I have indicated earlier, the pagination of the original edition is identical to that of the second, paperback edition (New York: Harper & Row, 1985), though not to the first paperback edition (New York: Bantam Books, 1975).

tic forms, the shaping styles and the envisioning substance, are at perennial odds with one another, contradictory or, worse perhaps, tautologous—"age-old," as we say—and no figure in American nature writing is more aware of the odds or their heritage than the aspiring pilgrim at Tinker Creek. No figure in American nature writing is more aware of the "conveniences and refined indulgences of civilized life," the essential needs satisfied by the "walls of human presumption," the periodic senses of place and security provided by the neatly organized tunnels, subways, and haystacks of the mind. None is more aware of the capacities these subways lend us to name, detail, and explain—to locate ourselves, with some marginal semblance of composure, in tentative relation to the elements of what we call our surroundings. And none is more aware, almost simultaneously, of the threats to consciousness (and self-consciousness)—the warnings to knowledge and self-knowledge, to self and other—which these tunneled, stacked presumptions and conveniences regularly and readily signal—the too-often stultifying (and hence vulnerable) state of mind and body occasioned by unreflecting dependence upon them—the considerable risks to what we call freedom and self-control embedded in unwitting reliance upon the refined indulgences of "civilized life"—the hazards to independence and originality, the double and sometimes triple jeopardy to the American pilgrim's dream.

No figure in American nature writing is more openly and desperately concerned to compose and settle herself and her immediate surroundings; none more concerned to relate her compositions of self and place to the overarching, sanctioning and justifying, terms of traditional Western thought, both classic and contemporary, both scientific and religious. And yet no figure in American nature writing is more openly (if not obsessively) engaged in resisting such sanctioned forms of settlement, none more given (or driven) to unsettling things and to keeping them unsettled. None, not even Thoreau, is more given to "the extravagant gesture," to radical conceits and overt paradoxes—"only a total unself-consciousness will permit me to live with myself" (p. 199). None is more resistant to the processes and methods of conventional explanation, or more disposed to the wild and extreme, to the manifestly unexplainable, and even on occasion to the irresponsible—to finely crafted, spontaneous shouts of joy—to blatant exclamations of surprise and wonder—"YIKE"— and especially, perhaps, to the indisputably predatory and blooded, the bitten and bloated, the flighty, the frenzied, and even on occasion the feral.

In conventional terms, no figure in American nature writing is more patently off her rocker—nor, in deeply traditional ways, more often on it. None, not even Thoreau, comes closer to conventional madness, to crossing and confusing the customary categories and discriminations of traditional Western thought. And yet none is more devoted to (or more self-consciously dependent upon) those same discriminations and categories, not to say the images, stories, and sciences that have developed upon them. None is more aware of the long strips of our historic apple–parings—nor more consistently enthralled by the fruit.

It is not too much to say, in fact, that no book of recent vintage comes closer than *Pilgrim at Tinker Creek* to capturing (and, hence, clarifying) the underlying heritage of American nature writing—that none comes closer to the often divisive and occasionally enlivening experience of trying to land oneself in America—that none is more openly devoted to the drama of impersonal science, spiritual autobiography, epistemology, and metaphysics—or more committed to the competing allegiances of self, other, and language. Certainly no work commonly aligned with nature writing does more to prove that the attempt to settle oneself in America—the effort to compose oneself and to fix the terms of one's environment, in this country so especially dedicated to human individuality and nonhuman other—is finally an epistemological and metaphysical struggle, an ongoing psychobiotic and philosophic scramble in which virtually every moment of innerving belief and hope is met with a coordinate moment of unnerving doubt, each instance of stabilizing facticity (each passage of solid reportage) followed by a meditation on the fragility and indeterminacy of fact, each image of energizing beauty or harmony accompanied by reminders of wasteful and wasting profligacy.

Not even *Walden* goes further than *Pilgrim at Tinker Creek* to expose the affinities between the self-conscious effort to settle nature's nation, even at its most scientific, and the fears, tremblings, and occasional tranquilities of classical Western metaphysics. On the banks of Tinker Creek, field guide and catechism are about as close as they can be, and the issues that inform American nature writing—the fixations embedded in William Bartram's travels, the obsessions hidden in the nut pines of John Muir's Yosemite, the hang-ups in the tree tops of Hawthorne's Sleepy Hollow—all in all, the dialectic legacies of *Walden* and *A Sand County Almanac*—are about as openly dramatized as they are ever likely to be.

"I propose to keep here," says the would-be pilgrim,

> what Thoreau called "a meteorological journal of the mind," telling some tales and describing some of the sights of this rather tamed valley, and exploring, in fear and trembling, some of the

unmapped dim reaches and unholy fastnesses to which those tales and sights so dizzyingly lead.

I am no scientist. I explore the neighborhood. An infant who has just learned to hold his head up has a frank and forthright way of gazing about him in bewilderment. He hasn't the faintest clue where he is, and he aims to learn. In a couple of years, what he will have learned instead is how to fake it: he'll have the cocksure air of a squatter who has come to feel he owns the place. Some unwonted, taught pride diverts us from our original intent, which is to explore the neighborhood, view the land-scape, to discover at least *where* it is that we have been so startlingly set down, if we can't learn why. (Pp. 11-12)

The idea and the ideal, of course—the American pilgrim's perennial dream—is to sustain "our original intent," to "see" with a naive eye, to explore without prejudice, and to record with an aboriginal, unwitting mind—to "see" as the "newly sighted" cataract patient is sometimes said to see, without preconceived perceptual forms, with a tabula rasa, perhaps—to perceive as Eve and Adam are supposed to have seen before they knew "what anything was," before they knew who and what they were, and well before they knew *where* they had been set down—to experience, know, and capture (or re-capture) "the world unraveled from reason, Eden before Adam gave names" (p. 30)—and, above all, not to think too much, certainly not about one's needs to "see," and even less, if possible, about names and language and style. For a moment at least, the idea is not to think about how one might locate Eden without names—nor about how, in the years since wide-eyed infancy, one has learned to fake it—and certainly not about the historic distinction between seeing and the written impression of seeing, or between things and words—for those inherited distinctions can only lead to diverting thoughts about "some unwonted, taught pride," some inescapable predisposition, that leads us to "the cocksure air of a squatter," some fated learning that divides us against ourselves and betrays our own and our infant's original intent.

The idea, then—and the underlying drama of the best American nature writing—is to hope against the forms and phrasings of one's hopes—to keep from thinking, if one can, about one's needs for names (or, worse, styles)—and to subdue one's consciousness of lan-guage and style and Eve or Adam (under circumstances that do little but call quite quotidian attention to them). The idea and the ideal—the almost debilitating effort and the utter need—are to de-termine in some intricate detail "*where* it is that we have been so startlingly set down"—to bring the details of our surroundings (and, coordinately, ourselves) into history, as it were—to locate ourselves and settle the terms of our environs—even as we continue to seek an original or aboriginal, "prelinguistic" and protohistoric, relationship to an everchanging, inconstant "nature," a cosmos and a wilderness forever opposed to our settling down or in.

To discover or establish terra firma—a sense of place—in a perpetual terra incognita—an unknown and finally unknowable territory—is, of course, an impossible and dividing task—prospectively redemptive, perhaps, but also destructive, alternately exalting and engulfing. And the pain of it, as well as the exhilaration—for both narrator and reader—is that neither of its antipodal concentrations, neither of its rather extreme states of mind and language, can be sustained for very long at all when they are entertained as wittingly as they are here.

In this conspicuously American "pilgrimage," the unassuming tales and sights of a "rather tamed valley" lead all but organically to "unmapped dim reaches" and "unholy fastnesses" of the mind— "fastnesses" which are nothing if not mapped places, strongholds, however remote or secret—unholy, perhaps, but necessary, especially to the process of discovering *where* we are. To find out where we are, in fact, seems to require becoming at least mental and psychic squatters—self-conscious explorers, certainly, if not even scientists of a kind—despite our age-old protestations to the contrary, despite (and, at least in part, because of) our "original intent." To find out where we are, to explore the tales and sights of the neighborhood, is to be led into the discontinuities and uncertainties of "unmapped dim reaches," into (but not through) the odds between form and content, to the unholy fastnesses we must create or discover to account for them. It is to indulge that unwonted pride again.

Against our "original intent," we inevitably violate the wild, the unfathomable, and the unmapped—if not by attempting to fathom them, then surely by naming them. We violate and betray our conception of the open-eyed, open-minded infant by speaking about his "frank and forthright" ways, by telling of his "aim." We undercut the "original" by remembering it, by placing it first in what we call time. There is a great desire to be silent here.

In something of this fashion, the would-be American "pilgrim" seeks the promise—the hope and the faith—of a release from history and time and language—through language and in time, of course, though not through a directed, concentrated journey to a historically sanctioned sacred place, through no mapped trudge to Canterbury or Jerusalem or Mecca—but rather as the "originating" American seeks "the promised land," as the "unprejudiced" ex-

ploration and discovery of one's own particular (and previously unfathomed) place, and with the enabling beliefs—first, no doubt, that
historically sanctioned "sacred places" are, by definition, profanations of both hope and despair—and, second, that all places in
this perpetually "new" world embody the sacred and the profane,
that any and all are places of worship and prospective redemption—
provided, of course, that they be entered as the bewildered "infant"
would enter them.

At the same time, of course, this aspiring pilgrim realizes—and
more fully than all but a very few of her nature-writing compatriots—that she and we are stuck, so to speak—stuck with our
learned fakings, caught by that classical unwonted pride, naturally
and inevitably diverted from our original intent—the more so, the
more we seek it—all in all, divided against ourselves. Indeed, it isn't
by any means clear that our nostalgic images of the clear-sighted
child, our visions of being able to enter a landscape innocently (or,
what is the same thing, our insistent aims to record it truly, as scientific description or impressionistic poem), aren't themselves the
proudest and most diverting of our prides—like our ideas of capturing it (or, worse, experiencing it) without craft, and especially
without historic, biotic, or psychic guile—and close kin as well to
our seemingly perennial complaints about being somehow diverted
from what we apparently must see and phrase as the unthinking
participation of infants, the "pure sensation unencumbered by
meaning" of the newly sighted cataract patient, or the "unedited"
sense impressions of one-celled animals—each itself a prospective
faking, an original and apparently inevitable squatting of sorts.

Of such things, it is not good to think too much, obviously. And
so, barely able to control the diverting masks of pride and age,
barely able to keep her phrasings from becoming openly self-reflexive, the pilgrim tries in her next sentence to bring herself back to
earth, to remind herself both of where she is and of her announced
purpose, her original intent. "So I think about the valley," she says,
in nearly overt self-defense, in what is by now a statement of almost
gritty determination.

What follows, however, is not what one might expect (or hope
for), some solidly conventional details of the valley, perhaps, or a
straightforward account of some experience in it, or a "childlike"
image or two. Despite her desires to pin things down—including,
especially, herself—despite her considerable needs to get into some
plain matters of customary fact, some "unedited" sense impressions—her approach to the "valley" remains extremely tentative,
cautious and oblique. "It is my leisure as well as my work"—it is, it
is—"a game," she says. It, the valley—my leisure and my work—"is

a fierce game I have joined *because* it is being played anyway" (p. 12) [italics mine]—a fierce (and, for the moment, largely abstract) game—in part, because her initial approaches to its phenomenal surfaces, earlier in her opening chapter, have proved manifestly discomfiting—but, finally—and in large part—because she is trying to sustain some vestigial sense of "freedom," some wry semblance of her "human" power to choose—full in the face of her "knowledge" (also quite "human," and all-too-immediate) that she hasn't (and hasn't had) any choice in the matter.

Having already pelted her mind with memories of blood sign left by the "old fighting" tomcat she once had, the one who, "in the middle of the night," would knead her "bare chest with his front paws, powerfully, arching his back, as if sharpening his claws, or pummeling a mother for milk,"—his markings "the rose of union" or "the blood of murder" (p. 1)—she is quite understandably wary about going on with her explorations. Having already virtually disfigured the preferred landscape of her mind with images of the giant water bug and the sucked frogskin, she is hesitant and provisional at best. Having already attempted to answer such blooded, urined discoveries with findings of a "grace wholly gratuitous"—with images of a free-falling mockingbird and the unpredictable lighting (the lighting ex nihilo, as she has put it) of Tinker Mountain and a "pale network of sycamore arms" (pp. 8, 10)—having unearthed this grace to answer cruelty and waste—and having found it no more stabilizing (more dazzling, perhaps, but also more chancy)— she is understandably guarded in her attempts at further overtures. Having taken a run at some steers, flailing her arms and hollering, "Lightning! Copperhead! Swedish meatballs!" (p. 4)—and having pulled (or tried to pull) grace into a tangled "rapture with violence" in the illuminated frenzy of feeding sharks (p. 8)—she is now shy of the landscape and the neighborhood. And with good reason.

Because even her initial explorations of her "rather tamed valley" have led directly to epistemological and metaphysical doubt— because she has already concluded, at least twice over, that "we don't know what's going on here" (pp. 8–9)—she is uneasy and even circumlocutory in her subsequent undertakings:

> It is a fierce game I have joined because it is being played anyway, a game of both skill and chance, played against an unseen adversary—the conditions of time—in which the payoffs, which may suddenly arrive in a blast of light at any moment, might as well come to me as anyone else. I stake the time I'm grateful to have, the energies I'm glad to direct. I risk getting stuck on the board, so to speak, unable to move in any direction, which hap-

> pens enough, God knows; and I risk the searing, exhausting
> nightmares that plunder rest and force me face down all night
> long in some muddy ditch with hatching insects and crusta-
> ceans. (P. 12)

Because, despite the concluding phrases of her previous paragraph,
the ostensibly straightforward process of discovering *where* we are
has already proven inseparable from the far more thought-ridden
effort to learn *why* we're here at all (or anywhere else)—because, in
other words, the process of attempting to identify and locate herself
has already proven inseparable from the basic questions of classical
epistemology and metaphysics—her seemingly innocent proposal
to tell some tales and describe some sights is already highly provisional and even protective, already troubled by shadows of fear and
trembling. "To explore the neighborhood" or "view the landscape,"
it would seem, requires more in the way of provisional accoutre-
ment and protective outfitting than one's vision of the clear-sighted
infant would suggest.

For a brief time, then—a very brief time—the valley may be a
game, a controlled (and momentarily controlling) diversion—like a
springtime, evening softball game or a round of pinochle or Par-
cheesi—in any case, an elaborate conceit, a stylistic device, itself a
bit of a game—in which, to begin with, one depends (for sanity's
sake) on the conventional distinction between games (recreational
diversions, as we call them) and real life, between artifice and nature, as we say—the whole designed to control what is now again all
but too present, the flipside of one's original intent, the underside of
the original, signified "object" of the conceit, life—my leisure and
my work—the recognition that the obverse of innocent exploration
and wide-eyed participation is what we call literal immersion in
one's surroundings, the awareness that the distinctions we draw
between sign and signifier, or conceit and reality, or games and real
life are kinds of biolinguistic defense mechanisms that enable us to
believe and act as if we are in control—the self-conscious nature
writer's understanding that both the games people play (including
those they play with language) and those they pretend not to play
enable them to deal with what they call insects and crustaceans,
among many other things.

It will not do, clearly, to be too open-minded in one's explorations. It is necessary, in fact, to be something of a stalker as well as
an explorer, or, as she puts it in the next paragraph but one, "the
instrument of the hunt itself"—and one's book "the straying trail of
blood" (p. 12). Having been in the gutted frogskin, however
briefly—having wondered whether what we call waking or waking

up is not a process of losing oneself in a "leafy interior, intent, remembering nothing" (p. 2)—having asked, "If the giant water bug
was not made in jest, was it then made in earnest?" (p. 7)—and
having again tried to think about the valley—only in the final sentences of the chapter can she gradually subdue the self and turn
again toward the fields, winds, and waters:

> When I cross again the bridge that is really the steers' fence, the
> wind has thinned to the delicate air of twilight; it crumples the
> water's skin. I watch the running sheets of light raised on the
> creek's surface. The sight has the appeal of the purely passive,
> like the racing of light under clouds on a field, the beautiful
> dream at the moment of being dreamed. The breeze is the
> merest puff, but you yourself sail headlong and breathless under
> the gale force of the spirit. (P. 13)

Finally, one might think, she has gotten herself back on the ground
of her original intent—were it not for the lingering echoes of crum-
pled skin and overwhelming light. Finally, one might say, she is
giving herself uncharily to the merest puff of breeze—were it not for
"the gale force of the spirit" juxtaposed with it.

By the time one reaches the end of the opening chapter of this
late twentieth-century attempt to settle oneself in America, the patterns and the issues are well established. The effort is to be (or
become) part and parcel of the valley—to be, as we say, at home
with oneself—but without sacrificing one's capacity to know that
one is at home, or to heave a long sigh of relief that one has (finally)
found a home—and above all, perhaps, without sacrificing the sustaining faith—the American dream, as it were—that the place has a
special wild, unfathomable, frontiered quality to it, for all its apparent tameness.

The causes, then—the motivations and the reasons, the wants
to be satisfied and the fears to be escaped—are deeply kin to the
underlying causes of *Walden* and *Sand County* and William
Bartram's *Travels*. The specific terms vary, of course—and so does
the timing or periodicity of tension—the intricacy of paradox and
the frequency of self-reflection—but the underlying concerns are
virtually identical. With some trepidation, the seemingly perennial
endeavor is to attempt to immerse oneself in one's surroundings, to
engage one's biotic neighborhood genuinely and fully—but not at
the cost of consciousness or self-knowledge—to participate, but to
participate knowingly, without sacrificing one's "freedom," while
preserving one's independence, and above all, perhaps, the inimi-

table novelty of one's experience (or at least the illusions of same). The ongoing effort is to attempt to work one's way, ever so slowly, away from the promises and threats of self-consciousness (or from what here is the same thing, stylistic self-reflexiveness)—away both from the senses of alienation and loneliness it seems to induce and (what is far more difficult for the self-conscious American) away from the "independence" and "originality" it seems to ensure and sustain. It is indeed a fierce game, played against the conditions of time, the writing no less risky than the thinking or the living—and finally, of course, inseparable from them.

Once again, it turns out that the business of attempting to locate oneself in America is closely and terribly tied up with the "learning" of why we are here at all, or why we should care about being anywhere in particular—and for good and telling historical and cultural reasons, for causes that have much to do with the American's traditional desire to eat one's natural cake while simultaneously preserving it—to be a part of the valley, while simultaneously knowing that one is a part—all in all, to resolve those inherited and classic conflicts between action (or participation) and contemplation (or understanding), between nature and history, fact and theory (or metaphor), emotion and reason, mind and body, subject and object, human self and nonhuman other, language and reality, word and thing, signified and signifier—in short, to "locate" (or, as some would say, "incarnate") in one's experience of a particular American place the perfection, the ultimate and original resolution, of Western history and thought.

What finally distinguishes this particular American pilgrimage from its nature-writing compatriots are not its underlying conditions and causes, and certainly not its competing allegiances, but, rather, the extreme rapidity with which its central figure shifts from one to another, and the almost unrelieved pressure that results. Like the central figure of *Walden*, she engages those competing allegiances with intensity, and takes their implications to extremes, consciously and self-consciously playing them off against one and other. At the same time, she goes her acknowledged predecessor one better (or, perhaps, one worse)—by shifting with even greater frequency among them—by moving with even more inordinate (and most often unexpected) speed from the straightforwardly referential and nonfigurative to (and most often through) the openly figurative and metaphoric to the overtly self-reflexive and self-referential. In one sense, at least, she is even less settled (and less inclined to settle) that her counterpart at Walden—less in need of the comforts of extended reportage, perhaps—but also more suspicious of the seeming securities of its conventions, more distrustful of the unwilling suspension of disbelief it seems to entail.

Someone might say—indeed, she herself might—that she is less the scientist, autobiographer, historian, or reporter than the descriptive and expository self of *Walden*—more the poet, metaphysician, and theologue—but the difference is finally less a matter of degree than it is of duration. Seldom does she allow herself (or her reader) more than half a paragraph to recover from a bout with uncertainty. Seldom is she able to sustain frank and forthright reportage for more than a sentence or two without interrupting herself or suggesting a mildly disturbing connection between some seeming matter of customary fact and some earlier upsetting experience—some epistemological dilemma, some fright, or some shadow of ecstasy. Her total time on the solid ground of referential statement and publicly confirmable truth may ultimately equal her Waldened compatriot's, but her landings and departures are more frequent, and her sojourns briefer.

In this blue-ridged valley of Virginia, about the best one can do for the unqueried ground of scientific information is this passage on newts from the chapter entitled "Spring":

> Newts are the most common of salamanders. Their skin is a lighted green, like water in a sunlit pool, and rows of very bright red dots line their backs. They have gills as larvae; as they grow they turn a luminescent red, lose their gills, and walk out of the water to spend a few years padding around in damp places on the forest floor. Their feet look like fingered baby hands, and they walk in the same leg patterns as all four-footed creatures—dogs, mules, and for that matter, lesser pandas. When they mature fully, they turn green again and stream to the water in droves. A newt can scent its way home from as far as eight miles away. (P. 109)

Reasonably straightforward passages even this extensive are extremely rare, however. And passages of unalloyed autobiography or history or anthropology are seldom any longer (and when they are, they are typically built upon quotations and paraphrastic elaborations of the expository prose of others, others—like Henri Fabre and Peter Freuchen—more given than she to the referential and verifiable). Fastnesses of a kind—almost unconditional, seemingly unpretentious, and ostensibly self-effacing—such expository and descriptive passages provide momentary fixings against fears and uncertainties that have derived from unsettling images and speculations immediately past—brief, if determined, approaches to more conventional runways of the mind, touchdowns from which she soon takes off again on flights of fancy or philosophic gambles.

Frequently, in other words—and at least half despite herself—she utterly needs the anchorhold of straightforward identification and explanation, if only for a moment. In this particular case—by no means one of her most notable—she has begun her exploration of "Spring" by speaking about languages and codes, about a time when she was young when she "fondly imagined that all foreign languages were codes for English," and then about the first day of her first French course, when she realized that she was "going to have to learn speech all over again, word by word, one word at a time"—and her "dismay knew no bounds" (pp. 104–5). The implications, of course, are several—for her own words as for their attempted boundings—and not the least of them is the notion that experiencing "spring" is (and, perhaps, ought to be) like the first day of one's first French course, at once utterly dismaying and enthrallingly boundless—that to the language of spring, as to French, there may be "no key," that " 'oui' will never make sense in our language but only in its own," that we may need "to start all over again, on a new continent, learning the strange syllables one by one"—and, perhaps—but just perhaps—that we will never make sense in our language (pp. 106–7).

With such a start to "Spring," it is hardly surprising that she should pause (there is a break in her paragraphing)—or that she should attempt to continue with a flatly declarative reminder, followed by an overt and apparently controlled statement of resolve:

> It is spring. I plan to try to control myself this year, to watch the progress of the season in a calm and orderly fashion. In spring I am prone to wretched excess. I abandon myself to flights and compulsions; I veer into various states of physical disarray. For the duration of one entire spring I played pinochle; another spring I played second base. One spring I missed because I had lobar pneumonia; one softball season I missed with bursitis; and every spring at just about the time the leaves first blur on the willows, I stop eating and pale, like a silver eel about to migrate. My mind wanders. Second base is a Broadway, a Hollywood and Vine; but oh, if I'm out in right field they can kiss me goodbye. As the sun sets, sundogs, which are mock suns—chunks of rainbow on either side of the sun but often very distant from it—appear over the pasture by Carvin's Creek. . . . I have no idea how many outs there are; I luck through the left-handers, staring at rainbows. . . . The players look so thin on the green, and the shadows so long, and the ball a mystic thing, pale to invisibility. . . . I'm better off in the infield. (Pp. 107–8)

The passage begins—as do so many others in the book—with an assertion, functionally a reassertion, of one of the facts upon which one can surely depend—"It is spring." In a "calm and orderly fashion," a self-consciously controlled (and barely controlling) syntax, the second sentence all but exposes the first, and virtually undermines its own and its author's terms—"I *plan* to *try* to *control* myself this year" [italics mine]. With its stylistic and conceptual tremors of at least three orders of consciousness, it barely veils her half-frighted, half-expectant desires to participate fully—unconsciously and even excessively—in what she calls "the progress of the season." It also suggests her considerable doubts about the efficacy and the virtues of language and self-control, and indeed her substantial fears that the season cannot be followed (much less captured or partaken of) as long as one is stuck with one's articulating human consciousness.

Like several of the sentences immediately following—and many throughout the book—this three-tiered resolution is a barely maintained defensive device, an attempt to control oneself, at least half against one's will—or, more accurately, at least half against one of one's wills. Like virtually every sentence that follows, it suggests the odds between "spring" and what we call spring, the tension between control and a real letting go, between civilized form and what we futilely try to capture as "wild formlessness"—each, alternately, half-needed (or half-desired) and half-feared. Thus, the restrained frugality (perhaps even the penury) of "In spring I am prone to wretched excess"—and the cautious discipline of "I abandon myself to flights and compulsions"—or the single-minded straightness of "I veer into various states of physical disarray"—or the concentration of "My mind wanders"—until, finally, she (and her syntax) can take it no more, and "second base is a Broadway, a Hollywood and Vine"; and she's almost out in right field, as "the sun sets," with "sundogs, which are mock suns"—saved only perhaps by the explanatory appositive, "chunks of rainbow on either side of the sun but often very distant from it"—sundogs and mock suns that "appear over the pasture by Carvin's Creek"—chunks that barely enable her to stay within the bounds of her place. "I'm better off in the infield," she says; and so, for the moment, are the rest of us.

There is another full pause here—another break in the paragraphing—which is followed by yet another attempt at a beginning, a reloading of sorts, in which she tries again to work her way toward some steadying matters of fact, some "unedited" sense impressions—a memory of an April walk in Adams' woods, a recalled glance at one particular praying mantis egg case, "the one tied to the mock-orange hedge by my study window," with one of its sides "chewed away, either by the ants or by something else, revealing a rigid froth slit by narrow cells," and "over this protective layer"—no longer quite so clearly past or protective as one might wish—the ants almost presently scrambling, "in a frenzy, unable to eat," "the actual mantis eggs" all but immediately lying "secure and unseen, waiting, deeper in" (p. 108).

For the moment, the images and their implications are encased in the past (or is it simply the past tense?), though nowhere near as securely as one might desire. "The morning woods" of the next two paragraphs, in turn—"utterly new"—are replete with remembered snakes ("I saw a bright, smashed one on the path")—butterflies ("vaulting and furling about")—phlox ("at its peak")—"long racemes of white flowers" hanging from locust trees—and an old Cherokee legend about the moon goddess, which accounts for the crescent shapes of the racemes—all of this and a bit more, if one can put it that way, before one gets to the more clearly ordinal relief of the newts, a relief short-lived at best.

Within three pages of those home-scenting newts, the pilgrim is about to leave Adams' woods—in the meantime having concluded again that "we *know nothing* for certain" [italics mine]—having recalled trying to catch a leaf tip in the act of springing, rising and shoving against its "enclosing flaps"—and having been unable to wait—though she "*knew* the leaf would be fully erect within the hour" (pp. 112–13) [italics mine]:

> I left the woods, spreading silence before me in a wave, as though I'd stepped not through the forest, but on it. I left the wood silent, but I myself was stirred and quickened. I'll go to the Northwest Territories, I thought, Finland. (P. 113)

She leaves Adams' woods, then, perhaps for as good a reason as she "went" there—and certainly with the same fundamental fears and incitements with which she entered—at once enlivened and guilty—but, no more than Thoreau, because she has several more lives to lead, and no more time to spend on this one. Rather, because in this exploratory analysis, as in others, and in spite of the conventions of our usage, there has once again proven to be only one life, whatever the reasons for living it; because Adams' woods and its newts, like the other side of the mountain, have revealed only more of same. What she has found, in fact, is that the effort to locate herself, the sometime seemingly innocent attempt to explore her surroundings, has once again disclosed as much about the would-be explorer as it has about her environment—quite enough (for the moment) about the aspiring pilgrim, and plenty as well about the processes and objects of her desiring worship.

What she has found, and what her pilgrimage continues to prove—at least half despite herself—is that the effort to determine *where* one is gets one all entangled in trying to figure out both *what it* is and how to account for it (or how it could possibly be accounted for)—and more, that the pursuit of one's frank and forthright original intent seems inseparable from the "straying trail of blood" of one's own hungerings and impulses, the attempt to account for one's own motivations in the first place, constantly treading in one's own tracks, as it were—and more even than that, that the answer to the question *"where* are we?" (or, worse, "where am *I?"*) is intimately bound up not only with the answers to "what are *they?"*—the newts, the giant water bugs, and the crescent-shaped clusters on the locust tree—but also, by close association, to *"what* are we?"—not to say, *"who* are we?" or "who am *I?"* or, worse, "who is it?"—and almost inevitably "why are we here?," "why are they?," and "why am I?"—or "am I?"

In Adams' woods as elsewhere, then, this "meteorological journal of the mind" is a more or less constant struggle—on the one hand, to establish and maintain a sense of self and a capacity for self-consciousness, an independence and a feisty originality that cannot be explained or explained away—on the other hand, to establish and maintain the independent, unconditional existence of the other, as a set of phenomena in no sense tied to (or dependent upon) one's own motivations or compositions—and all the while sustaining one's belief in the prospect of utterly losing one's self (and one's sense of self) in the other. On the one hand, to see through and beyond her own language, to see without words, so to speak; on the other hand, to recognize that the human can only "see" through language, that what she (and her readers) "see" here is a function (and solely and forever a function) of her own (and their) compositions.

With these deep-seated, competing allegiances as the antipodes of her world, already in the second chapter of the book she is driven (and drives herself) to confront head on the classic philosophic positions on perception and apperception, the theoretical options on "Seeing" and their apparent practical implications. Having begun the chapter by declaring that the world is "fairly studded and strewn" with perceptual pennies—bright, new coppers pretty much there for the taking—and then having wondered several times over why she so often seems to miss what's there to see, why she can't see any of three hundred or more red-winged blackbirds in an Osage orange tree, for example—until they fly out—in less than four pages, she has come to the point of acknowledging (and at least half-declaring) that she is no expert, that she cannot see or construct "the artificial obvious that those in the know construct"—that she just doesn't know "what the lover knows"—and, hence, is unable to see blackbirds, deer, and frogs with unconscious clarity or warmth. At the same time—and in the same space—she has come perilously (and perhaps a bit preciously) close to hinting that those who see with the specialist's unwitting clarity or the lover's unqueried affection—those who are able to "forget the naturally obvious"—are unknowing victims of their own constructs—that they can't see the phenomenal profligacy and fecundity of the forest for their obsessing trees (pp. 15-18).

In something of this fashion, she soon finds herself caught again (or, rather, catches herself) among at least three orders of consciousness. On the one hand, she separates and segregates herself from "those in the know," from those who see with ease what she can only try to see—"the artificial obvious is hard to see." She thus, at least half-enviously, isolates herself from her experts and lovers. On the other hand, she implies, if she does not state, that those in the know, with their artificially obvious "things," their seemingly effortless abilities to sort out their experiences, must inevitably miss the "naturally obvious," the pellucid edges where uncommon happenings blend into one another, the translucent patterns of color and light which she (despite, and at least in part because of, her lack of expertise) must be closer to—some slight self-saving grace perhaps. On still another hand, she implicitly (and at least half-reluctantly) acknowledges that she too is among those "in the know"—that she too (like others of her human kind, including both experts and lovers) sees only what she preconceives—"I see what I expect"—thus indirectly reestablishing her human kinship with the experts and lovers—and approaching (or reapproaching) the thought that no human has (or can have) access to the "naturally obvious"—that all humans, amateurs and experts alike, are by nature divorced from what we might call the naturally obvious—that, despite her deepest wishes, no human experience (and, perhaps, no "experience" at all) is unedited—and indeed that the "naturally obvious" is by no means naturally obvious. "No culture explains," she says, in a nearly self-defeating (and clearly self-reflexive) bit of not-so-pleasant irony: "I'm blind as a bat, sensing only from every direction the echo of my own thin cries" (pp. 17-18, 24-25).

In a considerable quandary now, and again much in need of a way out (or, rather, another model of the way in)—a way through or around these walls of human presumption, another side or angle of conception, another means to composure and continued composition—she turns to expert literature on cataract patients and tries again—and within a page, has all but immersed herself, with a kind of astonished envy, in the perceptions, if one can call them that, of those who are (or seem to be) entirely unknowing, the "newly-sighted" patients about whom she has read, and for whom, she says, "vision is pure sensation unencumbered by meaning" (p. 26). Expert opinion would indicate that these are multicelled, human perceivers whose perceptions are unedited, people who know no need of the artificially obvious, entirely open-minded receivers without perceptual expectations, people who see what we call "things" entirely naturally.

As further reading reveals, however—almost to the destruction of one's admiring, envious wonder—some of these newly sighted creatures are apparently frightened out of their wits by the naturally obvious, and very much in need of some expectations by which to maintain their self-control. So that, in no more than three additional pages—having briefly imagined (or tried in words to imagine) herself as a newly sighted seer in a depthless world of color-patches—having tried by example to unlearn her "sighted" ways—the exploring pilgrim has once again swung herself at least halfway back to where she started, stuck with her incapacities, unable, as she says, to "sustain the illusion of flatness," and at least half-troubled by the now apparent fact that she's "been around for too long." "Form," she says—half in abdication and half in self-defense—"is condemned to an eternal danse macabre with meaning" (p. 29). One may wonder in passing what the newly sighted cataract patient would make of a danse macabre, eternal or otherwise.

Within no more than another page she has worked herself even further back, perhaps, toward an apparently admissive (though again utterly tautologous) resignation of sorts—"seeing is of course very much a matter of verbalization" (p. 30)—and in two more brief paragraphs has once again swung rather boldly back the other way, as it were, to her determined, continuing, and completely antithetical insistence that "there is another kind of seeing that involves a letting go," a way of seeing, as she says, in which she sways "transfixed and emptied" (p. 31)—at least half like the newly-sighted cataract patient or the infant "who has just learned to hold his head up"—the way, as classical guides to mystic vision would have it, in which emptiness means not hollow, but capable of being filled—the way, as she puts it, of the "unscrupulous observer" (p. 31)—in this case, the paradoxical way of being filled, preoccupied and fixed, by the notions of being emptied and transfixed.

And so it goes throughout the book, as she continues to attempt to have it both ways, even as she "knows" better and "intends"

otherwise—scrupulous and unscrupulous, solidly settled and perpetually unsettled, firmly fixed and forever unfixed (not to say, unfixable). In the chapter entitled "The Fixed," after devoting five and
a half pages to details of praying mantises and their implications,
she speaks of "the scene . . . in the back of my brain all afternoon,
obscurely . . . beginning to rise from night's lagoon." "It really has
nothing to do with praying mantises," she writes, "but this afternoon I threw tiny string lashings and hitches with frozen hands,
gingerly, fearing to touch the egg cases even for a minute" (p. 59)—
thus trying once again to keep the elements of her surroundings
sufficiently in mind to sustain a particularizing and participating
sense of place, without being overwhelmed by her own needs for
such a sense (or by her awareness of those needs)—thus trying to
put and keep mantises and egg cases in place even as she tries to get
and keep herself in place.

The effort again is almost debilitating. Eight pages later—after
having almost literally spent herself in continued obsessions with
mantises, Polyphemus moths, and Pine processionaries—she declares: "I want out of this still air. . . . It is the fixed that horrifies us,
the fixed that assails us with the tremendous force of its mindlessness" (p. 67).

If, on its all-too-present upside, "The Fixed" is almost horri-
fyingly oppressive in its "mindlessness," its flipside, "The Present,"
soon to become its upside (one chapter and five pages later), is likewise mindless, though initially, at least, the opposite of horrifying. If
the fixed is "the world without fire . . . motion without direction,
force without power, the aimless procession of caterpillars round
the rim of a vase" (p. 68)—if it threatens to catch you, to reduce you
to an automaton, a creature of senseless, driving instinct—"The
Present," which soon replaces it in the mind's eye, "the spirit's un-
self-conscious state at any moment of pure devotion to any object"
(p. 82), is an utterly absorbing and at least initially absolving condition, a landscape sensed while working one's hand "automatically"
over a puppy's fur, "following the line of hair under his ears, down
his neck, inside his forelegs, along his hot-skinned belly":

> Shadows lope along the mountain's rumpled flanks; they
> elongate like root tips, like lobes of spilling water, faster and
> faster. A warm purple pigment pools in each ruck and tuck of
> the rock; it deepens and spreads, boring crevasses, canyons. As
> the purple vaults and slides, it tricks out the unleafed forest and
> rumpled rock in gilt, in shape-shifting patches of glow. These
> gold lights veer and retract, shatter and glide in a series of daz-
> zling splashes, shrinking, leaking, exploding. The ridge's bosses

> and hummocks sprout bulging from its side; the whole moun-
> tain looms miles closer; the light warms and reddens; the bare
> forest folds and pleats itself like living protoplasm before my
> eyes, like a running chart, a wildly scrawling oscillograph on the
> present moment. The air cools; the puppy's skin is hot. I am
> more alive than all the world. (P. 78)

It is a literally selfless condition, at least until the last sentence—a
condition much to be desired, if not sought. But it, too, proves un-
sustainable; for despite its apparent comforts, it (like the fixed)
threatens one's needs for self-control, one's sense of distinction and
one's vaunting human consciousness—"I am more alive than all
the world":

> This is it, I think, this is it, right now, the present, this
> empty gas station, here, this western wind, this tang of coffee on
> the tongue, and I am patting the puppy, I am watching the
> mountain. And the second I verbalize this awareness in my
> brain, I cease to see the mountain or feel the puppy. I am opaque,
> so much black asphalt. But at the same second, the second I
> know I've lost it, I also realize that the puppy is still squirming
> on his back under my hand. Nothing has changed for him. (Pp.
> 78–79)

Here as elsewhere in the American's pilgrimage, the experience
of what we call nature is by turns Hobbesian and Rousseauistic,
empiricistic and idealistic, enlivening and stultifying, consuming
and isolating. If, in one paragraph, the pilgrim succeeds in losing
her sense of self—her consciousness of human language and form—
in the next she reasserts it—the one the reciprocal of the other,
disengagement the answer to engagement, and each alternately de-
sirable (or necessary) and undesirable. If, in one paragraph, she is
an unwitting, integral participant of the scene, an un-self-conscious
perceiver and recorder—like the puppy, an unknowing part of the
landscape—in the next she is a knowing, self-conscious verbalizer,
divorced (and self-divorced) both from the scene and from her immediately past self, at once at least mildly distressed at having lost
contact, at having become "opaque" and, by implication, insensitive—and at least half pleased (however quietly) with the result, the
realization (previously unavailable) that "the puppy is still squirm-
ing on his back"—the *knowledge*, as humans are disposed to call it,
that "nothing has changed for him," the unthinking, nonhuman
animal.

At least half-lamenting her inability to participate as the puppy participates, she simultaneously and quietly asserts her own distinction and the distinguishing "mark" (however troublesome) of her species—the mark, if one can phrase it this way, not of consciousness per se, but of the *claim* to consciousness and of the protestation of self-consciousness, the mark of distinction and difference which she and her kind have for some time found it necessary to insist upon, even as that mark means divorce from the other. "It is ironic," she says, "that the one thing that all religions recognize as separating us from our creator—our very self-consciousness—is also the one thing that divides us from our fellow creatures. It was a bitter birthday present from evolution, cutting us off at both ends" (p. 79).

At least half at odds with herself and her heritage—her inherited views both of the unwitting puppy and of her own self-declared, conscious and self-conscious, kind—for the moment, she is unwilling, if not unable, to consider openly the several ironies of her own statement. What is ironic, someone might say—the puppy perhaps?—is that we, of all organisms, should consider this psycho- and sociobiotic state of affairs ironic—as if we were meant to live in some other way.

In such a near quandary, her quite immediate effort is to find some half-adequate, discriminating and justifying, ground upon which to continue to stand—some means of salvaging her articulate consciousness while simultaneously assuring herself of her ability to experience "the present" purely, as the puppy apparently does— some method again of being of and in one's place while simultaneously knowing it—some way of having one's participatory cake and simultaneously eating (or appreciating) it. Feeling half left out, at least, and at best half-happy in her divided state of mind, she is extremely reluctant to admit that consciousness may be inimical, as she puts it, to "living in the present":

> Consciousness itself does not hinder living in the present. In fact, it is only to a heightened awareness that the great door to the present opens at all. Even a certain amount of interior verbalization is helpful to enforce the memory of whatever it is that is taking place. The gas station puppy, after all, may have experienced those same moments more purely than I did, but he brought fewer instruments to bear on the same material, he had no data for comparison, and he profited only in the grossest of ways, by having an assortment of itches scratched.
>
> *Self*-consciousness, however, does hinder the experience of the present. It is the one instrument that unplugs all the rest. So

> long as I lose myself in a tree, say, I can scent its leafy breath or
> estimate its board feet of lumber. I can draw its fruit or boil tea
> on its branches, and the tree stays tree. But the second I become
> aware of myself at any of these activities—looking over my own
> shoulder, as it were—the tree vanishes, uprooted from the spot
> and flung out of sight as if it had never grown. And time, which
> had flowed down into the tree bearing new revelations like float-
> ing leaves at every moment, ceases. It dams, stills, stagnates.
>
> Self-consciousness is the curse of the city and all that
> sophistication implies. . . . Innocence is a better world. (P. 81)

The effort, then—the renewed effort, and for a brief time, the
success—is to distinguish between consciousness and self-consciousness, to insist (though not self-consciously) that the former, at
least in moderate amounts, is the key to the door of the fully appreciated present, and that the latter, which is the former taken to
extremes, is "the curse of the city and all that sophistication implies." The trick is, finally, to convince oneself that the unconscious
and un-self-consciousness use of language is categorically distinct
from (if not qualitatively superior to) a puppy's whines and bark-
ings—that a puppy's at-least-half-enviable way of being (or seeming
to be) is a lesser, grosser way than the way of the unconsciously (or
half-consciously) verbalizing human—that homeopathic doses of
what humans label "consciousness" do indeed enable one both to
profit from "the present" in qualitatively superior ways *and* to partake somehow of the puppy's unconscious purity.

And the trick works—as long as one can keep from thinking
about the odds between that conspicuously human need "to enforce the memory" of whatever's taking place and the happenings
which, no more than two pages ago, seemed hardly to demand en-
forcement, much less reinforcement—those once very-much-
present shadows, crevasses, and canyons—that sprouting, bulging,
bossed, and hummocked state of mind and being which seemed
only violated and polluted the moment ("the second") it was put in
the past. The trick works, in other words, only as long as one can
keep from viewing one's statements as the human equivalent of
whines or barks—only as long as one can keep an unconscious eye
on consciousness, self-consciousness, and verbalization. The persuasion persuades only as long as one can keep from sensing that
the most present substance of the all-but-present moment is neither
puppy nor tree nor board feet, but consciousness and self-consciousness. It is hardly any wonder, then, that the pilgrim should
conclude this first of several brief discourses on consciousness and
self-consciousness with an abstract advocacy of the concrete condi-

tion with which she had attempted to begin—"Innocence is a better world."—in an almost open recognition that both consciousness and self-consciousness—the methodical estimate of board feet and the estimation of one's estimate—the drawing of the fruit and the drawing of oneself drawing—are not so distinct from a puppy's whines or a tree's roots as she has just contended——and in a near admission that this business of discussing consciousness may well be a self-deceptive and self-defensive way of scratching an assort-ment of human itches.

The pattern is by now well established—at times all too well. To the degree she succeeds in convincing herself of her human distinc-tion—her knowledge and her knowing sense of a particular place, however painful—to just that degree she takes herself away from her own deeply held conception of what it means (or might mean) to be of a place—to just that degree, by her own admission, she vio-lates and pollutes her original intent. The quest to locate herself, the effort to explore her neighborhood and determine where she is, even if she can't discover why—is continuous and at best half-satisfying. "Where am I?" she asks openly (p.93), only to answer two pages later, "I am not here yet" (p. 95).

Plagued by memory, consciousness, and all-too-frequent self-consciousness—by her desire to be a part and her fears of becoming too much a part, by her needs to be apart and her dissatisfaction at being or becoming too much apart—over and over again she tries to lose herself in the wonderful intricacy of suspended newts or tulip-tree leaves, the "little masterpieces of masonry" of caddisfly cases, the exacting stability of "one hundred thirty-six atoms of hydrogen, carbon, oxygen, and nitrogen" arrayed around a single atom of magnesium in a molecule of chlorophyll—the amazing fact that an atom of iron substituted for the atom of magnesium produces a molecule of hemoglobin (p. 126)—or the "two hundred twenty-eight separate and distinct muscles in the head of an ordinary caterpil-lar" (p. 132)—only to find herself confronted (or to confront herself) with the almost overwhelming fecundity of ostracods, which she crunches "by the thousands" every time she sets foot in Tinker Creek (p. 132)—or the scandalous profligacy of an average goldfish eating her five thousand eggs as fast as she lays them (p. 167)— "mothers devouring their own offspring" (p. 169), offspring de-vouring their mothers (pp. 169–70), and blood flukes working their not-so-whilom way from human feces to snail guts to human intes-tines and back (p. 173).

By the time she gets through the blood flukes and the horsehair worms, she is asking, "Are my values then so diametrically op-posed to those that nature preserves?" "This is the key point," she says:

> Must I then part ways with the only world I know? I had
> thought to live by the side of the creek in order to shape my life
> to its free flow. But I seem to have reached a point where I must
> draw the line. It looks as though the creek is not buoying me up
> but dragging me down. . . . It looks for the moment as though I
> might have to reject this creek life unless I want to be utterly
> brutalized. Is human culture with its values my only real home
> after all? Can it possibly be that I should move my anchor-hold
> to the side of a library. This direction of thought brings me
> abruptly to a fork in the road where I stand paralyzed, unwilling
> to go on, for both ways lead to madness. (P. 176).

It is the classic American's dilemma in a nutshell—or, rather, in an
aphid's egg—history and human culture versus the by now all-too-
apparent revelations of a solitary involvement with what we call
nature—word versus thing, human subject versus nonhuman object, emotion versus reason, value (and metaphor) versus fact—desire, impulse, and instinct versus consciousness, self-consciousness, and knowledge. "Both ways lead to madness"—and, "for the
moment," one might assume, paralysis—the end of the book,
perhaps—but the inveterate American is unwilling (and, finally, unable)—despite (and in large part because of) her awareness of the
limitations and functions of language—to give up the ghost of the
dream, the original vision of finding some way through or out of the
conflicts, some incarnation of harmony between isolate human self
and nonhuman other.

Few "Europeans"—few people of historistic mind—can readily
and sympathetically comprehend this persistent concern to live "as
purely as we can, in the present"—this fear that "human culture
with its values" may be "my only real home after all?" Where else,
pray tell—one might ask—did you think you might live? Few people
of historistic and methodo-logical mind can do anything but respond with a wry smile to the disjointing effects of "I am not here
yet"—or the pronouncement "here we—so incontrovertibly—are"
(pp. 127–28), which much later in the book becomes, in slight echoing variation, "Here we so incontrovertibly are" (p. 240)—or the
dividing and slightly desperate "I want to think about trees" (p.
86)—or the several reminders of "I am sitting under a sycamore by
Tinker Creek" (p. 85) which accompany it—interspersed with the
likes of "Where do I live anyway?" and "Where am I?" (p. 93)—
repeated throughout the second section of the sixth chapter, "The
Present"—as stays against temporal and spatial confusion—"My
back rests on a steep bank under the sycamore" (p. 89)—"I am
sitting under a sycamore tree" (p. 92)—"I am sitting under a
bankside sycamore" (p. 92)—"I am sitting under a sycamore by

Tinker Creek" (p. 94)—each at best a half-willing, if urgent, reclamation of some sense of customary time and place, each a near-
admission of the failings of one's visionary explorations.

The historically methodo-logical mind can understand, of
course, the desire to "live" outside time—the effort to transcend or
escape history—perhaps even in or through some present configuration or incarnation of what we call the eternal or the timeless—but
in the configuration of a muskrat?—or through a bluegill? In or
through a particular cedar, of course, but only if it clearly partakes
of the long-sanctioned and sanctioning cedars of Lebanon—not if
it's one particular cedar, lighted or no, of the Tinker Creek valley of
Virginia. That, one might say, is the American's dilemma—to find in
the particulars of one's American surroundings sanctioning meaning and significance which shall match (if not surpass and comprehend) their European counterparts and progenitors.

The ongoing and by now traditional American effort is to discover and engage the substance of one's local and previously unknown place, to shape one's life to one's given environment, to lend
it some substantial and, hence, historic (or historistic) stature and
significance—while simultaneously avoiding both the decomposing
underside of nature and the discomposing madness of historic institutions, the library and all it signifies. The attempt is to find within
one's previously unknown place—one's humble, energizing, and
humbling American surroundings—some justifying (if not redemptive) substance and meaning which are neither historic nor
cultured—and thus to lend oneself, if not something of sainthood,
then something at least of classical despair. It is to be possessed of
and by one's local American place, while simultaneously experiencing the dispossessing insight of the classical mystic—to know and
be of one's immediately local world while somehow being emptied
of all things worldly. It is to find eternity in a grain of sand or a blade
of grass, but in the particular grains of sand one finds in the washes
and spawning beds of Tinker Creek, and in the grasses and clovers
chewed and cached by one very particular, provincial muskrat. It is
to stalk the phenomenal surfaces of one's previously unstoried surroundings and to find in them the intuitions of Newton and Buddha:

> In summer, I stalk. Summer leaves obscure, heat dazzles,
> and creatures hide from the red-eyed sun, and me. I have to seek
> things out. The creatures I seek have several senses and free
> will; it becomes apparent that they do not wish to be seen. I can
> stalk them in either of two ways. The first is not what you think
> of as true stalking, but it is the *Via negativa*, and as fruitful as
> actual pursuit. When I stalk this way I take my stand on a bridge

> and wait, emptied. I put myself in the way of the creature's pas-
> sage, like spring Eskimos at a seal's breathing hole. Something
> might come; something might go. I am Newton under the apple
> tree, Buddha under the bo. Stalking the other way [the *Via ac-
> tiva*], I forge my own passage seeking the creature. I wander the
> banks; what I find, I follow, doggedly, like the Eskimos haunting
> the caribou herds. I am Wilson squinting after the traces of elec-
> trons in a cloud chamber; I am Jacob at Peniel wrestling with
> the angel. (P. 184)

Someone might say that these allusive images, and the concepts associated with them, are mainly or purely "evocative"—that
she can't be serious, that she's simply playing games, that the tone
is too light. To some degree, of course, the tone is indeed light, even
too light; and she isn't, as we say, serious. To some extent she is
making fun of herself and the serious claims she has been making
both for herself and for her very limited neighborhood. The apparent "fun," however—the openly egotistic identification with
Newton and Buddha (which no one in his "right mind" would take
seriously)—is more than half-belied by the seriousness of things
that both precede and follow it—the former an account of Eskimo
women and children "netting little birds":

> They have devised a cruel and ingenious method: after they net
> a few birds with great effort and after much stalking, they thread
> them alive and squawking through their beaks' nostrils, and fly
> them like living kites at the end of long lines. The birds fly franti-
> cally, trying to escape, but they cannot, and their flapping efforts
> attract others of their kind, curious—and the Eskimos easily net
> the others. (P. 183)

One does not want to pursue too closely here latent analogies between the present, stalking expositor—whose methods seem so often to prove futile, who so often seems to miss her mark—and these
long-suffering Eskimo hunters—whose very successful stalkings
are as patently brutal as they are ingenious. One does not want to
pursue too doggedly these "innocent" women and children. For one
might easily be caught in one's own half-fascinated, half-terrifying
net—or, worse perhaps, be taken unwittingly with others of one's
animal kind.

Neither does one wish to attend too adroitly or inventively to
similarly lurking analogies between oneself and the image of three
bluegills that follows immediately upon Jacob's evocative wres-
tlings:

> Fish are hard to see either way. Although I spend most of the summer stalking muskrats, I think it is fish even more than muskrats that by their very mystery and hiddenness crystalize the quality of my summer life at the creek. A thick spawning of fish, a bedful of fish, is too much, horror; but I walk out of my way in hopes of glimpsing three bluegills bewitched in a pool's depth or rising to floating petals or bubbles. (Pp. 184–85)

The near-reminders of one's own bewitchment, of one's own instinctive risings—to petals or bubbles?—are not quite as quiescent as one might like, no more dormant and no less in need of control than the images of Eskimo women and children or netted birds frantically trying to escape. In their reflective lights and entangling depths, the apparently playful allusions and analogues juxtaposed with them—the near-identification of one's humbled American self with Newton, Buddha, Wilson, and Jacob—and each, by implication, with the others—are finally at least as serious as the events on either side of them. Despite (and indeed because of) their manifest playfulness—their blatant egotism and their open craziness—they provide seriously therapeutic interludes in what is otherwise an all-too-threatening drama, brief respites of sorts that enable the two-sided stalker to prepare for yet another metaphysical and epistemological foray:

> The very act of trying to see fish makes them almost impossible to see. My eyes are awkward instruments whose casing is clumsily outsized. If I face the sun along a bank I cannot see into the water; instead of fish I see water striders, the reflected undersides of leaves, birds' bellies, clouds and blue sky. So I cross to the opposite bank and put the sun at my back. Then I can see into the water perfectly within the blue shadow made by my body; but as soon as that shadow looms across them, the fish vanish in a flurry of flashing tails. (P. 185)

Virtually every extended image contains the seeds of its author's (and frequently its reader's) discomfiture; and the workable responses tend to be two—a smile (or some comparable recognition of one's craziness) or further, serious exploration of one's prospects. Contemplative or active, the experience of (or, more accurately, the quest for) "nature in America" puts the very fabric of classical Western thought—the basic forms and structures of one's sanity and control—at considerable risk:

> I am coming around to fish as spirit. The Greek acronym for
> some of the names of Christ yields *ichthys*, Christ as fish, and
> fish as Christ. The more I glimpse the fish in Tinker Creek, the
> more satisfying the coincidence becomes, the richer the symbol,
> not only for Christ but for the spirit as well. (Pp. 185–86)

Christ comes perilously close to becoming a local bluegill, Tinker
Creek to becoming the Sea of Galilee, and the narrator to becoming
a self-declared Virginia saint, a recipient of an ichthyic grace, an
original apostle kneeling not to a cross but to a flurry of flashing
tails. "To say that holiness is a fish," as the pilgrim says here, "is a
statement of the abundance of grace"—a statement and a declaration, by doubly self-reflexive definition, of the abundance of grace—
a statement that barely veils a substantial, telling desperation in her
quest—an almost openly spoken fear that one's statements and sayings are not much more than that, are not being heard or
answered—that what we call the external world is not responding,
that the other (nonhuman or suprahuman, natural or supernatural)
bears little if any resemblance to one's articulated needs, that one
may be once again "blind as a bat, sensing only from every direction the echo" of one's own thin cries.

Faced once again with the prospect of such a self-reflexive conclusion—and no closer than she ever has been to finding out where
she is—her response, quite understandably, is to try to forget the
fish—despite their crystallizing mysteriousness—and to turn, first,
to a green heron (p. 187) and then to a particular dragonfly (p. 188)
and then to a water strider (p. 189)—and finally to an extensive
engagement with muskrats, the most sustained encounter with a
single species or phenomenon in the entire book:

> One hot evening three years ago, I was standing more or less
> *in* a bush. I was stock-still, looking deep into Tinker Creek from a
> spot on the bank opposite the house, watching a group of
> bluegills stare and hang motionless near the bottom of a deep,
> sunlit pool. I was focused for depth. I had long since lost myself,
> lost the creek, the day, lost everything, but still amber depth. All
> at once I couldn't see. And then I could: a young muskrat had
> appeared on top of the water, floating on its back. Its forelegs
> were folded langorously [sic] across its chest; the sun shone on
> its upturned belly. Its youthfulness and rodent grin, coupled
> with its ridiculous method of locomotion, which consisted of a
> lazy wag of the tail assisted by an occasional dabble of a webbed
> hind foot, made it an enchanting picture of decadence, dissipa-
> tion, and summer sloth. I forgot all about the fish. (Pp. 190–91)

It is not easy to forget the fish, obviously; and neither is it easy to concentrate. To focus for depth, or to recall such a focus, it is best not to think (or write) too much about focusing. "Focusing" is not for meditation, but for handbooks of meditation. To lose oneself (much less the creek, the day, and "everything, but still amber depth"), it is best not to think (or write) too much about losing oneself (much less about the creek or the day or "everything, but still amber depth"). To "see" or experience the muskrat in its own right, it is best not to think or write too much about pictures of decadence or dissipation or sloth. In fact, to lose oneself in a muskrat, it is best to go exclusively with forelegs and an upturned belly, with rodents perhaps (but not with a rodent "grin"), with a tail and a webbed hind foot.

Losing oneself to a muskrat (or even to the remembered image of one)—immersing oneself in nature, as we say—is, in fact, a risky business. It requires (or seems to require), and it certainly produces, an almost constant vigilance—a slow, watchful, and above all self-protective "approach"—in fact, for every approach a withdrawal, for every advance a retreat, for every "appearance" a "disappearance"—the former simultaneously engrossing and engulfing, the latter at once disheartening and disencumbering—at least one guarded, psychic step backward for every move forward. Otherwise one might easily lose both oneself and the object of one's quest:

> [I]n my surprise at having the light come on so suddenly, and at having my consciousness returned to me all at once and bearing an inverted muskrat, I must have moved and betrayed myself. The kit—for I know now it was just a young kit—righted itself so that only its head was visible above water, and swam downstream, away from me. I extricated myself from the bush and foolishly pursued it. It dove sleekly, reemerged, and glided for the opposite bank. I ran along the bankside brush, trying to keep it in sight. It kept casting an alarmed look over its shoulder at me. Once again it dove, under a floating mat of brush lodged in the bank, and disappeared. I never saw it again. (P. 191)

To "betray" oneself in such a situation is also, and tellingly, to save oneself, or one's sense of self. To "extricate" oneself from "the bush"—as the muskrat swims "away," and then to pursue it "foolishly"—is to anticipate and forestall further and deeper entanglement. It is to "extricate" and "rescue" oneself from the all-too-present threat of utter psychic entrapment, from a prospective "disappearance" at least as ominous as it may be redemptive. Mo-

mentarily, at least, it is to "invert" the tone of the relationship between self and other, to increase their distance, and to reverse one's
psychic direction.

Gone now—out of "sight," and almost out of mind—the youthful muskrat almost returns in the next few sentences, along with
others of its fascinating kind:

> (Nor have I ever, despite all the muskrats I have seen, again seen
> a muskrat floating on its back.) But I did not know muskrats
> then; I waited panting, and watched the shadowed bank. Now I
> know that I cannot outwait a muskrat who knows I am there.
> The most I can do is get "there" quietly, while it is still in its
> hole, so that it never knows, and wait there until it emerges. (P.
> 191)

One clearly doesn't want to get too close to a muskrat too soon, not
even to a remembered muskrat. One needs to prepare for such an
encounter, to think one's methods through, before one can under-
take further floating inversions and sleek divings:

> But then all I knew was that I wanted to see more muskrats.
>
> I began to look for them day and night. . . . That summer I
> haunted the bridges, I walked up creeks and down, but no
> muskrats ever appeared. You must just have to be there, I
> thought. You must have to spend the rest of your life standing in
> bushes. It was a once-in-a-lifetime thing, and you've had your
> once.
>
> Then one night I saw another, and my life changed. After
> that I knew where they were in numbers, and I knew when to
> look. It was late dusk; I was driving home from a visit with
> friends. Just on the off chance I parked quietly by the creek,
> walked out on the narrow bridge over the shallows, and looked
> upstream. Someday, I had been telling myself for weeks, some-
> day a muskrat is going to swim right through that channel in the
> cattails, and I am going to see it. That is precisely what hap-
> pened. I looked up into the channel for a muskrat, and there it
> came, swimming right toward me. Knock; seek; ask. It seemed
> to swim with a side-to-side, sculling motion of its vertically flat-
> tened tail. It looked bigger than the upside-down muskrat, and
> its face more reddish. In its mouth it clasped a twig of tulip tree.
> One thing amazed me: it swam right down the middle of the
> creek. I thought it would hide in the brush along the edge; in-
> stead, it plied the waters as obviously as an aquaplane. I could
> just look and look.

> But I was standing on the bridge, not sitting, and it saw me.
> It changed its course, veered toward the bank, and disappeared
> behind an indentation in the rushy shoreline. I felt a rush of
> such pure energy I thought I would not need to breathe for days.
> (Pp. 191–92)

Though it is hardly more detailed than its earlier slothful associate,
this second muskrat is in no way "ridiculous," in no sense languor-
ous or decadent or grinning. In general, it is more wonderful—a fair
amount bolder and a tad less concerned with the observing human
self. It casts no alarmed look over its shoulder, and it leaves the
scene with a nearly oblivious calm, with but one glance in the direction of the amazed self. Its stay, however, is even briefer than the
first's—and not surprisingly. For the frustration or the human de-
fensiveness—the sense of isolation, the self-doubt, the occasional
good-humored pique, or the feeling of personal triumph—which its
smooth, nonhuman indifference might otherwise (and elsewhere)
provoke—is all but subdued and absorbed in a statement of outright
amazement and worshipful admiration—an almost self-obliterating
disclosure of aweful pleasure.

Like the first, then, this second muskrat rather quickly disappears—as it must. The third, however—which follows it after two
pages of distancing (and almost entirely impersonal) exposition—
proves far less easy to deal (or dispense) with. This third muskrat, in
fact, is at once more intricately enchanting and more complexly
baleful than either of his rodentian predecessors, as engrossing and
as threatening as any single organism or phenomenon in the book.
He may even be seen as the pilgrim's last extensive effort to get
deeply into the details of her given place; and the terms of her preoc-
cupation with him are some considerable, and at least four-sided,
sign that she may slowly be coming toward an end:

> The wonderful thing about muskrats in my book is that they
> cannot see very well, and are rather dim, to boot. They are ex-
> tremely wary if they know I am there, and will outwait me every
> time. But with a modicum of skill and a minimum loss of human
> dignity, such as it is, I can be right "there," and the breathing
> fact of my presence will never penetrate their narrow skulls. (P.
> 194)

The approach again is gradual—self-defensive, self-reflexive, and at
least marginally self-controlled. And a reader, like the pilgrim, must
be constantly on guard, so as not too easily to become entrapped in

his own preconceptions. Like the pilgrim—whether she's writing about muskrats, or writing about herself watching muskrats, or about muskrats watching her sometimes concentrated, sometimes desperate, and often "foolish" self—a reader must be at least marginally self-conscious, so as not to be caught too unwittingly by his own conceptions of books, words, and muskrats—so as not to be led too far astray from the object of *his* concentration, so as not to confuse too readily the pilgrim's words with the "reality" of muskrats or giant water bugs, so as not to identify too unknowingly the pilgrim's book with "nature," so as not too unwillingly to suspend his disbelief. If the phrase "in my book," without any offsetting commas, isn't some sign of the extent of self-reflexiveness in this pilgrim's explorations—her passing acknowledgment (if not her worry) that she may be listening to her own thin cries, blind as a human—if there isn't some considerable, half-proud self-reflexiveness in the perceptual limitations of these muskrats, in their dimness and dimwittedness—then certainly there ought to be in the recognition that, within the next five and a half pages, not only will she prove herself a bit dimwitted again—in her self-conscious "anthropocentricity"—but she will also lose a bit more of her "human dignity" than she finds comfortable—and she will find herself on the verge of "kicking" yet a fourth muskrat, on the verge of giving him the boot.

The idea, then—if not the necessity—in reading this book is to be "extremely wary," perhaps not to outwait the pilgrim, but certainly to maintain a modicum of skill in one's reading, and without too much loss of one's own dignity—so that something of its author's competing allegiances may penetrate one's narrow skull:

> What happened last night was not only the ultimate in muskrat dimness, it was also the ultimate in human intrusion, the limit beyond which I am certain I cannot go. I would never have imagined I could go that far, actually to sit beside a feeding muskrat as beside a dinner partner at a crowded table. (P. 194)

In strictly narrative terms, it may be worth remembering, only two dinner partners are (or will be) seated at this "crowded table":

> What happened was this. Just in the past week I have been frequenting a different place, one of the creek's nameless feeder streams. It is mostly a shallow trickle joining several pools up to three feet deep. Over one of these pools is a tiny pedestrian bridge known locally, if at all, as the troll bridge. I was sitting on

the troll bridge about an hour before sunset, looking upstream about eight feet to my right where I know the muskrats have a den. I had just lighted a cigarette when a pulse of ripples appeared at the mouth of the den, and a muskrat emerged. He swam straight toward me and headed under the bridge.

Now the moment a muskrat's eyes disappear from view under a bridge, I go into action. I have about five seconds to switch myself around so that I will be able to see him very well when he emerges on the other side of the bridge. I can easily hang my head over the other side of the bridge, so that when he appears under me, I will be able to count his eyelashes if I want. The trouble with this maneuver is that, once his beady eyes appear again on the other side, I am stuck. If I move again, the show is over for the evening. I have to remain in whatever insane position I happen to be caught, for as long as I am in his sight, so that I stiffen all my muscles, bruise my ankles on the concrete, and burn my fingers on the cigarette. And if the muskrat goes out on a bank to feed, there I am with my face hanging a foot over the water, unable to see anything but crayfish. So I have learned to take it easy on these five-second flings.

When the muskrat went under the bridge, I moved so I could face downstream comfortably. He reappeared, and I had a good look at him. He was eight inches long in the body, and another six in the tail. Muskrat tails are black and scaled, flattened not horizontally, like beavers' tails, but vertically, like a belt stood on edge. In the winter, muskrats' tails sometimes freeze solid, and the animals chew off the frozen parts up to about an inch of the body. They must swim entirely with their hind feet, and have a terrible time steering. This one used his tail as a rudder and only occasionally as a propeller; mostly he swam with a pedaling motion of his hind feet, held very straight and moving down and around, "toeing down" like a bicycle racer. The soles of his hind feet were strangely pale; his toenails were pointed in long cones. He kept his forelegs still, tucked up to his chest. (Pp. 194-96)

"What happened was this"—one seemingly direct step forward, toward the object of one's desired concentration, followed by several half-steps backward, to situate oneself and set the scene—"Just in the past week I have been frequenting a different place, one of the creek's nameless feeder streams. It is mostly a shallow trickle joining several pools. . . . Over one of these pools is a tiny pedestrian bridge. . . . I was sitting on the troll bridge. . . . I had just lighted a cigarette. . . ."—all to get set for the tension to come—the excitement, the pain, the revelations, and the doubt—"a pulse of ripples appeared at the mouth of the den, and a muskrat emerged. He swam straight toward me and headed under the bridge." One bold, giant-step forward.

In fact, it seems, too bold too soon—because the pilgrim backs off for an entire paragraph—to consider herself and to discuss her methods and their implications—before allowing the muskrat (or herself) to come nearer. She is careful, in other words, to prepare her own and the muskrat's way—to attempt to assure herself that the upcoming and much-desired experience will not be as awkwardly intoxicating as she knows, from frequent past experience (and despite her preparations), it is likely to be.

Even as she readmits this third muskrat to consciousness, she is concerned to quiet prospective ecstasy and pain—"When the muskrat went under the bridge, I moved so I could face downstream *comfortably*" [italics mine, of course]. When he fully reappears, and she has "a good look at him"—when he comes directly into closeup view—appearing in his own right, as it were—without the open intercessions of the uneasy human "I"—as he comes very close indeed—she literally sizes him up—"He was eight inches long in the body, and another six in the tail"—and then immediately pulls back from him. As his tail becomes immediate, and all but unmediable, she reestablishes (or attempts to reestablish) and reasserts her "knowledgeable" human distance from it (and from him) by turning to a generically impersonal voice—by turning to no muskrat tail in particular, and to several muskrat tails in general: "Muskrat tails are black and scaled, flattened not horizontally, like beavers' tails, but vertically, like a belt stood on edge."

And for a brief moment the defensive move is successful. Her turn toward the "knowledge" of the library, the generic probabilities and averages of science, enables her to gain a much-needed and temporarily unconscious perspective on what she is seeing. But this way, too, almost immediately leads back toward consciousness—and its seemingly inevitable outcome, self-consciousness—"In the winter, muskrats' tails sometimes freeze solid, and the animals chew off the frozen parts up to about an inch of the body. They must swim entirely with their hind feet, and have a terrible time steering." The images threaten to become openly self-reflexive. It is all but clear that the pilgrim is having at least as terrible a time steering as the generic, wintered muskrats who chew off their own frozen tails—and a much harder time than the particular muskrat who has just reappeared from beneath the bridge. Both "ways" seem to be leading toward madness again, or at least to considerable discomfiture.

Having tried to place this muskrat and his tail in provisional, generic context—and having again come perilously close to "discovering" herself, rather than some satisfying "knowledge" of the object of her desire—she has little choice but to turn back to the muskrat at hand, alternately promising and threatening as he may be—while trying to avoid reflections upon his successful and apparently untroubled swimmings, while trying again to lose herself (and her sense of self) in his clamberings, chompings, and slidings—without thinking too much about her instinctive needs for some limited human dignity—and trying again to find some workable blend between human self and nonhuman other, without thinking too much about her needs for same—"This one used his tail as a rudder and only occasionally as a propeller; mostly he swam with a pedaling motion of his hind feet, held very straight and moving down and around, 'toeing down' like a bicycle racer. The soles of his hind feet were strangely pale; his toenails were pointed in long cones. He kept his forelegs still, tucked up to his chest."

The effort, then, is to maintain a modicum of human skill—to propel and sustain one's human self—"like a bicycle racer," "as a carpenter feeds a saw," or as "somebody eating celery sticks"—without thinking too much about the strange paleness of the muskrat's hind feet or its seemingly unerring maneuvers and "unthought" nurturings:

> The muskrat clambered out on the bank across the stream from me, and began feeding. He chomped down on a ten-inch weed, pushing it into his mouth steadily with both forepaws as a carpenter feeds a saw. I could hear his chewing; it sounded like somebody eating celery sticks. Then he slid back into the water with the weed still in his mouth, crossed under the bridge, and, instead of returning to his den, rose erect on a submerged rock and calmly polished off the rest of the weed. He was about four feet away from me. Immediately he swam under the bridge again, hauled himself out on the bank, and unerringly found the same spot on the grass, where he devoured the weed's stump. (P. 196)

The idea—and at least temporarily the need—is to "take it easy," and not to get caught (or catch oneself) in some "insane position," some position that threatens the breakdown of one's instinctive categories. It is to keep the show going—to see more than mere crayfish—to see what one came to see, in fact—and not to get stuck watching or thinking of oneself. It is, above all, to keep from thinking about the all-too-apparent odds between human similes and nonhuman phenomena—to keep from thinking, in other words, about one's needs to think of the muskrat as unthinking. It is to sustain one's admiration and respect for the muskrat without becoming jealous of its "unerring" ways, to keep from being (or becoming) critical or vindictive or bitter—or, worse, "superior." Because such "superiority," once it becomes conscious, can do little but undercut the only thing one apparently has to go on, the only distinguishing trait one can sensibly claim in this chomping, chewing world. It is to maintain one's human dignity—one's capacity to appreciate, admire, and tolerate—until one can no longer help oneself:

> All this time I was not only doing an elaborate about-face every time his eyes disappeared under the bridge, but I was also smoking a cigarette. He never noticed that the configuration of the bridge metamorphosed utterly every time he went under it. Many animals are the same way: they can't see a thing unless it's moving. Similarly, every time he turned his head away, I was free to smoke the cigarette, although of course I never knew when he would suddenly turn again and leave me caught in some wretched position. The galling thing was, he was downwind of me and my cigarette: was I really going through all this for a creature without any sense whatsoever? (P. 196)

Given the previous paragraph, the "about-face" here is considerable. The metamorphoses, though covert, are quite noticeable to the discerning eye—and certainly not to the muskrat's. In this conspicuously "human" state of mind and body, it isn't at all clear but what the normal, "sane" human observer—the one who isn't on his or her apperceptive toes—is one of the "many animals" dependent for perception upon motion. The muskrat's motions and prospective motions—its trips under the bridge and the turnings of its head—certainly determine a good deal of what the human pilgrim can and cannot see (not to mention what she can and cannot do). In this manifest human condition, it isn't at all clear that "freedom" means what one might habitually take it to mean. It means, apparently, momentary "freedom" from the muskrat's gripping eyes, "independence" from at least some of its turnings; but it also means the "freedom" to turn (or return) to one's normal human habits—the smoking of the cigarette—the satisfaction of one's distinctly human needs—though hardly for more than half a sentence. In the long run, it may mean no more than the substitution of one fixation for another; and that thought may well lead one to wonder about the referent of that "creature without sense" in the final sentence—about just who or what it is that demands these sacrifices.

Once again about all one can accomplish is another elaborating "about-face"—another attempted turn away from one's seemingly inescapable, and apparently complicating, human consciousness— another turn toward the comings and goings of what we call the muskrat. And the further one goes, the "closer" the relationship seems to become—not, unfortunately, in the sanguine, popular sense of getting "closer to nature," but in the sense that it becomes harder and harder to distinguish one's own motivations and methods from one's muskrat's, and indeed to distinguish "the muskrat"—and, for that matter, one's self—from one's own half-predatory, half-nervous terms:

> After the weed stump was gone, the muskrat began ranging over the grass with a nervous motion, chewing off mouthfuls of grass and clover near the base. Soon he had gathered a huge, bushy mouthful; he pushed into the water, crossed under the bridge, swam towards his den, and dove.
>
> When he launched himself again shortly, having apparently cached the grass, he repeated the same routine in a businesslike fashion, and returned with another shock of grass.
>
> Out he came again. I lost him for a minute when he went under the bridge; he did not come out where I expected him. Suddenly to my utter disbelief he appeared on the bank next to me. The troll bridge itself is on a level with the low bank; there I was, and there he was, at my side. I could have touched him with the palm of my hand without straightening my elbow. He was ready to hand.
>
> Foraging beside me he walked very humped up, maybe to save heat loss through evaporation. Generally, whenever he was out of water he assumed the shape of a shmoo; his shoulders were as slender as a kitten's. He used his forepaws to part clumps of grass extremely tidily; I could see the flex in his narrow wrists. He gathered mouthfuls of grass and clover less by actually gnawing than by biting hard near the ground, locking his neck muscles, and pushing up jerkily with his forelegs.
>
> His jaw was underslung, his black eyes close set and glistening, his small ears pointed and furred. I will have to try and see if he can cock them. I could see the water-slicked long hairs of his coat, which gathered in rich brown strands that emphasized the smooth contours of his body, and which parted to reveal the paler, softer hair like rabbit fur underneath. Despite his closeness, I never saw his teeth or belly.
>
> After several minutes of rummaging about in the grass at my side, he eased into the water under the bridge and paddled to his den with the jawful of grass held high, and that was the last I saw of him. (Pp. 196–97)

Given the intensity and the extent of this engagement, it is hardly surprising that, despite his seemingly final "disappearance," this muskrat should prove extremely difficult to get rid of. As one might expect by now, in the next few sentences he returns (or what is the same thing, returns to mind)—and with a near-vengeance:

> In the forty minutes I watched him, he never saw me, smelled me, or heard me at all. When he was in full view of course I never moved except to breathe. My eyes would move, too, following his, but he never noticed. I even swallowed a couple of times: nothing. The swallowing thing interested me because I had read that, when you are trying to hand-tame wild birds, if you inadvertently swallow, you ruin everything. The bird, according to this theory, thinks you are swallowing in anticipation, and off it goes. The muskrat never twitched. Only once, when he was feeding from the opposite bank about eight feet away from me, did he suddenly rise upright, all alert—and then he immediately resumed foraging. But he never knew I was there.
>
> I never knew I was there, either. For that forty minutes last night I was as purely sensitive and mute as a photographic plate; I received impressions, but I did not print out captions. My own self-awareness had disappeared; it seems now almost as though, had I been wired with electrodes, my EEG would have been flat. I have done this sort of thing so often that I have lost self-consciousness about moving slowly and halting suddenly; it is second nature to me now. And I have often noticed that even a few minutes of this self-forgetfulness is tremendously invigorating. I wonder if we do not waste most of our energy just by spending every waking minute saying hello to ourselves. Martin Buber quotes an old Hasid master who said, "When you walk across the fields with your mind pure and holy, then from all the stones, and all growing things, and all animals, the sparks of their soul come out and cling to you, and then they are purified and become a holy fire in you." This is one way of describing the energy that comes, using the specialized Kabbalistic vocabulary of Hasidism. (Pp. 197–98)

"I never knew I was there, either"—as this very particular, shmoo-shaped, black-eyed, foraging muskrat literally disappears for the last time, the pilgrim attempts an about-face to end all her previous about-faces. She announces and authors an abrupt and radical, if seemingly light-toned, shift in perspective, an inversion of sorts, that for the next few pages at least, will supersede and all but subsume her previous metamorphoses, while virtually undercutting both the muskrat and the sometime-jealous, sometime-loving figure on the troll bridge. "I never knew I was there, either"—to believe this statement, to go with it, it is necessary to dis-believe—to dis-regard and put out of mind—the many difficulties and frustrations she has experienced (or claimed to experience) over the last several pages—her considerable and more or less continuous efforts to sustain "a modicum of skill" and some semblance of "human dignity" in the face of the muskrat—the conscious and even self-conscious pains she has taken to be, as she has previously put it, "there," to be ready and capable of receiving, if and when the muskrat should appear—the many elaborate about-faces she has undertaken and undergone on the "tiny pedestrian bridge" over a pool no more than three feet deep—and, in general, her many struggles to come to terms both with the muskrat and with her own hopes and fears. "I never knew I was there, either"—to go with this statement, or to continue with it, one must, in fact, recast virtually the whole of last night's "events" as one presently knows them—either that, or one must ignore them, putting them firmly and sharply down.

"For that forty minutes last night I was as purely sensitive and mute as a photographic plate; I received impressions, but I did not print out captions. My own self-awareness had disappeared"—to suspend one's disbelief here, willingly or unwillingly, one must forget the several active "responses" to the muskrat over the last three pages. One must put out of mind, if not out of time, all memory of all images of oneself as a living, reacting being in the "events" of "last night" (not to mention any psychological rejoinders or philosophical quandaries implicit in them). One must forget one's "elaborate" twistings and turnings on the troll bridge, skillfully "comfortable" though they may have been. One must leave behind the occasional tricky drag on the cigarette, and especially any thought that one may have wondered, at the time, why the muskrat didn't seem to scent or sense it (much less oneself). One must forget that one "lost" the muskrat every time he went under the bridge or dove to enter his den. One must ignore the implications—facial, physiological, and psychological—in the "utter disbelief" one felt when the muskrat "suddenly" appeared on the bank. And one must consign to oblivion the moving eyes, the breathing, and the swallowing—all one's own—of one's immediately previous paragraph—almost the last things that had been on one's mind.

Over the last few pages, in fact—and throughout the "events" of "last night"—the pilgrim has been far less a photographic plate than (pardon the figure) a living, desiring, shifting two-way mirror—one side reflective, the other all too transparent. At least half to her own dissatisfaction, she has "seen" and recorded as much of herself as she has of the muskrat. Her efforts to capture those "forty minutes" of experience with the nonhuman other have proven to be at least as nascently unsettling as settling—at best tensely "mute"— and at least as much reactive as "purely sensitive." And they continue to prove so, despite her declarations to the contrary.

In fact, her declarations to the contrary are the proof in and of the unfinished and unsettled psychic pudding—the intimacy between self and nonhuman other—she has been trying to thicken (without curdling) throughout the book. Her declarations of pure sensitivity and muteness are yet additional and continuing attempts somehow to lose that sense of self which has proved so difficult to handle in the face and body of the muskrat. Her insistences that for "forty minutes" she simply "received impressions," that she "did not print out captions," that her "own self-awareness had disappeared," are, despite themselves, yet additional captions to the incomplete and impure (because finally undevelopable) "photographs" of the last few pages. Together, in fact, these several abstract and distinctly human theorizations provide a psycho-logical (if not philosophical and theo-logical) photograph of their own kind, a photograph (or, rather, a moving picture) of the pilgrim turning (or trying to turn) as un-self-consciously as possible toward the library—away from the muskrat, the troll bridge, and "creek life," and toward the "other way," the way of "human culture with its values."

Now that the muskrat is gone (as at some point, it must go), the pilgrim can "freely" shift the anchor-hold of her thoughts (as she must and does, directly). No longer faced with any clear and present threat to her human dignity—no immediate image or impression of unerring (and apparently unconscious), nonhuman skill—she can give "free" and apparently "unerring" voice to that "state" of mind and body in which, as we say, we lose not only all sense of self but all consciousness. "Free" now of the muskrat and the concrete impressions of last night's events, she can speak (or attempt to speak) in an unqualified, "un-self-conscious," and almost entirely abstract voice about the disappearance of her own "self-awareness," about losing herself (and her sense of self) to the other. Forgetting the muskrat, she can now "remember" how her "own self-awareness had disappeared," and she can think without significant self-consciousness or self-reflection about how often she has noticed "that even a few minutes of this self-forgetfulness is tremendously invigorating."

With the muskrat gone, in other words, she can turn to being the distinctly (and here largely unconscious) human creature she "is," the creature who would claim to have participated fully in the unconscious processes of "nature," while simultaneously being able, consciously, to know and appreciate its participation—the creature who would claim in words, and after the fact, to have been "purely sensitive" and "mute"—the creature, in short, who would have its unconscious natural cake while consciously savoring it, and without descending to the level of the clambering, chomping animal. Faced (and facing herself) with the muskrat's disappearance, her quite human effort is to substitute the condition and the concept of "self-forgetfulness" for the details of "creek life," to plug in for the intricacies of the half-desiring, half-troubled figure on the troll bridge the "invigorating" concept of the "purely sensitive" self, the idea of the self lost to nature (as if the self were ever lost or found in any other condition). The effort and the method are to identify human conception with human and nonhuman substance, to equate human method with the object of human method—in large part *because* they have proven so difficult to blend in the immediately preceding paragraphs.

This sharp, determined turn toward the "library," toward Buber and the old Hasid master, works, then, only to the extent that the pilgrim can keep from thinking about her "captions"—about the unresponsive, inert, inorganic qualities of a "photographic plate"—about the patent odds between the "self" in the term "self-forgetfulness" and the condition to which that term is said to refer—about the small, thin, and logically troublesome cries of that "I" in the likes of "I have done this sort of thing so often that I have lost self-consciousness." She can comfort herself and recover from the events of last night only as long as she can speak without trembling about how "even a few minutes" of "self-forgetfulness" is "tremendously invigorating"—only as long as she can generalize and theorize without thinking of that particular shmoo-shaped muskrat—and only to the extent that she can wonder "if we do not waste most of our energy just by spending every waking minute saying hello to ourselves," without allowing the "content" and the form of her wondering to reflect upon themselves, without thinking of this clause (and all others before it) as self-reflecting, species-specific salutations—the echoes sensed from every direction of one's own thin cries.

It is by now an age-old move; and for the most part it works, for at least another four pages—but only because the pilgrim is able to subdue her sense of herself and her language as organic phenomena—only because she is able to keep from reflecting upon her phrases and conceptions as reflexes—and only as long as she can ignore the considerable frictions between method and object or form and content which, though she here tempers and controls, are just beneath the surface of her "human" consciousness—the same odds, as she will soon discover again, that have troubled all her earlier stalkings.

For the immediate present—and in spite of these shadows of doubt—the way of "human culture" and its "values" seems distinctly more promising than the way of "creek life." At this point, in fact, she hasn't much choice in the matter. Though both "ways" have long-since proven their potential for madness, the insanity of the creek is far more immediately threatening than the insanity of the "library." Bound and determined to continue to play this game—the one she has joined because it is being (and will be) played anyway—she is much in need of some sustaining defenses, some extended restoration of the human dignity she has taken to the edge of its limits on the troll bridge. Thus the highly "cultured" note of her next several pages—and the almost feisty, solidly anthropoid, tone of her last two encounters with muskrats.

As she continues her "retreat" from the "events" of "last night"—at once the nadir and the zenith of her stalkings at creekside—as she labors to bring these meditations toward a close, by gradually regaining some sense of historically sanctioning perspective—she returns inevitably to two brief interludes with a fourth and a fifth muskrat, still seeking some means of coming to terms with them, some "frame of mind" in which to place their promises and threats. In the first of these interludes, she recalls working her way skillfully toward a muskrat who was "feeding on a bank by the troll bridge," "taking as many gliding steps towards him as possible while his head was turned," spreading her "weight" as evenly as she could, so that he wouldn't feel her "coming through the ground," so that whenever she "became visible to him," she could "pause motionless until he turned away again without having to balance too awkwardly on one leg":

> When I got within ten feet of him, I was sure he would flee, but he continued to browse nearsightedly among the mown clovers and grass. Since I had seen just about everything I was ever going to see, I continued approaching just to see when he would break. To my utter bafflement, he never broke. I broke first. When one of my feet was six inches from his back, I refused to press on. He could see me perfectly well, of course, but I was stock-still except when he lowered his head. There was nothing left to do but kick him. Finally he returned to the water, dove, and vanished. I do not know to this day if he would have permitted me to keep on walking right up his back. (P. 199)

Clearly these muskrats are difficult to get rid of. Even in retrospect, they threaten to expose one's considerable, human accomplishments. How, then, to handle them?—if not by taking another distinctly "human" tack?

> I have read that in the unlikely event that you are caught in a stare-down with a grizzly bear, the best thing to do is talk to him softly and pleasantly. Your voice is supposed to have a soothing effect. I have not yet had occasion to test this out on grizzly bears, but I can attest that it does not work on muskrats. It scares them witless. I have tried time and again. Once I watched a muskrat feeding on a bank ten feet away from me; after I had looked my fill I had nothing to lose, so I offered a convivial greeting. Boom. The terrified muskrat flipped a hundred and eighty degrees in the air, nose-dived into the grass at his feet, and disappeared. The earth swallowed him; his tail shot straight up in the air and then vanished into the ground without a sound. Muskrats make several emergency escape holes along a bank for just this very purpose, and they don't like to feed too far away from them. The entire event was most impressive, and illustrates the relative power in nature of the word and the sneak. (P. 200)

The underlying issues are very much the same as they were with the third muskrat, but the tone has changed as the pilgrim's most immediate needs have changed. In the appearances and disappearances of these last two muskrats, there is no longer any sense of disappointed expectations, no sense of the human observer being left behind to suffer lonely, conscious (and self-conscious) separation from the nonhuman other—no sense of frustration, and none of alienation. Quite the contrary, in fact. Though the threats to one's human dignity are still quite apparent, the fears and self-doubts of the human "intruder" are kept well under control. The potentially embarrassing thought that "I broke first" barely ripples the surface of consciousness; and the mock-heroic implications of "I refused to press on"—anthropocentric undercurrents that "last night" would almost certainly have provoked serious self-reflection—are here left undeveloped—all in the interest of a distinctly human wit, a self-aggrandizement and even a kind of "sneaky," smiling pride, which, however short-lived, demonstrates the power of "consciousness" even as it declares (without significant apology) the superiority of the human species.

Still in retreat from the events of last night, the pilgrim can now forthrightly (and almost unconditionally) celebrate her own special, human talent:

> Stalking is a pure form of skill, like pitching or playing
> chess. Rarely is luck involved. I do it right or I do it wrong; the
> muskrat will tell me, and that right early. Even more than base-
> ball, stalking is a game played in the actual present. At every
> second, the muskrat comes, or stays, or goes, depending on my
> skill. (P. 200)

Now almost entirely in "cultured" control—"the muskrat comes, or
stays, or goes, depending on *my* skill"—and no longer openly concerned with the odds between human method and nonhuman object, or form and content (or motive)—having found in them, if anything, ironic reflections of a peculiarly and solely human
condition—she can declare again, and even more forcefully, her capacity to lose herself to the other, without worrying in the least
about the loss, and without allowing herself to reflect openly on the
considerable limitations, logical if not psychological, of her attempted phrasings and stylings:

> Can I stay still? How still? It is astonishing how many people
> cannot, or will not, hold still. I could not, or would not, hold still
> for thirty minutes inside, but at the creek I slow down, center
> down, empty. I am not excited; my breathing is slow and regular.
> In my brain I am not saying, Muskrat! Muskrat! There! I am
> saying nothing. If I must hold a position, I do not "freeze." If I
> freeze, locking my muscles, I will tire and break. Instead of going
> rigid, I go calm, I center down wherever I am; I find a balance
> and repose. I retreat—not inside myself, but outside myself, so
> that I am a tissue of senses. Whatever I see is plenty, abundance.
> I am the skin of water the wind plays over; I am petal, feather-
> stone. (Pp. 200–201)

Committed now as firmly to the "way" of the "library" as she was
"last night" to "creek life"—given (and driven) not to muskrats or
clovers or weed stumps, but to *notions* of centering down, to the
classical *concept* of stillness and the *idea* ("the spiritual state," as
we call it) of emptiness—she can speak about her "methods"
without openly troubling self-reflection, about the dangers of "lock-
ing" one's muscles or the risks of "going rigid" and "freezing,"
without allowing the rigidity of the images to disturb her present,
receptive "concentration." With no immediate fear of freezing—
with no immediate muskrat—she can "open" herself fully, as we
say, to the nonhuman other. With no thought of appearing ridiculous, and no sense of being intrusive, she can give herself "freely"
to notions and images of freely giving oneself to the other.

Now that the muskrats are "gone," she can (and does) abstract (and abstract herself) from the events of her creekside stalkings—and with good reason (or cause)—quite understandably—and even naturally. For now—and only now—can she "retreat" without reflecting on her retreat as a strategic withdrawal, as the reaction of a living, competing organism. Only as she moves toward "human culture with its values," in other words, can she readily (or easily) conceive herself solely as passive receptor or emptied vessel. Only now, in fact, can she afford to.

It is far easier, after all, to "empty" one's mind in the "library"—to fill it with notions and images of pure receptivity—than it is at creekside when one of one's feet is "six inches" from the back of a muskrat. It is far easier to speak of centering down or going "calm" when a muskrat, "terrified" by one's "convivial greeting," has "flipped a hundred and eighty degrees in the air, nose-dived into the grass . . . and disappeared." The closer one gets to the "library," in fact—and the further one gets from muskrats—the easier it is to speak of retreating "outside" oneself, to conceive oneself a balanced, reposeful "tissue of senses," a "petal" or "featherstone" (though not a muskrat or a weed stump). The closer one gets to "human culture with its values," the easier it is to subdue not only the muskrat but one's worrisome self as well, and (most importantly) one's sense of oneself as an organism—provided, of course, that one can keep from thinking about that other "way" to madness.

For the moment, then, the necessity and the method are to convince oneself—to declare outright—that in situations like "last night's," "I am not excited," that "my breathing is slow and regular," that in those now retrospective "forty minutes," at least—if not in this abstracting moment—"I am saying nothing." The trick, if one can accomplish it, is to be as unconsciously and unerringly "human" as one has previously imagined the muskrat to be "non-human." The repeated effort, though now in a distinctly "cultured" venue, and with an alternate "object" of concentration, is not to get caught (or catch oneself) in some awkwardly "insane position." It is to avoid at all costs the madness of the "library," and to keep from cutting oneself off at *both* ends.

Now is not the time to gaze self-consciously at one's "cultured," linguistic and stylistic, navel. Now is not the time to note the considerable odds between one's "human" medium—one's methods, one's phrases, and one's statements—and one's desired "substance" or "content." Now is the time to skim over, if one can, those otherwise all-too-obvious (and all-too-telling) contradictions between syntactic or logical form and semantic vision or desire. Now is the time to subdue one's "human" sense of "logical" and "illogical" relations, to ignore and repress one's sense of paradox and tautology, to say—if one can—"In my brain I am not saying, Muskrat! Muskrat! There!," without saying in one's brain (or anywhere else, for that matter) "Muskrat! Muskrat! There!"—to say, in the manner of the writing or speaking mystic, if one can, "I am saying nothing," without "saying" anything, or while only saying "nothing"—without thinking about the humbling "impossibilities" of one's sayings, without allowing one's senses of circularity and self-contradiction to surface.

The trick, then—the classical trick for a member of this pilgrim's "culture"—is to try to capture in a kind of perpetual present tense the condition, here at least half-past, of "emptiness"—to compose oneself in words, as we say, with thoughts of a wordless, thoughtless state of mind and body—without allowing the necessary limitations of one's words to trouble one's consciousness. The modus vivendi of "human culture with its values"—the effort to calm oneself and settle down—the now "cultured" means of continuing to play this game—is to contend against "last night's" several suggestions to the contrary that language is transparent, that one's present words do not betray some untoward, unwonted reaction to the discomfitures of "last night," that one's stylistic methods are entirely adequate to the "object" of one's desires and thoughts.

It is a difficult task for someone otherwise so given to discovering herself in her neighborhood explorations; and it succeeds only as long as she can avoid that alternate kind of self-consciousness occasioned by the "way" of the library. It succeeds, in fact, for no more than two ensuing pages. For within two paragraphs she is finding "in quantum mechanics a world symbolically similar to my world at the creek" (p. 202); and within another page she is deep into "The Principle of Indeterminacy"—"The electron is a muskrat; it cannot be perfectly stalked":

> It is not that we lack sufficient information to know both a particle's velocity and its position; that would have been a perfectly ordinary situation well within the understanding of classical physics. Rather, we know now for sure that there is no knowing. You can determine the position, and your figure for the velocity blurs into vagueness; or, you can determine the velocity, but whoops, there goes the position. The use of instruments and the very fact of an observer seem to bollix the observations; as a

> consequence, physicists are saying that they cannot study nature per se, but only their own investigations of nature. And I can only see bluegills within my own blue shadow, from which they immediately flee. (P. 203)

Now deep into the way of the library, she has moved her anchor-hold almost too far. She is perilously close once again to the madness of "human culture with its values," to that alternate form of self-consciousness that seems as inevitably to follow from epistemic reflection and analysis as it does from the contemplation of what we call a muskrat. She is perilously close to being on a cultural and philosophic troll bridge. The odds between form and content (or method and object), which she had kept from consciousness in attempting to calm herself—the doubts about the adequacy of her "human" and linguistic medium, which she had kept from surfacing as she "retreated" outside herself—are now all-but-openly present to mind again. The move toward the library is leading almost inexorably to the flipside of that self-conscious sense of isolation occasioned by "last night's" muskrat. The move toward Heisenberg and the Principle of Indeterminacy is threatening to turn the "retreat" outside oneself of two pages past into a self-deceiving echo of "inside" things. What had been, however momentarily, a receptive "emptying" of self to the other, is on the edge of becoming solely an active projection of self, a worrisome sense of inescapable anthropo-morphism (or, worse, ego-morphism), a sense of the complete limitations of the human and cultured self, the impossibility of knowing the other, and the open recognition that all one's explorations of one's "neighborhood" are explorations of oneself, that one can hear only the echoes of one's own thin cries again.

Under the aegis of Heisenberg, Eddington, and Jeans, the muskrat is threatening to become a social (or, worse, a personal) construct, a configuration of human method and desire, rather than a creature of bankside or bridge. Even its unerring otherness is on the verge of becoming a human (and personal) wish. In a sense—an increasingly strong sense—the muskrat is on the verge of "disappearing" again—or, rather, its "author" is on the verge of thinking that it never did (and never could) "appear," not, as we say, in its own right—that the events of "last night" and indeed all creekside events are (and have been) what Eddington calls "mind-stuff":

> The Principle of Indeterminacy turned science inside-out. Suddenly determinism goes, causality goes, and we are left with a universe composed of what Eddington calls, "mind-stuff." Lis-

ten to these physicists: Sir James Jeans, Eddington's successor, invokes "fate," saying that the future "may rest on the knees of whatever gods there be." Eddington says that "the physical world is entirely abstract and without 'actuality' apart from its linkage to consciousness." Heisenberg himself says, "method and object can no longer be separated. *The scientific world-view has ceased to be a scientific view in the true sense of the word."* Jeans says that science can no longer remain opposed to the notion of free will. Heisenberg says, "there is a higher power, not influenced by our wishes, which finally abides and judges." Eddington says that our dropping causality as a result of the Principle of Indeterminacy "leaves us with no clear distinction between the Natural and the Supernatural." And so forth. (Pp. 203–4)

"The Principle of Indeterminacy" is clearly threatening to turn far more than science inside-out. The way of the library is looking more and more like another cul-de-sac; and the pilgrim looks more and more to be cutting herself off once again at both ends. "Method and object can no longer be separated," she aims to say, in a sentence that pointedly (syntactically and formally) separates the two. Method and object, form and content, are identical—as one has wanted to believe they were for those "forty minutes" last night— but now their identity, their inseparability, is at least potential cause for alarm. Now the inseparability of method and object or word and thing or self and other, far from being the essence of a reposeful retreat outside oneself, is a reflection, if not a reminder, of the continuous limitations of being human, a recognition that a retreat outside oneself is necessarily (and only) an extension of oneself, the last thing one wanted two pages ago—a reminder not just that the Principle of Indeterminacy "leaves us with no clear distinction between the Natural and the Supernatural," but an all-but-openly-stated recognition that it leaves us as well with no clear distinction between the Natural and the Human, between the muskrat (or the giant water bug or the tree with lights in it) and our humanoid methods and motives—no clear distinction between the muskrat and oneself. Petal and featherstone, muskrat and troll bridge, are perilously close to losing their otherness, to becoming metaphors for human circumstance and desire, dangerously close to becoming little more than words, in fact.

About the only saving grace here may be the wry recognition, no more than half-satisfying, that comes from "thinking" about "mind-stuff," the recognition that "The Principle of Indeterminacy" likewise leaves us with no clear distinction between the Principle itself and our anthropo-morphic impulses—the self-reflexive recognition that the form and content (or method and object) of the Principle are themselves at odds with one another, that The Principle of Indeterminacy is quite clearly determined and determining, that uncertainty is quite certain, and that only as we take the Principle at what we call face value (only as we respond to it "unconsciously," as a muskrat might) are its "method" and its "object" inseparable—"we know now for sure that there is no knowing."

Like the ·madness threatened by creek life—by water bug, bluegill, and muskrat—the insanity of the library is barely beneath the surface of the pilgrim's prose—and hardly any more controllable. The alternate frights and near-ecstasies of one's creekside meditations are met by the alternating tones of one's philosophic and methodological speculations—first, perhaps, in one's efforts to accept the limitations of one's anthropo-logical condition, to resign oneself to the constraints of one's motives and methods—and, second, in the self-conscious recognition that the "way" of philosophic and methodological analysis is, finally, little different from the "way" of what we call the muskrat (or musquash or ratsmusques or, for that matter, *Ondatra zibethica*)—that all one's observations, classifications, and experimentations are finally defensive (or offensive)—and even that the smile induced by that recognition—the wit and humor (if not the laughter) of the library—are little more than awkwardly therapeutic, marginally satisfying at best, and once again all but discomposing.

The near ecstasy of losing oneself to a preening bankside muskrat—the self-conscious vanity, the half-smiling self-indulgence of preening one's own text—the literal fright of losing control (at worst, perhaps, to one's own imagery)—the madness of the library and the madness of creek life—these are antipodes of the American pilgrim's world. To all intents and purposes, it is a world in which one resists to one's death the establishment or discovery of an equator. It is "all touch and go" (p. 204), as she says.

Object and method, content and form, fact and metaphor—or, as she soon speaks of them, corruption and beauty, place and placelessness, knowledge and vision—these are "The Horns of the Altar" on which she constantly finds herself impaled, and at which she is slowly, if half-reluctantly, learning to worship—the Old World and the New, the fixed and the unfixed (or unfixable). Recollecting a "motionless" copperhead, "its head still hung in the air" above a sandstone rock, she thinks of "poking at it with a weed," but rejects the "notion." Still, wishing "it would do something," she notes its tail, tapering to "nothingness," slides her eye "down its body slowly," and wishes that she "tapered like that somewhere"—an object of beauty, she might say, with only the slightest of desiring, envying smiles—wondering, in at least half-sly response to her own figure, "What if I were a shaped balloon blown up through the tip of a finger":

> . . . this blood-filled, alert creature, this nerved rope of matter, really here instead of not here, splayed soft and solid on a rock by the slimmest of chances. It was a thickening of the air spread from a tip, a rush into being, eyeball and blood, through a pinhole rent. . . . From tail to head it spread like the lines of a crescendo, widening from stillness to a turgid blast; then at the bulging jaws it began contracting again, diminuendo, till at the tip of its snout the lines met back at the infinite point that corners every angle, and that space once more ceased to be a snake. (Pp. 225–26)

Beauty, desire, and fascination—met almost at once by the predacious instincts of a female mosquito:

> While this wonder engaged me, something happened that was so unusual and unexpected that I can scarcely believe I saw it. It was ridiculous.
>
> Night had been rising like a ground vapor from the blackened quarry pool. I heard a mosquito sing in my ear; I waved it away. I was looking at the copperhead. The mosquito landed on my ankle; again, I idly brushed it off. To my utter disbelief, it lighted on the copperhead. It squatted on the copperhead's back near its "neck," and bent its head to its task. I was riveted. I couldn't see the mosquito in great detail, but I could make out its lowered head that seemed to bore like a well drill through surface rock to fluid. . . .
>
> To the best of my knowledge, it lasted two or three full minutes; it seemed like an hour. I could imagine the snake, like the frog sucked dry by the giant water bug, collapsing to an empty bag of skin. But the snake never moved, never indicated any awareness. At last the mosquito straightened itself, fumbled with its forelegs about its head like a fly, and sluggishly took to the air, where I lost it at once. I looked at the snake; I looked beyond the snake to the ragged chomp in the hillside where years before men had quarried stone; I rose, brushed myself off, and walked home. (Pp. 226–27)

Engagements and disengagements, approaches and withdrawals, fascinations and fears, spreadings and contractions, penetrations and receptions—the boundaries between self and nonhuman other, between subject (or method) and object, are at best unstable:

> Is this what it's like, I thought then, and think now: a little blood here, a chomp there, and still we live, trampling the grass? Must everything whole be nibbled? Here was a new light on the intricate texture of things in the world, the actual plot of the present moment in time after the fall: the way we the living are nibbled and nibbling—not held aloft on a cloud in the air but bumbling pitted and scarred and broken through a frayed and beautiful land. (P. 227)

For the time being, virtually "anything can happen in any direction"; and "the world is more chomped than I'd dreamed." In extended contemplation of the "ten percent of all the world's species [that] are parasitic insects"—the immature fleas feeding on their parents' feces—the flies living "in the stomachs of horses, zebras, and elephants . . . in the nostrils and eyes of frogs"—the over one hundred thousand species of parasitic wasps, "so many that some parasitic wasps have parasitic wasps"—the almost disordering "insect order that consists entirely of parasitic insects called, singly and collectively, stylops," the female of which is a "formless lump," her "vestigial mouth and anus . . . tiny, degenerate, and nonfunctional"—and the "unfortunate" insects on which she feeds, those which, "although they live normal life spans, frequently undergo inexplicable changes," their colors brightened, their gonads " 'destroyed'," as they "not only lose their secondary sexual characteristics," but "actually acquire those of the opposite sex"—the pilgrim can only ask, no more than half-rhetorically (and half against her fascinated, extravagant will), "What kind of devil's tithe do we pay? What percentage of the world's species that are *not* insects are parasitic? Could it be, counting bacteria and viruses, that we live in a world in which half the creatures are running from—or limping from—the other half?" (pp. 229–33).

As is so often the case in this meteorological journal of the mind, what might be the supervening question, or the ensuing (and all-too-clearly self-reflexive) configuration, is just beneath the surface of discourse—an interrogative image, perhaps, of an entirely parasitic world, one hundred percent of the world's species parasitizing each other, if not themselves—the writer feeding upon the stylops, the reader upon the writer, and so on, all running and limping—from themselves, if from nothing else:

> Parasitism: this itch, this gasp in the lung, this coiled worm
> in the gut, hatching egg in the sinew, warble-hole in the hide—is
> a sort of rent, paid by all creatures who live in the real world with
> us now. It is not an extortionary rent: Wouldn't you pay it, don't
> you, a little blood from the throat and wrists for the taste of the
> air? Ask the turtle [the foot-long snapper with leeches, "stretch-
> ing and snapping wildly in the air," born aloft by a little boy (p.
> 228)]. True, for some creatures it is a slow death; for others, like
> the stylopsised bee, it is a strange, transfigured life. For most of
> us Western humans directly it is a pinprick or scabrous itch here
> and there from a world we learned early could pinch, and no
> surprise. Or it is the black burgeoning of disease, the dank bap-
> tismal lagoon into which we are dipped by blind chance many
> times over against our wishes, until one way or another we die.
> Chomp. It is the thorn in the flesh of the world, another sign, if
> any be needed, that the world is actual and fringed, pierced here
> and there, and through and through, with the toothed condi-
> tions of time and the mysterious, coiled spring of death. (P. 234)

Here as elsewhere, about the only way to "conclude" is to continue,
to take another tack, a tack that looks, at least initially, as if it might
preserve one's sense of participation and self-knowledge without
reducing one's self and one's actions, including one's writing, to
some function of a universal parasitism. About the only way
through these all-but-discomposing reflections is the way, in other
words, of alternative composition, the attempt to restore some
semblance of sanity by taking on another and alternative term, in
this case by returning to one's handbook or field guide and by trying (or trying on) the conventional distinction between parasite and
predator, all the while trying as well to resign oneself to "the present
moment in time after the fall," or "the toothed conditions of time
and the mysterious, coiled spring of death"—trying, in other words,
to assure oneself that "the thorn in the flesh of the world" is not an
extortionary rent. Parasites, then, are one thing; predators are quite
another—or so one hopes:

> Outright predators, of course, I understand. I am among
> them. There is no denying that the feats of predators can be just
> as gruesome as those of the unlovely parasites: the swathing
> and sipping of trapped hummingbirds by barn spiders, the occa-
> sional killing and eating of monkeys by chimpanzees. If I were to
> eat as the delicate ladybug eats, I would go through in just nine
> days the entire population of Boys Town. Nevertheless, the most

> rapacious lurk and charge of any predator is not nearly so sinis-
> ter as the silent hatching of barely visible, implanted eggs. With
> predators, at least you have a chance. (Pp. 234–35)

But the alternative composition barely works, or it works only for
two and a half pages, when, having tried to keep "an informal list"
of "the ones that got away," of the many "living creatures" who
carry on in "various states of disarray"—the mean (that is to say,
normative) condition of the harvestmen and daddy-longlegs
without their appointed eight appendages—the tiger swallowtails
and swallowtailed sparrows with incomplete tails—the Antarctic
crab-eater seals bearing the scars and slashes of feeding killer
whales—one comes again to the apparently inescapable conclusion:
"Any way you look at it, from the point of view of the whale or the
seal or the crab, from the point of view of the mosquito or copperhead or frog or dragonfly or minnow or rotifer, it is chomp or
fast" (pp. 235–37).

For the time being, then, "it is chomp or fast." To participate—
to be of and in one's place—is to eat and be eaten: "The summer is
old. . . . The world is festering with suppurating sores. Where is the
good, whole fruit?" The only apparent alternative is to starve and
starve oneself, with longing—and, hence, to lose touch with a good
part of one's neighborhood, if not with oneself: "the world is old, a
hungry old man, fatigued and broken past mending. Have I walked
too much, aged beyond my years?" (pp. 237–38):

> "In nature," wrote Huston Smith, "the emphasis is in what
> is rather than what ought to be." I learn this lesson in a new way
> every day. It must be, I think tonight, that in a certain sense only
> the newborn in this world are whole, that as adults we are ex-
> pected to be, and necessarily, somewhat nibbled. It's par for the
> course. Physical wholeness is not something we have barring
> accident; it is itself accidental, an accident of infancy, like a ba-
> by's fontanel or the egg-tooth on a hatchling. . . . I think of the
> beautiful sharks I saw from a shore, hefted and held aloft in a
> light-shot wave. Were those sharks sliced with scars, were there
> mites in their hides and worms in their hearts? Did the mock-
> ingbird that plunged from the rooftop, folding its wings, bear in
> its buoyant quills a host of sucking lice? Is our birthright and
> heritage to be, like Jacob's cattle on which the life of a nation
> was founded, "ring-streaked, speckled, and spotted" not with
> the spangling marks of a grace like beauty rained down from
> eternity, but with the blotched assaults and quarryings of time?
> (Pp. 238–39)

It is a difficult lesson for the American pilgrim, an almost subversive recognition. Even the questions are threatening—"Where is the good, whole fruit?"—for they cut at the heart of the original and originating myth of nature's nation, the sustaining and protohistorical idea of *America*—"Out here on the rocks the people don't mean to grapple, to crush and starve and betray, but with all the good will in the world, we do, there's no other way. We want it; we take it out of each other's hides; we chew the bitter skins the rest of our lives" (pp. 239–40). Just how early, one might ask, did we learn that the world could pinch?—and have we learned that "the good, whole fruit" is available here no more or less than any place else?

It is a difficult lesson, the recognition that health is accidental— that "physical wholeness," ecosystemic balance, and natural harmony or symbiosis, if they occur, are utterly fortuitous—not something given, and certainly not something to be programmatically restored or reclaimed, much less redeemed—"What happened to manna? Why doesn't everything eat manna, into what rare air did the manna dissolve that we harry the free live things, each other? . . . I wonder how many bites I have taken, parasite and predator, from family and friends; I wonder how long I will be permitted the luxury of this relative solitude" (p. 239).

It wasn't supposed to be like this in the New World; but it is, and incontrovertibly—and in some way one must come to terms with it, without sacrificing the dedications of one's American heritage. Somehow one must come to terms with the historical, and largely European, origins of America, the originating and sustaining promise of the New World—the only apparent cause to continue exploring one's neighborhood, the only justification for one's American being, if not the last, best hope for Western civilization—without succumbing to the seemingly interminable recognition of one's own immediate and historical experience, that this world meant to be new is as old and frayed as the hills. Somehow, in other words, one must sustain one's New World enthusiasm for wide-eyed exploration, one's belief in the wholeness of the newborn, one's commitment to the revelations of an unmediated (and unprecedented) experience of the cosmos, of nature and the originally wild—even as one's credulous discoveries constantly reveal the old truths of necessary imperfection, the original and originating lesson that all explorations are mediated, and that this one especially is precedented. Somehow one must learn to live this American life of seemingly perpetual displacement and dislocation, this life the more disjointing and disjunctive for all its original, conjunctive promises:

The only way I can reasonably talk about all this is to address you directly and frankly as a fellow survivor. Here we so incontrovertibly are. *Sub specie aeternitatis* this may all look different, from inside the blackened gut beyond the narrow craw, but now, although we hear the buzz in our ears and the crashing of jaws at our heels, we can look around as those who are nibbled but unbroken, from the shimmering vantage of the living. Here may not be the cleanest, newest place, but that clean timeless place that vaults on either side of this one is noplace at all. "Your fathers did eat manna in the wilderness, and are dead." There are no more chilling, invigorating words than these of Christ's, "Your fathers did eat manna in the wilderness, and are dead." (P. 240)

The keys to the American pilgrim's condition are to be found both in that latter-day declaration so difficult for European and historistic minds to take seriously—"Here we so incontrovertibly are"— that curious combination of resignation and release, that admission, at least half-liberating, to the constraints of time and the needs of place; and in its tonal counterpoint, the continuing echo of the very tradition from which it seeks relief, the tradition of the "redeemer nation"—here recalled and celebrated as "the shimmering vantage of the living."

The images and the thoughts are at once encumbering (or re-encumbering) and disencumbering, as the pilgrim seeks once again both disenthrallment and enthrallment, both dis-illusionment and re-illusionment—the one as she attempts to qualify the original dream of "the cleanest, newest place," the "world unraveled from reason, Eden before Adam gave names," and the other both as she seeks to acknowledge that "unwonted, taught pride" again, that pride that "diverts us from our original intent"—the bitter skins of consciousness and language—and as she attempts to reinforce the "newly" found wonders of quite quotidian places and times (the phrases, of course, are redundant) with the age-old recognition that the "clean timeless place" of the original Western and American dream "is noplace at all."

For the mind bound to the New World, the discovery of the Old is at least as invigorating as it is chilling. However paradoxically, or momentarily, it provides relief from the pressures of "Timelessness," a kind of temporal redemption from the historic burdens of "Emancipation," a deliverance of sorts from the "Independence" of nature's nation, a release from the burdens of Transcendentalism, and an appeasement of the originating (and all-too-often troubling) dreams of redeeming time and history in America. But the revelation of the Old-World in the New is also as chilling as it is invigorating. While it may soften and assuage one's "original intent," it can easily quench one's desires and quell one's sense of wonder. Its promise is the promise of affinity and participation. Its risk—for the American a considerable risk—is the risk of compromise and mitigation. Hence, the pilgrim's persisting rejoinders:

> I cannot in all honesty call the world old when I've seen it new. On the other hand, neither will honesty permit me suddenly to invoke certain experiences of newness and beauty as binding, sweeping away all knowledge. But I am thinking now of the tree with lights in it, the cedar in the yard by the creek I saw transfigured.
>
> That the world is old and frayed is no surprise; that the world could ever become new and whole beyond uncertainty was, and is, such a surprise that I find myself referring all subsequent kinds of knowledge to it. And it suddenly occurs to me to wonder: were the twigs of the cedar I saw really bloated with galls? They probably were; they almost surely were. (P. 241)

Initial appearances to the contrary, a large part of the "old" and "knowledgeable" in the first paragraph is the memory, the persistence, of the transfigured cedar in the yard by the creek—the ancestry, as one might call it, of the new and whole. Similarly, and contrarily, a large part of the "newness" in the second paragraph is the discovery, the revelation as one might call it, of the old—the "suddenly" occurring "wonder" and the thought that follows from it, the recognition, here virtually a bolt out of the blue, that the twigs of the tree with lights in it were almost certainly bloated with galls—the novel experience, by now as much astounding as galling, of the old and frayed—all in all, the transfiguration of the "transfigured" cedar of the first paragraph.

Only for an *American* pilgrim, perhaps, can the frayings and nibblings of age be original discoveries—or original sin a revelation and a release. Strange as it may sometimes seem to European and historistic minds—or to any mind dedicated solely to the logic of either-or—the determination of the American pilgrim is not simply to survive this disjointing life, but to live it and, quite literally, to appreciate it. It is indeed to find (and perhaps to be driven to find) the shades of Christ in a local bluegill—and the shadows of original sin in the galls of one personal and particular cedar. It is to discover with a kind of dumbfounded surprise the festerings of age and the wearings of history, and thus to resist the thought that novelty and beauty may be explained or worn away. It is to insist, conversely, on the traditional notion of perpetual new discoveries—including awed findings of the corruptions and frayings of age—and thus to resist, in turn, the thought that continuous new discoveries in any way mitigate corruption or soften the effects of age. It is to worship at an altar of contraries—in tones and styles quite different from those of Gilbert White or Darwin or Richard Jefferies or Jane Austen:

> Can I say then that corruption is one of beauty's deep-blue speckles, that the frayed and nibbled fringe of the world is a tallith, a prayer shawl, the intricate garment of beauty? It is very tempting, but I honestly cannot. But I can, however, affirm that corruption is not beauty's very heart. And I can I think call the vision of the cedar and the knowledge of these wormy quarryings twin fiords cutting into the granite cliffs of mystery, and say that the new is always present simultaneously with the old, however hidden. The tree with lights in it does not go out; that light still shines on an old world, now feebly, now bright.
>
> I am a frayed and nibbled survivor in a fallen world, and I am getting along. I am aging and eaten and have done my share of eating too. I am not washed and beautiful, in control of a shining world in which everything fits, but instead am wandering awed about on a splintered wreck I've come to care for, whose gnawed trees breath a delicate air, whose bloodied and scarred creatures are my dearest companions, and whose beauty beats and shines not *in* its imperfections but overwhelmingly in spite of them, under the wind-rent clouds, upstream and down. (P. 242)

Corruption and beauty, knowledge and vision, the shining and the splintered, the scarred and the companionable—though the enactments of history and the nibblings of survivorship are clear and inescapable—and indeed because they are—to the inveterate American pilgrim they mean as much excitement as sufferance, and, for the moment at least, more exaltation than acquiescence. Awesome manifestations in their own rights, the "blotched assaults and quarryings of time" are to be met head on, so to speak, reveled in, one might even say intemperately:

> I am a sacrifice bound with cords to the horns of the world's rock altar, waiting for worms. I take a deep breath, I open my eyes. Looking, I see there are worms in the horns of the altar like live maggots in amber, there are shells of worms in the rock and moths flapping at my eyes. A wind from noplace rises. A sense of the real exults me; the cords loose; I walk on my way. (P. 242)

In the short run, at least, there is no putting this pilgrim down. She is not about to give up or play down any of the inordinate distinctions of her condition—neither her unbending affirmations of the new and beautiful, nor her extravagant empathies with the old and suppurating. If it is worms we are given, then let there be worms, if not with vengeance, then certainly with extravagance. If it is scars, then scars aplenty there shall be—and maggots in amber—and "the new" shall be "always present simultaneously with the old, however hidden"—as it is in that sentence, and in the "worms in the horns of the altar"—and not much hidden at that—as she attempts to beat and shine some beautiful corruption (what some would call "corrupt beauty") against the wind-rent clouds.

The tree with lights in it may be shining feebly at the moment, but it is shining nonetheless—in her own sentence as in this one. Fiords and "fiords" may seem distinctly out of their Old World places in the Tinker Creek valley of Virginia, but that of course is just the point. "Vision" and "knowledge" are hardly new—nor are cedars, or "beauty" for that matter; but then "wormy quarryings" certainly is, and so is the association of sucking lice and Jacob's cattle—and the identification of a view *sub specie aeternitatis* with a view "from inside the blackened gut beyond the narrow craw."

"A wind from noplace rises. A sense of the real exults me; the cords loose; I walk on my way"—again one might reasonably think, perhaps even hope, that the book would end. But it's only the end of a chapter, one of those brief respites from the pressures of a pilgrimage that does little if it doesn't repeat itself, and insist on repeating itself. Within a page, the pilgrim is back at it again, off on yet another tack, another approach to the concerns and desires that have troubled and fascinated her from the beginning—"more of same," one might readily say:

> In September the birds were quiet. They were molting in the valley, the mockingbird in the spruce, the sparrow in the mock orange, the doves in the cedar by the creek. Everywhere I walked the ground was littered with shed feathers, long, colorful primaries and shaftless white down. I garnered this weightless crop in pockets all month long, and inserted the feathers one by one into the frame of a wall mirror. They're still there; I look in the mirror as though I'm wearing a ceremonial headdress, inside-out.
>
> In October the great restlessness came, the *Zugunruhe*, the restlessness of birds before migration. After a long unseasonable hot spell, one morning dawned suddenly cold. The birds were excited, stammering new songs all day long. Titmice, which had hidden in the leafy shade of mountains all summer, perched on

the gutter; chickadees staged a conventicle in the locusts, and a sparrow, acting very strange, hovered like a hummingbird inches above a roadside goldenrod. (P. 243)

So far so good, one might say. Certainly this is better than maggots in amber or moths flapping in one's eyes.

In a pattern by now familiar—perhaps all too-familiar—the penultimate chapter of *Tinker Creek* begins with what in another book one might think of as little more than innocent recordings or recallings, with what Jonathan Culler has called a "descriptive residue" perhaps. In this book, however—and in others of its kind— such plain matters of fact are far less a "residue" than another in a continuing series of descriptive and psychic counterweights, an opposition and at best a short-lived recovery, which the pilgrim knows all too well are only deceptively "reportorial" or comforting.[1]

As the pilgrim knows all too well, the claims against this Tinker-Creeked estate—the debts and bequests that must be satisfied, and the odds and ends that survive—are far less innocent and far more innerving than "residual" mockingbirds or "plain or simple" chickadees could ever indicate—if one could capture them. As the previous chapter, if no other, has made clear, there are in this world no plain and simple chickadees, nor residual mockingbirds— nor innocent pilgrims, nor purely descriptive phrases. Like virtually all other "plain facts" in this book, the mockingbird in the spruce, the titmice on the gutter, and the chickadees who staged a "conventicle" are at least as much binding as soothing, at least as much burdensome as comforting. While they may provide some momentary freedom from the "corruption" and "beauty" of the all-too-immediate past, they simultaneously reoccupy the mind, turning it toward creek life once again, and fixing it upon the stirrings of an autumnal season that almost immediately becomes as spiritual and theological as it is climatological and biological.

Momentarily restorative perhaps, the mockingbird in the spruce and the strange, hovering sparrow are soon no less engrossing and unsettling than the "worms in the horns of the altar." If they haven't already turned inside-out the mirror-image of a ceremonial headdress—if they haven't already committed the pilgrim to another stammering song—they have certainly set the tone for one; and within a paragraph they are leading her into another and fully fledged round of the tune she has been singing all along:

> I watched at the window; I watched at the creek. A new wind lifted the hair on my arms. The cold light was coming and going between oversized, careening clouds; patches of blue, like a

> ragged flock of protean birds, shifted and stretched, flapping and
> racing from one end of the sky to the other. Despite the wind, the
> air was moist; I smelled the rich vapor of loam around my face
> and wondered again why all that death—all those rotten leaves
> that one layer down are black sops roped in white webs of mold,
> all those millions of dead summer insects—didn't smell worse.
> When the wind quickened, a stranger, more subtle scent leaked
> from beyond the mountains, a disquieting fragrance of wet bark,
> salt marsh, and mud flat. (P. 244)

The shiftings and stretchings of the mind are irrepressible and inex-
orable—and quite as contradictory as they are complementary. On
the one hand, the pilgrim would immerse herself completely and
appreciatively in the great restlessness of the remembered season—
both its racing patches of blue and its millions of dead summer
insects. She would smell again the rich vapor of loam around her
face, and wonder "why all that death . . . didn't smell worse." On
the other hand, she would resist too close an identification with the
Zugunruhe. She would recall "a stranger, more subtle scent" from
over the mountains, and turn it into "a disquieting fragrance of wet
bark, salt marsh, and mud flat"—without elaborating upon its not-
so-subtle reminders of the distant evolutionary past, and without
further appreciation of its particular kind of disquietude.

    In yet another and another dialectic effort, she would fill her
mind with activities, and then wish it empty—in both ways seeking
once again to discover her neighborhood, to participate fully in her
place, by losing herself (and, more so, her sense of self) in the other.
On the one hand, she would occupy herself with floating tulip
leaves, swarming ants, and spreading flocks of goldfinches—engaging herself fully in this October restlessness—"worse than any
April's or May's . . . more pure, more inexplicable, and more
urgent." On the other hand, she would speed this urgency on its
way, wish it gone—"colder, colder than this, colder than anything,
and let the year hurry down!"—in short, get rid of it and its complicating events (pp. 244–45).

    She would fix in mind and language an image of herself stand-
ing, gazing, "unfixed," beneath autumnal trees, "tulips and ashes,
maples, sourwood, sassafras, locusts, catalpas, and oaks"—

> I let my eyes spread and unfix, screening out all that was not
> vertical motion, and I saw only leaves in the air—or rather, since
> my mind was also unfixed, vertical trails of yellow color-patches
> falling from nowhere to nowhere. Mysterious streamers of color
> unrolled silently all about me, distant and near. Some color
> chips made the descent violently; they wrenched from side to

> side in a series of diminishing swings, as if willfully fighting the
> fall with all the tricks of keel and glide they could muster. Others
> spun straight down in tight, suicidal circles. (P. 245)

—until the fixings of mind and the conceits of language threaten to
come unglued—until the diminishing swings of her much-desired
color chips threaten to become ebbings of mind and imagery, the
not-so-willful moves of a less-than-knowing, if art-full, human voyager—until the "impossible" and "irrational" simile (of leaves and
color chips willfully fighting the fall) threatens to become a self-
reflexive statement of her own condition, a thinly veiled suggestion
that "all" she may be doing is mustering her own tricks of stylistic
keel and analogic glide against the fall. The less said at this point
about those who spin "straight down in tight, suicidal circles," no
doubt the better.

These are the horns of the altar again, the antipodes of the pilgrim's world, her implacable wrenchings from side to side. On the
one hand, there is the cautious approach to "a long, slanting mown
field near the house," where she watches "a flock of forty robins"
from the unthreatening distance of a "fringe of trees," observing the
old and dreaming with the young, with the "fledglings from summer's last brood," "still mottled on the breast, embarking on their
first trip to unknown southern fields"—"At any given moment as I
watched, half of the robins were on the move, sloping forward in a
streamlined series of hops." On the other hand, there is the step
into the field, at which all the robins "halted":

> They stopped short, drew up, and looked at me, every one. I
> stopped too, suddenly as self-conscious as if I were before a firing
> squad. What are you going to do? I looked over the field, at all
> those cocked heads and black eyes. I'm staying here. You all go
> on. I'm staying here. (Pp. 250–51)

On the one hand, there is the desire to go, to engage oneself fully in
the motions and motives of the season, to unfix and uproot oneself,
to fly off toward those unknown southern fields, to light out for the
Territory. On the other hand, there is the quite reasonable fear of
those unknown and unsettling fields, with their continuing and
complicating engagements. If the south with its continuing entanglements won't do, perhaps the north with its seasonal simplifi-
cations will oblige:

> A kind of northing is what I wish to accomplish, a single-minded trek toward that place where any shutter left open to the zenith at night will record the wheeling of all the sky's stars as a pattern of perfect, concentric circles. I seek a reduction, a shedding, a sloughing off.
>
> At the seashore you often see a shell, or fragment of a shell, that sharp sands and surf have thinned to a wisp. There is no way you can tell what kind of shell it had been, what creature it had housed; it could have been a whelk or a scallop, a cowrie, limpet, or conch. The animal is long since dissolved, and its blood spread and thinned in the general sea. All you hold in your hand is a cool shred of shell, an inch long, pared so thin it passes a faint pink light, and almost as flexible as a straight razor. It is an essence, a smooth condensation of the air, a curve. I long for the North where unimpeded winds would hone me to such a pure slip of bone. (P. 251)

On the one hand, then, there is the desire to go—if not into the entanglements of the south, then surely toward the reductions of the north—the active longing for a classical perfection, a complete unhousing, a dissolution, a cleansing, and a resulting clarification—but only to a point, and as the better part of valor and sanity would seem to dictate, only to midparagraph:

> But I'll not go northing this year. I'll stalk that floating pole and frigid air by waiting here. I wait on bridges; I wait, stuck, on forest paths and meadow's fringes, hilltops and banksides, day in and day out, and I receive a southing as a gift. The North washes down the mountains like a waterfall, like a tidal wave, and pours across the valley; it comes to me. (P. 251)

On the other hand, there is the desire to stay, to settle down and in, and to wait—to wait to *be* engaged, to be entirely engulfed *by* the washings and wishings of the season, to be dispossessed of oneself and of one's desires for engagement—and, hence, to be clarified—in short, to wait empty and expectant once again, and then to be filled (or refilled)—without despairing in the meantime either of one's desires or of the inadequacies of one's language.

It is, of course, an impossible task—and always has been—this filling of one's mind with notions of emptiness—this series of fixations on the unfixed and unfixable—this attempt to say without expectation or hope that "you wait in all naturalness without expectation or hope"—and this inevitably interceding image of standing

"under wiped skies directly, naked, without intercessors" (p. 259).
And because these things are true, because "beauty beats and
shines" not *in* the imperfections of this splintered wreck, but "over-
whelmingly in spite of them"—this utterly American pilgrim is not
about to temper her wrenchings and swingings.

If the washings of the North are an autumnal "southing," a
benefaction awaited and received in the fall—if an autumnal
"northing" is a much-desired reduction brought on by the too-nu-
merous engagements of summer—then one might well think that
the shuckings of the "southing" to come will bring on a springtime
longing for an antonymous "southing," an addition or multiplica-
tion of engagements and associations, and a waiting for an alternative and just as antonymous "northing," the springtime northward
washings of the South. For the short run, at least, there is no easy
coming to terms with one's neighborhood.

If the Principle of Indeterminacy has left us "with no clear distinction between the Natural and the Supernatural"—or between
object and method, fact and metaphor, word and thing—except, of
course, the ones asserted (or reasserted) in those phrases—so the
contemplations of "Northing" have left us with little clear distinction between northing and southing, and but slight distinction between seeking and waiting. And so other of the pilgrim's endeavors
have left us and her with little settled distinction between meditation and action or the human and the nonhuman. And still others,
coordinately, have unsettled conventions of innocence and experience, or tradition and novelty—not to say self and other, or place-
ment and displacement.

The fixed and the unfixed, the new and the old, the corrupt and
the beautiful—these are not only the horns of the altar or the "twin
fiords cutting into the granite cliffs of mystery"; they are also "The
Waters of Separation" and "the gaps" of the pilgrim's last chapter;
and they are as well "the twin silver trumpets of praise," her final
word—in short, they are her conclusions, the only possible conclusions she can draw. They are, in fact, the dramatic essentials to
each of her engagements and disengagements with mockingbirds,
muskrats, and giant water bugs—the occasional composure and frequent discomposure of her meditations on self and others—at once
the classical dilemmas of Western thought and culture and the extreme expressions of those dilemmas which define her American
condition—both the inherited orders and the delights and fears in
disorder that enable her to get along:

> This Tinker Creek! It was low today, and clear. On the still
> side of the island the water held pellucid as a pane, a gloss on

runes of sandstone, shale, and snail-inscribed clay silt; on the faster side it hosted a blinding profusion of curved and pitched surfaces, flecks of shadow and tatters of sky. These are the waters of beauty and mystery, issuing from a gap in the granite world; they fill the lodes in my cells with a light like petaled water, and they churn in my lungs mighty and frigid, like a big ship's screw. And these are also the waters of separation: they purify, acrid and laving, and they cut me off. I am spattered with a sop of ashes, burnt bone knobs, and blood; I range wild-eyed, flying over fields and plundering the woods, no longer quite fit for company.

Bear with me one last time. In the old Hebrew ordinance for the waters of separation, the priest must find a red heifer, a red heifer unblemished, which has never known the yoke, and lead her outside the people's camp, and sacrifice her, burn her wholly, without looking away. . . . Into the stinking flame the priest casts the wood of a cedar tree for longevity, hyssop for purgation, and a scarlet thread for a vein of living blood. It is from these innocent ashes that the waters of separation are made, anew each time, by steeping them in a vessel with fresh running water. This special water purifies. A man—any man— dips a sprig of hyssop into the vessel and sprinkles—merely sprinkles—the water upon the unclean, "upon him that touched a bone, or one slain, or one dead." So. But I never signed up for this role. The bone touched me. (Pp. 266–67)

Pellucid and profuse—petaled and churning—these waters "purify, acrid and laving, and they cut me off." These waters purify? Or is it that these ordinanced "purifications" are meant to remind me of my separation? The pilgrim hardly needs reminding. Of separation she's got quite enough, thank you.

In patterns quite consonant with her "American heritage" (itself an awkward phrase), the pilgrim's condition is, at best, divided: engaged, desiring, almost entranced—and yet complaining and resistant, if not totally disengaged. Simultaneously beguiled and bedeviled by these "waters of separation"—seeking (and finding) them both in the previously uncoded runnels of Tinker Creek and in the well-ordinanced ancient Hebrew ceremony—she is once again cut off at both ends. Or, rather, she cuts herself off, and at least half against one of her wills—cuts herself off not only from the stinking flames of Old World ceremonies, not only from the blemished history of those ordinances that originally sanctioned and sanctified the very condition in which she finds herself, but from her New World surroundings as well—and all because she will not compromise. Indeed because she cannot, because she cannot (must not) surrender that part of her "heritage" which is ineluctably American, whatever it may owe to the Old Testament—because she must somehow sanction the waters of Tinker Creek (and, hence, herself) in terms at least equal to the terms of the old Hebrew ordinances, because she must ratify the giant water bug and the muskrat and the tree with lights in it—both their mind-blowing beauty and their fascinating corruption—and hence establish the significance of her experiences with each—because, in short, she must "fix" the phenomenal surfaces of her location, and appreciate the patterns of her identity, even if their only distinguishing characteristic should prove to be (as it certainly has) what she calls "a fixed tension between veering and longing" (p. 260), a kind of perpetual and less-than-circadian tilting between the twisted guts of predation and the twirlings of ecstasy.

The "trouble," of course—a perennial trouble for the American pilgrim—is that both the urgent and original need to fix one's location, and the seemingly inescapable consequent need—the need just-as-urgent (and, for that matter, original) to appraise and appreciate the unfixed—lead inevitably back toward the very ordinances and ceremonies one originally set out to escape or perfect, to the very terms and images with which we began this trek. It is Columbus, broken in spirit again, on the day of Epiphany at Veragua. It is William Bradford in the scrub oaks of eastern New England, unable to climb a literal Pisgah to view from "this wilderness" a more hopeful country. It is Sarah Kemble Knight in a canoe west of Providence, her hands gripping the gunnels, her eyes straight ahead, not daring to move her tongue from one side of her mouth to another, nor even to think on Lot's wife—"for a wry thought would have oversett our wherey."[2] It is William Bartram on a sultry afternoon at the "unparalleled" cascades of Falling Creek. It is Hawthorne attempting to compose himself in Sleepy Hollow. And it is certainly the pilgrim at Tinker Creek, complaining that she never signed up for this role—and standing, alone, with the world swaying.

About all one can do, then, on this pilgrimage in exile, this Exodus to Tinker Creek or Walden Pond or Plainville, or Bemidji or Flat Rock or Beaver, is to persist in inordinate variations upon the terms, categories, and imagery one has been given, in affirmation when doubt is most threatening, in danger when safety is most tempting. "I am a fugitive and a vagabond," says the pilgrim, "a sojourner seeking signs" (p. 267)—but, be it noted, an unrelenting fugitive, an active and unyielding seeker, and a celebrant of this disjointing life—one who, if she must contemplate her own sacrifice on the horns of the world's rock altar, will do so with a flair—one who would not stoop to "the enormous temptation in all of life to diddle around making itsy-bitsy friends and meals and journeys for itsy-bitsy years on end"—one who would all but excoriate the self-consciousness which, however blighting, has proven to be her own most distinguishing trait—one who would all but rage against those who (including a good part of herself), having "rightly" concluded that the world's grace is unmerited, that life is illogical and therefore immoral, then "sulk along" the rest of their days "on the edge of rage":

> It is so self-conscious, so apparently moral, simply to step aside from the gaps where the creeks and winds pour down, saying, I never merited this grace, quite rightly, and then to sulk along the rest of your days on the edge of rage. I won't have it. The world is wilder than that in all directions, more dangerous and bitter, more extravagant and bright. We are making hay when we should be making whoopee; we are raising tomatoes when we should be raising Cain, or Lazarus.
>
> Ezekiel excoriates false prophets as those who have "not gone up into the gaps." The gaps are the thing. The gaps are the spirit's one home, the altitudes and latitudes so dazzlingly spare and clean that the spirit can discover itself for the first time like a once-blind man unbound. The gaps are the clifts in the rock where you cower to see the back parts of God; they are the fissures between mountains and cells the wind lances through, the icy narrowing fiords splitting the cliffs of mystery. Go up into the gaps. If you can find them; they shift and vanish too. Stalk the gaps. Squeak into a gap in the soil, turn, and unlock—more than a maple—a universe. This is how you spend this afternoon, and tomorrow morning, and tomorrow afternoon. *Spend* the afternoon. You can't take it with you. (Pp. 268–69)

This conspicuously American pilgrim lives in "tranquility and trembling," and sometimes she dreams, of paring herself or of being pared, that she too "might pass through the merest crack"—"a gap" she knows is "there in the sky." Sometimes she opens, and sometimes she closes. Sometimes she is "porous as old bone, or translucent," gazing around her self "in bewilderment," fancying she casts no shadow. And sometimes she "rides a bucking faith while one hand grips and the other flails the air," like any daredevil, gouging her heels for blood—"for a wilder ride, for more."

For the time being, then, the idea—and, more than anything else, the determination—is to stalk "the gaps," to dream of going through them, perhaps, but more than anything else to go *into* them—as best and as often as one can. The desire for the time being—the need, in fact—is to live these gaps, to enter or squeak into them as often as one can, to celebrate them, and to thrive on the radical transformations they produce, including especially those transformations "you may not have bargained for":

> There is not a guarantee in the world. Oh your *needs* are guaranteed, your needs are absolutely guaranteed by the most stringent of warranties, in the plainest, truest words: knock; seek; ask. But you must read the fine print. "Not as the world giveth, give I unto you." That's the catch. If you can catch it it will catch you up, aloft, up to any gap at all, and you'll come back, for you will come back, transformed in a way you may not have bargained for—dribbling and crazed. (P. 269)

There is no guarantee in this pilgrim's world—except, perhaps, for that one. "There is no accounting for one second of it" (pp. 261-62)—except, perhaps, for that one. There are only your needs, and the gaps. And you must read the fine print again: "The waters of separation, however lightly sprinkled, leave indelible stains." "You see the creatures die, and you know you will die. And one day it occurs to you that you must not need life. Obviously. And then you're gone. You have finally understood that you're dealing with a maniac" (pp. 269-70)—yourself or God?—or both?

Object and method, word and thing, self and other—knowledge and vision, place and placelessness, division and unity—for the time being, there is no mediating among their claims, and no comfort in their estrangements—no living means of transcending their competitions, and precious little clarity in their relations. Nor must there be. There is, of course, the division of "division and unity," along with the knowledge of "knowledge and vision" and the place of "place and placelessness"; but there is also the other of "self and other" (or is it the self?), and the method of "object and method" (here as much object as method), and the words of "word and thing" (which are here unquestionably both). The old and the new, the facts and the fictions, the time and the timelessness—like Israel's priests, one may offer to and receive from them sacrificial gestures, "together, freely, in full knowledge, for thanksgiving"; and one may say that "neither gesture was whole without the other, and both meant a wide-eyed and keen-eyed thanks." But one must read the fine print, and wonder again what it might mean to give them "freely"—and whether the "full knowledge" in which they are given does not include the knowledge that the givings are far from free (are necessary, in fact)—and one must appreciate the duality entailed in conceiving them whole, the analysis that simultaneously excites and defeats all living attempts at synthesis.

Still seeking signs of her neighborhood and herself, the American pilgrim, this vagabond, gapes "appalled, or full of breath," and alternately. There is no other way. And there must not be. For both the giant water bug and the tree with lights in it, for both beauty and corruption, for both the settlings and the unsettlings, this veering, longing sojourner can only offer the last and next in the series of gestures she has been making from the beginning—as "freely" as she can—with as much "full knowledge" and thanksgiving as she can muster—and with as much in the way of vision as she has been able to accomplish—her final image of herself in unfixed place—"in and out of Shadow Creek, upstream and down, exultant, in a daze, dancing, to the twin silver trumpets of praise" (pp. 270–71).

Epilogue

With thinking we may be beside ourselves in a sane sense. By a conscious effort of the mind we can stand aloof from actions and their consequences; and all things, good and bad, go by us like a torrent. We are not wholly involved in Nature. I may be either the drift-wood in the stream, or Indra in the sky looking down on it. I *may* be affected by a theatrical exhibition; on the other hand, I *may not* be affected by an actual event which appears to concern me much more. I only know myself as a human entity; the scene, so to speak, of thoughts and affections; and am sensible of a certain doubleness by which I can stand as remote from myself as from another. However intense my experience, I am conscious of the presence and criticism of a part of me, which, as it were, is not a part of me, but spectator, sharing no experience, but taking note of it; and that is no more I than it is you. When the play, it may be the tragedy, of life is over, the spectator goes his way. It was a kind of fiction, a work of the imagination only, so far as he was concerned. This doubleness may easily make us poor neighbors and friends sometimes.

HENRY THOREAU, *Walden*

Is the difference in the trees, or in me?

ALDO LEOPOLD, *A Sand County Almanac*

If the giant water bug was not made in jest, was it then made in earnest?

ANNIE DILLARD, *Pilgrim at Tinker Creek*

I went farther into the alders, as if by doing so I could either find an answer or, better yet, forget that I had asked.

DIANA KAPPEL-SMITH, *Wintering*

So, I am sanest when I live in two worlds, when I am swept away by veils of light and at the same time caught on the sounds of my dumb drinking dog, who reminds me of where I am and of what I am.

PAUL LEHMBERG, *In the Strong Woods*

Apparently to write about nature is to write about how the mind sees nature, and sometimes about how the mind sees itself.

SHARON CAMERON, *Writing Nature: Henry Thoreau's Journal*

itting or unwitting, paradoxes are the essence of American nature writing, paradoxes of the kinds produced when the needs of an individual human animal meet the needs of lands which he or she conceives alternately as redeeming (or liberating) and encumbering; paradoxes of the kinds produced when the rhetorics of systematic science meet the rhetorics of spiritual autobiography and personal narrative; paradoxes of the kinds that result when metamorphic and metaphoric are so closely intertwined that each takes on aspects of the other; paradoxes, in short, of the kinds that typify *Walden* and *A Sand County Almanac* and *Pilgrim at Tinker Creek*. These, it seems to me, comprise the underlying "drama" of American nature writing, and they go a long way toward explaining its variable form, its shifting (and only partially narrative) point of view, its frequently changing grammatical moods and tenses, its oscillations between the systematically impersonal and the reflectively personal—all in all, its seemingly relentless dedication to isolate human self and nonhuman environment.

These paradoxes—or, if you prefer, these incompatible allegiances—are the psychobiotic consumers and producers in terms of whose workings American nature writing has developed, from the time of William Bartram through the time of Thoreau and John Muir to the time of John Hay and Annie Dillard. As Edward Abbey writes in *Desert Solitaire*:

> Standing there, gaping at this monstrous and inhuman spectacle of rock and cloud and sky and space, I feel a ridiculous greed and possessiveness come over me. I want to know it all, possess it all, embrace the entire scene intimately, deeply, totally, as a man desires a beautiful woman. An insane wish? Perhaps not—at least there's nothing else, no one human, to dispute possession with me.

The snow-covered ground glimmers with a dull blue light, reflecting the sky and the approaching sunrise. Leading away from me the narrow dirt road, an alluring and primitive track into nowhere, meanders down the slope and toward the heart of the labyrinth of naked stone. Near the first group of arches, looming over a bend in the road, is a balanced rock about fifty feet high, mounted on a pedestal of equal height; it looks like a head from Easter Island, a stone god or a petrified ogre.

Like a god, like an ogre? The personification of the natural is exactly the tendency I wish to suppress in myself, to eliminate for good. I am here not only to evade for a while the clamor and filth and confusion of the cultural apparatus but also to confront, immediately and directly if it's possible, the bare bones of existence, the elemental and fundamental, the bedrock which sustains us. I want to be able to look at and into a juniper tree, a piece of quartz, a vulture, a spider, and see it as it is in itself, devoid of all humanly ascribed qualities, anti-Kantian, even the categories of scientific description. To meet God or Medusa face to face, even if it means risking everything human in myself. I dream of a hard and brutal mysticism in which the naked self merges with a non-human world and yet somehow survives still intact, individual, separate. Paradox and bedrock. (Pp. 5–6)*

Paradox indeed!—and echo upon echo of the divided figures at Veragua and Sleepy Hollow and Walden Pond and Tinker Creek—hoping against one's own all-too-knowing hope—one's medium at all-too-obvious odds with one's deepest desires—and yet setting out once again on that ancestral trek—to evade the cultural apparatus (itself a cultural apparatus, like "God," "ogre," "juniper," and even "the"), to deny the human self (and thus affirm, if not the human self, the category of the human self), to merge the self with "a non-human world" of "quartz," "vulture," and "spider" (each itself a human term, at once Kantian and "scientific"), and to do so with only the most thinly veiled self-consciousness, a self-consciousness that comes tellingly close to self-hate, a barely restrained if perennial frustration.

To possess one's environment entirely, to know it all, and to be utterly dispossessed by it, if not of it—this is the kind of self-conscious paradoxism that simultaneously innervates and plagues the most extravagant (and, therefore, most revealing) forms of American nature writing—the kind of intentionally irresolvable ambiguity that typifies *Walden* and *Pilgrim at Tinker Creek*, among several

---

*Both this quotation and the one with which I conclude my ruminations are taken from the original edition of *Desert Solitaire* (New York: McGraw-Hill, 1968).

other works of their inordinate, exemplary type. The solitary figure here, reflecting both upon himself and the predawn light of east-central Utah (in geographic fact, no more than fifty miles as the raven flies from Paradox, Colorado), is another of those selves who, seeking location in *America*, find themselves almost constantly dislocated—in part because of the visions they continue to hold for themselves and their surroundings, in part because of their own quite basic needs and motivations, and in part because they have found themselves wanting to write these engrossing places, to bring their "neighborhoods" (and, hence, themselves) into history, science, and art.

Like the pilgrim at Tinker Creek, the figure here in the approaching sunrise is no civil reformer, finally—no clear-minded, programmatic renovator of the world's ways—lamenting in some public and political forum the discord between nature and culture in the modern world. This is no panelist at some well-lighted and much-nourished academic symposium, complaining that modern man has lost touch with nature. No, this is a figure—a prototypical figure in American nature writing—who finds the discord between nature and culture very much, too much, within himself. What others might call "our environmental problems" are his immediate and psychic troubles, including his troubles as a user of language—his deepest desires to lose himself in his surroundings, his most basic needs to compose himself and his environmental place, his very substantial self-doubts, and the occasional outbreaks of egotism that inevitably and naturally follow. His lonely cries into the canyons against society are far less the gestures of a cultural critic than they are cries against himself, his human language, and his inherited dreams. The medium of his "hard and brutal" mysticism, his dream of merging self and other, is at least half at odds with the merging he would dream—and, unfortunately, he knows it. The "humanly ascribed qualities" against which he rails—"the categories of scientific description" he would utterly escape—are, as he well knows, the inescapable tools of his kind, and inseparable from his "dream" of escaping them. The "naked" self he imagines merging with "a non-human world"—and yet remaining "intact, individual, separate"—this self clothed in an essentially traditional language—is deeply kin to the figure in *Pilgrim at Tinker Creek* who stands "under wiped skies directly, naked, without intercessors"—and kin as well to the figure at Walden Pond who would drive life into a corner—and to the figure in Hawthorne's Sleepy Hollow who would not take up pen a second time.

With Abbey's figure at the arches, as with the figure at Walden Pond or the man in Sand County, it's not just that culture and na-

ture are at odds with one another "out there," in Denver or Hobo-
ken, on the Kaibab or at Three Mile Island—but also, and at least as
painfully, that they are at odds with one and other "in here," right
here, in the dreaming and the thinking and, most pointedly
perhaps, in the writing—especially in the thinking and writing
about "nature," that nonhuman world which is the crux of the
"hard and brutal mysticism" the anxious, admiring American
would seek at virtually all costs. For the American who would *land*
himself, completely and utterly, the writing is a problem, the words
and the book are troubles, and not just because they are difficult to
style. Rather, because they are at irreconcilable odds with that ultimate merging in the predawn wilderness—because language and
writing (and science and art) are history and society and civilization, "the cultural apparatus" the original, questing American
would leave behind.

Here, as in so much American nature writing, it would be all for
the good if one could "eliminate for good" the personification of the
natural, if one could suppress one's human, cultural self—and still
survive "intact"—as a separate, knowing, and appreciating individual. It would be all to the natural and personal good if one could
merge with a nonhuman world, and yet not merge, not that final
meeting in the predawn kingdom. If only one could be a part while
simultaneously remaining appreciatively apart. If only one could be
(and continue to be) a comprehending and appreciating human self,
while escaping the trammelings of "humanity" and history, and
simultaneously merging with a nonhuman environment.

The conflicting desires and the resulting paradoxes have remained essentially unchanged from the time of William Bartram to
the time of Edward Abbey. In their most self-conscious and self-
reflexive forms, in the likes of *Desert Solitaire* and *Walden* and *Pilgrim at Tinker Creek*, they are made explicit and overt, for many
readers all too overt. They are flushed out into the open, as it were,
or scrambled after in creek beds, without reserve, or with as little
reserve as the self can muster. They are confronted and even desired directly, wantonly—not in the protective custody of conventional backporch observation and sanguine musing, but in the delights of aching knees and scratched hands, in the elations of alder
swamps, crevasses, and mud flats—and by no means least in the
quite biotic effort of trying to find the right name or phrase, in the
tired eyes and worn pages of trying to place oneself in writing, in the
frequent despairs and occasional delights of discovering that one
has contradicted oneself, that the mind-prints of one's words are as
good an indicator of one's daily or seasonal wants and fears as are
the tracks and tunnels of a January meadow mouse.

Only the most philosophic of nature writers, obviously, have been able to tolerate the kinds of side-trackings and back-trackings occasioned by stylistic and linguistic self-consciousness—the interruptions to personal experience coherently recalled, the diversions from impersonal environments consistently and schematically rendered. Obviously, too, only the most self-conscious nature writers have been able to explore fully the stylistic and psychic interplay of narration, description, and exposition as they oscillate between the highly personal and the systematically impersonal.

Only a Thoreau, perhaps—or a Dillard or an Abbey—can explain the phoebe as a figure of speech and, then, in the next sentence or paragraph consider and explain himself and his words (including his explanation of the phoebe) as biological phenomena. Only a Dillard, perhaps—or a John Janovy—can openly present and explain herself as a creature of her environment and, then, just as openly present and explain the creatures of her environment (including herself) as functions of her perceptual habits and her language. Only an Abbey no doubt—or a Thoreau or an Eiseley—can explore the boundaries of instinct and intention, openly wonder whether the exploration itself is instinctual or intentional, and yet not allow abstract questions to destroy concrete presentation. Only the most self-conscious of nature writers can engage fully and regularly each of the dialectic elements of American nature writing, momentarily succumbing to each, but finally to none.

The underwriting elements of the dialectic, however, are in no sense peculiar to Thoreau—nor to Dillard nor to Abbey nor to Janovy. The fluctuating prose forms and points of view, the shifting allegiances and varying tenses, are present in the work of all the acknowledged nature writers of America—the Bartrams as well as the Leopolds, the Muirs as well as the Zwingers—and so are the questions (and the alternating answers) raised by those forms and points of view, even if only implicitly, even if unintentionally.

What the Abbeys and the Dillards and the Thoreaus do is to expose the dialectic of American nature writing, to lay open to view both questions and answers that are at least implicit (or, in varying degrees, explicit) in the writings of all their compatriots, precursors as well as successors: Are human beings to be explained finally as functions of their geobiotic environments? Am I? To what extent? To what extent are human beings and human behavior to be identified and explained as functions of wants and fears in habitat? To what extent should they be? To the extent that those explanations and these questions are themselves conceived and understood in energetic or ecosystemic terms—and those terms as well—and these? *Can* human behavior be so explained, consistently, without meaningless tautology or debilitating infinite regress? What does it "practically mean" to explain human beings as psycho- and sociobiotic creatures, as functions of their ecosystemic places? Can a person so explain humankind (much less herself or himself) without risking what these days is sometimes called, quite logocentrically, a logocentric circularity—and thus endangering his representations and explanations (if not himself)? Contrarily, can a person describe and explain what we call the nonhuman environment (much less his or her own part in it) without risking still other forms of circularity, and hence undercutting both the descriptions and the explanations? To what extent is what we call (and represent and explain as) the nonhuman environment a figure of what we call thought and speech, a configuration of what we are inclined to call the human condition, varying through time and space as humans vary? To what extent is it a defensive and offensive mechanism designed, developed, and asserted to sustain our identity as what we call a species? Is it possible (and, if so, how, or to what extent) to escape through logic or language the limitations of our psycho- and sociobiotic conditions—or the limits of language and human conception through a muskrat or a juniper tree? Or are logic and language (even in their "highest forms") species-specific responses to ecosystemic contingencies? And, if they are, how are we to evaluate statements that claim to have in mind the best interests of so-called nonhuman species (much less the best interests of our own)?

If only a Thoreau or a Dillard or an Abbey can tolerate the open ambiguities of such questions, if it takes an Abbey or a Janovy or an Eiseley to press their alternate answers and implications toward their limits, to explore fully their edges, both the questions and the shifting answers and the patterns established by their openly self-conscious explorers go a long way toward explaining the seemingly more settled work of an Aldo Leopold or a John Hay, and an even longer way perhaps toward explaining the words, straightforwardly informative and most often conventionally hopeful, of a John Muir or a Sigurd Olson or an Ann Zwinger. If it takes an Abbey or a Thoreau or a Dillard to range the emotional and philosophic edges of self and place in America—and if the vast majority of American nature writing avoids those edges like the plague, preferring to stay much closer to conventional scientific and aesthetic homes—the extreme rangings of the former—their often radical declarations of identity and independence, and their just as radical images and thoughts of self-effacement—go a long way toward explaining the fears and wants of their more conventional and ostensibly less disturbed kinfolk.

Reading Thoreau and Dillard and Janovy—and juxtaposing their best known works with the writings of Ann Zwinger or Henry Beston or Joseph Wood Krutch, or John Muir or Edwin Way Teale or Sally Carrighar—one gets the distinct impression that deep within the historical and cultural soil of conventional American nature writing lie both an original fear, a formative dis-ease, and a coordinate (and just as formative) determination—that beneath or behind the doggedly informative science and the solidly orthodox aesthetic of so much American nature writing (and indeed of the many other cultural forms now dedicated to "nature in America") lie the original "broken spirits" of Columbus, among many others, and a coordinate determination to answer his unsettled psyche—not only with an unflagging drive to fix in systematic and empirically confirmable detail just *where* we are, but to sustain against all suggestions to the contrary the original dream of an unblemished and epiphanic *land*, the dream by now an essentially catechistic vision of nature's beautiful nation—and if and when the evidence should ever suggest otherwise, to legislate and plan its "preservation," to design and even to engineer its "restoration," to manage its "reclamation" and "conservation"—in short, to marshall all our forces, all our powers of appreciative, nostalgic, and saddened mind and body on its behalf (if need be, even against the contrary evidences of the modern science to which we are otherwise so devoted).

What lies behind the persistent fixings of so much American nature writing—its steadfast taxonomic notations, its simple naming, its plain exposition, and its formulaic (if not clichéd) appreciation—is the same unspoken doubt that underlies our quests for a systematic "theory of animal rights," or a comprehensive and formal "environmental ethic," or the development of "environmental law"—the fear that things are neither as fixed nor fixable as they were meant to be, nor even so easily locatable, and nowhere near as redeeming or redeemable. What lies behind the vast majority of American nature writing, or so it seems to me—what runs beneath those reassuring columns and essays that appear regularly in local newspapers and popular periodicals, in *Wilderness* and *Audubon* and *National Wildlife*—is the same original, and at least half-hopeful, uncertainty that underlies virtually all our efforts in "natural resource management" and "nature appreciation"—the uncertainty (the radical indeterminacy, as it were) of the rule of law and method and *scientia* in the much desired "world of nature," the fear which is half a fear, and the "knowledge," the still deeply hopeful sense, which is only half a knowledge, that nature is inimical to law and method and *scientia*, that both art and science are utterly incommensurate to wilderness—that America, as the systematic and programmatic perfection of originally European method, is self-defeating, if not self-destructive.

These are some of the extreme uncertainties—the radical hopes and fears—that the Thoreaus and the Dillards and the Abbeys delight in pressing toward the edges—nooks and crannies of American landscapes they are unable to pass by. Do trees have legal standing? Do I? Should animals be *given* "rights?" Does anyone or anything have a right to continued existence of any particular kind or quality in this old and fraying, extravagant, evolutionary, and ecosystemic world? At times it seems the strips of our apple-parings are becoming very long indeed.

On the one hand, there is the abiding commitment to—and, yes, even on occasion, the original experience of—"nature"—the confrontation and identification with an unfixed and unfixable wilderness, as we say—in textual configuration and, hence, in fact—an experience and a commitment that explain both the "wildness" of a good part of *Walden* or *Desert Solitaire* and the continuing popularity of their far more formulaic cousins; both the uncompromising profligacy of *Pilgrim at Tinker Creek* and the increasing annual sales of field guides and nature writing; both the hard and brutal mysticism of Edward Abbey—and indeed the isolate anger of the seeker at the arches—as well as the popularity of nature study and nature areas—and indeed the literature, art, science, politics, commerce, and law of nature (or ecology or environment or wilderness) in America. On the one hand, then, there are multitudinous and multiplying signs of the ancestral hope, now far more than a credo, that language and experience, literature and nature, human self and nonhuman other, will finally mesh in America—indeed that they must.

On the other hand, there is a just as abiding fear (and, on occasion, a hopeful and deeply ironic comprehension) that all such art, literature, science, commerce, politics, and law are—and, in the last analysis, can only be—violations and pollutions of that original experience, and profanations of that ancestral hope. Occasionally, then—as with a Thoreau or a Dillard or an Eiseley or an Abbey or a Barry Lopez—there is the agonized, guttural cry or, alternatively, a loud, therapeutic laugh—with a John Muir or a Sigurd Olson perhaps a deep sigh of relief, a real release, insofar as any human can attain it—the recognition and the knowledge that one's book and one's writing, even at their most appreciative, are just such violations and profanations, however natural. There is a recognition that art and literature and science—especially if they are well and convincingly done—can only undercut one's experiences and com-

mitments, can only violate the objects of one's worship—that civilization being what it is—that law, science, literature, art, and commerce being what they are—one cannot have one's wilderness in art
or literature or science while continuing to enjoy it in what we call
fact or experience—that art or literature and nature are indeed, and
in most painful fact, inimical to one and other—that untrammeled
or undiscovered nature and the languages and literatures of undiscovered nature are at inescapable odds with one another—that in
fairly painful biological, economic, and political fact—in the biopol-
itics, sociobiology, and even in the environmental ethics of things—
the literature and art and science of nature are no more immaculate
or inexpensive than "technology" or "commerce"—in short, that
nature writing and writing about nature writing are not, cannot be,
and never have been innocent.

So Edward Abbey once authored a final "word of caution," at
least half in hopes that *Desert Solitaire* would be a lost cause:

> Do not jump into your automobile next June and rush out to
> the canyon country hoping to see some of that which I have
> attempted to evoke in these pages. In the first place you can't see
> *anything* from a car; you've got to get out of the goddamned
> contraption and walk, better yet crawl, on hands and knees,
> over the sandstone and through the thornbush and cactus.
> When traces of blood begin to mark your trail you'll see some-
> thing, maybe. Probably not. In the second place most of what I
> write about in this book is already gone or going under fast. This
> is not a travel guide but an elegy. A memorial. You're holding a
> tombstone in your hands. A bloody rock. Don't drop it on your
> foot—throw it at something big and glassy. What do you have to
> lose? (P. xiv)

In this business of nature and nature writing in America, there is a
great desire to cry out, to warn and forewarn as well as to celebrate—but there is also a great and coordinate desire to be silent.

NOTES

Chapter One: Preliminary Concerns

1. For contemporary discussions of what is sometimes called the "nature writing" of Britain, see especially W. J. Keith's *The Rural Tradition* (Toronto: University of Toronto Press, 1975) and Raymond Williams's *The Country and the City* (New York: Oxford University Press, 1973). In their different ways, both Keith and Williams have convincingly demonstrated that British nature writing is fundamentally a literature of countrylife, a literature dedicated for the most part to the "country" customs of otherwise urban people, to "country" (and, occasionally, to rural) society and character—in essence, a literature that grows out of (and refers back to) agri-culture and changing agronomic patterns. The distinction between countrylife and rural life is Williams's, but both he and Keith make abundantly clear the characteristic traits of a literary tradition quite different from the tradition of Thoreau and Burroughs and Muir.

The country (or rural) tradition has, of course, had its numerous practitioners and advocates in the United States. Indeed, truly rural literature has been far more influential and popular in America than it has been in Britain. But the tradition of Thoreauvian nature writing, in which an essentially asocial individual confronts alone a scientifically rendered nonhuman environment, has had very little, if any, place in British literary history, or for that matter in any other national literature.

For a representative collection of British nature writing, see E. D. H. Johnson, ed., *The Poetry of Earth* (New York: Atheneum, 1974); and for a different but related sense of the "historical"—that is to say, social and institutional—dimensions of British writing on nonhuman environments, see David Elliston Allen, *The Naturalist in Britain: A Social History* (London: Allen Lane, 1976; Harmondsworth, Middlesex: Penguin Books, 1978) and Lynn L. Merrill, *The Romance of Victorian Natural History* (New York: Oxford University Press, 1989).

2. Though the prevailing concerns of the best American nature writers have been consistently psychobiotic, they have anticipated many of the underlying conceptions (and not a few of the controversies) of sociobiology. Like many a professional in wildlife or fisheries management, like many a field biologist, and not a few in the laboratory, they have become so obsessed and absorbed by the objects of their quests, so identified with them, that they have come to consider themselves and their own behavior in the same basic

terms—as parts of the same systems, and driven by the same fundamental needs or forces. In fact, it may be no accident that sociobiology—like professional resource management, national parks, legislated wilderness areas, and legally designated wild rivers—has gotten its start in America.

3. These quotations are, of course, purely exemplary. Each is regularly included in standard anthologies of American literature; and their essentially evangelical messages could be duplicated over and over again with comparable quotations from hundreds of American sources, some better known, many of considerably lesser renown.

The power and the ironies of redemptive vision in American culture are, perhaps, nowhere better demonstrated than in the now two-centuries-old reception and interpretation of Crevecoeur's *Letters from an American Farmer*. Though a strong case can be made that the best-known "letters" of Crevecoeur's farmer James are fairly typical pieces of eighteenth-century satiric irony, it is still quite common to find American teachers and scholars taking them at face value, in much the same way they rightly take the statements of Paine and Channing.

The specific sources cited here are, in order of appearance, "Common Sense," in *The Complete Writings of Thomas Paine*, ed. Philip S. Foner (New York: Citadel Press, 1945), 1:21,30–31; J. Hector St. John de Crevecoeur, *Letters from an American Farmer* (New York: E. P. Dutton, 1957), 39; and William Ellery Channing, "Remarks on National Literature," in *The Works of William E. Channing* (Boston: American Unitarian Association, 1889), 133.

4. Among the many works that might be said to consider the issue of location in early America more or less directly, see especially Wayne Franklin, *Discoverers, Explorers, Settlers: The Diligent Writers of Early America* (Chicago: University of Chicago Press, 1979); Edmundo O'Gorman, *The Invention of America* (Bloomington: Indiana University Press, 1961); Howard Mumford Jones, *O Strange New World* (New York: Viking, 1964); William Goetzmann, *Exploration and Empire: The Explorer and the Scientist in the Winning of the American West* (New York: Knopf, 1966) and *New Lands, New Men: America and the Second Great Age of Discovery* (New York: Viking Penguin, 1986); David Scofield Wilson, *In the Presence of Nature* (Amherst: University of Massachusetts Press, 1978); both of Antonello Gerbi's justly famous works, *The Dispute of the New World* and *Nature in the New World* (Pittsburgh: University of Pittsburgh Press, 1973 and 1985), each translated by Jeremy Moyle; Gaile McGregor, *The Noble Savage in the New World Garden: Notes toward a Syntactics of Place* (Toronto: University of Toronto Press, 1988); and Robert Lawson-Peebles, *Landscape and Written Expression in Revolutionary America* (New York: Cambridge University Press, 1988). Franklin, particularly, does the kind of intricate analysis of seemingly unassuming American texts that should prove to any close reader that few early Americans found themselves in ordinary situations. Gerbi analyzes both American and European texts with such historical depth and philosophic insight as to prove beyond reasonable doubt extensive and intricate connections between the composition and development of the Americas, on the one hand, and the underlying logic and epistemology of modern science, on the other. Lawson-Peebles's study, a rich complement to (and indeed an amplification of) Franklin's, provides a nice blend of readings of both fiction and nonfiction of revolutionary and republican America, and a

mine of bibliographic information. Had it appeared before the present book had gone to press, it would have occupied a more prominent place in my own ruminations.

5. In no ordinary sense of the word have the best American nature writers been "evangelical," or for that matter politically programmatic. All of them have been suspicious of practical philosophy and the culture of problem-solving. They have not taken readily to the suggestions contained in books like Nelson Rockefeller's *Our Environment Can Be Saved* (Garden City, N.Y.: Doubleday, 1970); and they have regularly found at least mildly ironic our efforts to legislate wildness and redeem or reclaim "the environment." They have likewise found phrases such as "environmental management" and "ecological engineering" telling expressions of plain human hubris (instances of the sin of pride) rather than hopeful indications of better things to come. For them there has been no ready way, scientific or theological, to escape what David Ehrenfeld has called "the arrogance of humanism"—the trials and tribulations of anthropocentricity or anthropomorphism—though they have clearly been at least as troubled by their homocentric conditions as have any of their ancestors or successors (for Ehrenfeld's views see *The Arrogance of Humanism* [New York: Oxford University Press, 1978]). Their affinities have run finally to the *classical* mystics rather than to such hopeful contemporary figures as Teilhard de Chardin, much less to contemporary celebrants of "deep ecology." One senses indeed that their continuing awareness of elementary psychobiotic needs and impulses has made it impossible for them to accede to Teilhard's (or anyone else's) prospects of systematically raising consciousness or deepening conscience. Perhaps there is something in the experience (or the memory of the experience) of American lands that undermines one's faith in the prospects of humankind.

6. On these notes, see Keith Thomas's *Man and the Natural World: A History of the Modern Sensibility* (New York: Pantheon Books, 1983). For what are perhaps obvious reasons, "nature" in America has only been partly what it has been in Europe, or even in England—in large part because for many, including some Europeans, American nature has always been more or less than a matter of "sensibility" (a historic end, perhaps, or a national cause, and frequently a personal condition). Aligning himself with Epicurus and Lucretius, Robert Frost once called it "the Whole Goddam Machinery," pointedly juxtaposing (and rhyming) that classical conception with the thoroughly modern and oh-so-civilized "Pretty Scenery" of college deans. To a large extent, in fact, the history of "man's" relations to "nature" in America has been a matter of trying to make "modern" conceptions which, in a European sense, are thoroughly ancient.

7. The specific sources cited here are, in order of appearance, Ann Zwinger's *Beyond the Aspen Grove* (New York: Random House, 1970; New York: Harper & Row, 1981), 200; John Muir's *The Mountains of California* (Garden City, N.Y.: Doubleday, Anchor Books, 1961), 72; and John Hay's *Nature's Year: The Seasons of Cape Cod* (Garden City, N.Y.: Doubleday, 1961; New York: Ballantine, 1971), 76–77.

8. These quotations and those immediately following them are taken directly from René Descartes, *Discourse on Method and The Meditations*, trans. F. E. Sutcliffe (London and New York: Penguin Books, 1968), 78–79.

For a recent, clear discussion of the place of these and other Cartesian max-
ims in the history of Western thought, see John Rodman's delightful and
incisive "The Dolphin Papers," *Antaeus* 57 (Autumn 1986): 252–80.

9. These quotations are also, of course, entirely exemplary. Like most
others I have cited, they could be replicated in kind several thousand times
over with quotations from other standard sources, the types of sources regularly consulted by American nature writers. The specific sources cited here
are, in order of appearance, Eugene P. Odum, *Fundamentals of Ecology*, 3d
ed. (Philadelphia: W. B. Saunders, 1971), 274; Ramon Margalef, "On Certain
Unifying Principles in Ecology," *American Naturalist* 97 (1963): 361, reprinted in Edward J. Kormondy, *Readings in Ecology* (Englewood Cliffs,
N.J.: Prentice-Hall, 1965), 215–19; and George A. Petrides, *A Field Guide to
Trees and Shrubs*, 2d ed. (Boston: Houghton Mifflin, 1972), 292–93.

10. In much the same way, my own efforts throughout this section of
the Introduction are to maintain some fundamental and unexamined distinctions both between myself and the so-called figure (narrator and expositor) I posit (and appeal to my readers' understanding of) in what we too easily
call "Hay's writing" *and* between my own ostensibly descriptive language
and the language (not to say the subjects) of what we still need to call something like "Hay's text." Until this very moment, in fact, I have been unwilling
and unable to let down my logical, philosophic, and psychological guard, to
admit to myself (or to others) that I am (and have been) playing the expositor
of "Hay's expositor," or that I have just now become the expositor of the
expositor of Hay's expositor. To some substantial degree, I have been (and
still am) resisting suggestions of association (much less identity or equiva-
lence) between myself and the "human figure" who I have been contending
is puzzling over the ghostly Indian pipe. In short, I have been (and still am)
maintaining my objective distance, so to speak, both from Hay's text and
from its narrator, as well as from the Indian pipe and the process of attempting to pin things down—though I must say the distance has gotten considerably less objective over my last few sentences.

Obviously, the process of self-reflection cannot go on for very long, for it
rather quickly comes to threaten one's control (of both subject and self), and
it takes one away from the objects and subjects of one's concern, in this case
not only (or even primarily) Indian pipe and saprophyte, but the business of
making sense of the Indian pipe, and indeed the business of making sense—
of American nature as well as American nature writing. Still, it is this kind of
overt self-reflection (however momentary) and this kind of open consideration of distinctions and relationships between word and thing or mystery
and fact that distinguish the nature writing of a Thoreau or a Janovy from
the nature writing of John Hay—and both, in turn, from the far less self-
reflexive nature writing of Muir and Zwinger, or John Burroughs and Hal
Borland, or Sigurd Olson and Josephine Johnson. It is this kind of self-consciousness that produces passages like the following in *Walden*:

> With thinking we may be beside ourselves in a sane sense. By a
> conscious effort of the mind we can stand aloof from actions and their
> consequences; and all things, good and bad, go by us like a torrent. We
> are not wholly involved in Nature. I may be either the drift-wood in the
> stream, or Indra in the sky looking down on it. I *may* be affected by a

theatrical exhibition; on the other hand, I *may not* be affected by an actual event which appears to concern me much more. I only know myself as a human entity; the scene, so to speak, of thoughts and affections; and am sensible of a certain doubleness by which I can stand as remote from myself as from another. However intense my experience, I am conscious of the presence and criticism of a part of me, which, as it were, is not a part of me, but spectator, sharing no experience, but taking note of it; and that is no more I than it is you. When the play, it may be the tragedy, of life is over, the spectator goes his way. It was a kind of fiction, a work of the imagination only, so far as he was concerned. This doubleness may easily make us poor neighbors and friends sometimes. (Pp. 134–35)

Like all quotations from *Walden* in this book, this one is taken from the Princeton edition, ed. J. Lyndon Shanley (Princeton: Princeton University Press, 1971).

11. Contrary to the recent suggestions of John Hildebidle (*Thoreau: A Naturalist's Liberty* [Cambridge: Harvard University Press, 1983]), I would argue that the style of Thoreau and the style of Darwin—and, hence, Thoreauvian nature writing and natural history—are, in this one critical way, at least, fundamentally and formally distinct. Like the vast majority of America's nature writers and all natural historians, Darwin consistently respects conventional, modern distinctions between metaphor and fact, subject and object, conjecture and observation. He takes at face value the relationships we customarily establish between well-managed statements of fact and the things to which we say they refer. In no reasonable sense could he be a scientist or natural historian without doing so. Thoreau, on the other hand, only partly respects the logical, epistemological, and methodological categories of modern scientific culture. At times, as Hildebidle and many others have indicated, Thoreau straightforwardly follows the methods and categories of the conventional, post-Cartesian thinker—scientist, historiographer, or poet. At times, he uses similes and metaphors (as well as factual statements) in precisely the same way Darwin or any decent writer of history or natural history would, in the same way any conventional biologist or autobiographer would. At other times, however—and just as frequently— Thoreau pointedly does not follow the methods or the categories of post-Cartesian thought. Frequently, as many critics have shown (and as Hildebidle himself acknowledges), Thoreau adopts those methods and categories only to expose and exploit them, to turn them over on themselves, so to speak, if not indeed to undermine them entirely.

Despite my disagreements with Hildebidle, both he and I are obviously and ultimately concerned with the same issue. For him, as for me and others of our ilk, it is partly a matter of trying to answer what he calls the "worrisome" question of "what to call Thoreau"—natural historian, poet-naturalist, or nature writer?—and partly a matter of trying to find some good formal and stylistic evidence for the rather loose connections devotees of nature writing have for years drawn not only between Thoreau and Darwin, but between Thoreau and Gilbert White and Muir and Burroughs and a hundred other British and American nature writers. My disagreements with Hildebidle, then, are completely sympathetic. I agree with him that neither "poet-naturalist" nor "nature writer" has the ring of respectability appropriate to Thoreau's writing. I agree as well that "natural historian" and "natural history" carry the kinds of connotations both he and I are seeking, connotations simultaneously less popular and less apt to be misconstrued than "nature writing" or "nature writer." Still, it seems to me that in the long run our only recourse is to develop some refinements upon those last two terms—partly because I believe we stand a better chance of refining popular usage than we do of changing it entirely, but largely because in my own efforts to draw comparisons and distinctions among the works of naturalists, nature writers, and natural historians (both British and American), I have continually come up against insurmountable philosophic, stylistic, and "substantive" barriers to any other alternative.

It simply will not do to argue, as Hildebidle inclines to, an underlying similarity between the styles of Darwin and Thoreau (much less to suggest a common generic identity for *Walden, Cape Cod,* and *The Voyage of the Beagle*) simply because one can show that both authors indulge in wordplay, or that Darwin (like Thoreau) was a conscious literary artist, or that Thoreau frequently follows the methods of natural history. Too often in Thoreau's works what initially appears as punning or wordplay is (or soon becomes) a serious questioning of the very method whereby we conventionally distinguish wordplay from what we call the straightforward, representational use of language, both figurative and nonfigurative—the very method whereby we distinguish natural history from nature. In Darwin's works, on the other hand—as in natural history generally—language, language-use, and personal linguistic habit are simply not relevant (or even visible) subjects. Darwin's works, like all conventional works of science, are simply not self-reflexive. Thoreau's works, on the other hand, frequently force a reader's attention to the page, the phrase, and even occasionally to the punctuation—if not indeed to that reader's own linguistic habits and associations. Thoreau is, at best or worst, a hyper-self-conscious user of language—as Darwin and the vast majority of naturalists (and nature writers) are not.

Thus it seems to me that in our efforts to classify the works of Thoreau (and, coincidentally, much of the writing of Eiseley, Leopold, Abbey, Dillard, Janovy, and Lopez) we should begin not (as Hildebidle does) by refining or modifying conventional notions of history, nor by attempting to modify the customary meaning of "natural history," but by refining and modifying conventional modern conceptions of nature, specifically by amplifying them to incorporate human language and the human language user, including both reader and writer (or narrator-expositor). By doing so, I would argue, we will be reintroducing a more ancient or classical conception of "nature"—a conception in tune with at least one of Thoreau's own—and simultaneously bringing the criticism of nature writing into closer alignment with contemporary philosophy and literary theory. (Throughout this book, the position I take on Thoreau and Thoreau's writings is closer, finally, to Joan Burbick's than it is to Hildebidle's, and closer still no doubt to Sharon Cameron's. See Burbick's *Thoreau's Alternative History: Changing Perspectives on Nature, Culture, and Language* [Philadelphia: University of Pennsylvania Press, 1987] and Cameron's *Writing Nature: Henry Thoreau's Journal* [New York: Oxford University Press, 1985]. Like Burbick, I view Thoreau's writings in dialectic terms, but with a different dialectic. What Burbick tends to see as moments of synthesis [or even as epiphanies], I tend to see as moments, most often brief, of un-self-conscious writing. What Burbick sees as "moments of disrupture," I tend to see as *attempted* epiphanies, seldom if ever achieved, because most often too self-conscious. Like Cameron, I find radical discontinuities in Thoreau's prose; but I find them in *Walden* as well as the journals; and at times they seem almost periodic or circadian. Like Burbick, I find that "Thoreau remains a genuine transcendentalist committed to the universality of the human mind and the transparency of language" [Burbick, 150]; but I find that he remains as well a genuine antitranscendentalist, committed to the individualities of human minds [especially his own] and to the inescapable opacity of language.)

In my understanding, then, Thoreau is a nature writer, and Darwin a naturalist or natural historian. The discriminations we customarily draw between the two are both sensible and reasonably accurate. Unlike Thoreau, Darwin consistently maintains his allegiance to conventional distinctions between figurative and nonfigurative language. His puns are clearly and cleanly puns. His plays on words are plays on words rather than stimulae to serious logical or epistemological—bio-logical, anthropo-logical, and psycho-logical—questionings. Thoreau may frequently be having fun, more frequently than Darwin certainly, but his "fun" is often hard-earned fun, fun purchased at the considerable cost of our own conventional sense as well as his own. Thoreau's extended (and often mixed) metaphors—his overtly para-doxical phrasings and his elaborate conceits—are more than decorative elab-orations of the underlying scientific methods of a natural historian. His sub-jects, unlike Darwin's or Gilbert White's or William Howitt's, are too often overtly philosophic or "literary" (and even, on occasion, stylistic) for his works (including significant portions even of his later essays) to be classified as natural history.

If the styles of Thoreau and Darwin (or Thoreau and Gilbert White) are thus distinct, at least in this one singular regard—if Thoreauvian nature writing and Darwinian natural history are thus different forms of writing (and, as I would argue, representatives of different genres)—what is one to make of the vast majority of American nature writing, of the writings of Muir or Burroughs or John Hay or Sally Carrighar? Are their writings more appro-priately aligned with Darwin or with Thoreau? Is what they have written natural history or nature writing?

Obviously, it is best here not to draw too many fine distinctions among genres. Obviously, too, there are many ways in which the forms and pur-poses of nature writing and natural history overlap. In the pages that follow, I will attempt to show that natural history was one of several historical pre-cursors and contributors to the development both of Thoreauvian nature writing and of its less self-reflexive and more popular American descendants (one of the most significant contributors, certainly, but no more significant than spiritual autobiography or romantic landscape art).

In the meantime, it may be worthwhile here to reiterate some of the obvious differences between Darwin's writings and the writings of Muir or John Hay or Ann Zwinger—between the vast majority of American nature writing and the writing of what we customarily call natural history. Appeal-ing, then, both to my readers' general knowledge of American nature writers and to the exemplary passages from Zwinger, Muir, and Hay cited above, I would note that American nature writers are *not* generally in the process of making or trying to make "scientific discoveries," that they are not generally (or do not generally portray themselves as being) in the service of institutional (or even methodological) science (John Janovy and, to a lesser extent, Muir are perhaps the clearest well-known exceptions to this rule, though Janovy's views of science and scientific method are critically different from the views of most natural historians, including Darwin's). Though American nature writers characteristically couch their "discoveries" in scientific terms, those discoveries are usually "personal discoveries," personal discoveries of scientific truths, if one may phrase things in such a way. In what may be a tellingly American way, the "scientific truths" of almost all American nature writing are noninstitutional (and, hence, as a rule, nonmethodological as well). Though John Hay may be employed partly as a naturalist in West Brewster, Massachusetts, he does not portray himself (or his narrators) as such in his best known and most popular works. The central narrating and expository figures of Muir and Zwinger—like those in the works of Mary Austin, Henry Beston, Joseph Wood Krutch, Sigurd Olson, Eiseley, and Dillard, among many many others—are, to all intents and purposes, "unemployed." Unlike Darwin (or Darwin's narrators)—and the narrators of Gilbert White, W. H. Hudson, and Richard Jefferies—the central figures of American nature writing are not engaged in (and they generally do not mention) the daily and institutionally appointed rounds of their parishes or their holdings. Unlike Hudson, H. J. Massingham, and Henry Williamson, they are generally not even gardeners going about the necessary business of controlling weeds or vermin to produce better crops. In short, though they may be doing something that seems like natural history, their endeavors are generally "ahistorical." They are not, generally, participants in ongoing institutional business; and they generally lack both institutional identity and institutional affiliations. (The notable exceptions to this almost unvarying American rule—a rule which, as many critics have noted, also prevails in most classic American fiction—are, again, Janovy and, to a lesser extent, Muir, Abbey, and the later Thoreau.)

If these differences between the works of American nature writers and the works of Darwin (or Agassiz or Nuttall, as well as the works of Gilbert White, Hudson, and Jefferies) are not enough to discriminate them—if, on the whole, the central figures of American nature writing are not consciously dedicated to institutional science or even to scientific method—it may be worth noting that the time and space of their works are also generally nonhistorical, often even when they discuss history. Though the places of their works have generally been local (or, at best, regional)—like the places of White, Massingham, and Hudson—unlike their British counterparts (including Darwin), they have not been inclined to populate those places with developed characters other than themselves, much less to define or develop them in social, economic, or political terms. Very few have been the narrators of American nature writing who have had associates or aids in the field. The time of their American places, in turn, has generally not been the routine, institutional time of waking, laboring, eating, and sleeping—or even, perhaps a bit surprisingly, the time of recreating—but rather an irregular and generally nonlinear time—the time (or times) of an interior monologue, perhaps, but almost never a developmental or accruing time—and only periodically a teleologically evolutionary or seasonal time—in short, seldom the time of natural history or scientific expedition or geographic exploration.

(The later essays of Thoreau, perhaps, and, in different ways, portions of the works of Burroughs, Muir, and Sigurd Olson provide at least partial exceptions to this rule.) In one common sense of the word, in fact, the time of American nature writing has been only partially "narrative."

Though the term "nature writing" may not have the prestigious ring of "natural history," it seems to me time (indeed well past the time) for students of literature to begin noting the kinds of rather obvious formal and stylistic traits that will discriminate the two while at the same time acknowledging their similarities—and likewise to distinguish each of them from rural (or country) literature and from the literature of travel.

12. Despite the regeneration Americans apparently gather from violence, violence has generally been lacking in the vast majority of American nature writing. So, on the whole, have open expressions of fear and rapacity. Human predation in American literature has, for the most part, been left to filmmakers, novelists, poets, and what are sometimes called outdoor writers (those who specialize in writing about fishing, hunting, and trapping). Unlike many of their angling, shooting, British counterparts, American outdoor writers have generally been thought to be distinctly subliterary; and the subjects (as well as the motives) of outdoor writing have generally been considered out of place (if not unnatural) in American nature writing. Predation—or at least human predation—has been out of place in most of America's natural Edens, as selfish or interested quests and needs have been out of place in good science and respectable landscape art. On violence and regeneration in American literature and culture see, of course, Richard Slotkin's *Regeneration through Violence: The Mythology of the American Frontier, 1600–1860* (Middletown, Conn.: Wesleyan University Press, 1973) and its sequel, *The Fatal Environment: The Myth of the Frontier in the Age of Industrialization, 1800–1890* (New York: Atheneum, 1985).

13. Thoreau, *Walden*, 306, 308, 216.

14. My point here, I hope obviously, is not to argue that Thoreau (or the central narrating figure of *Walden*) is consistently self-reflexive, or that the reading of *Walden* occasions continuous self-reflection. My point is, rather, that *Walden* is frequently self-reflexive, and that close readers must be prepared (often against their own wishes and inclinations) to suspend their own willing or unwilling suspensions of disbelief, to reflect upon their own habits of belief. My point, then, is that the central figure of *Walden* is sometimes a naive dreamer and sometimes pointedly not.

My point is also, again I hope obviously, to indicate that, in this self-conscious or self-reflexive regard, the narrator-expositor of *Walden* is unlike the central figures of more conventional American nature writing, and quite akin to the central figures in the nature writing of Eiseley, Leopold, Abbey, Dillard, and Lopez—sometimes self-conscious and sometimes not.

By saying or implying that the narrating figure of John Hay's *Nature's Year* is a naive dreamer, or that he struggles unknowingly (and, in this case, successfully) to sustain a naive dreamer's state of mind and psyche, in no way do I mean to imply that the naturalist, nature writer, and published author John Hay is somehow incapable of self-consciousness or self-reflection. In fact, I would be inclined to argue just the opposite solely on the basis of my reading of his published work (as I probably would not in the case of

John Burroughs or John Muir). To say that a narrating or narrative figure is a naive dreamer is not, of course, to say that the author of the work is unaware of the needs or desires of the figure he has cut, or for that matter of the reasons he has cut it as he as.

For an informative, penetrating discussion of the place of the naive dreamer, "the naive eye," in American literature and culture, see Tony Tanner's *The Reign of Wonder: Naivety and Reality in American Literature* (Cambridge: Cambridge University Press, 1965). For confirmation of the disposition among America's nature writers to divorce themselves and their nonhuman surroundings from institutional history see, among other well-known studies of American literature and art, R. W. B. Lewis, *The American Adam: Innocence, Tragedy, and Tradition in the Nineteenth Century* (Chicago: University of Chicago Press, 1955); Richard Chase, *The American Novel and Its Tradition* (Garden City, N.Y.: Doubleday, Anchor Books, 1957); A. N. Kaul, *The American Vision* (New Haven: Yale University Press, 1963); Daniel Hoffman, *Form and Fable in American Fiction* (New York: Oxford University Press, 1965); Richard Poirier, *A World Elsewhere: The Place of Style in American Literature* (New York: Oxford University Press, 1966); Barbara Novak, *Nature and Culture: American Landscape and Painting, 1825–1875* (New York: Oxford University Press, 1980); Larzer Ziff, *Literary Democracy: The Declaration of Cultural Independence in America* (New York: Viking Press, 1981); and Irving Howe's brief but telling *The American Newness: Culture and Politics in the Age of Emerson* (Cambridge: Harvard University Press, 1986). For confirmation of the inclinations of America's nature writers to divorce their narrators and expositors even from considerations of gender, family, and sex, see D. H. Lawrence's essays "The Spirit of Place" and "Fenimore Cooper's Leatherstocking Novels" in *Studies in Classic American Literature* (New York: Seltzer, 1923; reprint, New York: Viking Press, 1961); Leslie Fiedler's trilogy, *Love and Death in the American Novel* (New York: Criterion Books, 1960), *Waiting for the End* (New York: Stein & Day, 1964), *The Return of the Vanishing American* (New York: Stein & Day, 1968); and, in a slightly different vein, Annette Kolodny's two books, *The Lay of the Land: Metaphor as Experience and History in American Life and Letters* and *The Land before Her: Fantasy and Experience of the American Frontier, 1630–1860* (Chapel Hill: University of North Carolina Press, 1975 and 1984). On this last set of issues, it is probably worth noting that both males and females among America's nature writers have generally dissociated their central narrating figures from familial and sexual relations and concerns. Annie Dillard's *Pilgrim at Tinker Creek* (New York: Harper's Magazine Press, 1974) is the only work of American nature writing I know of in which considerations of gender or sex play anything like a significant role in the configuration of self or surroundings, and even in *Pilgrim* such considerations are fundamentally psychobiotic rather than social or familial.

15. See again, Odum, *Fundamentals of Ecology*, 283.

Chapter Two: The History and
Criticism of Nature Writing

1. Of the many studies that might be said to deal, at least indirectly, with the places of nature writers and the functions of nature writing in

American social, intellectual, and political history, see Hans Huth, *Nature and the American: Three Centuries of Changing Attitudes* (Berkeley and Los Angeles: University of California Press, 1957); Samuel P. Hays, *Conservation and the Gospel of Efficiency: The Progressive Conservation Movement, 1890–1920* (Cambridge: Harvard University Press, 1959); Arthur A. Ekirch, *Man and Nature in America* (New York: Columbia University Press, 1963); Roderick Nash, *Wilderness and the American Mind*, 3d ed. (New Haven: Yale University Press, 1982); Peter J. Schmitt, *Back to Nature: The Arcadian Myth in Urban America* (New York: Oxford University Press, 1969); Edward Halsey Foster, *The Civilized Wilderness: Backgrounds to American Romantic Literature, 1817–1860* (New York: Free Press, 1975); Donald Worster, *Nature's Economy: The Roots of Ecology* (San Francisco: Sierra Club Books, 1977; reprint, Garden City, N.Y.: Doubleday, Anchor Books, 1979); Bernard Rosenthal, *City of Nature: Journeys to Nature in the Age of American Romanticism* (Newark, Del.: University of Delaware Press, 1980); Barbara Novak, *Nature and Culture: American Landscape and Painting, 1825–1875* (New York: Oxford University Press, 1980); Lee Clark Mitchell, *Witnesses to a Vanishing America: The Nineteenth Century Response* (Princeton: Princeton University Press, 1981); and Frederick Turner, *Beyond Geography: The Western Spirit against the Wilderness* (New Brunswick, N.J.: Rutgers University Press, 1983). Of the many other works, both scholarly and popular, that consider the lives of naturalists and the roles of natural history in American culture, see Max Meisel, *A Bibliography of American Natural History*, 3 vols. (New York: Premiere Publishing, 1924); N. Bryllion Fagin, *William Bartram: Interpreter of the American Landscape* (Baltimore: Johns Hopkins Press, 1933); Donald Culross Peattie, *Green Laurels: The Lives and Achievements of the Great Naturalists* (New York: Simon & Schuster, 1936); William Martin Smallwood, *Natural History and the American Mind* (New York: Columbia University Press, 1941); Josephine Herbst, *New Green World* (New York: Hastings House, 1954); Virginia S. Eifert, *Tall Trees and Far Horizons: Adventures and Discoveries of Early Botanists in America* (New York: Dodd, Mead, 1965); Alexander B. Adams, *Eternal Quest: The Story of the Great Naturalists* (New York: G. P. Putnam's, 1969); Henry Savage, Jr., *Lost Heritage: Wilderness America through the Eyes of Seven Pre-Audubon Naturalists* (New York: William Morrow, 1970); Joseph Kastner, *A Species of Eternity* (New York: Knopf, 1977); Wayne Hanley, *Natural History in America: From Mark Catesby to Rachel Carson* (New York: Quadrangle/New York Times Book Co., 1977); and David Scofield Wilson, *In the Presence of Nature* (Amherst: University of Massachusetts Press, 1978). For still additional, and for the most part popular, illustrations of the developing canon, see not only such now forgotten works as Henry Chester Tracy, *American Naturists* (New York: Dutton, 1930); and Herbert Faulkner West, *The Nature Writers: A Guide to Richer Reading* (Brattleboro, Vt.: Stephen Daye, 1939)—but also, and more recently, Stewart Udall, *The Quiet Crisis* (New York: Holt, Rinehart & Winston, 1963); Frank Graham, Jr., *Man's Dominion: The Story of Conservation in America* (New York: M. Evans, 1971); and Paul Brooks, *Speaking for Nature: How Literary Naturalists from Henry Thoreau to Rachel Carson Have Shaped America* (Boston: Houghton Mifflin, 1980)—as well as the several anthologies of American "nature writing," which, however disparate, suggest a slowly developing conviction that something is distinct in this vaguely defined region of nonfiction

prose. From my point of view, the most notable of these anthologies—because formally the most consistent—are the two that were put together by
practicing nature writers: Joseph Wood Krutch's *Great American Nature
Writing* (New York: Wm. Sloane, 1950), of which I will have much more to
say below, and Hal Borland's *Our Natural World* (Philadelphia: J. B. Lippincott, 1969). The several others that have followed in the wake of the popular
"ecology movement," have depicted considerably more diverse and uneven
notions of "nature writing," in part no doubt because they have been intended less as representations of a kind of writing than as textbooks for
college courses in the broad reach of American literature and history or as
stimulants to "environmental action." See, for example, Jean Vermes, ed.
The Wilderness Sampler (Harrisburg, Pa.: Stackpole, 1968); William
Schwartz, ed. *Voices for the Wilderness* (New York: Ballantine, 1969); David
D. Anderson, ed., *Sunshine and Smoke: American Writers and the American Environment* (Philadelphia: Lippincott, 1971); Robert J. Gangewere,
ed., *The Exploited Eden: Literature on the American Environment* (New
York: Harper & Row, 1972); John Conron, ed., *The American Landscape: A
Critical Anthology of Prose and Poetry* (New York: Oxford University Press,
1973); Frank Bergon, ed. *The Wilderness Reader* (New York: New American
Library, 1980); Robert C. Baron and Elizabeth Darby Junkin, eds., *Of Discovery and Destiny: An Anthology of American Writers and the American
Land* (Golden, Colo.: Fulcrum, 1987); Thomas J. Lyon, ed., *This Incomperable Lande: A Book of American Nature Writing* (Boston: Houghton Mifflin,
1989). Though each of these anthologies has brought renewed attention to
the literature of American lands—and, hence, to many of the works whose
type Krutch and Borland sought to illustrate—each has also tended to
neglect the issues of literary types and their functions by lumping the various types together and by tying them to the "ecological issues" and "environmental problems" of the most recent politicization and commercializa-
tion of "nature in America."

As a general rule, historians concerned with the "nature" and "nature
writing" of Britain have been both fewer in number than their Americanist
counterparts and less inclined to separate the study of history from the study
of style, or the history of ideas from literary analysis—less inclined, in other
words, to divorce the politics, economics, aesthetics, and ethics of land use
from the intricacies of style, image, and construct. In fact, the discrimination
between history and literature—between land and text or land-use and style
that seems to characterize American studies of nature, nature writing, and
related matters—as well as the difference I find between the contributions of
intellectual, political, and economic historians, on the one hand, and literary
historians and critics, on the other—is far less clear in related studies of
"nature in Britain." So much so, at times it seems, that one is tempted not
only to note again the by now fairly well-recognized fact that "nature" (like
"wilderness," "land," "environment," and "ecology") tends to be a far more
discrete category in American historiography than it does in the historiography of Britain, but also to recite its underlying consequence—that the
dualism of nature and culture—like the distinction between nature and history, or thing and word, or reality and rhetoric—tends to be more extreme
(sharper, if you will) in America than it is in Britain—and this despite the fact
that American historians seem far more devoted to the "culture of nature"

than their British counterparts. Certainly the differences between "nature in Britain" and "nature in America"—in historiography as in nature writing and philosophy, if not indeed in science—at least partly reflect the daily and ideological fact that "nature" and the management of natural resources are (and historically have been) less "public" and legislative in Britain than they are (or have been) in the United States (and even in Canada)—less matters of national, regional, or even local policy or program, and more matters of class-consciousness, conscience, and custom, if not indeed of individual or familial aesthetic and ethical taste. Whatever the reasons, many (perhaps most) influential studies of "nature in Britain" have been more devoted than their American counterparts to the details of style and imagery—even when, like Raymond Williams's *The Country and the City* (New York: Oxford University Press, 1973), they have been concerned with the economic and political history of "nature."

By some of these same broadly ideological tokens, however, the study of "nature" and "nature writing" in Britain has tended to slight (if not to ignore completely) those so-called minor figures and works so central to much of the social, intellectual, and political history of nature in America. In America, at least we can say that our historians have acknowledged the functions of nature writing and the roles of nature writers, whatever the disposition of our literary critics. In Britain, by contrast, scholarly recognition for "nature writing" and "nature writers"—however different they may be from their American counterparts, and despite their considerable and continuing popularity—has been far slower in coming, except of course for the one or two figures (Darwin and Hudson are perhaps the best candidates) who are occasionally considered to have made it into the elite canon of "literary" greats.

Williams's *The Country and the City* and, more recently, Keith Thomas's *Man and the Natural World: A History of the Modern Sensibility* (New York: Pantheon Books, 1983) have both provided promising paradigms that may eventually lead to greater recognition and more detailed study of the nature writing of Britain; but so far, to the best of my knowledge, only W. J. Keith (*The Rural Tradition: William Cobbett, Gilbert White, and Other Non-Fiction Prose Writers of the English Countryside* [Toronto: University of Toronto Press, 1975]) has undertaken any extended study of the many, many works of British nature writing. Ironically, and perhaps tellingly, even the pervasive literature of British "country life"—the essentially urban vision of "country" so deeply criticized by Williams—continues to receive extremely short shrift from serious historians and critics—except, of course, where it enters into the "higher," "aesthetic" forms of fiction, poetry, drama, and landscape art.

Without some intimate experience of British bookstores, in fact—or the catalogues of used-book dealers—or an acquaintance with Keith's *The Rural Tradition*, non-British readers (including even those many Americans whose inclinations run to "nature books") would be hard pressed to discover the nearest thing to American nature writing in Britain. Without some knowledge of *The Rural Tradition* or *The Country and the City* or E. D. H. Johnson's *The Poetry of Earth: A Collection of English Nature Writings from Gilbert White to Richard Jefferies* (New York: Atheneum, 1974), even those non-British scholars who consider themselves well versed in English literature of the nineteenth and twentieth centuries would be hard-pressed to find much if anything in British literary and historical scholarship to lead them to the works (or even the names) of a Massingham, a Howitt, a Stuart, or a Henry Williamson (much less a Maurice Wiggin, a Gavin Maxwell, a Derek Tangye, or a John Stewart Collis), among dozens of other British nature writers. Non-American readers, by comparison, would find the works of at least a few "unknown" American writers on nature—Bartram, Muir, and George Perkins Marsh, for example—or Audubon, Burroughs, and George Bird Grinnell—considered at some length in several respectable histories of American culture. As it turns out, even *The Natural History of Selborne* seems to be of more interest to Americanists than it does to historians and critics of British literature.

The point to be made here, then, is that though historians and critics of "nature in Britain" have tended—far more than their Americanist peers—to emphasize issues of style and text, they have done comparatively little to acknowledge the voluminous nature writing of Britain or to place it and its authors in social, intellectual, and political contexts—and even less to extend it detailed critical attention. With precious few exceptions, literary and historical scholars of Britain continue to view nature writers and nature writing as subliterary and, at best, of coincidental historical and cultural significance. Historians of "nature in America," on the other hand—including at least a few literary historians—have done quite a good deal to bring nature writers and nature writing to the public eye—much to abstract from them and to place them in social, political, and intellectual contexts—but almost nothing to lead their audiences into the intricacies of imagery, logic, and metaphor in nature writing (the works of Thoreau excepted, of course), or to bring the styles and forms of nature writing into the historical arena. What one needs, it would seem, is some blending of the two scholarly traditions, some meshing of the Americanist's disposition to extend the "literary" canon, some synthesis of the American scholar's emphasis on the facts of nature and environmental action, on the one hand—and some of the "British" scholar's attention to style, transferred from Wordsworth's poetry or the verse of the country house, on the other hand—all in all, some blending of the essentially nonstylistic historiography of America with the pointedly stylistic historiography of Britain.

For other exemplary views of nature and nature writing in Britain see not only such classic studies as Myra Reynolds, *The Treatment of Nature in English Poetry between Pope and Wordsworth* (Chicago: University of Chicago Press, 1909); Christopher Hussey, *The Picturesque* (New York: G. P. Putnam's, 1927); Samuel Holt Monk, *The Sublime* (1935; reprint, Ann Arbor: University of Michigan Press, 1960); Joseph Warren Beach, *The Concept of Nature in Nineteenth-Century English Poetry* (New York: Macmillan, 1936); Charles Raven, *English Naturalists from Neckham to Ray* (Cambridge; Cambridge University Press, 1947); Marjorie Hope Nicolson, *Mountain Gloom and Mountain Glory: The Development of the Aesthetics of the Infinite* (Ithaca: Cornell University Press, 1959)—but also, and more recently, Edward Malins, *English Landscaping and Literature, 1660–1840* (London: Oxford University Press, 1966); John Barrell, *The Idea of Landscape and the Sense of Place, 1730–1840: An Approach to the Poetry of John Clare* (Cambridge: Cambridge University Press, 1972); David Elliston

Allen, *The Naturalist in Britain: A Social History* (London: Allen Lane, 1976; Harmondsworth, Middlesex: Penguin Books, 1978); U. C. Knoepflmacher and G. B. Tennyson, eds., *Nature and the Victorian Imagination* (Berkeley and Los Angeles: University of California Press, 1977); James Turner, *The Politics of Landscape: Rural Scenery and Society in English Poetry, 1630–1660* (Cambridge: Harvard University Press, 1979); Lynn L. Merrill, *The Romance of Victorian Natural History* (New York: Oxford University Press, 1989); and, on a more deeply personal note, the opening chapter, "An Inherited Perspective," of Ronald Blythe's *Characters and Their Landscapes* (New York: Harcourt, Brace, 1983).

It may be worth pointing out here that, for all their philosophic and historiographic differences, these historians and critics of Britain and America nonetheless seem to share one fundamental and distinguishing trait—their interest in "nature" and things "natural"—as well as their interests, however undeveloped, in the linguistic and literary forms in which such things have been couched. As one looks in vain for a French or German or Brazilian Gilbert White, much less a Spanish or Chinese Thoreau (the Russian Mikhail Prishvin is the clearest exception I know of to the apparent rule against nature writing outside the Anglo-American world), so one looks in almost equal vain on the European continent—or in Asia, Africa, and Latin America—for scholarly counterparts to these British and American historians and critics of "nature" and "the environment."

2. I speak here primarily about literary historians and critics of America, about those whose chief concerns are American authors and texts. Those *very* few who have seriously considered the so-called nature writing of Britain (such as Raymond Williams and W. J. Keith) seem to me to have done a creditable, though even more inaugural, job—both of framing the extensive cultural history of British "nature writing" and of noting its essential stylistic and substantive traits. Among the several noteworthy American studies one should mention, see first those four or five "classics" which, however superficial or incomplete, called original attention to nature writing and, hence, gave credence and support to others which followed—particularly and especially, Selden Whitcomb, "Nature in Early American Literature," *Sewanee Review* 2 (1893–1894): 159–179; Norman Foerster, *Nature in American Literature* (New York: Macmillan, 1923); Philip Marshall Hicks, *The Development of the Natural History Essay in American Literature* (Philadelphia: University of Pennsylvania, 1924); Fagin, *William Bartram*, the only one of these early studies to devote significant attention to the details of style and their implications; and Krutch, "Prologue" to *Great American Nature Writing*, 2–95. On this same originating note, one should also mention Leo Marx's *The Machine in the Garden: Technology and the Pastoral Ideal in America* (New York: Oxford University Press, 1964), not because it deals specifically with nature writing, but because it came on the critical scene at a particularly influential time.

Given the virtual plethora of "nature books" and "environmental studies"—historical, political, sociological, anthropological, and philosophic—that followed in the wake of "ecology" in the late 1960s and 1970s, one might find somewhat surprising the comparative paucity of detailed literary studies—informed studies of nature writing—unless one remembers that Anglo-American literary critics have generally been slow to acknowledge the

complexities of nonfiction prose, and even slower to appreciate those forms
of it that deal in the vocabularies, logics, and major metaphors of science. As
far as I know, no knowledgeable literary critic has taken on the broad issue of
nature writing as genre since Richard Lillard addressed the matter in 1969.
In an essay that deserves to be better known than it is—"Books in the Field:
Nature and Conservation," *Wilson Library Bulletin* (October 1969): 159–
77—Lillard noted (albeit for a popular audience, and for the most part abstractly) several of the obviously distinguishing formal traits of what he
called the "nature book." Having done so, he went on to distinguish the
nature book, in turn, both from the literature of conservation and from natural history (as well as its modern "ecological" variants). Indeed, Lillard's
essay might well be read as an attempted elaboration and further specifica-
tion of the terms Krutch initially proposed for nature writing as a distinct
genre in 1950. And so might the brief "Taxonomy of Nature Writing" proposed more recently by Thomas J. Lyon as the first chapter of *This Incomperable Lande.*

   In the "environmental" years of the 1970s and 1980s, many other interested parties have no doubt written or delivered still additional, and for
the most part popular, accounts of nature writing as genre (see, for example,
Dennis Ribbens, "Nature Writing: A Definition," *Wisconsin Academy Review* [September 1984]: 9–12); but none that have caught my eye have gone
further than Lillard's in providing the essentials of a comprehensive view of
nature writing as a literary type. In fact, the most helpful refinements and
amplifications of Krutch's and Lillard's terms—and the most promising addi-
tions to an understanding of the forms and types of nature writing—have
come from one or two studies devoted mainly to novel readings of individual
figures and texts. I think here of David Scofield Wilson's *In the Presence of
Nature*, not because of its devotion to the terms "nature reporter" and "nature reportage," but because of its close readings of works by Jonathan
Carver, John Bartram, and Mark Catesby—because the philosophic issues
with which it begins, when brought to the daily lives of these early Americans, enable one to move beneath and beyond the conventional (and naively
realistic) view that natural history or reporting on nature is simply a matter
of contributing to an ever-increasing scientific knowledge, or to its popular-
ization—enable one, in fact, to move into the psycho- and sociolinguistic
entanglements of the early American naturalist's text. I think also of John
Hildebidle's *Thoreau: A Naturalist's Liberty* (Cambridge: Harvard University Press, 1983), not because it advocates the term "natural history" for the
works of Thoreau—and, hence, slights both the anxieties and the egoism of
spiritual autobiography, as well as the serious and philosophic doubts Thoreau frequently entertained about his own (and others') dependence upon
natural history—but because it takes seriously that part of Thoreau's works
(as well as Gilbert White's and Darwin's) defined by the stylistic mode and
"methodology" of natural history—because, in other words, it takes seriously the logical forms and syntax of natural science.

   Such studies as Wilson's and Hildebidle's seem to be clear exceptions,
however, to the going rule on nature writing, both scholarly and popular. All
in all, one must say, the literary history and criticism of nature writing remain several decades behind the history and criticism even of other forms of
nonfiction prose, if not indeed behind the initial views proposed by Krutch

and Lillard some years ago. A sample of contemporary views might be run with a cursory reading of part 4 of the recent issue of *Antaeus* (Autumn 1986) devoted to "Essays on Nature," an issue that otherwise contains some excellent pieces of nature writing. As a supplement to contributions from Annie Dillard, Barry Lopez, Robert Finch, Jim Harrison, and several others, the editors of *Antaeus* have seen fit to add what is meant to be a bibliographic aid to interested readers, a section (part 4) that includes two lists of exemplary titles. The first—"Natural History: An Annotated Booklist"—is a compilation of titles and comments by the several writers who contributed to the autumn issue. The second is a more straightforward bibliography prepared by Thomas J. Lyon entitled "American Nature Writing: A Selective Booklist on Nature and Man-and-Nature." The first list on "natural history" mentions, among many other titles, *Moby-Dick*, Whitehead's *Science and the Modern World*, Henry Nash Smith's *Virgin Land*, Von Frisch's *The Dancing Bees*, Laurens van der Post's *The Heart of the Hunter*, Whitman's "Song of Myself" and *Specimen Days*, as well as *Walden, My First Summer in the Sierra*, and the tenth-century collection of 1,111 Japanese poems known in English as *The Kokinshu*. The second, and admittedly "selective," list on "American Nature Writing" offers hardly any more help; for it catalogues not only the likes of Barry Lopez's *River Notes* and Muir's *The Yosemite*, among other anticipated fare, but several scholarly works (such as Nash's *Wilderness and the American Mind* and Annette Kolodny's *The Land before Her: Fantasy and Experience of the American Frontier, 1630–1860*), a few works of travel literature, and numerous scientific and semiscientific studies that bear precious little formal or stylistic resemblance to *Walden* or *The Yosemite* or, for that matter, to one another—works such as Durward Allen's *Wolves of Minong: Their Vital Role in a Wild Community* (Boston: Houghton Mifflin, 1979), for example, or E. O. Wilson's *Sociobiology: The New Synthesis* (Cambridge; Harvard University Press, 1975).

The difficulties with such conglomerate lists of "nature writing" (or, worse, "natural history") are, of course, several—and in America they have been repeated many times over in the years since *Silent Spring*. More than anything else, perhaps, such ecumenical listings prove the contemporary resilience of that popular Romantic enthusiasm for all things seemingly "natural," whatever their forms and styles. In their enthusiasm for nature, they reinforce (even if unintentionally) that sometime Romantic (and very much American) disposition to look through the many historical shapes of the medium to the heart-felt depths of the uniform natural message—and, hence, they tend to retard (rather than advance) our understandings of the compositions of nature.

As one might expect under such cultural circumstances, only the works of Thoreau have received the kinds of extended attention to style that might deepen and detail our appreciations of the forms and types of nature writing. See, especially, Joseph J. Moldenhauer, "The *Extra-vagant* Maneuver: Paradox in *Walden*," *Graduate Journal* 6 (Winter 1964): 132–46, revised and reprinted as "Paradox in *Walden*," in *Twentieth Century Interpretations of "Walden*," ed. Richard Ruland (Englewood Cliffs, N.J.: Prentice-Hall, 1968), 73–84; Albert McLean, "Thoreau's True Meridian: Natural Fact and Metaphor," *American Quarterly* 20 (1968): 567–79 (The "and" of McLean's title is to be emphasized.); Charles R. Anderson, *The Magic Circle of Walden*

(New York: Holt, 1968); Sherman Paul, *The Shores of America: Thoreau's Inward Exploration* (Urbana: University of Illinois Press, 1972); Stanley Cavell, *The Senses of Walden* (New York: Viking Press, 1972) (Cavell's plural "senses" is also to be emphasized.); Lawrence Buell, *Literary Transcendentalism: Style and Vision in the American Renaissance* (Ithaca: Cornell University Press, 1973), especially chaps. 7, 8, 10, and 11; James McIntosh, *Thoreau as Romantic Naturalist: His Shifting Stance toward Nature* (Ithaca: Cornell University Press, 1974); Richard Bridgman, *Dark Thoreau* (Lincoln: University of Nebraska Press, 1982); Hildebidle, *Thoreau: A Naturalist's Liberty*; Sharon Cameron, *Writing Nature: Henry Thoreau's Journal* (New York: Oxford University Press, 1985); Robert Richardson, *Henry David Thoreau: A Life of the Mind* (Berkeley and Los Angeles: University of California Press, 1986); Linck Johnson, *Thoreau's Complex Weave: The Writing of "A Week on the Concord and Merrimack Rivers"* (Charlottesville: University Press of Virginia, 1986); Joan Burbick, *Thoreau's Alternative History: Changing Perspectives on Nature, Culture, and Language* (Philadelphia: University of Pennsylvania Press, 1987).

As even a cursory reading of these and many other, shorter studies will indicate, the essentials of a more detailed criticism of nature writing have been in place for quite some time; and yet very little has been done to extend the kinds of rhetorical, psychological, and philosophical analysis now characteristic of Thoreauvian criticism to the works of Thoreau's nature-writing associates. Even studies of John Muir's writings, for all their recent popularity, have remained for the most part traditionally biographical and historical—ideational, political, "scientific," and popularly didactic: see, for example, Michael Cohen's *The Pathless Way: John Muir and American Wilderness* (Madison: University of Wisconsin Press, 1984); the more promising biography by Frederick Turner, *Rediscovering America: John Muir in His Time and Ours* (San Francisco: Sierra Club, 1985); and the special issue of *Pacific Historian*, vol. 29 (Summer/Fall 1985), devoted exclusively to essays on Muir. And with very few exceptions, the same can be said of the criticism of even the best-known and best-received of contemporary nature writers—Leopold, Eiseley, Hay, Abbey, Lopez, and Dillard, for example. For one of those few welcome exceptions, see John Tallmadge's nicely tuned study of figure and configuration in *A Sand County Almanac*, "Anatomy of a Classic," in *Companion to* A Sand County Almanac: *Interpretive and Critical Essays*, ed. J. Baird Callicott (Madison: University of Wisconsin Press, 1987), 110–27; for another, see David Stuart Miller, "An Unfinished Pilgrimage: Edwin Way Teale and American Nature Writing" (Ph.D. diss., University of Minnesota, 1982); for a few more see the several appreciative reviews and essays that have begun to bring to the writings of Loren Eiseley the kinds of attentions that typify the best criticism of Thoreau—I think here especially of the review of Eiseley's *The Unexpected Universe* that W. H. Auden originally wrote for the *New Yorker* in 1970 and which now appears as the "Introduction" to the posthumous collection of Eiseley's essays entitled *The Star Thrower* (New York: Harcourt Brace Jovanovich, 1978); but I think as well of E. Fred Carlisle's "The Heretical Science of Loren Eiseley," *Centennial Review* 18 (Fall 1974): 354–77; of James M. Schwartz's "The 'Immense Journey' of an Artist: The Literary Technique and Style of Loren Eiseley" (Ph.D. diss., Ohio University, 1977) and of his "Loren Eiseley: The Scientist as Literary Artist," *Georgia Review* 31 (1977): 855–71; of some sections of Deborah Hawkin Pickering's "The Selves of Loren Eiseley: A Stylistic Analysis of the Essays in *The Immense Journey, The Night Country,* and *All the Strange Hours*" (Ph.D. diss., University of Iowa, 1982); and of the second chapter, "*The Immense Journey*: The Making of a Literary Naturalist," of Warren French's *Loren Eiseley* (Boston: Twayne, 1983).

As the authors of these exceptions occasionally note themselves, literary critics—weaned as they have been on traditional forms of belles lettres—continue to have a hard time with nature writing, even when they acknowledge its successful or influential exemplars. As John Elder has said, in at least partial explanation of the phenomenon, "it is interesting, in fact, how often, from Thoreau on, American literature's most intense engagements with nature have issued into uncategorizable books" (*Imagining the Earth: Poetry and the Vision of Nature* [Urbana: University of Illinois Press, 1985], 175).

3. For further bibliographic information on Hicks, Tracy, Fagin, and Krutch, see the notes immediately above. For Burroughs's many essays on writing about nature, see the twenty-three volumes of the Riverby edition of *The Writings of John Burroughs,* originally published, updated, and republished by Houghton Mifflin, and recently reissued complete (with *The Last Harvest* [Boston: Houghton Mifflin, 1922] as the final volume) by Russell & Russell (New York, 1968). Of the five specific essays mentioned here, only "The True Test of Good Nature Literature," *Country Life* 6 (May 1904): 51–53, seems not to have made it into the final edition of Burroughs's writings. The others may be located as follows: "The Literary Treatment of Nature" in vol. 12, *Ways of Nature,* 191–208; "Nature in Literature" in vol 10, *Literary Values and Other Papers,* 225–27; "Henry D. Thoreau" and "Gilbert White's Book" in vol. 8, *Indoor Studies,* 3–47 and 177–192, respectively. Like virtually all of Burroughs's writings, each of these essays was originally published in a popular magazine before being printed and reprinted in similarly popular book form in the decades that followed: "Nature in Literature," *Critic* 1 (July 1881): 185; "Henry D. Thoreau," *Century Magazine* 24 (May, 1882): 368–79; "Gilbert White's Book," *Lippincott's* 38 (August 1886): 133–40; and "The Literary Treatment of Nature," *Atlantic Monthly* 94 (July 1904): 38–43. Francis Halsey's "The Rise of Nature Writers" appeared in *American Monthly Review of the Reviews* 26 (November 1902): 567–71.

It is difficult and finally no doubt unimportant to indicate when the concern with nature writing as a particular ideational, stylistic, and substantive type began. Certainly the discussion dates at least to Burroughs's earliest essays, popular magazine writings that derived, in turn, from late-nineteenth and early-twentieth-century enthusiasm for what are sometimes called "nature poetry" and "nature study"—from the search for Wordsworth's ancestors, Bryant's predecessors, and especially the progenitors and successors of Thoreau—and in general from the study of the forms and fashions of the Romantics' appreciations of NATURE, in painting as well as in literature, in prose as well as in verse. Certainly, too, a part of this slowly growing historical and critical interest in nature writing derived from closely related late-nineteenth and early-twentieth-century attempts to elucidate the history of biology (especially taxonomic or systematic biology) and the lives of the great naturalists (see Meisel's *Bibliography of American Natural History*).

If one cannot be precise with originating dates, one can certainly document broadly cultural motivations—the development of ecology and various forms of natural resource management (in forestry, fisheries, wildlife, hydrology, and soil science), for example—and even more generally, the back-to-nature movement of the first decades of the twentieth century—all in all, the movements, concepts, and professions that gave rise to national and local parks, forests, and wildlife refuges—the social and intellectual trends which found expression in Teddy Roosevelt and Olive Thorne Miller (the pen name of Harriet Mann Miller, author of immensely popular nature books from the 1870s through the First World War), in Gifford Pinchot and George Bird Grinnell, in Mabel Osgood Wright (whose *Citizen Bird* [New York: Macmillan, 1897] was illustrated with the first significant series of published drawings by Louis Agassiz Fuertes), in Frederick Law Olmsted, Florence A. Merriam, and the founding of numerous Audubon Societies, the Sierra Club, and the Boy Scouts, among many other associated things. For exemplary sources on "nature" in America at the turn of the century, see Schmitt, *Back to Nature*; Nash, *Wilderness and the American Mind*; Hays, *Conservation and the Gospel of Efficiency*; Graham, *Man's Dominion*; Worster, *Nature's Economy*; and Brooks, *Speaking for Nature*.

At least by 1904, in "The Literary Treatment of Nature," Burroughs was seeking to distinguish "the literary treatment of natural history" from its "scientific treatment," and coordinately to discriminate the successful "essay-naturalist" from the "nature-fakir," the writer who sought to "interpret" nature rather than to observe, record, and legitimately appreciate it. Again and again, over and over, in one popular periodical after another, Burroughs wrote that the literary naturalist observed and admired, while the nature-fakir personified and humanized. The former kept human desire and emotion distinct from the rational and empirical rendering of nonhuman nature. The latter confused them.

As John Hildebidle has recently pointed out (*Thoreau: A Naturalist's Liberty*, 53–59), the amount of time Burroughs spent writing about nature in literature and the literary treatment of nature is some indication of the difficulty he was having both in characterizing his own writing and in discriminating among the works of other "literary naturalists." In logical and conceptual fashions that foreshadow the efforts of virtually all later critics of nature writing, he sought valiantly to distinguish those nature writers who kept their own and their readers' feet on solid, scientific ground from those who went off on wild or childish "anthropomorphic" trips, reading human motive and conception into things and arrangements where good modern thought said they must not go. No one gave Burroughs more trouble than Thoreau: "His mood was subjective rather than objective. He was more intent on the natural history of his own thought than on that of the bird. . . . He had no self-abandonment, no self-forgetfulness; he could not give himself to the birds or animals: they must surrender to him" ("Henry D. Thoreau" in *Indoor Studies*, vol. 8 of *Writings of John Burroughs*, 39, 41). The true nature writer (Thoreau was as much false as true) was not a scientist exactly—"The essay-naturalist observes and admires; the scientific naturalist collects"—but neither was he an artist: "The aim of art is the beautiful, not

over but *through* the true. The aim of the literary naturalist is the true, not
over but through the beautiful; you shall find the exact facts in his pages,
and you shall find them possessed of some of the allurement and suggestive-
ness that they had in the fields and woods. Only thus does his work attain to
the rank of literature" ("The Literary Treatment of Nature" in *Ways of Nature*, vol. 12 of *Writings of John Burroughs*, 191, 208).

> To attribute human motives and faculties to the animals is to caricature
> them; but to put us in such relation with them that we feel their kinship,
> that we see their lives embosomed in the same iron necessity as our own,
> that we see in their minds a humbler manifestation of the same psychic
> power and intelligence that culminates and is conscious of itself in
> man,—that, I take it, is the true humanization. ("The Literary Treatment
> of Nature," 195)

Despite Hildebidle's suggestions (*Thoreau: A Naturalist's Liberty*, 58–
59)—or, rather, in amplification of them—the difficulty Burroughs was having with the definition and characterization of literary naturalism was less a
function of science leaving the rich variances of the outdoors and the field for
the controlled experiments of the laboratory—less a function of the amateur
naturalist's observation and appreciation of "locality" and "context" gradually giving way to the modern scientific desire to abstract from "natural"
and local places—less, in other words, a function of some "reorientation of
science" that led scientists away from contexts "actually observable" to
"some artificial and limited recreation in laboratory or museum" (Hildebidle, 58)—than it was (and with the vast majority of nature-writing's critics,
including Hildebidle, still is) a function of that clean philosophic dualism that
juxtaposes the rich and notably "natural" contexts of field study with the
sterile (and by implication "unnatural"), "contextless," and even emotion-
less environments of the laboratory or the museum—that same classical,
and especially post-Cartesian, dualism that depends upon categorical distinctions not only between nature and the laboratory, or the natural and the
artificial, but also (as in Burroughs's case) between the subjective and the
objective, or fact and art, or true humanization and false (and misleading)
personification.

   This is the dualism—the presumed and assumed breakdown of the bi-
cameral mind—the split between science and literature (or art), as between
human and nonhuman, that puts "nature" clearly outside the library and
the laboratory (and most often well beyond the city and the suburb), as the
"object" of human science and art—as that which human language and
artifact partake of and participate in (if they do) only when and where the
birds are singing. This is the dualism that declares the laboratory and the
museum "placeless," "contextless," and even unnatural, the dualism that
has plagued the history and criticism of nature writing from Burroughs's
time onward. It is this way of thinking that enables even a contemporary
critic of nature writing to say, without apparent irony, that "modern experimental science depends upon the control and limitation of context" (Hildebidle, 58)—the same way of thinking that makes Watson and Crick's *The Double Helix* or Heisenberg's *Physics and Philosophy* or Ammons's poetry
difficult reading for so many true believers—and certainly the way of think-

ing that made *Walden* and Thoreau difficult for Burroughs.

By Burroughs's time, it wasn't just that scientific labor and poetic or natured leisure were separate—or that one couldn't be both scientist and poet—but that even a person of Burroughs's ilk was struggling with the modern form of Cartesian "practical philosophy," wherein one had to avoid the anthropomorphic and anthropocentric. At least half of the clear object of nature writing was to respect the object—to avoid, at all apparent costs, confusing or, for that matter, relating it to the interests of the human observer, classifier, or experimenter. By Burroughs's time, then (and against the suggestions of Michelson, Morley, Bohr, Planck, Einstein, Heisenberg, and Freud, among others in both literature and science), Western (and especially American) appreciators of nature had moved well beyond the active, participating ego of Thoreau and had come to believe deeply that the essential mind-set of science could (and would) take them beyond self-interest and anthropomorphism and free them not only from vested sectarianism of one kind or another, but apparently from their basic psychobiotic interests as well. The surprise, if there is one, is that the people of nature's nation—including its critical appreciators of nature writing—have gone little further in the century that has followed. In America, at least, we still very much need to believe that we can step into a forest or a marsh—that we can enter the wilderness—and even do research in it, without affecting or influencing that which we would observe and admire or worship.

4. Though he never says so explicitly, like most other critics and historians, Krutch clearly viewed nature writing as a form of prose rather than verse, a prose form dedicated in substantial part to extended scientific description and exposition. In terms of customary conception and conventional usage, he was right, of course. Little if any nature writing—and even less scientific writing—has been done in verse in the modern, Western world—not so much because verse forms are somehow by nature or definition inappropriate or unamenable to extended scientific description and exposition, but because they have customarily been thought to be (and treated as if they were), perhaps since the time of Lucretius, and certainly since the seventeenth century. As a matter of what we call empirical fact, then, Krutch and those others who have seen nature writing as a form of prose have so far been quite correct; and those critics who have found nature writing somehow transcending genre and even culture have been wrong, in several senses. By the same tokens of critical and theoretical custom, however, both Krutch and his associates might well have taken a lesson or two from those who have found "nature writing" in "poetry"—because, in the modern Western world, only "poetry," including "prose poetry" and "prosaic verse," has conventionally been thought susceptible to revealing or interesting stylistic analysis—and the association of nature writing with scientific prose has kept critic after critic from taking at least one of the defining formal traits of the genre seriously.

5. For Leopold's wise and humbling statement, see *A Sand County Almanac and Sketches Here and There* (New York: Oxford University Press, 1949), 200.

6. Henry David Thoreau, *Walden*, ed. J. Lyndon Shanley (Princeton: Princeton University Press, 1971), 327.

7. No one is more aware than I am that my suggestions here, and

elsewhere throughout this book, are running at least half against the NATU-
RAL grains of so much of American culture—just how much perhaps no one
makes clearer than Myra Jehlen, in whose *American Incarnation: The Individual, the Nation, and the Continent* (Cambridge; Harvard University
Press, 1986) one can find a thought-provoking, theoretical and historiographic, countercase to my own. Both Jehlen and I are much concerned with
the formative myth of America; and both of us take the position that "the
crucial characters in that myth were [and are] the individual and the land"
(Jehlen, 227). Both of us are concerned as well with the distinguishing
marks and peculiarities of American literature and culture, especially as
they may be contrasted and compared with their European counterparts.

As Jehlen sees "the drama of America's discovery," it "describes an
archetypal conjunction of personal identity and national identification coming together in the very earth of the New World." In her phrasing, "the decisive factor shaping the founding conceptions of 'America' and of 'the American' was material rather than conceptual; rather than a set of abstract ideas,
the physical fact of the continent" (Jehlen, 2–3).

To many readers, perhaps especially American readers, Jehlen's ideas
(and even her phrasings) may seem identical to my own. The differences,
however, are substantial between Jehlen's conceptions and mine, both of
"the physical fact of the continent" and of the essentially Emersonian ways
of thinking that "enabled" "the archetypal conjunction" and underwrote
the "incarnation" in America of self, national identity, and land or nature.
Jehlen is far more convinced than I am (or can be) that many Americans
(most especially Emerson, but also the likes of Thoreau and William
Bartram) actually achieved the unity of vision—the transcendent harmony
of self, nation, and continent—which they professed to achieve. She is also
far more convinced than I am both that "the notion of unlimited possibilities" mono-polized American literature and thought of the eighteenth and
nineteenth centuries and that "the monism of the American incarnation"
has gradually given way to a querying "dualism" of the twentieth century, a
dualism that, in her view, both "unearths" the "ideal concepts of America
and American" and brings them "down to earth" (Jehlen, 234–35, 226).

In my view, "early" American experience (American thought, literature,
and even material culture of the sixteenth and seventeenth as well as the
eighteenth, nineteenth, and twentieth centuries) was (and continues to be) at
least as much dualistic as monistic, despite (and to a large extent because of)
the powerful, founding myth of harmony incarnate in America, despite (and
because of) Emerson's vision of American nature as "an infinitely permeable
medium for personal expansion" (Jehlen, 231). In no sense do I wish to deny
the power, even in twentieth-century America, of Emerson's "transcendent
vision" or of the myth of American incarnation. But I do wish to suggest, as I
argue throughout this book, that the peculiar power of that myth and the
surprising resilience of Emerson's "vision" are direct (and ongoing) responses to the radical dualism—the often extreme (because ineffectively mediated) juxtapositions of self and other, individual and environment, that
seem to me almost endemic to early and formative American experience.
The shape of American literature and culture seems to me less a story of a
gradual shift from a transcending monism to an earthbound dualism—less a
linear story moving from horizons and open frontiers to closed frontiers and

boundaries—than an ongoing and repetitive set of interactions between hori-
zon and home, or line and circle—a dialectic of the competing allegiances of
monism and dualism, Nature and the Indian pipe, the abstract and the concrete (as we say), deduction and induction, self and other, and, by no means
least, space and place—a literature and a culture in which the attractions to
each are generally far stronger, and more intensely couched, than they traditionally have been in Europe, because in America the relationships between
them have been less intricately defined and modulated. (On many of the
intricate relations between space and place, see Yi-Fu Tuan, *Space and
Place: The Perspective of Experience* [Minneapolis: University of Minnesota
Press, 1972].)

Because Jehlen is unabashedly and self-consciously committed to recap-
turing what she sees as the optimism especially of nineteenth-century
America, a frontiered vision she finds alien to twentieth-century American
culture (and entirely alien to "historical" and "dialectic" Europe)—and because she rightly sees that vision defining America (providing its one distinguishing cultural trait)—she speaks of "profound differences between American and European understandings of the nature of the interaction between
characters and their worlds" (Jehlen, 148). I, in my turn, find these differences significant and discriminating, but nowhere near as profound (or,
for that matter, as clear) as Jehlen does. My assumed position is that though
American conceptions of the contrasts between American and European
understandings of character and world (or individual and environment) do
indeed often presume "profound differences" between the two cultures,
these differences are less differences in fundamental (biological, psychological, and cultural) kind than they are differences in degree or extent. As I see
them, almost all facets of *American* culture are best and most accurately
viewed as radical expressions and inordinate phrasings of the underlying
and conflicting allegiances of classical Western civilization. What makes for
the "profound differences" between Europe and America, it seems to me, are
two rather simple and more or less inescapable historical and psychological
"facts"—first, that in "early" America (which for some people was the seventeenth century and for others is the twentieth) relations between character
and world (or self and other) have been less intricately mediated and modulated by the orders of established institutions than they have been at comparable times in Europe—and, second, that for reasons having much to do with
the decades of America's several declarations of independence, Americans
have been (and continue to be) ideologically opposed to what have seemed to
them the compromises and, hence, the threats of such "historical" mediations and modulations.

In Jehlen's terms, my perspective on American culture is no doubt too
"historical," too dialectical, and even too "European" to represent America
adequately, especially as I tend to deny the capacity (though by no means the
desire or the dream) of Americans (and especially of American nature writers) to transcend or escape the limitations of their conditions and to reform
or re-create themselves and the worlds around them. At the same time, and
much in the same vein, I tend to undercut "the physical fact of the continent." I tend, in other words—and too frequently for advocates of the myth of
American incarnation—to see even "the very earth of the New World," as
well as the Indian pipe and the phoebe, as a conceptual, psychic, and linguis-

tic phenomenon. By now I hope it is obvious that I take this "European" and dialectical position not because I wish to deny or undercut the root mythos of American culture—nor even so much because I see American thinkers and writers constrained by what we call "history"—but because I wish to emphasize (and because, like Jehlen, I participate in) a second root mythos of American culture, inseparable from the first, and one of the central convictions of almost all American nature writers (and, coincidentally, of many other Americans), the conviction that we are finally and inescapably *constrained* not so much by history as by nature—or, in an alternate phrasing (Jehlen's, of course), "that the decisive factor shaping the founding conceptions of 'America' and of 'the American' was . . . the physical fact of the continent" (Jehlen, 3)—a conviction and a condition I believe to have been as central to seventeenth-and nineteenth-century America as it is to the twentieth.

As Jehlen's study and many others of its philosophic kind illustrate (albeit for the most part unknowingly), this latter conception—this second root mythos—is at least as crucial to the ongoing shapings of "America" and "the American" as the Emersonian (and originally European) vision of transcendent harmony. It, too, was, of course, originally European, especially perhaps as a theoretical (philosophic and theological) position; and it, too, seems to me essential not only to an understanding of American nature writing but to an understanding of the daily condition of many "early," landed Americans, from Columbus and William Bradford, through my own Norwegian and Swedish ancestors, to contemporary migrant workers and, especially perhaps, to those many urban Americans (including several distinguished cultural critics) who have recently discovered (or rediscovered) the land.

If, as Jehlen and several others have indicated, American intellectuals seem to have given up on Emerson's version of harmony, if Emerson seems out of date, substitute versions of Emersonian harmony have been (and are) regularly found (or "discovered," as we are inclined to say)—if not in the harmonies of "ecology," then in nature writing and the mythology of the Sioux or the Kiowa—even in these days of an apparent earthbound dualism. In several forms, Emerson's vision lives on—even as we claim to "bring it down to earth"—in popular culture as in historical and critical avatars, in "the physical fact of the continent" as contemporary ding an sich, and in our visions of getting (or going) "beyond geography." (For a well-written and committed statement of this persuasion, the persuasion that apparently underlies Jehlen's work as well, see Frederick Turner's *Beyond Geography*; for another and philosophically similar discussion, see John Vernon's *The Garden and the Map: Schizophrenia in Twentieth-Century Literature and Culture* [Urbana: University of Illinois Press, 1973], in which the typos and mythos of the garden are essentially and existentially conjunctive and restorative, while their mapping opposite is disjunctive, divisive, and destructive—the one mythic, poetic, and even religious, the other ratioinactive and scientific.) Despite (and indeed because of) the strength of Jehlen's claims— despite (and because of) Turner's and Vernon's—and because of the desperation that so often seems to characterize Emerson's—I think we Americans at least half deceive ourselves by professing to get or go beyond geography. By claiming to get beyond the charts, maps, and diagrams of *scientia*—by celebrating the "ecological" harmonies of Sioux or Chippewa mythology in scholarly tomes, anthologies, and workshops—we give renewed expression to the original myth of American incarnation, and simultaneously neglect the conspicuously "European" forms and styles (and indeed the logics and methodologies) by which we construct and map our "newfound" lands and altars, in much the same way Emerson "neglected" the form and style of the conventional sermon in his essays. We thus continue to give largely unwitting voice to our original monistic dreams in fashions and forms at dualistic odds with our visions—to construct "new" dualistic pairings in which the "old," alienating dualism is set radically against some "new" holistic vision. No wonder the Sioux are occasionally suspicious.

In defense of my position, then, I would simply argue both that American culture has been more "historical" and dialectic than Jehlen indicates (and than many Americans like to believe) and, what is more important, certainly in the case of American nature writing, that much (if not all) of American culture has been heavily influenced by another kind of temporal restraining order, a restraining order deeply and definitively biological (and "biological"). Finally, I would argue that a deeply "biotic" sense—a sense of (and a need for) what we currently call biology—is as dialectic and, hence, as threatening to America's quest for transcendence as is the "historical" sense of Europe. Indeed, I do not believe that history and biology, or wilderness and civilization, or land and landscape, or garden and map, can be as readily or easily dissociated as we sometimes seem to think. By the same token, however, neither do I believe that they can be easily or miraculously blended in some associating and transcending third or fourth or fifth term. Americans (and perhaps especially American historians and critics) need, I think, to be reminded frequently that "immersing oneself in nature" or "the garden"— or going "beyond geography"—is as fully constraining as it is uplifting or liberating, as likely to induce fear and confusion as it is to lead to ecstasy and clarity, and indeed that this kind of "clarity"—the clarity of the mystic—is as often frightening as it is enrapturing—in short, that "human kind cannot bear very much reality."

We would do better by way of "America" and "the American," it seems to me, first to distinguish between Emerson and Thoreau and then to recognize that a good deal of the story of America can be told by examining the interplay between the two, with a Louis Agassiz or an Asa Gray thrown in to balance Emerson. Indeed, I would argue that we would better comprehend many of the basics of American culture (and not a little of American literature) if we took Thoreau as our central model (he of beans, phoebes, railroads, and woodchucks—all in some methodical detail—as well as he of higher laws—he, in other words, whose "nature" is disciplined and concrete *as well as* abstract) and considered Emerson (he even whose gardening seems not to have involved dirty knees) a crucial but partial and one-sided influence. Thus, I would argue that, though (as Jehlen has shown in nicely pointed detail), a part, even a large part, of the American artist's (and coincidentally the American's) anxiety was (and is) a function of the originating myth that America had been "discovered already complete and perfect (as nature is complete and perfect)" (Jehlen, 150)—and, therefore, that the American writer was (and is) faced with the awesome (and sometimes seemingly overwhelming) task of *re*-creating the whole of reality from scratch, as it were—another and no less significant part of the American

writer's anxiety (an anxiety of artists as well as more ordinary citizens) is
(and was) a function of quite quotidian efforts to underwrite that originating
myth—to fix America and the American in daily working detail, to create a
reality (at times it must have seemed that almost any would do), rather than
to re-create the honored world of high European culture.

As I see the story (and the anxiety) of American culture and literature,
then, it is the story (finally a dialectic story) partly of facing the awesome
task (in Jehlen's terms) of "replacing" completely "the actual" of respected
Europe (a prospect Emerson professed, at least, to find more exhilarating
than Hawthorne or Melville did) and partly of quite literally having to construct the details of operative, daily worlds, whether they "replaced" their
European predecessors or not, and even if they parroted them. For this reason, what Jehlen calls "Emerson's vision of the infinite reach of individual
creativity" (Jehlen, 150) is, to me, far more a hyperbolic sign of anxiety—a
rather desperate attempt to lend oneself and one's surroundings significance—than it is the vision of a self-conscious American soothsayer.
Methinks he declaims too much. The "infinite reach of individual creativity"
thus, to me, not only *produces* anxiety (in Hawthorne, Melville, and many
others, who seem to have feared more than Emerson their interventions in
an American nature already incarnate), but it also *expresses* an anxiety; and
it masks a considerable uncertainty, an uncertainty of the kind produced by
discovering, as so many Americans early and quickly discovered, that the
mythic (pre- and antihistorical) American Nature, which they had been
asked to take as given and predestined, did not *exist* in daily, working
terms—or, in other words, that the founding myth of Nature's Nation (of
perfection incarnate) in no sense prepared them to deal with the details of
daily psychobiotic life—and, worse perhaps, that long, utterly exhausting
effort would be required to adjust the terms of daily life to the transcending
terms of the original myth—that both the original myth and "the physical
fact of the continent" had to be brought into daily, historic, biotic, and psychic time, if you will.

It is one thing to recognize, as Jehlen and several others have recently,
that Perry Miller's notion of a "vacant wilderness" (upon which early Americans projected their fantasies) is itself a fantasy (Jehlen, 28). It is quite
another thing to say, as Jehlen does in the sentence following that recognition, that "of course the wilderness was not vacant," as if that latter statement were a recording of the finally known "facts"—an all-knowing, archeo-
logical, scientific, and historical report on the ding an sich, the wilderness as
it really was—rather than (as is just as probable) a restatement and reaffir-
mation of one of the versions of the original myth, in this case the version
that emphasizes fullness and plentitude, or at least complexity.

For reasons that I hope by now are clear, my view of William Bartram's
Travels, for example—among many other exemplary American texts—is at
considerable odds with Jehlen's. Though I agree completely with her that
one must entitle chapters in a book about American conceptions of nature
with "ands" rather than "ors"—as in "Civilization *and* Wilderness" or
"Conquest *and* Conservation"—and that the distinction is crucial to the difference between British and American culture—in no sense can I agree with
her or others that "in Bartram's vision and in the earlier texts [texts of Jefferson, Benjamin Rush, and Noah Webster, among others], the identity of land

and landscape, of America and the continent, the incarnation of the idea of the former in the body of the latter, has achieved a fundamental reconciliation" (Jehlen, 59). Oh, that it were so easy. Had it been, Bartram would have been less anxious than he was, would have worked considerably less hard than he did to learn Linnaean names and categories—those distinctly Latinate terms—perhaps would have felt little need to send specimens and samples to Peter Collinson and Linnaeus himself, and certainly little need to attempt to bring vocabularies of the sublime and picturesque to Georgia wetlands and Florida valleys, much less to publish them. Were the "identity of land and landscape"—the "fundamental reconciliation" of America and mosquito or alligator or Indian pipe (much less oneself)—so easy to achieve, Bartram's *Travels* would be less replete with long Linnaean catalogues or "scientific" descriptions of individual species, or any one of a number of other indications of fundamentally and originally European notions of American nature (as if the two could ever be separated), such as alligators and bears on the immediate fringes of one's campsite, or Indian maidens picking strawberries in a picturesque "vale."

Make no doubt about it, Bartram wished very much to reconcile land and landscape, America and the continent (as we are inclined to say), American nature and scientific understanding (as well as his own historical and institutional identity and the "feelings" of Romantic landscape art)—and that wish is, without question, the premier wish of America, the American dream incarnate; but it is still a wish; and as any close reading of the vocabularies and styles of Bartram's works (and virtually all other such American works) will reveal, Bartram did not succeed. Perhaps he thought he had succeeded (though about that, too, there must remain considerable doubt). Certainly he tried (and tried hard) to wed land, self, and landscape—to reconcile scientific and personal "fact" with aesthetic, moral, and even theological nature—but he was almost entirely constrained (historically, psychologically, and even physiologically) by the terms he had at his disposal (well over 90 percent of which were European not simply in point of origin but in meaning and phrasing), and by his inherited notions of significant identity (both for himself and for individual species as well as for landscapes).

8. See, for example, Leo Marx's *The Machine in the Garden* and his earlier essay, "Thoreau's Excursions," *Yale Review* 51 (1962): 363-69, as well as Buell's *Literary Transcendentalism*, Hildebidle's *Thoreau: A Naturalist's Liberty*, and Linck Johnson's *Thoreau's Complex Weave*. This may be as good a place as any to mention several other contributions Marx has made to the discussions and issues that underlie and underwrite much of my book: "The Two Thoreaus," originally published in *New York Review of Books* (1978) and now reprinted in *The Pilot and the Passenger* (New York: Oxford University Press, 1988); the "Introduction" to *Pilot*; "The Pilot and the Passenger: Landscape Conventions and the Style of *Huckleberry Finn*," in *Pilot* (from *American Literature*, 1956); the original "The Machine in the Garden," in *Pilot* (from *New England Quarterly*, 1956); "American Institutions and Ecological Ideals," in *Pilot* (from *Science*, 1970); "The Neo-Romantic Critique of Science," in *Pilot* (from *Daedalus*, 1978); "American Literary Culture and the Fatalistic View of Technology," in *Pilot* (from *Alternative Futures*, 1978); "The Puzzle of Anti-Urbanism in American Literature," in *Literature and the Urban Experience, Essays on the City and Literature,*

ed. Michael C. Jaye and Ann Chalmers Watts (New Brunswick, N.J.: Rutgers University Press, 1981); "Susan Sontag's 'New left Pastoral': Notes on Revolutionary Pastoralism," in *Literature in Revolution*, ed. George Abbott White and Charles Newman (New York: Holt, Rinehart & Winston, 1972); and "The American Revolution and the American Landscape," in *America's Continuing Revolution*, ed. Stephen J. Tonsor (Washington D.C.: American Enterprise Institute for Public Policy Research, 1975). For an update on the dialectic argument of *The Machine in the Garden*, see Leo Marx, "Pastoralism in America," in *Ideology and Classic American Literature*, ed. Sacvan Bercovitch and Myra Jehlen (New York: Cambridge University Press, 1986), 36–69.

9. In that little-known essay mentioned in the notes above, Richard Lillard had many similar things to say about nature writing, as he attempted to elaborate upon Hal Borland's notion of the "nature book." Among other things, Lillard wrote, "The nature book is not philosophical as such . . . nor autobiographical as such . . . not strictly scientific, historical, or folkloristic . . . not a practical how-to-do or how-to-survive book. It has nothing to do with pets, or zoos, botanical gardens, and other end results of domesticating or collecting, including gardening or crop growing" ("Books in the Field," 159)—none of which suggestions is inconsistent with Krutch's original intimations or with the criteria I am attempting to outline.

Chapter Three: Science and Our Declarations of Dependence:
A Prolegomenon to the Study of Nature Writing

1. R. D. Laing, *Self and Others* (New York: Random House, Pantheon Books, 1961), 19.

2. Aldo Leopold, *A Sand County Almanac and Sketches Here and There* (New York: Oxford University Press, 1949), 201, 101. Like all quotations from *Sand County* in this book, this one is taken from the original edition.

3. Eugene P. Odum, *Fundamentals of Ecology*, 3d ed. (Philadelphia: W. B. Saunders, 1971), 65. By no means do I intend here (or elsewhere) to single out Eugene Odum for criticism. I cite his *Fundamentals of Ecology* not because it is particularly blameworthy or fallible, but because it is perhaps the most respected and influential textbook in the profession. The quotation from Odum, like several others cited earlier, and more than a few to follow, is purely exemplary. Its logical and philosophical analogues can be found in hundreds of books and articles in the professional literature of ecology, and in thousands of popular essays that seek to celebrate the field.

4. A slightly fuller citation of Thoreau's famous dictum reads as follows:

> The West of which I speak is but another name for the Wild; and what I have been preparing to say is, that in Wildness is the preservation of the World. Every tree sends its fibres forth in search of the Wild. The cities import it at any price. Men plow and sail for it. From the forest and wilderness come the tonics and barks which brace mankind. Our ancestors were savages. The story of Romulus and Remus being suckled by a

wolf is not a meaningless fable. The founders of every state which has
risen to eminence have drawn their nourishment and vigor from a similar
wild source. It was because the children of the Empire were not suckled
by the wolf that they were conquered and displaced by the children of the
northern forests who were.

I believe in the forests, and in the meadow, and in the night in which
the corn grows. We require an infusion of hemlock spruce or arbor-vitae in
our tea. There is a difference between eating and drinking for strength
and from mere gluttony. The Hottentots eagerly devour the marrow of the
koodoo and other antelopes raw, as a matter of course. Some of our northern Indians eat raw the marrow of the Arctic reindeer, as well as various
other parts, including the summits of the antlers, as long as they are soft.
And herein, perchance, they have stolen a march on the cooks of Paris.
They get what usually goes to feed the fire. This is probably better than
stall-fed beef and slaughter-house pork to make a man of. Give me a wildness whose glance no civilization can endure,—as if we lived on the marrow of koodoos devoured raw. ("Walking," in *Thoreau: The Major Essays*,
ed. Jeffrey L. Duncan [New York: E. P. Dutton, 1972], 209)

As even a cursory reading of this passage will indicate, "the West" and "the
Wild" of which Thoreau speaks are not to be identified primarily (and certainly not solely) with the popular, twentieth-century (and almost exclusively American) notion of literal "wilderness," as in "wilderness area." In
fact, many of the behaviors, experiences, emotions, and thoughts Thoreau
advocates in "Walking" would be distinctly "out of style," if not entirely
unacceptable, in the conventional "wilderness experience" of most twentieth-century Americans.

5. John P. Milton, "Earth: The End of Infinity," in *Wilderness: The
Edge of Knowledge*, ed. Maxine E. McCloskey (New York: Sierra Club, 1970).
Again I do not mean to single out for particular criticism John Milton or
Maxine McCloskey or the Sierra Club. Milton's statement, too, is entirely
representative; and I choose it because it is reputable. Its underlying philosophy—its ontology, if you will—is echoed thousands of times over in the literature of environmental politics, management, and concern—not only of the
last quarter century, but even of the hundred years preceding the publication of *Silent Spring*. The underlying logic—one might almost say, the escha-
tology—is classically Western, of course; and even its modern, managerial
phrasings date at least to George Perkins Marsh's *Man and Nature* (1864).

Chapter Four: The Musquito in My Garden:
Early American Selves and Their Nonhuman Environments

1. These Latin binomials are present-day tags for the aforementioned
avians. To induce a bit of the early American's puzzlement and uncertainty
over names, naming, and phenomena, I leave it to concerned readers to
search the various field guides and taxonomies for the colloquial names.

2. Wayne Franklin, *Discoverers, Explorers, Settlers: The Diligent
Writers of Early America* (Chicago: University of Chicago Press, 1979), 2–3.
My debts to Franklin are substantial. Although he is interested specifically in
the literature of travel to and in America, we are both finally concerned with

"the constitution of America . . . as a verbal construct, as an artifact" (Franklin, xi).

3. For Franklin's discussion of Columbus's difficulties with Veragua and Epiphany see both the prologue and the introduction to *Discoverers, Explorers, Settlers*, xi–xiii, 1–19. I can not recommend them too highly. For the specific phrases cited here, see (in order of my borrowings) Franklin, 7, 7, 1, 6, 6–7.

4. Ibid., 6.

5. For first-hand evidence of Columbus's "severe displacement" (the phrase is Franklin's), see "The Digest of Columbus's Log-Book" and the letters and narratives of the four voyages in *The Four Voyages of Christopher Columbus*, ed. and trans. J. M. Cohen (Baltimore: Penguin Books, 1969). For Columbus's accounts of the mouth of the Orinoco and the pains of Epiphany at Veragua, see pp. 217–24 and 291.

6. For Captain John Smith's "glistering tinctures" and "guilded" ground see the opening section of book 2 of *The Generall Historie of Virginia, New England, and the Summer Isles*. The specific source cited here is *The Complete Works of Captain John Smith*, ed. Philip L. Barbour (Chapel Hill: University of North Carolina Press, 1986), 2:102. For the absence of Pisgah in William Bradford's *Of Plymouth Plantation*, see the famous passage on the landing of the pilgrims, which is reprinted in virtually every anthology of early American literature: "Neither could they, as it were, go up to the top of Pisgah to view from this wilderness a more goodly country to feed their hopes; for which way soever they turned their eyes (save upward to the heavens) they could have little solace or content in respect of any outward objects." The specific source cited here is *Of Plymouth Plantation*, ed. Samuel Eliot Morison (New York: Knopf, 1953), 62. For Jonathan Dickinson's struggles, see *Jonathan Dickinson's Journal, or God's Protecting Providence: Being the Narrative of a Journey from Port Royal in Jamaica to Philadelphia between August 23, 1696 and April 1, 1697*, ed. Evangeline Walker Andrews and Charles McLean Andrews, rev. ed. (New Haven: Yale University Press, 1961), 50.

7. For Jonathan Edwards's attempted meditations, see the first few pages of virtually any printing of his "Personal Narrative," another one of those standard entries in anthologies of early American literature. For John Woolman's contemplations, see the fourth chapter of his *Journal*. The edition cited here is *The Journal of John Woolman and A Plea for the Poor* (New York: Corinth Books, 1961), 71. For Thomas Jefferson's experiences with the "Natural Bridge," see *Notes on the State of Virginia* (New York: Harper & Row, 1964), 21–22. Wayne Franklin discusses this famous, one-paragraph episode in some detail in *Discoverers, Explorers, Settlers*, 24–33. So does Robert Lawson-Peebles in *Landscape and Written Expression in Revolutionary America* (New York: Cambridge University Press, 1988), 177–83.

Each of the figures and events cited here is representative and exemplary. So, too, is the passage from Nathaniel Hawthorne's notebooks that I quote at length. So, too, are the passages to come from John Banister's "Collectio insectorum, atque aliarum rerum naturalium in Virginia" and William Bartram's *Travels*. The basic drama of each of these passages and much of the works of which they are parts could easily be duplicated thousands of times over by citing comparable passages from other early American journals, diaries, autobiographies, and scientific catalogues.

I have chosen Hawthorne's notebook entry of July 27, 1844, for extended analysis in part because Leo Marx used segments of it as cornerstones to the argument of *The Machine in the Garden: Technology and the Pastoral Ideal in America* (New York: Oxford University Press, 1964) and in part because (since Marx has made it reasonably familiar to students of American literature and culture) its familiarity may enable me to illustrate in some detail just how deep and intricate are the conflicts and relations between self and nonhuman surroundings in early America—just how incomplete, in other words, were Marx's first-time readings. For the source of my lengthy quotation from Hawthorne, see volume 8 of *The Centenary Edition of the Works of Nathaniel Hawthorne, The American Notebooks*, ed. Claude M. Simpson (Columbus: Ohio State University Press, 1972), 245–50. The bracketed numbers are the page numbers to Hawthorne's manuscript notebooks.

8. For de Tocqueville's justly famous statement, see *Democracy in America*, ed. J. P. Mayer and Max Lerner, trans. George Lawrence (New York: Harper & Row, 1966), 456: "Each citizen of a democracy generally spends his time considering the interests of a very insignificant person, namely, himself. If he ever does raise his eyes higher, he sees nothing but the huge apparition of society or the even larger form of the human race. He has nothing between very limited and clear ideas and very general and very vague conceptions; the space between is empty."

I have added to the huge apparitions of "society" and "the human race" the seemingly even larger form of NATURE because it seems to me that both that grand abstraction and the quotidian minutiae of biological and geological surroundings (to which NATURE is so often related in American literature) rather nicely fit de Tocqueville's implicit, and almost prophetic, model—especially when the "insignificant" self is moving (or trying to move) between them.

9. R. W. B. Lewis, *The American Adam: Innocence, Tragedy, and Tradition in the Nineteenth Century* (Chicago: University of Chicago Press, 1955), 13.

10. Neither here nor elsewhere do I mean to deny the significance of the literature and culture of politics, law, and theology in America—nor the literature of more explicitly "social" forms and economics. Nor do I wish to deny the significance of those many "early" Americans whose initial and formative experiences were (and still are) urban. I mean, rather, to redress what I see as an imbalance in the contemporary history and criticism of American literature—to recall forms of American writing that, despite their considerable and continuing popularity, tend to be neglected in contemporary literary criticism (in part, no doubt, because these forms are too much "scientific," and today's literary critics receive little training in the vocabularies and styles of science)—in other words, I wish to recall critical and historical attention to the landed, "early" American, and by implication to the urbanite or ex-urbanite who finds herself or himself participating in or puzzling over that immense part of the culture of the United States devoted to what is variously called "nature" or, nowadays, "the environment," "the ecology," and "the ecosphere."

11. For the finally poignant story of the Reverend John Banister, see Joseph Ewan and Nesta Ewan, *John Banister and His Natural History of Virginia, 1678–1692* (Urbana: University of Illinois Press, 1970). For the specific passage cited here, see p. 291. Born in 1650, chaplain at Magdalen College from 1676 until he left for Virginia in 1678, Banister may have been one of a number of ministers (or, rather, prospective ministers) sent to Virginia by Charles II in response to continuing requests of the Virginia Assembly. The detailed causes and conditions of Banister's move in 1678, like his whereabouts and functions in Virginia for at least the next ten years, are difficult to trace. Before coming to Virginia, he apparently stopped in Barbados; by April of 1678, he apparently was witness to a deed of William Byrd, Sr., then resident at the falls of the James River; by 1680 he had put together the essentials of his "Collectio insectorum," a manuscript in quarto of fourteen pages (four of which deal with Mollusca) to which he added occasional notes and refinements in later years. By April of 1688, Banister was married; by late spring of that year, he was ordering books and materials for drawing through Byrd's agents in London, and Byrd was representing him to the group of naturalists who met at the Temple Coffee House—in a manner that suggests that Banister may for some time have been on assignment (and intermittently on some sponsor's payroll) as a collector and field-naturalist. By early 1690, his name was being mentioned as one of two to be honored in the establishment of a college in Virginia. Unfortunately, the college (William and Mary) did not receive its charter until a year after Banister died, shot while he was botanizing, apparently, along the Roanoke River.

On one matter or another, Banister's career seems to have been closely interwoven with Byrd's plans, prospects, and identities in Virginia and London. Not until 1689 is there any official record of Banister's acts as a minister; and he may not even have been fully inducted until then. All in all, one gets the image of a college-educated young man struggling to make a go of it without the wealth of his "friends" and associates—a "prospective" minister to Virginia who found that he might stock his larder to slightly greater effect by turning to those in England who were speculating in natural history. Whatever his role as a clergyman, he clearly identified himself (or sought to identify himself) as a naturalist. In his fourteen years in America, he "collected, described, and sent specimens of approximately 340 species of plants, 100 'Insecta,' twenty 'Mollusca,' and some fossils and rocks to colleagues in England." He "sketched more than eighty species of plants, a few insects, a number of shells"; and he "composed part of his Natural History and part of his account 'Of the Natives' " (Ewan and Ewan, *John Banister*, 26)—very small parts one might note. For his work he was much appreciated in London by those who used his collections, drawings, and descriptions in their own publications. John Ray was not the least of those to miss him upon his death.

In one important respect, there is little that is special about the Reverend John Banister. He never attained the stature of an Agassiz or an Audubon—nor even of a William Bartram or a John Lawson (see *A New Voyage to Carolina*, ed. Hugh Talmage Lefler [Chapel Hill: University of North Carolina Press, 1967], originally published in London, 1709). One gathers that he simply did not have the time or the energy. And that, of course, is just my point, here and elsewhere throughout this chapter. I mention him and his work because in most crucial regards he was an ordinary early American, taking advantage of his location even as he sought to make a name for himself, however small. I hope his name and his works, however slight, may stand for hundreds of others of their kinds in the first three and more centuries of the composition of America.

12. For the story of Agassiz's life and works, see Edward Lurie, *Louis Agassiz: A Life in Science* (Chicago: University of Chicago Press, 1960). For Powell's place in the science and settlement of the American West, see Wallace Stegner, *Beyond the Hundredth Meridian: John Wesley Powell and the Second Opening of the West* (Boston: Houghton Mifflin, 1954). For Powell's best-known work, see his *Report on the Lands of the Arid Region of the United States*, ed. Wallace Stegner (Cambridge: Harvard University Press, 1962), originally published in 1878 as 45th Cong., 2d sess., H. R. Exec. Doc. 73. For the full text of Henry Rowe Schoolcraft's best-known work, see his *Narrative Journal of Travels from Detroit Northwest through the Great Chain of American Lakes to the Sources of the Mississippi River in the Year 1820* (Albany: E. & E. Hosford, 1821); facsimile rept. (Ann Arbor: University Microfilms, 1966). For a brief sketch of Schoolcraft's life see Mentor L. Williams, introduction to his "modernized" edition of Schoolcraft's *Narrative Journal of Travels* (East Lansing: Michigan State College Press, 1953), 1–24. These figures and their works are likewise purely exemplary, of course.

No one is more aware than I am of the risks involved in an argument based on name-dropping and allusions. I can only hope that my appeals to the likes of Agassiz, Powell, and Schoolcraft (who might as well have been Frederick Pursh or Thomas Nuttall) are various enough (while not being too numerous) to provoke responsive chords in my readers, and that others will follow the suggestive leads I am trying to provide with close readings of Hawthorne and Bartram by extending comparable treatment to the many figures and documents that make up the literature of the nonhuman environment in America.

13. *The Travels of William Bartram: Naturalist's Edition*, ed. Francis Harper (New Haven: Yale University Press, 1958), 216–17. Because of its faithfulness to the original (Philadelphia: James & Johnson, 1791), Harper's edition is much to be preferred to the much "modernized" edition of Mark Van Doren (n.p.: Dover Publications, 1928). Bartram's *Travels* was originally published as *Travels through North & South Carolina, Georgia, East & West Florida, the Cherokee Country, the Extensive Territories of the Muscogulges, or Creek Confederacy, and the Country of the Chactaws; Containing an Account of the Soil and Natural Productions of Those Regions, together with Observations on the Manners of the Indians.*

14. Bartram, *Travels*, ed. Francis Harper, 215–16. The numbers in brackets in this excerpt (taken here verbatim from Harper) are the page numbers of the original edition of 1791.

Chapter Five: Nature Writing and America

1. Raymond Williams, *The Country and the City* (New York: Oxford University Press, 1973); W. J. Keith, *The Rural Tradition* (Toronto: University of Toronto Press, 1975).

2. Annie Dillard, *Pilgrim at Tinker Creek* (New York: Harper's Maga-

zine Press, 1974), 5–6. The pagination of the original edition of *Pilgrim at Tinker Creek*, which I cite here and elsewhere, varies somewhat from the first paperback edition (New York: Bantam Books, 1975), though not from the later paperback reprinting of the original (New York: Harper & Row, 1985).

3. For Richard Chase's account of the distinguishing features of the classic American romance-novel see, especially, the introduction and the first chapter, "The Broken Circuit," of *The American Novel and Its Tradition* (Garden City, N.Y.: Doubleday, Anchor Books, 1957; reprint, Baltimore: Johns Hopkins University Press, 1980). As any reader of Chase will be able to tell, I have borrowed liberally from his terms and phrasings in my attempts to discriminate American nature writing both from its British counterparts and from their analogues in the United States.

4. For the full citation of John Hay's phrase, see *In Defense of Nature* (Boston: Atlantic Monthly Press and Little, Brown, 1969), 139. The sentiment and the desire embodied in this self-defeating phrase—"order of time-lessness"—are echoed time and again, and most often unknowingly, in hundreds of other works of American nature writing.

5. John Kieran, *Natural History of New York City* (Boston: Houghton Mifflin, 1959). For further proof that the American nature writer is committed to a "nature" that transcends customary sociopolitical boundaries between city and country, see Louis J. Halle's celebration of nature in Washington, D.C., *Spring in Washington* (New York: Harper & Brothers, 1947).

6. Insofar as I can trace it, the phrase in quotation marks is a variant of R. W. B. Lewis's "The Case against the Past," for which see chapter 1 of *The American Adam: Innocence, Tragedy, and Tradition in the Nineteenth Century* (Chicago: University of Chicago Press, 1955). Though I can in no sense agree with Lewis's one-sided view of Thoreau—"Thoreau knew not evil" (p. 27)—like many others I more than acknowledge the influence of Lewis's discussion of the antihistorical persuasion of much early American literature and culture.

7. For a wide-ranging discussion of the motives and forms of pastoralism in American politics and culture, see Leo Marx's "Pastoralism in America," in *Ideology and Classic American Literature*, ed. Sacvan Bercovitch and Myra Jehlen (New York: Cambridge University Press, 1986), 36–69.

8. For thoughts on these and related traits of American literature, see Tony Tanner, *The Reign of Wonder: Naivety and Reality in American Literature* (New York: Cambridge University Press, 1965). The specific phrases I cite in this paragraph and the one following it appear on Tanner's pages 336–37.

9. For Kuhn's updated thoughts on normal and revolutionary science, see *The Structure of Scientific Revolutions*, 2d ed. enl. (Chicago: University of Chicago Press, 1970).

Chapter Six: Walden *and Paradox: Thoreau as Self-Conscious Ecologist*

1. Stanley Cavell, *The Senses of Walden* (New York: Viking Press, 1972), 12; Sharon Cameron, *Writing Nature: Henry Thoreau's Journal* (New York: Oxford University Press, 1985), 10. I do not wish to recite here the

intricacies of my agreements and disagreements with the many critics of
Thoreau and *Walden*. Most of the important ones I have tried to cover in the
notes to chapter 1. I do wish, however, to pay particular tribute to Sharon
Cameron's analysis of Thoreau's *Journal*, because her argument that the
Journal "confounds" distinctions upon which "our determinations about
how to treat discourse conventionally depend" (Cameron, 16) is essentially
the argument I would make about *Walden* and, what may be as much to the
point, about the best of *Walden*'s successors—about the nature writings of
Loren Eiseley, as about the likes of Aldo Leopold's *A Sand County Almanac*,
John Hay's *Nature's Year*, Edward Abbey's *Desert Solitaire*, Annie Dillard's
Pilgrim at Tinker Creek, Barry Lopez's *River Notes*, and John Janovy's
Keith County Journal.

As I set out on my brief and grossly oversimplified run at *Walden*, I
would note (in Cameron's words) that each of these works "presents us with
discontinuities (between nature and the self, between one part of nature and
another . . . between private and public)"—discontinuities that inevitably
upset our conventional applecarts, but discontinuities that are far from peculiar to Thoreau's *Journal* (Cameron, 16). While I honor her reading of Thoreau's *Journal*, then, I cannot agree with Cameron "that *Walden* and the
Journal . . . make competitive claims and establish competitive alliances"
(Cameron, 22); for the discontinuities I find in the one (as apparently she
does not), I also find in the other (as she does as well, and most tellingly); and
the only significant differences I can see between the two are matters of what
I might call periodicity. As I see them, the discontinuities and dislocations of
Thoreau's *Journal* are philosophically—logically, epistemologically, ethi-
cally, metaphysically, and psychologically—identical to those in *Walden*. A
reader's experiences of the two works are different not because the underlying issues are different—nor because the one is "public" and the other
"private"—but because the distortions of perspective, the discontinuities
and dislocations, are more frequent and less "predictable" in the *Journal*
than they are in *Walden*. Conversely, one might say, the continuities and
"locations"—the passages in which we know with comfort where we are—
are slightly longer in *Walden* than they are in the *Journal*.

Most of Cameron's crucial claims about Thoreau's *Journal* I would thus
extend to *Walden*—"important passages of the Journal raise questions
which resist the very answers that apparently are requisite," (Cameron, 11),
for example, or "because Thoreau calls into question how natural phenomena are to be named, conceptualized and delimited by boundaries, he also
implicitly makes problematic our procedures for identifying the quotations
that are to represent these subjects" (Cameron, 20), or "such organizational
acts by which we make sense of literary texts violate the forms of disorder
the *Journal*'s discourse works to preserve" (Cameron, 21)—though not, of
course, such claims of Cameron's as "forty-seven manuscript volumes
which add up to nothing if not to a record of man's harmony with nature"
(Cameron, 9), and certainly not "Thoreau consistently refuses to anthropo-
centrize what he sees" (Cameron, 11).

Even against her wishes, then, I would extend the details of Cameron's
method and the broad outline of her argument to *Walden*, and take special
notice of the several cautions she raises about quoting from Thoreau:
"Quotation from Thoreau's *Journal* is further rendered suspect by Tho-

reau's aggressive attempt to disorganize the categories and conventions by which we customarily conceive of natural phenomena. . . . Where, for example, in any given case, are we to begin and end a quotation when the work's most prevasive critique derides the stability of such demarcations?" (Cameron, 20). It is a caution I take particularly to heart at the moment, because it bears directly both upon the method I use in this chapter, the method of isolating passages from their contexts, and especially perhaps upon those passages I cite at the beginning in my attempts to identify the voice of the philosophic environmentalist, passages so seemingly straightforward and transparent. What I share with Cameron, finally, is a conviction that even these seemingly "innocent," reportorial passages are "alternative orders of significance," alternate and oscillating ways of attempting to redefine vision and stabilize experience: "Perhaps such attempts to redefine vision by making it literally contingent upon nature . . . account for the fact that while it often seems easy to assign meaning to an excerpted journal passage, that same passage, returned to the journal context, presents us with not simply different foci, but ones which appear to be hierarchically competitive" (Cameron, 9). As I begin this chapter by isolating excerpts from *Walden* to which it may seem especially "easy to assign meaning," I am well aware that my "organizational acts" have violated the "forms of disorder" that *Walden*'s discourse, like the discourse of the *Journal*, "works to preserve." In my own defense, I can only say that, as Thoreau well knew, there is no other comprehensible and communicable way—that only settled perspectives can be truly unsettled, that applecarts must be set up before they can be upset, that woods and woodmen can be known only by comparing them with towns and townsmen, and vice versa.

Chapter Seven: A Sand County Almanac
and the Conflicts of Ecological Conscience

1. For representative and convincing evidence of the wide and varying appeal of *Sand County*, see *Companion to* A Sand County Almanac: *Interpretive and Critical Essays*, ed. J. Baird Callicott (Madison: University of Wisconsin Press, 1987).

Chapter Eight: Composition and Decomposition at Tinker Creek

1. For Jonathan Culler's notion of a "descriptive residue" see the chapter entitled "Poetics of the Novel" in *Structuralist Poetics: Structuralism, Linguistics, and the Study of Literature* (Ithaca: Cornell University Press, 1975), 192ff., and especially the initial pages of the section entitled "Narrative Contracts":

> If the basic convention governing the novel is the expectation that readers will, through their contact with the text, be able to recognize a world which it produces or to which it refers, it ought to be possible to identify at least some elements of the text whose function it is to confirm this expectation and to assert the representational or mimetic orientation of fiction.

> At the most elementary level this function is fulfilled by what one might
> call a descriptive residue: *items whose only apparent role in the text is
> that of denoting a concrete reality (trivial gestures, insignificant objects,
> superfluous dialogue). In a description of a room items which are not
> picked up and integrated by symbolic or thematic codes (items which
> tell us nothing about the inhabitant of the room, for example) and
> which do not have a function in the plot produce what Barthes calls a
> "reality effect."* . . . The pure representation of reality thus becomes, as
> Barthes says, a resistance to meaning, an instance of the 'referential illu-
> sion', according to which the meaning of a sign is nothing other than its
> referent. [italics mine]
>
> Elements of this kind confirm the mimetic contract and assure the
> reader that he can interpret the text as about a real world. It is possible, of
> course, to trouble this contract by blocking the process of recognition,
> preventing one from moving through the text to a world, and making one
> read the text as an autonomous verbal object. But such effects are possi-
> ble only because of the convention that novels do refer. (Pp. 192–93)

Though I may seem to complain here specifically about Culler's notion of
a descriptive residue, my complaint is in no sense a criticism of him or of his
formulations of structuralist theory. Quite the contrary, in fact. If anything,
my complaint is a kind of final appeal to literary theorists and critics of
Culler's caliber and persuasion to turn some of their attentions to the "contracts" of nature writing, to extend to the likes of *Pilgrim at Tinker Creek*,
but also to more "purely" representational nature writing, the kinds of well-
informed analysis that Culler in particular has provided for poetry, and more
so for the novel. In short, I am exploiting Culler's explanation of the functions of descriptive residues in prose fiction, and complaining, as I think he
would, about those critics who seek to extend his quite sensible notion of
purely mimetic residues in the novel to works such as *Walden* or *Pilgrim at
Tinker Creek*, in which the apparently "mimetic" so often turns out to be
impure and unstable—or even to such a dominantly "representational"
work as John Muir's *The Yosemite*, in which the "purely" representational
occupies well over half a reader's time and attention. In other words, because
the works I am calling nature writing are only partly narrative, it is inappropriate to label their often dominant descriptive components as "residues"—
as leftovers, as things that remain after other and more significant claims
have been satisfied.

I think here, for example, of a moment in Joan Burbick's discussion of
Thoreau's journal in which she finds parts of the following passage (and
other descriptive details of Thoreau's entry for June 11, 1851) to impart
"what Barthes and other structuralists call the 'reality' effect"—and, then, in
support of her analysis, cites in an endnote the italicized part above of Culler's definition of "descriptive residue":

> I now descend round the corner of the grain-field, through the pitch pine
> wood into a lower field, more inclosed by woods, and find myself in a
> colder, damp and misty atmosphere, with much dew on the grass. I seem
> to be nearer to the origin of things. There is something creative and pri-
> mal in the cool mist. This dewy mist does not fail to suggest music to me,
> unaccountably; fertility, the origin of things. An atmosphere which has
> forgotten the sun, where the ancient principle of moisture prevails. It is

laden with the condensed fragrance of plants and, as it were, distilled in
dews. (*The Journal of Henry D. Thoreau*, ed. Bradford Torrey and Francis
H. Allen [1906; reprint, New York: Dover Publications, 1962], 2:237)

Burbick concludes her analysis of this passage (and of the brief narrative of
which it is a kind of culmination) in the following terms:

> The movement through the topography of Concord imparts what Barthes
> and other structuralists call the "reality" effect. [At this point she cites
> Culler.] Enough details of time and place accumulate to create the illusion
> of the "here and now." This reality of time and place is then made con-
> tingent on both history and transcendence. The "origin of things" be-
> comes "nearer" to human time and space. It projects the walker back in
> time and space to an original moment at one with all living phenomena.
> (*Thoreau's Alternative History: Changing Perspectives on Nature, Cul-
> ture, and Language* [Philadelphia: University of Pennsylvania Press,
> 1987], 41–42, 159)

Burbick may indeed have a point here. In fact, I am sure she does; but it
is not a point that benefits much from Culler's definition of "descriptive
residue." Perhaps "the grain-field," "the pitch pine wood," and "much dew
on the grass" are Culler's "insignificant objects"—"items whose only apparent role in the text is that of denoting a concrete reality"—but the same
cannot be said of "descend" or "corner" or "lower" or of any of those other
inclosing words by which the narrating figure works himself into a "colder,
damp and misty atmosphere." Indeed, the ambiguous modifier in "find myself . . . with much dew on the grass" suggests that virtually everything here
is "picked up by symbolic or thematic codes." Even "the grain-field" and
"the pitch pine wood" tell us something about the "walker" who inhabits
the place; and each has a clear function in the "plot," however primitive, of
this particular entry.

What Burbick has missed here—or, rather, what she has neglected of
Culler's discussion of narrative contracts—is his telling statement that the
satisfaction of a reader's referential expectations (and indeed both the status
and the functions of "descriptive details") are closely related to the narrative
stance of a work, to the presence or absence of an identifiable, if not consistent, narrator. If I read Culler rightly, he would not identify any of the "items"
in this passage from Thoreau's journal simply as descriptive residues; and,
at least by the end of the passage, he would be speaking as much of a desiring "thinker" (if not of a writer) as he would of a "walker"—and in virtually no sense of "Thoreau" as recorder.

As I hope I have made clear by now, large parts of American nature
writing (if that is what we are going to call it) depend on codes and expectations that differ fairly markedly from those that tend to govern traditional
"literary" forms of narrative prose, including the novel, and even autobiography. If there are affinities to be found between the governing conventions
of American nature writing and those that generally govern narrative fiction,
they are most likely to be found, it seems to me, not in the defining codes of
traditional novels but in the patterns of those novels which Culler identifies
as extremes. Works such as *Pilgrim at Tinker Creek* and *Walden* and signifi-

cant segments of Thoreau's journal tend to trouble conventional narrative contracts in at least two of the ways Culler identifies—first, in their self-reflexive tendencies, by calling attention to themselves as compositions, by "preventing one from moving through the text to a world," by "making one read the text as an autonomous verbal object," by lifting "our attention away from a supposed object to the process of writing itself" (Culler, 193)—or, as I would phrase the point, by making one think of the text (and occasionally perhaps even the reading of the text) as verbal behavior—not, in other words, as a set of conventional truth-claims or mimetic representations, but as animal behavior, as an expression of psychobiotic need. In this regard, *Walden* and large parts of Thoreau's journal and *Pilgrim at Tinker Creek* are formally (if not philosophically) kin to the *Dans le labyrinthe* of Robbe-Grillet, which Culler cites in illustrating what he calls first-level violations of conventional narrative contracts—and kin as well to the likes of Ford Madox Ford's *The Good Soldier* or John Barth's "Lost in the Funhouse."

But *Walden* and *Pilgrim at Tinker Creek*, and a few others among their nature-writing compatriots, are also inclined to trouble the contracts of traditional narratives in yet a second way, often within the same page or paragraph—in a way that aligns them with the writings of William Bartram or John Muir or Darwin or Edwin Way Teale. As Culler says, if the process of recognition, the satisfaction of the referential function, is not blocked at the first level, "then the reader will assume that the text is gesturing towards a world which he can identify and will, after assimilating this world, attempt to move back from world to text so as to compose and give meaning to what has been identified":

> This second move in the cycle of reading can be troubled if the text under-
> takes an excessive proliferation of elements whose function seems purely
> referential. Enumerations or descriptions of objects which seem deter-
> mined by no thematic purpose enable the reader to recognize a world but
> prevent him from composing it and leave him with flawed or incomplete
> meanings which are still applied to the world or to his own experience by
> virtue of their prior recognition. The fundamental character of a truly
> 'realistic' or referential discourse is, as Philippe Hamon says, to deny the
> story or to make it impossible by producing a thematic emptiness. (Culler,
> 194)

Here, I suspect, are many of those long catalogues of species one finds not only in William Bartram's *Travels* but in so much of the early literature of American exploration and promotion. Here, too, are many of the extended and essentially impersonal, nonnarrative descriptions and explanations of individual species (or, indeed, of individual plants and glaciers) that one finds not only in the notebooks of John Banister or the writings of John Muir, but in the works of John Hay and Ann Zwinger as well. And here, too, I continue to suspect, is a large part of the "story" of American nature writing, that "drama" at best sporadically narrative which alternately troubles over the destined *history* of American lands and then drives toward their systematic and schematic codification, drives not so much to re-produce a world, but to give it some kind of sanctioned identity, to "compose" it through nomination and descriptive explication, and generally to shy away from any but the most clichéd thematic or symbolic meanings.

Large segments of American nature writing, including especially its most conventional works, but including as well whole paragraphs of *Walden* and substantial parts of Thoreau's journal (though only the briefest of passages in *Pilgrim at Tinker Creek*), are, thus, like some of the descriptions of Flaubert which Culler notes in explaining that "a mania of precision produces *une thématique vide*":

> By blocking access to concepts Flaubert shows his mastery of what Barthes calls the indirect language of literature: 'the best way for a language to be indirect is to refer as constantly as possible to things themselves rather than to their concepts, for the meaning of an object always flickers, but not that of the concept' (*Essais critiques*, p. 232). Relying on this referential function, Flaubert produces descriptions which seem determined only by a desire for objectivity and thus leads the reader to construct a world which he takes as real but whose meaning he finds difficult to grasp.
>
> The referential function may be affirmed by descriptive details but it also depends to a considerable extent on the narrative stance implied by the text. The difficulty of reading a novel like Pierre Guyotat's *Éden, Éden, Éden* derives in part from the fact that we are unable to identify any narrator and so do not know how to situate its language. If we could read it as some speaker's account of a situation, real or imagined, we would be some way towards organizing it; but instead we have a sentence which lasts for two hundred and fifty-five pages, 'as if it were a question of representing, not imagined scenes, but the scene of language, so that the model of this mimesis is no longer the adventures of a hero but the adventures of the signifier: what happens to it'. There are, however, few novels of this kind. (Culler, 194–95; the final quotation is from Roland Barthes's "Ce qu'il advient au significant, " the preface to *Éden, Éden, Éden* [Paris, 1970], 9)

There may be few novels of this kind, but there are many works of American nature writing that depend upon this stance—many, in fact, that are dominated by it. Some, perhaps most, works of American nature writing are so little or sporadically narrative, and so driven to extended denotation or exposition, that in Culler's terms they do indeed leave their readers with "flawed or incomplete meanings," able "to recognize a world," perhaps, but unable to compose one. The points I would make about such works—the best known of John Muir or Ann Zwinger, for example—are perhaps obvious by now: that the near obsession with precise description and systematic denotation in so much American nature writing is a function in part of the originally indeterminate and still flickering meaning of the "natural object" in America—and that the disappearance (if not the effacement) of a narrator that regularly follows from such a dedication to impersonal description is at least loosely related both to the indeterminacy of self in America and to that original and Romantic desire to lose oneself in one surroundings—so that the drama, if one can call it that, becomes not (except most implicitly or extra-textually) the adventures of the signifier, but almost solely the science of the signified.

In either way, the designative in American nature writing—the descriptive and the expository—is far from residual. At their worst, perhaps, description and exposition are all but obsessive. At their best, they are impure and unstable—and nowhere more so than in *Pilgrim at Tinker Creek*. In *Pilgrim* as in substantial segments of *Walden* and the nature writing of Loren Eiseley—in the most self-reflexive American nature writing—the dilemmas that face Culler's readers of the *nouveau roman*, the satisfactions and disappointments of narrative contracts and expectations, are often the satisfactions and disappointments of descriptive contracts as well (if not generally of linguistic contracts). They are, in other words, the dilemmas faced by a "narrator" who is as often namer and expositor, if not philosopher and critic, as settled and dependable speaker or actor. To account for the codes of American nature writing, it seems to me, we must draw the best we can from theorists and critics of the novel—there is much of value to be found—but we must come up with a "poetics" in which the systematically descriptive and expository are the opposite of residual. One of the governing conventions of a good deal of American nature writing, after all—a convention shared with the writings of field naturalists and laboratory scientists—is *not* so much "the expectation that readers will, through their contact with the text, be able to recognize a world which it produces or to which it refers," but the expectation that they will be introduced to a world previously uncoded and fundamentally apersonal. To a theorist or critic of narrative fiction, the ironies implicit in such a convention, particularly when it is satisfied by catechistic formulae—may be substantial, as it were—but so, I continue to suspect, are the underlying needs and implicit instabilities.

2. For Sarah Kemble Knight's wry reflection upon her own considerable fright see *The Journal of Madame Knight* (Boston: David R. Godine, 1972), 5.

BIBLIOGRAPHY

I have made no effort here to provide a comprehensive listing of every title or author mentioned in the text or notes of this book. I have tried, rather, to construct a representative listing of sources and references—both primary and secondary—that, when put together with notes and index, will be of aid to an audience of varying, if not widely divergent, interests and concerns.

A BIBLIOGRAPHIC SAMPLER OF AMERICAN NATURE WRITING

In no sense should this bibliographic sampler be taken to be anything more than suggestive—and woefully incomplete. I list here only those works of American *nature writing* (and a few of the writings of those authors) I have elsewhere alluded to or cited or discussed at length. Though each of the works listed generally satisfies the formal criteria I have outlined for the nature writing of the United States, the list could go on and on. A more complete register, even of the seemingly restricted form of nature writing with which I am concerned, would require additional years (and no less than two or three volumes) of purely bibliographic research.

Works of so-called British nature writing (writings of the "rural tradition" characterized by W. J. Keith) are listed in a companion sampler. Works of the rural tradition in America—the few I have cited in text or notes—and other works related to the development, style, and interpretation of what I call the nature writing of America are listed under Other References and Works Cited.

Abbey, Edward. *Desert Solitaire: A Season in the Wilderness.* New York: McGraw-Hill, 1968.
Arbib, Robert. *The Lord's Woods: The Passing of an American Woodland.* New York: W. W. Norton, 1971.
Arthur, Elizabeth. *Island Sojourn.* New York: Harper & Row, 1980.
Austin, Mary. *The Land of Little Rain.* Boston: Houghton Mifflin, 1903.
Beebe, William. *The Log of the Sun.* New York: Holt, 1906.
_____. *Unseen Life of New York: As a Naturalist Sees It.* New York: Duell, Sloan & Pearce, 1953.
Beston, Henry. *The Outermost House.* New York: Holt, 1928.
Borland, Hal. *Hal Borland's Book of Days.* New York: Knopf, 1978.
Brooks, Paul. *Roadless Area.* New York: Knopf, 1964.

Burroughs, John. *The Writings of John Burroughs*. 23 vols. New York: Russell & Russell, 1968.

Carrighar, Sally. *One Day on Beetle Rock*. New York: Knopf, 1944.

———. *One Day at Teton Marsh*. New York: Knopf, 1947.

Cowles, Raymond. *Desert Journal: Reflections of a Naturalist*. Berkeley and Los Angeles: University of California Press, 1977.

Dillard, Annie. *Pilgrim at Tinker Creek*. New York: Harper's Magazine Press, 1974.

Eckert, Allan. *Wild Season*. Boston: Little, Brown, 1967.

Eiseley, Loren. *The Immense Journey*. New York: Random House, 1959.

Errington, Paul. *Of Men and Marshes*. New York: Macmillan, 1957.

Finch, Robert. *Common Ground*. Boston: David R. Godine, 1981.

———. *The Primal Place*. New York: W. W. Norton, 1983.

———. *Outlands: Journeys to the Outer Edges of Cape Cod*. Boston: David R. Godine, 1986.

Hall, Leonard. *Stars Upstream: Life along an Ozark River*. Chicago: University of Chicago Press, 1958.

Halle, Louis J. *Spring in Washington*. New York: Harper & Brothers, 1947.

Hay, John. *The Run*. Garden City, N.Y.: Doubleday, 1959.

———. *Nature's Year: The Seasons of Cape Cod*. Garden City, N.Y.: Doubleday, 1961.

———. *The Great Beach*. Garden City, N.Y.: Doubleday, 1963.

———. *In Defense of Nature*. New York: Atlantic Monthly Press and Little, Brown, 1969.

———. *Spirit of Survival: A Natural and Personal History of Terns*. New York: E. P. Dutton, 1974.

———. *The Undiscovered Country*. New York: W. W. Norton 1981.

———. *The Immortal Wilderness*. New York: W. W. Norton, 1987.

Hoover, Helen. *The Long-Shadowed Forest*. Thomas Y. Crowell, 1963.

———. *The Gift of the Deer*. New York: Knopf, 1966.

Janovy, John. *Keith County Journal*. New York: St. Martin's, 1978.

———. *Yellowlegs*. New York: St. Martin's, 1980.

Johnson, Josephine. *The Inland Island*. New York: Simon & Schuster, 1969.

Kappel-Smith, Diana. *Wintering*. Boston: Little, Brown, 1984.

Kieran, John. *Natural History of New York City*. Boston: Houghton Mifflin, 1959.

Klees, Fredric. *The Round of the Year: An Almanac*. New York: Macmillan, 1963.

Krutch, Joseph Wood. *The Twelve Seasons*. New York: Wm. Sloane, 1949.

———. *The Desert Year*. New York: Wm. Sloane, 1952.

———. *The Voice of the Desert: A Naturalist's Interpretation*. New York: Wm. Sloane, 1955.

———. *Grand Canyon*. New York: William Morrow, 1957.

———. *The Forgotten Peninsula: A Naturalist in Baja California*. New York: William Morrow, 1961.

LaBastille, Anne. *Woodswoman*. New York: E. P. Dutton, 1976.

Lehmberg, Paul. *In the Strong Woods*. New York: St. Martin's, 1980.

Leopold, Aldo. *A Sand County Almanac and Sketches Here and There*. New York: Oxford University Press, 1949.

Lopez, Barry. *Desert Notes: Reflections in the Eye of a Raven*. Fairway, Kans.: Sheed, Andrews & McMeel, 1976.

_____. *River Notes: The Dance of Herons*. Fairway, Kans.: Sheed, Andrews & McMeel, 1979.

_____. "The Stone Horse." In *Crossing Open Ground*. New York: Charles Scribner's Sons, 1988.

Mitchell, John Hanson. *Ceremonial Time: Fifteen Thousand Years on One Square Mile*. Garden City, N.Y.: Doubleday, 1984.

Muir, John. *The Mountains of California*. Garden City, N.Y.: Doubleday, Anchor Books, 1961.

_____. *The Yosemite*. Garden City, N.Y.: Doubleday, Anchor Books, 1962.

_____. *My First Summer in the Sierra*. Sellanraa, Dunwoody, Ga.: Norman S. Berg, 1972.

_____. *John of the Mountains: The Unpublished Journals of John Muir*. Edited by Linnie Marsh Wolfe. Madison: University of Wisconsin Press, 1979.

Nichols, John. *On the Mesa*. Salt Lake City: Peregrine Smith, 1986.

Olson, Sigurd. *The Singing Wilderness*. New York: Knopf, 1956.

_____. *Listening Point*. New York: Knopf, 1958.

_____. *The Lonely Land*. New York: Knopf, 1961.

_____. *Runes of the North*. New York: Knopf, 1963.

_____. *Open Horizons*. New York: Knopf, 1969.

_____. *Reflections from the North Country*. New York: Knopf, 1976.

Peattie, Donald Culross. *An Almanac for Moderns*. New York: G. P. Putnam's, 1935.

_____. *Singing in the Wilderness*. New York: G. P. Putnam's, 1935.

_____. *A Prairie Grove*. New York: Simon & Schuster, 1938.

Petite, Irving. *The Elderberry Tree*. Garden City, N.Y.: Doubleday, 1964.

_____. *The Best Time of Year*. Garden City, N.Y.: Doubleday, 1966.

Rand, Christopher. *The Changing Landscape: Salisbury, Connecticut*. New York: Oxford University Press, 1968.

Schultheis, Rob. *The Hidden West: Journeys in the American Outback*. New York: Random House, 1982.

Skutch, Alexander. *A Naturalist on a Tropical Farm*. Berkeley and Los Angeles: University of California Press, 1980.

Smith, Dwight. *Above Timberline: A Wildlife Biologist's Rocky Mountain Journal*. Edited by Alan Anderson, Jr. New York: Knopf, 1981.

Teale, Edwin Way. *The Lost Woods*. New York: Dodd, Mead, 1945.

_____. *North with the Spring*. New York: Dodd, Mead, 1951.

_____. *Autumn across America*. New York: Dodd, Mead, 1956.

_____. *Journey into Summer*. New York: Dodd, Mead, 1960.

_____. *Wandering through Winter*. New York: Dodd, Mead, 1965.

Thoreau, Henry David. *The Journal of Henry D. Thoreau*. Edited by Bradford Torrey and Francis H. Allen. Boston: Houghton Mifflin, 1906. Reprint, New York: Dover Publications, 1962.

_____. *Cape Cod*. New York: Thomas Y. Crowell, 1961.

_____. *Walden*. Edited by J. Lyndon Shanley. Princeton: Princeton University Press, 1971.

_____. *The Maine Woods*. Edited by Joseph J. Moldenhauer. Princeton: Princeton University Press, 1972.

_____. *Thoreau: The Major Essays*. Edited by Jeffrey L. Duncan. New York: E. P. Dutton, 1972.

_____. *Early Essays and Miscellanies*. Edited by Joseph J. Moldenhauer and William Moser, with Alexander C. Kern. Princeton: Princeton University Press, 1975.

_____. *A Week on the Concord and Merrimack Rivers*. Edited by Carl Hovde, William L. Howarth, and Elizabeth Hall Witherell. Princeton: Princeton University Press, 1980.

_____. *Journal 1: 1837–1844*. Edited by Elizabeth Hall Witherell et al. Princeton: Princeton University Press, 1981.

_____. *Journal 2: 1842–1848*. Edited by Robert Sattelmeyer. Princeton: Princeton University Press, 1984.

Wallace, David Rains. *Idle Weeds: The Life of a Sandstone Ridge*. San Francisco: Sierra Club Books, 1980.

_____. *The Klamath Knot: Explorations of Myth and Evolution*. San Francisco: Sierra Club Books, 1983.

Wright, Mabel Osgood. *Citizen Bird*. New York: Macmillan, 1897.

Zwinger, Ann. *Beyond the Aspen Grove*. New York: Random House, 1970. New York: Harper & Row, 1981.

A BIBLIOGRAPHIC SAMPLER OF BRITISH "NATURE WRITING"

This bibliographic sampler is, of course, even more incomplete than the one above. This listing is restricted to the few authors of the British tradition I have cited directly in text or notes; and it provides nothing but representative titles for each of them. Richard Jefferies, for example, authored at least eighteen separate books of "nature writing," and who knows how many uncollected narratives, essays, and sketches for periodical publication. W. H. Hudson authored an even greater number; and I have not even mentioned the many works of Mary Russell Mitford or George Borrow or George Bourne or Edward Thomas or Henry Williamson. For additional information on the writings of these authors (and, except for William Howitt, John Stewart Collis, and Edward Storey, of all those listed below), see the extensive bibliographies to W. J. Keith's *The Rural Tradition*. For the many works of other, and more contemporary, purveyors of the tradition—Maurice Wiggin, perhaps, or Derek Jones, or Derek Tangye, or John Wyatt—I can only recommend lengthy visits to British bookstores.

For the works listed below, works less familiar to American readers than *Walden* or John Muir's *The Yosemite*, I have included in brackets, where appropriate, dates of original publication.

Cobbett, William. *Rural Rides* [1830]. Harmondsworth, Middlesex: Penguin Books, 1967.

Collis, John Stewart. *The Worm Forgives the Plough*. Harmondsworth, Middlesex: Penguin Books, 1975.

Howitt, William. *The Book of the Seasons, or The Calendar of Nature*. London: Henry Colburn & Richard Bentley, 1831.

Hudson, W. H. *Hampshire Days*. London: Longmans, Green, 1903.

_____. *The Collected Works of W. H. Hudson*. 24 vols. London: Dent, 1922–1923.

Jefferies, Richard. *Wildlife in a Southern County* [1879]. London: Lutterworth, 1949.

_____. *The Gamekeeper at Home* [1878]. Rhyl, Flintshire: Tideline Books, 1973.

Massingham, H. J. *Country*. London: Cobden-Sanderson, 1934.

_____. *A Countryman's Journal*. London: Chapman & Hall, 1939.

_____. *The Wisdom of the Fields*. London: Collins, 1945.

_____. *The Curious Traveller*. London: Collins, 1950.

Storey, Edward. *The Solitary Landscape*. London: Victor Gollanz, 1975.

White, Gilbert. *The Natural History of Selborne* [1789]. New York: Dolphin · Books, n.d.

_____. *Gilbert White's Journals*. Edited by Walter Johnson. New York: Taplinger, 1970.

OTHER REFERENCES AND WORKS CITED

Adams, Alexander B. *Eternal Quest: The Story of the Great Naturalists*. New York: G. P. Putnam's, 1969.

Allen, David Elliston. *The Naturalist in Britain: A Social History*. London: Allen Lane, 1976.

Anderson, Charles R. *The Magic Circle of Walden*. New York: Holt, 1968.

Auden, W. H. Introduction to Loren Eiseley, *The Star Thrower*. New York: Harcourt Brace Jovanovich, 1978.

Banister, John. "Collectio Insectorum, atque Aliarum Rerum Naturalium in Virginia." In Joseph Ewan and Nesta Ewan, *John Banister and His Natural History of Virginia, 1678–1692*. Urbana: University of Illinois Press, 1970.

Barrell, John. *The Idea of Landscape and the Sense of Place, 1730–1840: An Approach to the Poetry of John Clare*. Cambridge: Cambridge University Press, 1972.

Bartram, William. *The Travels of William Bartram: Naturalist's Edition*. Edited by Francis Harper. New Haven: Yale University Press, 1958.

Beach, Joseph Warren. *The Concept of Nature in Nineteenth-Century English Poetry*. New York: Macmillan, 1936.

Bercovitch, Sacvan. *The Puritan Origins of the American Self*. New Haven: Yale University Press, 1975.

_____. *The American Jeremiad*. Madison: University of Wisconsin Press, 1978.

Bercovitch, Sacvan and Jehlen, Myra, eds. *Ideology and Classic American Literature*. New York: Cambridge University Press, 1986.

Berra, Tim M. *William Beebe: An Annotated Bibliography*. Hamden, Conn.: Shoestring Press, Anchor Books, 1977.

Berry, Wendell. *The Long-Legged House*. New York: Harcourt, Brace, 1965.

Beston, Henry. *Northern Farm: A Chronicle of Maine*. Holt, 1948.

Blasing, Mutlu Konuk. *The Art of Life: Studies in American Autobiographical Literature*. Austin: University of Texas Press, 1977.

Bly, Carol. *Letters from the Country*. New York: Harper & Row, 1981.

Blythe, Ronald. "An Inherited Perspective." In *Characters and Their Landscapes*. New York: Harcourt, Brace, 1983.

Borland, Hal. *Countryman*. Philadelphia: J. B. Lippincott, 1957.

_____, ed. *Our Natural World: The Land and Wildlife of America as Seen and Described by Writers since the Country's Discovery*. Philadelphia: J. B. Lippincott, 1969.

Bourjaily, Vance. *Country Matters*. New York: Dial Press, 1973.

Bridgman, Richard. *Dark Thoreau*. Lincoln: University of Nebraska Press, 1982.

Brooks, Paul. *Speaking for Nature: How Literary Naturalists from Henry Thoreau to Rachel Carson Have Shaped America*. Boston: Houghton Mifflin, 1980.

Bruss, Elizabeth W. *Autobiographical Acts: The Changing Situation of a Literary Genre*. Baltimore: Johns Hopkins University Press, 1976.

Buell, Lawrence. *Literary Transcendentalism: Style and Vision in the American Renaissance*. Ithaca: Cornell University Press, 1973.

Burbick, Joan. *Thoreau's Alternative History: Changing Perspectives on Nature, Culture, and Language*. Philadelphia: University of Pennsylvania Press, 1987.

Cameron, Sharon. *Writing Nature: Henry Thoreau's Journal*. New York: Oxford University Press, 1985.

Carlisle, E. Fred. "The Heretical Science of Loren Eiseley." *Centennial Review* 18 (Fall 1974); 354–77.

Cavell, Stanley. *The Senses of Walden*. New York: Viking, 1972.

Chase, Richard. *The American Novel and Its Tradition*. Garden City, N.Y.: Doubleday, Anchor Books, 1957. Reprint, Baltimore: Johns Hopkins University Press, 1980.

Clough, Wilson O. *The Necessary Earth: Nature and Solitude in American Literature*. Austin: University of Texas Press, 1964.

Columbus, Christopher. *The Four Voyages of Christopher Columbus*. Edited and translated by J. M. Cohen. Baltimore: Penguin Books, 1969.

Cooley, Thomas. *Educated Lives: The Rise of Modern Autobiography in America*. Columbus: Ohio State University Press, 1976.

Cooper, Susan Fenimore. *Rural Hours*. 1850. Rev. ed. Boston: Houghton Mifflin, 1887.

Couser, G. Thomas. *American Autobiography: The Prophetic Mode*. Amherst: University of Massachusetts Press, 1979.

Culler, Jonathan. *Structuralist Poetics: Structuralism, Linguistics, and the Study of Literature*. Ithaca: Cornell University Press, 1975.

Darwin, Charles. *The Voyage of the Beagle*. Edited by Leonard Engel. Garden City, N.Y.: Anchor Books, 1962.

Descartes, René. *Discourse on Method and The Meditations*. Translated by F. E. Sutcliffe. London and New York: Penguin Books, 1968.

Ehrenfeld, David. *The Arrogance of Humanism*. New York: Oxford University Press, 1978.

Ehrlich, Gretel. *The Solace of Open Spaces*. New York: Viking Press, Penguin Books, 1985.

Eifert, Virginia S. *Tall Trees and Far Horizons: Adventures and Discoveries of Early Botanists in America*. New York: Dodd, Mead, 1965.

Ekirch, Arthur A. *Man and Nature in America*. New York: Columbia University Press, 1963.

Elder, John. *Imagining the Earth: Poetry and the Vision of Nature*. Urbana: University of Illinois Press, 1985.

Fagin, N. Bryllion. *William Bartram: Interpreter of the American Landscape*. Baltimore: Johns Hopkins Press, 1933.

Fiedler, Leslie. *Love and Death in the American Novel*. New York: Criterion Books, 1960.

_____. *Waiting for the End*. New York: Stein & Day, 1964.

_____. *The Return of the Vanishing American*. New York: Stein & Day, 1968.

Flader, Susan L. *Thinking like a Mountain: Aldo Leopold and the Evolution of an Ecological Attitude toward Deer, Wolves, and Forests*. Columbia: University of Missouri Press, 1974.

Foerster, Norman. *Nature in American Literature*. New York: Macmillan, 1923.

Foster, Edward Halsey. *The Civilized Wilderness: Backgrounds to American Romantic Literature, 1817–1860*. New York: Free Press, 1975.

Fox, Stephen. *John Muir and His Legacy: The American Conservation Movement*. Boston: Little, Brown, 1981.

Franklin, Wayne. *Discoverers, Explorers, Settlers: The Diligent Writers of Early America*. Chicago: University of Chicago Press, 1979.

French, Warren. "*The Immense Journey*: The Making of a Literary Naturalist. " In *Loren Eiseley*. Boston: Twayne, 1983.

Gerbi, Antonello. *The Dispute of the New World*. Translated by Jeremy Moyle. Pittsburgh: University of Pittsburgh Press, 1973.

_____. *Nature in the New World*. Translated by Jeremy Moyle. Pittsburgh: University of Pittsburgh Press, 1985.

Glacken, Clarence J. *Traces on the Rhodian Shore: Nature and Culture in Western Thought from Ancient Times to the End of the Eighteenth Century*. Berkeley and Los Angeles: University of California Press, 1967.

Goetzmann, William. *Exploration and Empire: The Explorer and the Scientist in the Winning of the American West*. New York: Knopf, 1966.

_____. *New Lands, New Men: America and the Second Great Age of Discovery*. New York: Viking Penguin, 1986.

Hanley, Wayne. *Natural History in America: From Mark Catesby to Rachel Carson*. New York: Quadrangle/New York Times Book Co., 1977.

Hartz, Louis. *The Founding of New Societies: Studies in the History of the United States, Latin America, South Africa, Canada, and Australia*. New York: Harcourt, Brace, 1964.

Hawthorne, Nathaniel. *The American Notebooks*. Edited by Claude M. Simpson. Columbus: Ohio State University Press, 1972.

Hays, Samuel P. *Conservation and the Gospel of Efficiency: The Progressive Conservation Movement, 1890–1920*. Cambridge: Harvard University Press, 1959.

Herbst, Josephine. *New Green World*. New York: Hastings House, 1954.

Hicks, Philip Marshall. *The Development of the Natural History Essay in American Literature*. Philadelphia: University of Pennsylvania, 1924.

Hildebidle, John. *Thoreau: A Naturalist's Liberty*. Cambridge: Harvard University Press, 1983.

Hoffmann, Daniel. *Form and Fable in American Fiction*. New York: Oxford University Press, 1965.

Howe, Irving. *The American Newness: Culture and Politics in the Age of Emerson*. Cambridge: Harvard University Press, 1986.

Hubbell, Sue. *A Country Year: Living the Questions*. New York: Random House, 1983.

Hussey, Christopher. *The Picturesque*. New York: G. P. Putnam's, 1927.

Huth, Hans. *Nature and the American: Three Centuries of Changing Attitudes.* Berkeley and Los Angeles: University of California Press, 1957.

Jefferies, Richard. *The Story of My Heart: My Autobiography* [1883]. New York: E. P. Dutton, 1924.

Jehlen, Myra. *American Incarnation: The Individual, the Nation, and the Continent.* Cambridge: Harvard University Press, 1986.

Johnson, E. D. H., ed. *The Poetry of Earth: A Collection of English Nature Writings from Gilbert White to Richard Jefferies.* New York: Atheneum, 1974.

Johnson, Linck. *Thoreau's Complex Weave: The Writing of "A Week on the Concord and Merrimack Rivers."* Charlottesville: University Press of Virginia, 1986.

Jones, Howard Mumford. *O Strange New World: American Culture, The Formative Years.* New York: Viking Press, 1964.

Kastner, Joseph. *A Species of Eternity.* New York: Knopf, 1977.

Kaul, A. N. *The American Vision.* New Haven: Yale University Press, 1963.

Keith, W. J. *The Rural Tradition: William Cobbett, Gilbert White, and Other Non-Fiction Prose Writers of the English Countryside.* Toronto: University of Toronto Press, 1975.

Kirkland, Caroline M. *A New Home—Who'll Follow? or Glimpses of Western Life.* New York: C. S. Francis, 1839.

———. *Forest Life.* 2 vols. New York: C. S. Francis, 1842.

Knight, Sarah Kemble. *The Journal of Madam Knight.* Introduction by Malcolm Freiberg. Boston: David R. Godine, 1972.

Knoepflmacher, U. C., and Tennyson, G. B., eds. *Nature and the Victorian Imagination.* Berkeley and Los Angeles: University of California Press, 1977.

Kolodny, Annette. *The Lay of the Land: Metaphor as Experience and History in American Life and Letters.* Chapel Hill: University of North Carolina Press, 1975.

———. *The Land before Her: Fantasy and Experience of the American Frontier, 1630–1860.* Chapel Hill: University of North Carolina Press, 1984.

Krutch, Joseph Wood. Prologue to *Great American Nature Writing*, 2–95. New York: Wm. Sloane, 1950.

Laing, R.D. *Self and Others.* New York: Pantheon Books, 1969.

Lawrence, D. H. "The Spirit of Place" and "Fenimore Cooper's Leatherstocking Novels." In *Studies in Classic American Literature.* New York: Seltzer, 1923. Reprint, New York: Viking Press, 1961.

Lawson-Peebles, Robert. *Landscape and Written Expression in Revolutionary America.* New York: Cambridge University Press, 1988.

Lewis, R. W. B. *The American Adam: Innocence, Tragedy, and Tradition in the Nineteenth Century.* Chicago: University of Chicago Press, 1955.

Lillard, Richard. "Books in the Field: Nature and Conservation." *Wilson Library Bulletin* (October 1969): 159–77.

Lipset, Seymour Martin. *The First New Nation: The United States in Historical and Comparative Perspective.* Garden City, N.Y.: Doubleday, Anchor Books, 1967.

Lueders, Edward. *The Clam Lake Papers: A Winter in the North Woods.* New York: Harper & Row, 1977.

Lyon, Thomas J. "A Taxonomy of Nature Writing." In *This Incomperable*

Lande: A Book of American Nature Writing, 3–7. Boston: Houghton Mifflin, 1989.

Lyons, John O. *The Invention of the Self: The Hinge of Consciousness in the Eighteenth Century.* Carbondale: Southern Illinois University Press, 1978.

McGregor, Gaile. *The Noble Savage in the New World Garden: Notes toward a Syntactics of Place.* Toronto: University of Toronto Press, 1988.

McIntosh, James. *Thoreau as Romantic Naturalist: His Shifting Stance toward Nature.* Ithaca: Cornell University Press, 1974.

McLean, Albert. "Thoreau's True Meridian: Natural Fact and Metaphor." *American Quarterly* 20 (1968): 567–79.

Malins, Edward. *English Landscaping and Literature, 1660–1840.* London: Oxford University Press, 1966.

Marx, Leo. "Thoreau's Excursions." *Yale Review* 51 (1962): 363–69.

———. *The Machine in the Garden: Technology and the Pastoral Ideal in America.* New York: Oxford University Press, 1964.

———. "Pastoralism in America." In *Ideology and Classic American Literature.* Edited by Sacvan Bercovitch and Myra Jehlen. New York: Cambridge University Press, 1986.

———. *The Pilot and the Passenger.* New York: Oxford University Press, 1988.

Matson, Peter. *A Place in the Country: A Narrative on the Imperfect Art of Homesteading and the Value of Ignorance.* New York: Random House, 1977.

Meine, Curt. *Aldo Leopold: His Life and Work.* Madison: University of Wisconsin Press, 1988.

Meisel, Max. *A Bibliography of American Natural History.* 3 vols. New York: Premiere Publishing, 1924.

Merrill, Lynn L. *The Romance of Victorian Natural History.* New York: Oxford University Press, 1989.

Miller, David Stuart. "An Unfinished Pilgrimage: Edwin Way Teale and American Nature Writing." Ph.D. diss., University of Minnesota, 1982.

Miller, Perry. *Nature's Nation.* Cambridge: Harvard University Press, 1967.

Milton, John P. "Earth: The End of Infinity." In *Wilderness: The Edge of Knowledge.* Edited by Maxine E. McCloskey. New York: Sierra Club, 1970.

Mitchell, Lee Clark. *Witnesses to a Vanishing America: The Nineteenth Century Response.* Princeton: Princeton University Press, 1981.

Moldenhauer, Joseph J. "The *Extra-vagant* Maneuver: Paradox in *Walden.*" *Graduate Journal* 6 (Winter 1964): 132–46. Revised and reprinted as "Paradox in Walden." In *Twentieth Century Interpretations of "Walden."* Edited by Richard Ruland. Englewood Cliffs, N.J.: Prentice-Hall, 1968.

Monk, Samuel Holt. *The Sublime.* 1935. Reprint. Ann Arbor: University of Michigan Press, 1960.

Nash, Roderick. *Wilderness and the American Mind.* New Haven: Yale University Press, 1967; 3d ed., 1982.

Nicolson, Marjorie Hope. *Mountain Gloom and Mountain Glory: The Development of the Aesthetics of the Infinite.* Ithaca: Cornell University Press, 1959.

Novak, Barbara. *Nature and Culture: American Landscape and Painting,*

1825–1875. New York: Oxford University Press, 1980.

Odum, Eugene P. *Fundamentals of Ecology*. 3d ed. Philadelphia: W. B. Saunders, 1971.

O'Gorman, Edmundo. *The Invention of America*. Bloomington: Indiana University Press, 1961.

Olney, James. *Metaphors of Self: The Meaning of Autobiography*. Princeton: Princeton University Press, 1972.

Paul, Sherman. *The Shores of America: Thoreau's Inward Exploration*. Urbana: University of Illinois Press, 1972.

Peattie, Donald Culross. *Green Laurels: The Lives and Achievements of the Great Naturalists*. New York: Simon & Schuster, 1936.

Perrin, Noel. *First Person Rural: Essays of a Sometime Farmer*. Boston: David R. Godine, 1978.

———. *Second Person Rural: More Essays of a Sometime Farmer*. Boston: David R. Godine, 1980.

Persons, Stow, ed. *Evolutionary Thought in America*. New York: George Braziller, 1956.

Pickering, Deborah Hawkin. "The Selves of Loren Eiseley: A Stylistic Analysis of the Essays in *The Immense Journey, The Night Country*, and *All the Strange Hours*." Ph.D. diss., University of Iowa, 1982.

Poirier, Richard. *A World Elsewhere: The Place of Style in American Literature*. New York: Oxford University Press, 1966.

Prishvin, Mikhail. *Nature's Dairy* [1925]. Translated by L. Navrozov. Introduction by John Updike. New York: Penguin Books, 1987.

Raven, Charles. *English Naturalists from Neckham to Ray*. Cambridge: Cambridge University Press, 1947.

Reynolds, Myra. *The Treatment of Nature in English Poetry between Pope and Wordsworth*. Chicago: University of Chicago Press, 1909.

Richardson, Robert. *Henry David Thoreau: A Life of the Mind*. Berkeley and Los Angeles: University of California Press, 1986.

Rodman, John. "The Dolphin Papers." *Antaeus* 57 (Autumn 1986): 252–80.

Rosenthal, Bernard. *City of Nature: Journeys to Nature in the Age of American Romanticism*. Newark: University of Delaware Press, 1980.

Savage, Henry, Jr. *Lost Heritage: Wilderness America through the Eyes of Seven Pre-Audubon Naturalists*. New York: William Morrow, 1970.

Schmitt, Peter J. *Back to Nature: The Arcadian Myth in Urban America*. New York: Oxford University Press, 1969.

Schwartz, James M. "The 'Immense Journey' of an Artist: The Literary Technique and Style of Loren Eiseley." Ph.D. diss., Ohio University, 1977.

———. "Loren Eiseley: The Scientist as Literary Artist." *Georgia Review* 31 (1977): 855–71.

Shea, Daniel B. Jr. *Spiritual Autobiography in Early America*. Princeton: Princeton University Press, 1968.

Simonson, Harold P. *Radical Discontinuities: American Romanticism and Christian Consciousness*. East Brunswick, N.J.: Associated University Presses, 1983.

Slotkin, Richard. *Regeneration through Violence: The Mythology of the American Frontier, 1600–1860*. Middletown, Conn.: Wesleyan University Press, 1973.

_____. *The Fatal Environment: The Myth of the Frontier in the Age of Industrialization, 1800–1890*. New York: Atheneum, 1985.

Smallwood, William Martin, *Natural History and the American Mind*. New York: Columbia University Press, 1941.

Smith, Henry Nash. *Virgin Land: The American West as Symbol and Myth*. Cambridge: Harvard University Press, 1950.

Spengemann, William C. *The Forms of Autobiography: Episodes in the History of a Literary Genre*. New Haven: Yale University Press, 1980.

Tallmadge, John. "Anatomy of a Classic." In *Companion to* A Sand County Almanac: *Interpretive and Critical Essays*. Edited by J. Baird Callicott. Madison: University of Wisconsin Press, 1987.

Tanner, Thomas, ed. *Aldo Leopold: The Man and His Legacy*. Ankeny, Iowa: Soil Conservation Society of America, 1987.

Tanner, Tony. *The Reign of Wonder: Naivety and Reality in American Literature*. Cambridge: Cambridge University Press, 1965.

Terres, John, ed. *Discovery: Great Moments in the Lives of Outstanding Naturalists*. Philadelphia: J. B. Lippincott, 1961.

Thomas, Keith. *Man and the Natural World: A History of the Modern Sensibility*. New York: Pantheon Books, 1983.

Tichi, Cecilia. *New World, New Earth: Environmental Reform in American Literature from the Puritans through Whitman*. New Haven: Yale University Press, 1979.

Tocqueville, Alexis de. *Democracy in America*. Edited by J. P. Mayer and Max Lerner. Translated by George Lawrence. New York: Harper & Row, 1966.

Tuan, Yi-Fu. *Space and Place: The Perspective of Experience*. Minneapolis: University of Minnesota Press, 1972.

Turner, Frederick. *Beyond Geography: The Western Spirit against the Wilderness*. New Brunswick, N.J.: Rutgers University Press, 1983.

Turner, James. *The Politics of Landscape: Rural Scenery and Society in English Poetry, 1630–1660*. Cambridge: Harvard University Press, 1979.

Vernon, John. *The Garden and the Map: Schizophrenia in Twentieth-Century Literature and Culture*. Urbana: University of Illinois Press, 1973.

Weintraub, Karl J. *The Value of the Individual: Self and Circumstance in Autobiography*. Chicago: University of Chicago Press, 1978.

Williams, Raymond. *The Country and the City*. New York: Oxford University Press, 1973.

Wilson, David Scofield. *In the Presence of Nature*. Amherst: University of Massachusetts Press, 1978.

Worster, Donald. *Nature's Economy: The Roots of Ecology*. San Francisco: Sierra Club Books, 1977; Garden City, N.Y.: Doubleday, Anchor Books, 1979.

Ziff, Larzer. *Literary Democracy: The Declaration of Cultural Independence in America*. New York: Viking Press, 1981.

INDEX

Abbey, Edward: *Desert Solitaire,* 287–88, 295

America: Crevecoeur on, 9; as Eden, 6, 8, 13, 111–12; as epistemological problem, 10–11, 116–20; need to locate in, 7–8; as paradise, 14, 15; as perfection of history, 6, 9–10; preconceptions of, 7, 8–10; radical dualism in, 111–15; Thomas Paine on, 9; Wayne Franklin on, 116–18; William Ellery Channing on, 9–10

American literature, classic: similarities to nature writing, 158–59, 161–62, 168–69

American Notebook (Hawthorne), 129–30, 133–35, 148–52

Anglicanus, Bartholomew: *De Proprieteribus,* 44–45

Anthropomorphism: scientific knowledge as, 98–99

Anti-institutionalism: in American nature writing, 11–12, 158

Assertion: and skepticism in American nature writing, 6–7

Autobiography: as component of Thoreauvian nature writing, 3, 5; in *A Sand County Almanac,* 211–12; and systematic science in early America, 150–52; in Thoreau's *Walden. See also* Narrative

Banister, John, 329–30 n.11; "Collectio insectorum," 136–38

Bartram, William: *Travels,* 138–52

Cameron, Sharon: on Thoreau's *Walden,* 331–33 n.1

Channing, William Ellery: on America as perfection of history, 9–10

"Collectio insectorum" (Banister): 136–38

Columbus, Christopher: language and location in letters of, 117–19

Crevecoeur: *Letters from an American Farmer,* 9

Criticism, literary. *See* Literary criticism

Darwin, Charles: style of, compared with Thoreau, 301–5 n.11

Descriptive residue: in American nature writing, 333–38 n.1

Desert Solitaire (Abbey), 287–88, 295

Despair: of knowledge of The Wild, 15. *See also* Doubt; Skepticism

de Tocqueville: on self and society, 328 n.8

Dialectic: of American nature writing, 3, 4–7, 291; of assertion and skepticism in American nature writing, 6–7; in Dillard's *Pilgrim at Tinker Creek,* 275–80; of history and criticism of nature writing, 49–50; in Leopold's *A Sand County Almanac,* 210–12; in nature writing, 320–22 n.7; in Thoreau's *Walden,* 186, 188. *See also* Dualism

Dillard, Annie: *Pilgrim at Tinker Creek,* 160–61, 217–83

Doubt: and assertion in dialectic, 6–7. *See also* Despair

Dualism, philosophic: in Bartram's *Travels,* 138–52; in Leopold's *A Sand County Almanac,* 202–4; in nature writing, 317 n.3, 319 n.7;

351

Born and bred on the northern plains of an avid outdoor family, **Peter Fritzell** is inclined to note that he never got quite straight the conventional truths of mankind's relations to nature. "To be schooled in the Dakotas," as he puts it, "is to be more aware than most that modern Western peoples are not so far removed from nature as they are sometimes disposed to think." Author of several articles and essays on nature writing and the literature of the nonhuman environment, Mr. Fritzell is a professor of English and holder of the Patricia Hamar Boldt Chair in Liberal Studies at Lawrence University in Appleton, Wisconsin.